KU-301-627

How the
Stock
Markets
Work

How the Stock Markets Work

A GUIDE TO THE INTERNATIONAL MARKETS

COLIN CHAPMAN

CENTURY
BUSINESS

First published 1994
© Colin Chapman 1986, 1987, 1988, 1991, 1994, 1998
All rights reserved

Colin Chapman has asserted his rights under the Copyright,
Designs and Patents Act, 1988, to be identified as the author of
this work

This edition first published in the United Kingdom in 1998
by Century Ltd
Random House, 20 Vauxhall Bridge Road, London SW1V 2SA

Random House Australia (Pty) Limited
20 Alfred Street, Milsons Point, Sydney
New South Wales 2061, Australia

Random House New Zealand Limited
18 Poland Road, Glenfield
Auckland 10, New Zealand

Random House South Africa (Pty) Limited
Endulini, 5A Jubilee Road, Parktown 2193, South Africa

Random House UK Limited Reg. No. 954009

A CIP catalogue record for this book
is available from the British Library

ISBN 0 7126 7970 7

Typeset by SX Composing DTP, Rayleigh, Essex
Printed in Great Britain by
Mackays of Chatham PLC, Chatham, Kent

Companies, institutions and other organizations wishing to make bulk
purchases of any business books published by Random House should
contact their local bookstore or Random House direct:
Special Sales Director
Random House, 20 Vauxhall Bridge Road, London SW1V 2SA
Tel 0171 840 8470   Fax 0171 828 6681
www.randomhouse.co.uk
businessbooks@randomhouse.co.uk

Contents

Introduction and Acknowledgements

This book has survived, with substantial rewriting and many additions, six editions, and 12 years. Originally inspired by Big Bang, a set of changes which turned the London Stock Exchange inside out and upside down, it has now borne witness to Big Bang Two, which created less turmoil but also wrought major changes on the way shares are traded.

During this time there have been two global stock market crashes, countless financial scandals and frauds, and several attempts at creating a regulatory system that protects the average investor. In Britain there has been a change of government. As New Labour embraced the workings of the stock market with Gordon Brown enthusiastically initiating new trading techniques, it seemed hardly credible that the previous Labour chancellor of the exchequer had lunged at the City threatening 'to squeeze the pips until they squeak'. On the day Tony Blair's Labour was elected, the main stock market index rose to a new record.

This period has also seen the process of privatization almost completed in Britain. It is also well underway in many countries where the prospect of the state giving up control of major enterprises was once beyond imagination. As a result many millions of people worldwide have become shareholders. In Britain alone the number of private shareholders has risen to between eight and nine million: more than a quarter of all families. Those holding shares during this period have seen their value grow, despite occasional setbacks, by a degree that makes building society investments look derisory.

The London Stock Exchange, the oldest in the world, has also been halfway to hell and back. After managing well the precipitous changes of Big Bang, it lost focus and direction, and, for a while, seemed set for near terminal decline. But in recent years its self-confidence has been restored, and it is no longer in search of a role. London also has maintained its status as the world's most significant financial centre outside New York.

But if so much has changed, much remains the same. Science and technology have made share purchase easy, and the choice of investment opportunities has never been wider. Yet, as I said in my introduction to the fifth edition of *How the Stock Markets Work*, more people feel further away from the share markets than ever before. Giant institutions continue to dominate the markets, which are remote from the man in the street. To the average family shares are not part of everyday life, nor the topic of conversation. They should be, because for many millions of people in Britain and elsewhere, they provide the value for our children's futures.

Over the years most of the reporting in this book is the result of my own observations and research. I have continued to enjoy the assistance of colleagues at the *Financial Times*. People in many stockbroking firms, but particularly BZW, Merrill Lynch and Nomura, have been very open and helpful, as has the London Stock Exchange, the New York Stock Exchange and NASDAQ. But my most consistent supporter has been Susan Grice. When we met I was preoccupied with the concluding chapter of the first edition. Six editions later, she is still ready with the proofreader's pencil.

1 Globalization is the Name of the Game

On October 13 1997, Gordon Brown, the first Labour chancellor of the exchequer in Britain for more than 20 years, stood on the steps in the foyer of the London Stock Exchange in the heart of the City and declared his government's strong support for the trading system right at the heart of world capitalism. He then pressed a button to signal the start of a new, all-electronic form of buying and selling shares. Seconds later, the huge monitor behind him, replicating the trading screens in dealing rooms throughout London, turned a bright shade of red.

This change of colour was not a symbolic gesture signifying City support for New Labour, a party that had stripped itself of its dogma and adopted market capitalism. It meant that on the chancellor's earlier words, indicating that the Labour Government was not to be in the first group of countries joining European Monetary Union, large numbers of institutional investors were dumping British shares. On the screens in dealing rooms throughout London shares with falling prices are highlighted in red; those on the rise are in blue. On October 13 dealers took the view that by not joining EMU British interest rates would remain high, depressing business.

Thousands of miles to the east, in Kuala Lumpur, capital of Malaysia, angry crowds were burning an effigy of the billionaire investor, George Soros. Soros had previously sold Malaysian ringits, believing the currency to be overvalued. His action precipitated weeks of turmoil on Kuala Lumpur's money and share markets, leading the country's ascerbic prime minister, Mahathir Mohamad, to denounce him as a criminal.

One week later, almost ten years to the day to the great stock market crash of 1987, world markets were in chaos. In the Chinese city of Hong Kong, handed over by the British in a ceremony of pompous optimism only two months earlier, the city's Hang Seng index lost almost one fifth of its value. The Chinese governor of the former colony appealed for common sense and calm, his words almost a replica of those used by his British counterpart ten years earlier.

In Johannesburg Trevor Manuel, the finance minister, and Chris Stals, the governor of the Reserve Bank of South Africa, stood by wringing their hands as the Johannesburg Stock Exchange shed all its gains of the previous year. In two hours it saw its biggest one-day loss in nine years, sending panic through the bond and currency markets. This was despite a heroic economic performance by the Mandela government whose brave decisions had led to a huge fall in inflation and a steadily improving economy.

Although emerging markets were hit harder by the 1997 turmoil than the established markets of New York, London and Tokyo, no investor was immune from the sudden downturn. The more sensible of them realized, of course, that the correction was just that – a temporary halt to the onward march of the world's share markets, not a crash wiping out long term the value of sound and well-run corporations. Within three months the major markets had not only recovered their losses, but were trading at record levels.

The big lesson to be learned from these events is that as we approach the millennium we live in a global economy, and that no one politician, however powerful or even popular in his own country, can hope to influence the ebb and flow of world money. True power now lies in the markets, which dictate the fate of countries large and small. And in turn the markets are in the hands of the money masters and the money minders, men and women to whom, directly or indirectly, we have entrusted our savings. If they do not like the policies of a government, do not rate the performance of a corporation's executive, or do not believe that a country or company has the best interest of investors at heart, they can move the money in their care, at whim, within seconds, to anywhere they like. Under globalization, capital may be shifted to whichever country offers the best investment opportunities.

Of course globalization and the integration of national

economies means that the same principle applies to goods and services. Large numbers of those who like wine with their meals consume Chardonnays from Australia's Barossa Valley and reds from the Hunter region because, in quality and price, they compare with products from nearby France. We buy German cars, French brandy, Italian shoes, American computers. A holiday in Margate, Kwazulu Natal, seems better value for money than Margate, Kent, even after the airfare.

This globalization of products and services also impacts the financial markets. Companies that are truly global – British Airways, General Electric, ICI, BMW – are less exposed to the vagaries of one market than a purely national concern.

Of course globalization is not an entirely new phenomenon. Older readers will recall the vast expansion of European empires in the early part of this century. But there are differences. In the great migrations and shifts of capital that established the 'new world', people moved and took their money and possessions with them. They uprooted themselves and uprooted those whose countries they subsumed.

Today's globalization demands little movement of people. Most of the people stay put, for good or ill. It is a value driven system. Those who have money or, more accurately those who control investments, seek ways of achieving the best return on these investments. And, like those who founded the first stock exchange they are prepared to take risks. Stock markets are all about risk.

2   History

*'The howling of the wolf, the grunting of the hog,
the braying of the ass, the nocturnal wooing of the cat,
all these in unison could not be more hideous than the
noise which these beings make in the Stock Exchange'*
– Anonymous commentator on the scene in Change
Alley, London in 1695.

*'Stock-jobbing is knavish in its private practice, and
treason in its public'* – Daniel Defoe.

'Dictum meum pactum – My word is my bond' –
Handbook of the London Stock Exchange.

For most the stock markets epitomize the concept of risk and
reward. With not too much of the former, and the chance of
achieving a fair amount of the latter, the investor can be on
the road to riches. This has been true throughout the three
centuries of stock market activity.

Those who took a billion pound risk in investing in satellite television in Britain in 1990 were opting for the same
choice as the few backers prepared to chance £3,200 apiece
on the *Concepción* adventure in 1686. Then, a whiskery sea
captain from Boston called Phips sought investors for an
expedition to the north coast of Hispaniola to salvage a
sunken galleon. Nine months later the backers reaped their
reward – £250,000 worth of fine silver.

Then as now another major threat to any investment has
been that people cheat. There are big cheats and little cheats,
of course, and only a few of them have passed through the
cells of the Old Bailey. The excitement that greeted the trial
in London of the Guinness Five in 1990 or the humiliation of
the president of the House of Nomura a year later – or the
imprisonment of Ivan Boesky and Michael Milken in New
York, and Ronald Li in Hong Kong – was only a latter-day

repeat of events in Britain in the late seventeenth century.

In 1697, following a wave of market-rigging and insider trading, the British government brought in an Act designed to 'restrain the number and ill-practice of brokers and stock-jobbers'.

This followed a report from a Parliamentary Commission set up a year earlier which had discovered that:

> the pernicious art of stockjobbing hath, of late, so perverted the end design of Companies and Corporations, erected for the introducing or carrying on of manufactures, to the private profit of the first projectors, that the privileges granted to them have commonly been made no other use of – but to sell again, with advantage, to innocent men.

As a result of the 1697 Act all stockbrokers and stockjobbers had to be licensed before they plied their trade in the coffee shops, walks and alleys near the Royal Exchange in London. These licences were limited to 100 and were granted by the Lord Mayor of London and the Court of Aldermen. They cost only £2, and entitled the licensee to wear a specially struck silver medal embossed with the Royal Arms, once he had taken an oath that he would 'truly and faithfully execute and perform the office and employment of a broker between party and party, without fraud or collusion'.

The rules of operation were strict. Brokers were not allowed to deal on their own behalf, but only for clients. They could not hold any options for more than three days without facing the certainty of permanent expulsion. Commission was limited to five per cent, or less. Anyone who tried to operate as a broker without a licence was, if caught, exposed to three days in the City pillory.

Muscovy and Company

The trade in shares had started with City traders and merchants spreading the risk of two major entrepreneurial journeys: an attempt to investigate the prospects offered by the uncharted White Sea and Arctic Circle, and a voyage to India and the East Indies via the Cape of Good Hope.

These ventures were to lead to the world's first two public companies: the Muscovy Company and the East India Company, whose members did not follow previous practice of trading on their own account as private individuals, but contributed money to 'joint stock', through shares which were freely transferable.

The Muscovy Company emerged from a brave, if unsuccessful attempt by Sebastian Cabot in 1553 to find a North East trade route to China and the Orient. As one of the first shareholders explained at the time:

> Every man willing to bee of the societie, should disburse the portion of twentie and five pounds a piece: so that in a short time, by this means, the sum of six thousand pounds being gathered, three ships were brought.

Two of the three ships sank off Norway, and things looked bleak for the 250 merchants putting up £25 each. But one of the project leaders did make it to Moscow, where he persuaded Ivan the Terrible to sign a trade agreement.

The East India Company was more successful and was the first to raise equity capital on a substantial scale. It needed modern, armed ships for the difficult and dangerous voyage to the Orient, and substantial docks in London. Although it lost ships on voyages, and hovered close to bankruptcy, it managed to raise over £1.6m in 17 years. As the silk and spice trade developed, those who had invested in the original stock saw profit returns of 40 per cent a year.

Enterprising developers quickly realized that raising capital through shares had potential far beyond risky voyages. Why not try it at home? Francis, Earl of Bedford had a bold plan to drain the Fens, which would provide more fertile agricultural land as well as giving London its first supply of fresh water. So others topped up his own £100,000 contribution and 'The Government and Company of the New River brought from Chadwell and Amwell to London' was founded in 1609, to become Britain's first water stock. Although the water company operations were bought out by the Metropolitan Water Board in 1904, the company still exists as the oldest one quoted on the Stock Exchange.

The Stock Exchange Official List

By the end of the seventeenth century there was substantial dealing in shares of one sort or another. It was estimated by the historian W. R. Scott that by 1695 there were some 140 joint stock companies, with a total market capitalization of £4.5m. More by habit than by design, much of this took place in two coffee houses called Garraway's and Jonathan's near Change Alley. Change Alley is still there today in the narrow spit of land between Cornhill and Threadneedle Street. The coffee establishments of the seventeenth century had style. You could meet there fellow merchants and traders, discuss the latest ventures, and buy and sell shares. You could also run your eye down a sheet of paper containing prices of commodities and a few shares – called 'The Course of the Exchange and Other Things'; this was to be the precursor of the Stock Exchange Daily Official List.

A writer of the day set the scene:

> The centre of the jobbing is in the Kingdom of Exchange Alley and its adjacencies: the limits are easily surrounded in about a Minute and a half stepping out of Jonathan's into the Alley, you turn your face full South, moving on a few paces, and then turning Due East, you advance to Garraway's; from there going out at the other Door, you go on still East into Birchin Lane and then halting a little at the Sword-Blade Bank to do much mischief in fervent Words, you immediately face to the North, enter Cornhill, visit two or three petty Provinces there in your way West; and thus having Boxed your Compass, and sail'd round the whole Stock Jobbing Globe, you turn into Jonathan's again; and so, as most of the great Follies of Life oblige us to do, you end just where you began.

South Sea Bubble

This coffee society was to thrive for more than 50 years, and by 1720 Change Alley, and its coffee houses thronged with brokers, was the place to be. The narrow streets were impassable because of the throng of lords and ladies in their carriages. The Act regulating and restricting their operations had lapsed, by popular consent. And the eighteenth-century equivalent of the hit parade contained the following ballad:

> Then stars and garters did appear
> Among the meaner rabble
> To buy and sell, to see and hear
> The Jews and Gentiles squabble,
> The greatest ladies thither came
> And plied in chariots daily,
> Or pawned their jewels for a sum
> To venture in the Alley.

The principal attraction was the excitement caused by the booming share prices of the South Sea Company, which started in 1720 at £128 apiece, and swiftly rose as euphoria about their prospects was spread both by brokers and by the government. By March the price rose to £330, by May it was £550, and by 24 June it had reached an insane £1,050.

The South Sea Company had been set up nine years earlier by the British government, ostensibly with the aim of opening up trade and markets for new commodities in South America. It also had another purpose, which, these days, has a familiar ring about it, for it was to relieve the government of some £9m of public debt.

For eight years it did virtually nothing, and created no excitement. Its shares were static, and it had only one contract of any size: to supply black slaves to Latin America. The government then gave birth to the concept of privatization of a State concern, something much more audacious than the contemporary sales of British Telecom or British Gas. It offered shares in the South Sea Company to the public, hoping that it would raise enough money to wipe out the entire National Debt of some £31m.

The government was persuaded to do this by a wily operator, Sir John Blunt, who was a director of the company and effectively underwrote the issue. The issues were 'partly-paid'; an investor had to find only a small proportion at the start, and then pay the rest of the share price in instalments. The issue was heavily oversubscribed, and there was much irritation when it was discovered that Blunt's acquaintances, and others of influence, had received an extra allocation. To raise still more money, the company made loans to the public, secured on the shares themselves, provided the money was used to buy more stock. Blunt also proved adept at the use of public relations in pushing the share price up. There were promises of lavish dividends, the interest of prominent people was secured by thinly veiled bribes, and the peace negotiations with Spain were used for propaganda purposes, since the prospect of an end to conflict meant more trade with South America.

The smart money, including the prime minister, Sir Robert Walpole, sold out at the peak of the boom. The Prince of Wales, the Duke of Argyll, the chancellor of the exchequer and MPs too numerous to mention, made handsome gains before the bubble burst. Then the government, by bringing in the Bubble Act, designed to prevent a rash of similar competitive enterprises from springing up, triggered off the first ever bear market. So the bubble burst, and within eight weeks of passing £1,000, the share price had plunged to £175. By December it had sunk to £124, bringing ruin to those who had seen the South Sea Company as the chance of a lifetime. There was the inevitable Parliamentary inquiry, which concluded that the accounts had been falsified and a government minister bribed. The chancellor had no chance to enjoy his £800,000 capital gain; he was committed to the Tower after being found guilty of the 'most notorious, dangerous and infamous corruption'.

It was – and remains – the most notorious episode in British financial history, and it was a long time before the market got back into its stride. Indeed it was not until the next century that a large crop of joint stock companies was formed, a development brought about by an acute shortage of capital for major projects both at home and abroad.

Mines, Railways, Canals

By 1824, the end of the cyclical trade depression, there were 156 companies quoted on the London Stock Exchange, with a market capitalization of £47.9m. In the following twelve months interest in investment increased sharply. Prospectuses were issued for no less than 624 companies with capital requirements of £372m. The largest group were general investment companies, mostly with extensive interests overseas, which raised £52m. Canals and railways came next, raising £44m, followed by mining companies, £38m and insurance, a new industry, with £35m.

The railways proved a great boon for the promotion of investment, even if most of the investors lost their money. The Duke of Wellington had opposed the development of railways: 'Railroads will only encourage the lower classes to move about needlessly.' Not only did this prove to be the case, but investment in the railways also led to the spread of share ownership outside London and the ruling classes to the provinces. It also created a new word in the financial vocabulary: stag, a person who applies for an allotment of shares with the clear intention of selling them to someone else before he has to pay for them.

The stags were out in force in 1836 when George Hudson, a bluff Yorkshireman, raised £300,000 for the York and North Midland Railway under the slogan 'Mak' all t'railways coom t'York'. The £50 shares were oversubscribed and quickly gained a premium of £4 each. Within three years the line was opened, and the bells of York Minster pealed out in joyful celebration. Much of the joy was shortlived, however, for so many railway lines sprouted up across the country that many of them could not pay the wages of the train drivers, let alone the dividends for shareholders. Many of them also turned out to be overcapitalized, with the surplus funds vanishing into other ventures, to the shareholders' chagrin.

Even so, despite setbacks, by 1842 there were 66 railway companies quoted on the London Stock Exchange, with a capital of almost £50m. During the boom in railway issues, *The Economist* was moved to write an editorial, which, with the change of name and date, might well have fitted into the British Telecom era of 1985: 'Everybody is in the stocks now (sic),' it purred. 'Needy clerks, poor tradesmen's apprentices, discarding serving men and bankrupts – all have entered the ranks of the great moneyed interest.'

Provincial stock markets were also established. Local investment opportunities were featured in the advertisements of share auctions which regularly appeared in a Liverpool newspaper after about 1827. It was quite usual to use a property auction as the opportunity to dispose of a parcel of shares. By the middle of 1845 regional stock exchanges had been formed in 12 towns and cities, from Bristol in the South, to Newcastle in the North, with Yorkshire claiming the greatest number. But only five of them survived the trading slump of 1845 to become permanent institutions.

Government Debt

All through this period government debt had been growing, and its funding was providing the most lucrative and reliable form of income to sharebrokers. In 1860, British funds amounted to more than all the other quoted securities combined, and provided by far the widest market in the Exchange. Compensation to slave-owners, whose slaves had been freed, the cost of the Crimean War and the purchase by the government of the national telegraph system, all added to the cost.

Government stocks, or bonds, were bought daily from the Treasury by the City figure called the Government Broker, who then sold them on in the market-place. The idea was that these stocks, to become known much later as gilt-edged securities, would be used to cut back or even get rid of the National Debt. In effect, of course, they added to the debt, but they were a way of funding unpopular measures without resorting to excessive taxation. By the early twentieth century local authorities had also jumped on the bandwagon. The City of Dublin was the first to raise money through bonds, followed by Edinburgh, Glasgow and the Metropolitan Board of Works.

The First Exchange

The brokers and other money dealers had, of course, long since left their damp pitches in Change Alley, and the coffee houses had not only become too crowded but also too accommodating to groups which the more established professionals liked to call the 'riff-raff'. When Jonathan's was finally burnt down after a series of major fires around 1748, the broking industry sought refuge in New Jonathan's, rebuilt in Threadneedle Street, where they charged sixpence a day entrance fee, a sum sufficient to discourage tinkers, money-lenders and the other parasites that had frequented the previous premises. Soon afterwards they put a sign over the door: The Stock Exchange.

It continued in this way, more or less as a club, for 30 years, until its members decided something more formal was required. On 7 February 1801 its days as the Stock Exchange ended and it was shut down, to reopen one month later as the 'Stock Subscription Room'. It no longer cost sixpence a day to enter; members had to be elected and to pay a fee of ten guineas, and risk a fine of two guineas if they were found guilty of 'disorderly conduct', the penalty going to charity. There does not seem to be an accurate record of how much charities benefited from this provision. The Stock Subscription Room had a short life, for members quickly decided it was too small, and in the same year laid the foundation stone for a new building in Capel Court. The stone records that this was also the 'first year of the union between Great Britain and Ireland', and notes that the building was being 'erected by private subscription for transaction of the business in the public funds'.

Not all members of the public were impressed by this new monument; the old lady who sold cups of tea and sweet buns outside Capel Court moved away because, she said: 'the Stock Exchange is such a wicked place'. But with monuments come tablets, and it was not long before members were forced to draw up new rules of operation. Adopted in 1812, these still form the basis if not the letter of the present-day rule book. Neither members nor their wives could be engaged in any other business, failures had to be chalked up above the clock immediately so that there could be a fair distribution of assets to creditors, and members were informed that they had to give up 'rude and trifling practices which have long disgraced the Stock Exchange'.

The Capel Court building was to last a century and a half, and it was, in the end, not size but ancient communications that made it unworkable. The decision was taken to rebuild, and a new 'state-of-the-art' 26-storey concrete tower was established as the new London Stock Exchange in Throgmorton Street almost on the spot where New Jonathan's had once flourished. Opened by Queen Elizabeth in 1972, it stood as a seemingly unassailable bastion of capitalism in a climate where the City of London was often under political scrutiny and attack, and where Britain was in deep economic and industrial decline.

The early years in 'Throg Street' were good years for the practitioners in the market. While heavy industry had crumbled – and much of manufacturing industry had vanished under international competition from Europe and southeast Asia – the banks and other financial institutions that provided much of Britain's invisible exports thrived and prospered. Britain was still merchant banker to the free world, and overseas governments, corporations and individual potentates entrusted their dollars, gold and silver to financial houses in the square mile of the City of London. In the early 1980s more than £50-million worth of foreign currency changed hands each day in London, yielding banks and other exchange dealers large sums in commission, making London the dominant market in foreign exchange with one third of world business.

The City of London was a club, as cosy and impenetrable as any of the establishments in St James's two miles away which served diplomats and the officer class. Those invited to share its mysteries at generous lunches or livery dinners felt an uneasy air of narrow bonhomie and patrimony. Above all it was a closed shop.

The members of the London Stock Exchange were particularly well protected. No one could buy or sell shares except through one of their member firms, most of which had been in the hands of the same family for decades. And, as a consequence of an official over-manning policy, investors had to pay twice for each transaction; a commission for the stockbroker and a mark-up for the stockjobber.

Commissions were fixed, in the manner of most professional fees at the time. For a broker to discount a commission, even to a friend, was as serious an offence as a doctor committing adultery with a patient or a farm worker poaching a landowner's pheasants. Stockbrokers brandished a pocket guide, published by Messrs Basil, Montgomery, Lloyd and Ward, which until 1975 set out an elaborate sliding scale of charges.

In 1950 a share valued at 15 shillings (at the rate of 20 shillings to the pound and 12 pence to the shilling) cost a purchaser 15s. 5¼d, after paying government stamp duty of 3¾d and commission of a modest 1½d. A £5 share would cost £5. 2s. 9d, with the broker getting 9d for his pains. By 1952 commission rates had gone up – to 0.75 per cent, but the 15s share still cost the saver only ¾d more at 15s 6d, while the £5 share cost him £5.3s, with the broker getting a whole shilling instead of 9d for the trade. Ten years later the rates were much higher at 1.25 per cent, but in the case of transactions over £2,500, the broker could, at his discretion, reduce the commission to not less than half the standard rates, provided the business was not shared with an agent, in which case the full rate had to be charged. On 14 February 1975 there was another rise – to 1.5 per cent for the first £5,000 consideration, falling to 0.625 per cent for the next £15,000. Decimalization had made calculations simpler: the £5 share now cost the investor £5.1625, of which 10 pence went in stamp duty and 6.25 pence in commission.

At these levels and with the volumes of business that were available to the limited number of stockbrokers, it was a profitable and relatively stress-free occupation. Advertising was banned, so clients were obtained through personal networking – usually over a substantial lunch, a game of cards in the first-class rail compartment on the way home, or a round of golf. The better broking firms used some of their profits to undertake detailed research into the activities of major companies, the results of which were made freely available to the investing institutions and more moneyed private customers.

The stockbroker did not have to sully his hands in direct financial bargaining with other brokers; indeed, until 1986, he was prohibited from doing so. Share trading was in the hands of stockjobbers, colourful and resilient characters with strong constitutions who stood or perched on stools at the elevated benches on the floor of the London Stock Exchange. Many of them had a demeanour more akin to a barrow-boy or bookmaker than to a City gent, and their daily work had many similarities. The jobbers made the market, deciding at what price they would buy or sell the shares on offer. Their profit was the difference between the buying and selling price, known as the 'jobbers' turn'.

Jobbers never dealt with the investing public, at any level. They traded only with dealers, usually junior employees of stockbroking firms, who were based on the floor of the Exchange, and who took their instructions by telephone or by sign language from colleagues standing nearby. Trading started at nine and finished at four-thirty, with an hour's break for lunch, and, at peak times, provided a colourful spectacle to visitors peering down from the gallery above. Occasionally trading would be punctuated by the ringing of a bell, signifying an announcement to the Exchange, which would usually be followed by a roar of approval or derision, a quick revision by jobbers of their prices, and another burst of trading.

In trading both dealer and jobber had to display a certain amount of guile.

The Jobber's Pitch

In those days the stockbroker – or to be more accurate a dealer working for a firm of brokers – would hurry into the trading floor of the Exchange, armed with orders from clients, and make his way to one of the pitches, or stalls, specializing in the sector of the market in which he was interested. The operation was just like that of a shopper visiting a market to buy fresh vegetables. Just as the prudent buyer would check out the prices at a variety of stalls selling the same produce, so the dealer would seek quotes from the jobber at his pitch.

Although this system is no longer in use a modern version of it is still practised in many of the world's markets. So it may be instructive to understand how it worked. Let us assume, for the purpose of this example, that the dealer was seeking to buy shares in British Petroleum.

Without disclosing whether he was a potential buyer or seller, the dealer would seek a quote on BP's price. The jobber, in this example, replied '£5.36 to £5.40', indicating he would buy BP shares at the lower price or sell them at the higher. The gap provided the jobber's 'turn' or margin, in other words, his livelihood. With a share as well known as

BP, the jobber would more probably have answered 'thirty-six to forty', correctly assuming that any dealer would have known that the price was in the area of £5.

The dealer would then visit other stalls and obtain alternative quotes. Having settled on the most attractive, and still without disclosing whether he was a buyer or a seller, the dealer then reapproached one of the jobbers, reminded him of the quote he had made a few minutes earlier, and asked if there was a possibility of 'anything closer'.

The jobber, sensing the possibility of an imminent deal, would try to guess whether his client was a buyer or seller, and would then ask: 'Are you many?' 'Only 500,' said the broker, in the knowledge that small packages were usually attractive to jobbers, who, at the end of the trading account, have to balance up buyers with sellers. 'I'll make you thirty-six to thirty-nine and a half,' the jobber replied. In turn the broker said: 'I'll sell you 500 at thirty-six,' and a 'bargain' is struck. This would be recorded on a slip of paper in the notebook of each party.

Under Stock Exchange etiquette, the broker was obliged to deal at the time of the quote – he could not have returned ten minutes later, having haggled elsewhere. Had he decided not to deal, the jobber would have said formally: 'I'm off,' indicating that the quote was no longer valid.

The Big Bang

October 1986 was the most momentous month in the long history of the London Stock Exchange – a combination of forces for change known as Big Bang. One force was Margaret Thatcher: in her assault on trade unions' restrictive practices she determined that fixed commissions charged by stockbrokers should be abolished, and that all major financial institutions should have free and open access to the capital markets. The principal barriers between banks, merchant banks, investment institutions and stockbrokers should be broken down: all should be able to set up as one-stop financial supermarkets if they wished to. Why not allow one company to buy and sell shares for clients, raise capital for business, invest in new ventures, and trade in international securities like eurobonds?

But by far the biggest force for change was technology: the combination of hi-speed telecommunications and the micro-processor meant that international deals could be carried out anywhere. There was no need for any of the very large trades to pass through the Stock Exchange at all.

Immediately prior to Big Bang 62 per cent of the trading in one of Britain's largest companies, ICI, was being transacted off the London Exchange, mainly in New York. A large share of the buying and selling of other major British companies had also been taking place in the United States. This trading was by no means confined to American investors, for some of the big British institutions found that dealing across the Atlantic was a better proposition. An official of the Prudential Assurance Company explained: 'When we have a significant buying programme on we check all available markets. We take the attitude that we deal wherever we can get the best price.'

Effectively the big traders bypassed London, where the complicated system of brokers and jobbers was costing them much more in commission, government stamp duty and Value Added Tax.

So, for Sir Nicholas Goodison, chairman of the Stock Exchange and his colleagues on the Council, sweeping reform was the only answer. If the Stock Exchange was to compete with the giant American broking houses, it had to join them at their own game. There was no choice, when competition was creaming off the top business, both in value and volume. Otherwise there would be nothing left for the old-fashioned Stock Exchange, and the jobbers would be left standing at their pitches.

Effecting the necessary changes took time and consider-able resolution. It meant ending a way of life that had been a tradition for more than 100 years.

Even though its members saw the system was under threat, the Stock Exchange Council had to be given a firm nudge in the direction of change by the government. This happened almost by accident. The Office of Fair Trading had argued that stockbrokers should be treated no differently from other sectors of the community – solicitors, estate agents, motor traders, soap powder manufacturers – who had been barred from fixing prices amongst each other, and were now bound to offer some semblance of competition in the market-place. When the Stock Exchange demurred, the Government decided to take legal action, using the weight of the Monopolies Commission to take apart the entire rule book of the Exchange as a litany of restrictive practices. The proceedings were estimated to take five years to complete, and to cost at least £5m in legal fees. It was, of course, like using a sledgehammer to crack a nut and an absurd way of challenging an entire trading system. As Sir Nicholas Goodison, chairman at the time, was to say later:

> 'It was a foolish way to study the future of a great international market. It was a matter which needed long and close study, and preferably a public examination not constrained by the requirements of litigation or the strait-jacket of court procedure. Unfortunately the Government turned down the suggestion of such an examination, and we were forced into a position of defence of rules, not all of which we would necessarily wish to keep. Thus open debate became impossible because anything said could, as it were, be taken down in evidence and used in court. The case pre-empted resources, effort and thought.'

It did, however, concentrate the mind of the Stock Exchange Council. The government was clearly in no mood to set up a Royal Commission to inquire into the Stock Exchange; Ministers saw that as a waste of time. If the case went on, with each side producing volumes of written evidence, as well as witnesses for examination, cross-examination and re-examination, the Stock Exchange would end up in an unwinnable situation. There would also be unfavourable publicity. And even if the Exchange won, its joy would be shortlived, for such was the resolve of the Thatcher government to curb the restrictive power of trade unions that it could hardly spare as notorious a City club, and would then feel obliged to legislate to change the law.

In July 1983 the government offered Goodison a way out. It offered to drop the case against the Stock Exchange, if the Council would follow the example of New York in 1985 and abandon fixed commissions. It did so, and the die was cast for Big Bang.

Both the government and the Stock Exchange knew that

the abolition of fixed commissions would be the catalyst for major change, because without steady reliance on a solid income, more or less indexed to the rate of inflation, many stockbrokers could not exist. Competition over commissions might be acceptable in a bull market, but when the bears emerged in strength there would be trouble. A bull is the name for the optimist who believes that prices are likely to go higher, and who charges into the market to buy; if there are enough bulls, their confidence is sufficient to push up prices. A bear is the opposite market animal, who fears the worst, and expects a fall; when the bears run for cover, you have a bear market. For stockbrokers, a bear market generates fear, for although there are good commissions to be had when there is pronounced selling, the prices on which those commissions are based are lower, and interest dies.

Under the 'Big Bang', the Old Guard knew, life would never be the same again. Those who wanted to survive would have to behave like Chicago futures dealers. Life would become just like a job on the money or commodity markets, with young men and women arriving to a room full of telephones and computer terminals at 7.30 every morning, shouting at them and at each other for at least 12 hours, and leaving exhausted in the evening. This was a world where the midlife crisis came at the age of twenty-six.

And competition would be so fierce there would probably be less money in it anyway. With no fixed commissions, firms would have neither the time nor the resources to undertake company or sector research, let alone visit a firm and enjoy a steak and kidney pie in a country hotel with the chairman and managing director. Instead they would spend their days peering at monitors, and yelling down the telephone.

As for open ownership, well, the senior partners would sell out, pocket their millions, and go to live in Bermuda, whilst those left would not know who their bosses were, only that they worked for some large bank, most probably under foreign ownership.

Despite their defeat over commissions, the Old Guard held out against other reforms. However on 4 June 1985 the 4,495 members of the Stock Exchange were confronted with an historic choice: to face up to the future or face the consequences of living with the past.

Two resolutions were put to the members' vote on the floor of the Exchange. For Goodison, the issue was clear. It was about 'whether or not members want to keep the bulk of the securities business in this country and in the Stock Exchange', he wrote in a letter. 'It is about keeping and strengthening the Stock Exchange as the natural market in securities.'

The first resolution, which required only a simple majority, would enable outsiders – banks, mining finance houses, international conglomerates, money brokers – to own up to 100 per cent of a member firm, instead of only 29.9 per cent. The second resolution required a 75 per cent majority, and proposed changes in the Stock Exchange Constitution to shift ownership of the Exchange from individual members to member firms. Plans were to be devised whereby members could sell their shares in the Exchange to newcomers.

The first resolution was passed by 3,246 votes to 681, but the second failed by a very small margin, achieving 73.64 per cent instead of the required 75 per cent. For Goodison, this was a major setback, but for those who had voted against it, it was to prove an even greater blow.

Goodison had already warned members that to reject the proposal would be 'very serious and could cause substantial damage to the standing of the Stock Exchange', mainly because new entrants from America and elsewhere, if denied easy membership, would decide simply to bypass its activities. But he had one major card to play. Under his leadership the Stock Exchange's reputation and credibility had been high. In almost every other area of the City there had been scandal, but the Stock Exchange had retained its integrity, and had been shown to be a more effective policeman of those within its province than the Bank of England. Goodison was able to secure the Stock Exchange's right to self-regulation under the Conservative government's proposed financial services legislation, thus making it certain that those who wished to trade in British equities would want to be governed by its rules. The Exchange's Council then moved to create the new class of corporate membership effective from March 1986.

Corporate members would then each own one share, which gave them the right to take part in all of the Stock

Exchange's trading activities, and to use its settlement and other facilities. But there would be no need for any corporate member to have an individual member on either its board or staff, although all those in its employ who had contact with customers would have to be 'approved persons'. Thus, those members who had voted against the Council on the second resolution in the hope of getting better terms for selling their individual shares to new conglomerate members found that these shares were virtually worthless. The biggest group in the world could join the club for only one share, negotiating the price, not with old members, but with the Stock Exchange Council.

The World's First International Exchange

No sooner had the new deal gone through and the day of 'Big Bang' passed, relatively without incident, than Goodison achieved a major coup. As outlined earlier, one of the major threats to the London Stock Exchange was international equity trading bypassing London altogether. Even though the new rules made London less uncompetitive – and electronic dealing systems forced traders to work faster – there was still a large group of securities houses trading international stocks who saw no good reason why they should be part of the new Exchange.

They had formed themselves into ISRO, the International Securities Regulatory Organization, which, despite its grandiose title, showed very little affection for regulation. Its members traded in the stocks of about 400 of the world's major corporations for the benefit of about 80 institutions. It was an exclusive club for the big boys, who argued that since they all knew each other not many rules were needed.

Prior to 'Big Bang' ISRO and the London Exchange were not exactly the best of friends; indeed they often traded insults. Since international equities were stocks which were traded beyond their own country boundaries, it was argued they should not be subject to rigid domestic rules. And a new class of international equity was being spawned: issues by international corporations underwritten and distributed in alien countries. The first really large issue of this kind was British Telecom; when it was floated off by the British government a large proportion of the stock was successfully offered to institutions in North America, Europe and Japan.

Such international equity issues are organized by investment banks and securities houses who offer tranches of stock directly to favoured clients without touching the stock markets. Because of London's position at the centre of the world business time zone, most of this business has been conducted there. Goodison approached ISRO and suggested that sooner or later some form of ordered regulation for the conduct of global equity markets would be forced on it, if it did not form an international standard of its own; and since the London Stock Exchange offered the nearest to such a standard, why not merge with it?

From the Stock Exchange point of view the proposed deal averted the possibility of the world's financial giants setting up a competing market-place in London, and, according to Goodison, opened 'the way for a united securities market which will be a very powerful competitor for international business'.

On November 12 1986, members of the Stock Exchange voted for the merger, and the combined body became known as the International Stock Exchange of the United Kingdom and Northern Ireland. The old guard knew there was no choice – the new Exchange was going to be dominated by foreigners, but so what? The previous changes they had approved had already allowed foreign financial houses to take over two-thirds of large British broking firms, and so domination by the likes of Citicorp, American Express, Deutsche Bank, Merrill Lynch, Nomura, and the Swiss Banking Corporation was anyway inevitable. There was also a sweetener of £10,000 for each member when they retired or reached the age of sixty.

The New Conglomerates

The establishment of giant new conglomerates led to an undignified scramble as City and international broking firms, banks and finance houses rushed to jump into bed with each other. So unseemly was the haste that some parted company with new-found, if expensive, friends within days rather than weeks, in a kind of financial promiscuity which must have left old faithfuls gasping for breath. One major bank bought a firm of jobbers only to find that, by the time the ink was dry

on the contract, the best people had all left *en masse* to join
a rival. Since these people had been almost the firm's only
asset, the acquisition was more or less worthless. The Deputy
Governor of the Bank of England put his finger on the
problem:

> 'If key staff – and on occasions whole teams – can be offered
> inducements to move suddenly from one institution to another it
> becomes very difficult for any bank to rely on the commitment
> individuals will give to implementing its plans, and adds a
> further dimension of risk to any bank which is building its
> strategy largely around a few individuals' skills.'

The banks and merchant banks were the predators, but
they found even the very large broking firms only too willing
to submit. Typical of the alliances formed was Barclays de
Zoete Wedd, a merger between the investing banking side of
Barclays Bank plc, the large stockbrokers, de Zoete and
Bevan, and London's largest stockjobber in gilt-edged securities, Wedd, Durlacher & Mordaunt. Barclays became top
dog, owning 75 per cent of the shares. Another group was
Mercury, formed by S. G. Warburg and Co., with three
major broking and jobbing firms. Each of these two giants is
able to issue securities, to place them with its large clientele
base, and to buy and sell speculatively on its own account.

All but one of Britain's top twenty broking and jobbing
houses were absorbed into large new financial conglomerates. Among the leading firms, only Cazenove and Co.
remained independent. By taking this step, it benefited from
both institutions and private investors seeking out brokers
with no commercial link, and therefore no potential conflict
of interest with a bank, an insurance company or a unit trust
management company.

So were spawned new groups which can, in parallel, act as
bankers to a company, raise long-term debt or equity, make
a market in its shares, retail them to investors, and buy them
as managers of discretionary funds. How can the public be
sure that those at the marketing end of the firm are not privy
to insider information, and, if they are, how can they be pre-
vented from acting upon it? Sensitive information does not,
of course, have to be in written form in a report; a nudge and
a wink over lunch is a more subtle, more common, and less

detectable way of passing secrets. The official Stock Exchange answer to this problem is that 'Chinese Walls' must be erected between the various parts of a financial services company, so that the interest of the public or investors comes first.

The arrival of the new monoliths also upset the staid City career structure. Salaries rocketed as a game of musical chairs for all but the most mundane jobs got under way. Staffs of merchant banks and broking firms, whose only regular bright spot had previously been the annual bonus payment, suddenly found, to their wonderment, that they had taken over from soccer professionals as the group in society most likely to be able to bid up earnings without lifting their game. 'The trick,' one twenty-six-year-old woman employed by a Swiss bank told me, 'is to always appear to be in demand. If they think you are about to leave, they will offer more without you having to ask for it.'

One might have expected the level of poaching to diminish over time. But, more than ten years after Big Bang, generous offers were still being made to whole teams of analysts. One of the worst to suffer was Deutsche Morgan Grenfell, an institution formed out of an alliance between one of London's oldest firms and the powerful Deutsche Bank. But, in 1997, it lost its entire four-person emerging market bond team to the Japanese group, Daiwa Europe. In the same month its deputy chairman, Peter Cadbury, responsible for some of Morgan Grenfell's most important relationships management, left to become joint chairman of a large corporate finance institution.

Some of the individuals involved cut a very high profile, none more so than Nicola Horlick, mother-of-five from West London, who made the headlines when she parted company with Deutsche Morgan Grenfell after being seen having lunch with senior officers from another company. It was alleged that she was planning to leave the company, for whom her team had quadrupled the value of the funds under management, a suggestion she strenuously denied. But within six months, after a series of tear-jerking stories in the tabloids about how as a woman in the City she had been 'picked on', she was leaving her £3 million home shortly after dawn each morning for a new job at DMG's deadly rivals, the French-owned Société Generale Asset Management. She was joined there by an old friend, John Richards, who had been on 'gardening leave', a euphemism for sitting at home doing nothing, after resigning as head of institutional investment management at another rival, Mercury Asset Management. Horlick's lifestyle, her £1 million a year income package, and her huge responsibilities, led to her being dubbed 'superwoman', a highly sexist remark because no one would ascribe the title 'superman' to a male with comparable responsibilities.

On the other hand few would agree with Nicola Horlick's own description of herself as 'an ordinary person doing an ordinary job'.

Along with a move towards a super league of financial conglomerates came another switch of attitudes – an obsession with short-term performance.

It has become clear that fund managers – the men and women who manage the money in pension funds, life assurance companies and unit trusts – are no longer prepared to play safe by maintaining large holdings in giant but dull corporations. Not long ago the average institutional investor shared his portfolio between government gilt-edged securities (interest-bearing bonds) and blue-chip equities (shares in well-known companies like Unilever, BP and ICI).

Now they prefer to move their money around, terrifying corporate treasurers who watch, helpless, as large blocks of their companies' shares are traded for what seems fashion or a whim. A fund manager may desert GEC, as many did soon after Big Bang, and buy into Siemens of Germany, Microsoft of America or NTT of Japan, thereby gambling on future currency movements as well as on the future profitability of a company or market sector. Or he may buy eurobonds. And because of the risk of volatile movements in exchange or interest rates, he may protect himself by an options or futures contract (of which more later), or both. The result is that fund managers tend towards taking profits whenever they present themselves. The London Stock Exchange, or LSE, as it is now known is – like the companies whose equities it trades – a limited liability company, whose shareholders are its members. The governing council has been replaced by a board of directors, drawn from the Exchange's executive, its customers and its users. And membership ranges from the world's largest investment bank to small local firms. At the end of 1996 there were 2,171 listed companies on the LSE with a market value of £1,011 billion.

3 How It Works

*'It's paper anyway. It was paper when we started
and it's paper now'* – Sam Moore Walton, a very rich
American.

*'When stocks go down, shoeshines go down. It's
rough'* – Wall Street shoe cleaner.

Each morning as dawn breaks over the City of London, a
square mile of grey stone and cement built on north Thames
mud flats and bordered by the Tower of London to the east
and the Law Courts to the west, there is an early rush hour,
which starts and finishes long before the commuter trains
empty their cargo of long-faced office workers. It happens
quickly as new shiny cars – Mercedes, BMWs, Porsches,
Saabs, Jaguars and Lexuses – are driven, tyres squealing, into
some of the world's most expensive car parks. Many of the
young men and women striding through the Italian-marbled
entrance halls of securities houses have flushed faces and
carry sports bags, evidence of a 30-minute workout in a
nearby gymnasium while most Britons are still in their beds.

Upstairs, in a conference room with clocks showing the
London time at seven o'clock, Tokyo at three in the afternoon, and New York at two in the morning, there is already
a buzz of activity, and intense concentration. The pre-trade
meeting is about to get underway. The morning newspapers
have already been discarded as ancient history; a television
news channel carrying financial news flickers in the background, but over the fresh coffee and orange juice the emphasis of the dialogue among the two dozen present is on the
tasks immediately ahead. A senior member of the company
discusses developments in Asian markets over the phone
with a colleague in Tokyo, occasionally turning up the
volume on the speaker so everyone can hear. 'You are sure

it's a new trend: they're not following Wall Street?' he asks. 'No, but they might be ramping that particular stock again,' comes back the answer.

A director calls the meeting to order, and bids a younger colleague to speak. 'We've got a council meeting of the Bundesbank this morning, the US trade figures, and results from British Airways and Honkers and Shankers [The Hong Kong and Shanghai Bank]. Plus a whole series of other numbers, and you've seen the Dun and Bradstreet survey which shows things might be overheating.' There is a brief discussion about the US money supply figures, and it is generally agreed that Wall Street traders the night before had already anticipated them. The company's specialist analyst on airline and transportation stocks then enters the room, carrying a sheaf of papers, which he distributes to those present. 'I think BA might surprise us,' he says. 'It's tough-going out there but they have really taken the axe to their costs.' 'Yeah, but what about the long term?' asks a young dealer with blue-striped shirt and dark blue braces. 'They've got a fight on their hands on the Atlantic, and an ageing fleet of planes.'

The discussion continues for a few minutes in similar vein, half earnest, half jousting, as the market makers – the men and women who have to set the prices at which the securities house will trade shares – challenge the seemingly unassailable logic of the analysts. Analysts, some of them trained in accountancy, some of them investment specialists, a few of them former financial journalists, are steeped in knowledge of the companies in the sectors in which they specialize. Whereas a market-maker has to make a split-second judgement on the value of a stock – often reacting to a news report – an analyst usually has the time to pore over company reports and other published information, talk to company chairmen and finance directors, compare their views with those of rival executives, and even visit factories and other operations.

'I'll bet you a bottle of squiff that BA falls by more than five pence,' blue-braces offers as a parting shot, as the discussion moves on to results just announced from Hong Kong and Shanghai, showing profits sharply up. 'It might be time to look at bank stocks again,' comes a comment from a woman in another group in the corner of the room. She and her group form part of the other key element of the modern sharebroking house – the equity salesmen.

Their job is to get more business moving through the trading desks by persuading clients – many of them large investing institutions like life assurance companies, pension funds and unit trusts – to buy blocks of shares in the market. Some of these shares might already be in the possession of the securities house as a result of it being appointed to handle a rights issue. Others may have been acquired in a trading operation; some might have to be bought and sold on. Equally, an equity salesman may have a client who is interested in a particular share. He will walk over to the dealing desk, and ask a market-maker how much it would cost to get hold of them.

Well before eight o'clock the meeting is over, and it is time to get to work. The equity salesmen go out to their desks and make a list of potential clients they will approach by phone. The analysts retreat behind glass partitions to paper-strewn work stations, and contemplate their next reports. And the market-makers are busy at their terminals, keying in the prices to tell their counterparts across the world at what price they are prepared to deal. By eight thirty the atmosphere is like a television portrayal of the newsroom of a major newspaper, but a trifle more tense, with more fever and more bustle. Most people appear to be on the telephone, their fitful but fleeting dialogues always punctuated by taps at a keyboard, which reveal an array of coloured numbers on the bank of computer screens that dominate their desks.

Every few minutes someone gets up from his high-back swivel chair and shouts a message – or, plastic coffee beaker in hand, wanders across the floor to talk with a colleague. For the most part these dialogues are friendly and unobtrusive, but the occasional sharp-edged rejoinder reminds the observer that this is a place where serious money is at stake.

My description is of the equities floor of one of London's largest securities houses, where each working day tens of millions of pounds worth of shares change hands. Most trading floors look the same. Large stakes in major companies are bought and sold, small allotments in privatization issues are traded, money is won or lost.

Down on the floor, on the central desk, the lead salesman touches the flickering light on his telephone panel that indicates a call is waiting, picks up the phone, and rests one foot on a drawer of his desk. The caller is a fund manager from one of Britain's largest life assurance companies. He is looking to pick up a million shares in one of the big breweries. The salesman keys into his computer the first three letters of the company's name, and the screen reveals to him that the price of the stock is higher than it has been for several weeks.

But it also shows that the posted price is only available for the purchase of 50,000 shares or less. Buying a block twenty times that size could be difficult. 'Leave it with me, we'll see what we can do, the price is good, so someone might be prepared to sell,' he tells his client. After ringing off, the salesman, a man in his early thirties, shirt-sleeved and displaying wide Wall Street braces, makes a few more keystrokes. In quick succession, two graphs appear on the screen – one of them portraying the movement of the share price of the brewery group over a five-year period; the other tracking it against the progress of the Financial Times-Stock Exchange One Hundred Share Index, popularly known as the Footsie. The graph shows that although the shares have been rising they have been outperformed by the index.

The salesman smiles, reflecting that one of the brewery's major shareholders may well be prepared to sell, given the higher price of the stock, and the prospect that by reinvesting elsewhere there will be a more profitable return. He keys in a few more strokes, and a printer at the end of the desk produces a sheet of paper with a breakdown of the company's major shareholders, in order of size of holding. Most of the names on the list are investment institutions, life assurance companies competing with the salesman's client, pension funds, and unit trust companies. But there are also some international companies and a handful of names of wealthy individuals. The salesman calls over a junior colleague, and tells him: 'See if you can do anything with this. We need a million.'

The young man returns to his desk, picks up his telephone, and starts making calls. Within 40 minutes he is back. 'I've got them,' he says, glowing with pleasure at his swift if unexpected achievement. The salesman whoops with joy, hits his client's number on the phone pad, and passes on the good news. He then walks over to market-makers sitting at another, larger bank of computers, and asks them to execute the deal. As mentioned earlier, market-makers set the price for shares and, within limits, are obligated to buy and sell at the prices they set. One of them keys in both the purchase and the sale: and the deal is complete. The salesman is well pleased. His firm's commission on the transaction will be about £150,000. A small percentage of that goes towards his annual bonus.

What is a share worth? This is a simple enough question, and it deserves a simple answer. Unfortunately short answers, such as 'whatever the market determines' are facile and meaningless.

The market is not unlike that for airline tickets. You can pay £1,200 for a fully flexible economy return ticket to New York, and find yourself sitting next to someone who has paid £225 for the same class of seat, the identical meals service, and the same quarter bottle of Californian Chardonnay.

The situation is similar in buying and selling shares. Various investors buy the same share at prices which show widespread differences, depending on day or minute purchased, the volume bought, and the system used to buy them.

In share transactions in Britain a class system exists, just as such a system is pervasive in British life. However unlike the general class system, it is not based on royalty, privilege of birth or inherited wealth, but on real money and corporate power. As you might expect those with the most financial clout get the best deals and the hottest information. That this should be the case is of increasing concern to a number of consumer pressure groups and those few members of parliament who have had the wit to notice.

How it works in Britain is a depressingly familiar story. Those dealing in large blocks of shares in the companies that make up the FTSE 100 may post the price at which they are prepared to buy or sell their stock on the London Stock Exchange's electronic trading system. By doing this they can directly influence the market. If they effect a trade at the posted price they not only save on brokers' commissions but also on the profit the money-maker takes by the spread between the price he buys and that for which he sells.

The rest of us have to buy and sell our shares through the market-making system, which means that we buy or sell at a price set by a man – it usually is a man – in a busy dealing room. Since we cannot deal with market makers direct, we also have to pay a broker's commission as well as a dealer's spread. Those without a stockbroker pay even more, directly or indirectly. This group includes the majority of those who have acquired popular shares through privatization or the floating off of mutual assurance companies over the last few years. Abandoned largely to their own devices, they have sold out their share holdings through High Street banks and building societies, many of whose front counter staff not only are totally ignorant of the working of the stock markets, but compound their ignorance by attempting to persuade investors to buy unit trusts and other packaged investment products of doubtful quality. They would be better off logging on to the Motley Fool on the Internet. The Motley Fool web site is discussed in Chapter 15.

Another pernicious aspect of the stock market's class system is the way in which it extends to the provision of information. Anyone can buy the *Financial Times*, of course, and it can and should be mined for information from those involved in any level of investment. But real-time share prices, and other up to the second market information, is only available to a privileged few who will wish to purchase it, which usually means the professionals. Computer services with real time prices and up to date news cost in the region of £10,000. At the next level down are Internet services and television programmes such as those provided by Financial Times Television. These are free, but, of course you have to pay around £10 per month for an Internet connection, or around the same amount for a subscription to cable or satellite television. Finally there are services like the BBC's Ceefax teletext, where the share prices are not current but are updated several times a day.

If you watch the football scores during a match's progress on Ceefax or Oracle, the ITV equivalent, goals are marked up almost immediately. It is strange indeed that a goal in a game of football is considered more significant than a share price movement that may affect many thousands of investors. Out the other way round, would viewers be prepared to accept a ruling by the Football Association that publication of scores could be delayed for 15 minutes because the rights had been sold to a media mogul like Rupert Murdoch? It is unthinkable. Yet the world's most important stock exchanges, including those in New York and London, have for years been able to get away with an insistence that publication of prices should be delayed 15 minutes except for those information providers that pay the exchanges a hefty fee. It is not surprising that, in Europe at least, this practice is being examined by the European Competitions Commissioner.

In order to understand the class system of share dealing, it is worth examining in some detail the way it applies in the London market. This will also help small investors to comprehend why it is that it is very hard for them to compete in the day to day market-place, and why it is usually better for a private individual to stand back from the flurry of the trading floor and make medium-term, rather than short-term, judgements.

The principal shares traded in London are those in the companies that make up the Financial Times-Stock Exchange 100 index, or Footsie. Since mid October 1997 these shares have been traded on the Stock Exchange's order book system – known as SETS, an acronym for Stock Exchange Electronic Trading System. This matches orders placed electronically by prospective buyers and sellers, partly replacing the quote driven system where deals were done by telephone.

So instead of agreeing to trade at a price set by a market-maker, as described later, buyers and sellers of large blocks of stocks can advertise through their broker the price at which they would like to deal, and then choose to wait for the market to move in their favour, or to execute the deal immediately at the best price currently available. Only members of the London Stock Exchange can enter orders directly into SETS.

Under the system, investors wishing to deal will contact their broker by phone or by electronic mail, and agree the price at which they are willing to buy or sell a particular stock. The broker will enter the order directly into the order book, and it will be displayed anonymously to the entire market.

For example, the broker could open his screen on the stock and find an investor wants to sell 4,000 shares at once, at the 'best price' available. At the time the best 'buy' order available is for 17,800 shares at 938 pence. The 'sell' order for 4,000 shares will automatically trade against the 'buy' order – leaving 13,800 shares at 938 pence still on the order book. The second the order is executed, the trade is automatically reported to the Exchange, and the market informed immediately.

This is only one type of share trade using the order book system. Another common deal is the limit order. Here the investor posts specific details of the proposed trade – the number of shares, the price and the date upon which the offer will close. These limit orders sit on the SETS electronic order book until either they are matched or they pass the expiry date.

Another is the execute and eliminate order. It sounds like a command from the old Soviet KGB, but in fact is very similar to an 'at best' order, but with a limit price specified.

Automatic execution through the order book takes place between 08.30 until 16.30. From 08.00 there is a half-hour period during which orders can be added or deleted in readiness for the trading day. In the half-hour between the end of the trading day and 17.00 there is a housekeeping period during which orders that have not been executed may be deleted if brokers do not wish to leave them on the book overnight.

The introduction of this form of trading has made London more efficient, and brought it in line with its major competitors, who were threatening to take a great deal of institutional business because of the lower spreads and cheaper commissions available through order book trading. Until its introduction spreads in the old system gave market-makers a turn of an average of 0.6 per cent, the highest of any big market. France, Germany, Italy and Spain were operating on spreads of one sixth of this amount. It also created a big reduction in commissions.

Country	Size £bn	Type of Market
US-New York	4300	Floor auction with electronic order routing
US-Nasdaq	870	Electronic quote driven plus limit orders
Japan	1940	Floor auction and electronic order book
Britain	1150	Mixed electronic order book and quote driven system
Germany	480	Mixed floor auction and electronic order book
France	340	Electronic order book
Netherlands	325	Mixed floor quote driven and electronic order book
Canada	300	Electronic order book
Hong Kong	300	Partially electronic order book (input on floor)
Australia	180	Electronic order book
Italy	165	Electronic order book
Spain	130	Electronic order book

Source: Credit Lyonnais Laing

So, as the table illustrates, in London and the other large financial centres, shares are no longer traded on a floor. Gone are the days when visitors could climb two storeys at the London Stock Exchange to a public gallery and enjoy the spectacle of scores of dealers clutching paper orders and milling round the jobbers as they set the prices. On busy days there would be a crush, and a great roar would go up when an item of news was flashed across the ticker screen. The old floor looked not unlike a flea market; the analogy is a good one for real bargains were struck every minute of the trading day.

The excitement has now been transferred to the dealing rooms of the large securities houses where, despite the arrival of order-based trading, the focus is still on the market-makers. Market-makers set the prices for all transactions other than those booked through SETS. Although, at the time of writing, the London Stock Exchange hoped that at least half of the FTSE 100 trades would be conducted through SETS by the end of 1998, it seems inevitable that market-makers will still have the major role in share dealing until well beyond the year 2000.

So most of us will trade our shares on the quote driven system, SEAQ, short for Stock Exchange Automated Quotation System. It works like this.

The market-makers sit at their terminals all day, their only exercise swivelling in the chairs to shout across to a colleague or taking a 30-minute break to visit a gymnasium or squash club. Not all market-makers can trade all shares; their baili-wick is those sectors in which their firm has elected and been authorized to make a market. Like the jobbers of the past, the market-makers will typically specialize: for example, in oil stocks, the leisure sector, industrials, banks and so on. Once a bid and offer price have been entered, the market-maker is obliged to trade at that price, although of course he can alter his figures at any time in response to market condi-tions – in other words after he has seen what the opposition is doing. The SEAQ system covers more than 3,500 securi-ties, and is divided into three groups of stocks – alpha, beta, and gamma.

As the name implies alpha stocks are the most actively traded shares, and market-makers who buy or sell must immediately enter the trade into the SEAQ system. From SEAQ the trade details are passed instantly to the London Stock Exchange's electronic information service, which is available to traders, brokers and investors.

So, to take an example of an investor purchasing 500 shares in British Petroleum, how does the new system work? His broker or licensed financial intermediary will call out the BP page from the system, and see an array of offers from more than a dozen market-makers, each of them identified by a code. One line will say 'ML 36–40 1 × 1'. This means that Merrill Lynch, for example, are prepared to buy BP at £9.36 and to sell at £9.40, and that their figure applies for pur-chases or sales of 1,000 shares or less. Another line might say 'BZW 36–41 1 × 2', indicating that Barclays de Zoete Wedd will buy at the same price as Merrill Lynch, but that they will only sell BP at £9.41, and then only in units of up to 2,000.

Another page on SEAQ will reveal that ten minutes earlier there had been a large transaction of BP shares at £9.38. Assuming he wants to trade, the broker calls the dealing desk of his own or another firm and asks to buy BP at £9.40. If the broker's firm is also listed as a market-maker in BP, the bro-ker will try and keep the deal 'in-house' by persuading his own colleagues to match the Merrill offer, which they may or may not be willing to do. When the bargain is struck, the market-maker enters it into the BP SEAQ page; other market-makers, noting the transaction, readjust their offers accordingly.

Deals in beta stocks are concluded in exactly the same way, except that not all trades are logged, and there are fewer market-makers, perhaps only two or three, who will usually be firms that have decided to specialize in a particular sector, such as electronics, or insurance. In the case of gamma stocks, only indicative quotes are provided, so that any broker anxious to consider a purchase has to call the market-maker and negotiate a price, often based on volume. Many of the market-makers in the gamma section may be regional brokers, who know companies in their area well and are better placed to hold the book than a large London conglomerate.

For the technically-minded, the SEAQ system operates on two dedicated mainframe computers, designed to respond to entries within one second, update information at a peak rate of 20 items per second, and handle up to 70,000 transactions an hour. In the event of a computer crash, a major fire or bomb outrage at the Stock Exchange, all the records would be saved, for parallel computers operate in another part of London and, for double protection, in the United States. The entire capitalist system is not likely to fail because of a power cut!

Brokers and dealers get their information through a personal computer, connected to the SEAQ system either by direct data line or, in the case of the smaller user or provincial broker, by a leased telephone line. Those who wish to use the system only occasionally may do so through an ordinary phone line, connecting their computer to the jack via a standard modem. Those on the move may use a laptop computer plugged into the telephone.

While equities represent the most interesting aspect of stock market activity, and offer the investor the greatest degree of risk and reward, it is important not to overlook gilts, as they are known in Britain, or bonds everywhere else. Gilts is short for gilt-edged securities, and these, as the name suggests, are units of a loan tranche issued by the Government to fund its spending. Gilts are issued for a fixed term at a fixed rate of interest, but no one is obligated to hold them for the whole period. But like all fixed interest securities they offer the holder the security of regular interest payments, as well as repayment of the amount borrowed at maturity.

There is a substantial market in buying and selling these bonds, the prices of which vary according to how far out of line their fixed interest rates are with the standard rates of interest applying at the time in the economy. If interest rates are falling, then gilts with a higher rate will be sold at a premium of their basic price. As with equities prices are set by market-makers, drawn from 25 firms.

There are three types of gilts traded. Those with five years or less to run until redemption are known as shorts; those with a redemption period of between 5 and 15 years are mediums, while longs are those stocks with a redemption date of more than 15 years.

In the United States the equivalent to gilts are bonds known as Treasuries – because they are issued by the United States Treasury. Treasuries, particularly long bonds, have been popular over the years with Japanese investors, who have taken the risk that the rate of return in dollars will be greater than the decline of the dollar against the yen.

Large corporations also issue bonds, at rates of interest which are higher than government bonds, but which are also highly secure investments. Some of these offer the option to convert the bond to equities at a favourable price. It has also become fashionable for large corporations to raise money outside the country in which they are based and in another currency. These are known as Eurobonds, and almost one third of these securities are listed on the London Stock Exchange.

Another form of security is a warrant. This allows the holder the right to subscribe, at a fixed price, for shares in the company at some future date. Warrants are high-risk, and offer the holders neither dividends nor voting rights. If the holder decides not to subscribe for the underlying shares, then the paper is worthless.

These, and other even more exotic securities, are known as derivatives, and the interested reader should look out one of the many specialist books devoted to them, or read the regular surveys that appear in the *Financial Times*.

4 The Street

'I would rather be vaguely right than precisely wrong' – Warren Buffett

'Risk arbitrage is not gambling in any sense. Traditional stock investing is much closer to gambling than is risk arbitrage' – Ivan Boesky, in his book *Merger Mania.*

'The New York Stock Exchange is perhaps the most substantial and perfect financial temple in the world' – John Rodemeyer.

Wall Street is the term used to describe the financial district of New York, and, like the City, it occupies only a small area of the business capital of the United States. Wall Street is in lower Manhattan, facing out to the Statue of Liberty, and the stock market grew up there in support of the merchants and bankers who, two centuries ago, established themselves on the tip of the island, when it was the pre-eminent business centre of America.

In those days Wall Street was the most important thoroughfare. Cargo ships were moored on the nearby East River, and the commodities they brought were traded in offices and warehouses on what became known as 'The Street'. As in London, everything in the area was destroyed by a Great Fire: the one in Wall Street occurred in 1835, and the damage stretched from the present site of City Hall to the Statue of Liberty.

The New York Stock Exchange was founded on its present site, the block bounded by Wall, Broad and New Streets and Exchange Place, although it has been rebuilt several times since the construction in 1864 of Renwick's $2 million marble-fronted wooden building, highlighted by eight lacquered columns and a rococo cornice.

The first New York Stock Exchange was more like a gentlemen's club than a business centre. There were 1,100 members, and its books and records were as closely guarded as those of a Masonic lodge. There was an honorary president, with few duties, and two salaried vice-presidents, but they had little to do except open and close trading at the morning and afternoon sessions.

The Exchange conducted its business by way of auctions, not dissimilar to those used by Sotheby's in the fine art market. Sellers would hand in their shares to the vice-president, who would guard them rather like a cloakroom attendant at a large hotel. They would be auctioned in blocks, and sold to the highest bidder. Inevitably, as with real estate auctions, some deals took place outside the room, usually in the street, and a number of sub-exchanges grew up, often handling specialist shares.

One of these grew into an exchange of its own, operating from another building in Lower Broad Street, where it was known as the Open Board, so called because access was available to anyone prepared to pay a $50 membership fee. Once inside there was no auction, no organization and no records were kept: buyers simply met potential sellers and dealt. The Open Board operated six days a week, and kept open as long as there were sufficient people about.

Out of this chaos developed the ticker, telegraph machines which simply listed the latest prices at which stocks were traded. As access to the ticker spread beyond Wall Street and New York itself to other American cities, further share trading exchanges grew up, using the ticker as a guide to prices.

This development was viewed with some alarm by the elders of the New York Stock Exchange. Although the ticker services generated more business, their activities were outside NYSE control, their prices were sometimes wrong, and they led to the proliferation of rival trading locations. So in 1885 reporters of ticker companies were barred from the floor of the exchange, and forced to purchase the information. Within five years the New York Stock Exchange had control of the ticker, and was able to insist that the Western Union telegraph company which distributed it make it available only to licensed brokerages and other approved buyers. (This, as we shall see later, created an unfortunate precedent.)

By this time business had grown to such a level that the auction system could not cope. What took its place was a sub-system of specialist auctions within the trading floor. Legend has it that a broker called Boyd broke his leg and, finding hobbling around the floor on crutches difficult, remained at one post to trade his shares. After his leg had mended, he discovered that this mode of operation had become so profitable that he stuck with it, thus creating the specialist market-making auction system that still exists today.

I can find no evidence that this story is anything but apocryphal, but something like this happened, and provided the basis for present-day trading in New York. The NYSE believes it is the 'world's fairest, most open, and most technologically advanced marketplace'. These days about one quarter of the membership of the New York Stock Exchange are specialist market-makers, operating in 66 units. These units operate as principals in the shares in which they specialize.

These specialists form about a quarter of the professionals working on the floor of the exchange. The others are the people they deal with – the brokers and traders.

A broker buying or selling shares on behalf of a client in any of the over 2,000 issues listed on the New York Stock Exchange will go to one of the 22 trading posts. There he will approach market-makers, rather as in London, in the old days, brokers used to seek out jobbers, and seek a price. The market-maker is obliged to be ready to buy and sell, and he has to balance his own books. If he is left with an oversupply or shortage of stock at the end of the day he has to hold it in his own account.

In theory the market-maker only changes his prices by notches: thus he is not supposed to react to any dramatic turn of events by radical shifts. In practice he is human, and will not want to pay over-the-odds for a share which is tumbling. Running for cover is not encouraged. On the other hand when large institutions trade very large blocks of shares, it is unreasonable to expect an individual to hold out against a hurricane. The New York Stock Exchange attempts to keep market-makers on track by policing price movements very carefully, and by encouraging competition.

This competition exists, of course, within the exchange, but also from rivals. One of these rivals is known as the over-the-counter market, so called because sharebrokers anywhere in the United States or elsewhere can buy or sell stock for customers who drop by. This market is run by NASDAQ, an acronym for National Association of Securities Dealers Automated Quotation System.

NASDAQ

NASDAQ, which lists over 5,500 American and international companies, is the second largest and fastest growing equity market in the United States, though, of course, being only just over 25 years old, it starts from a smaller base. Even so it trades more shares than the NYSE, a total of 138.1 billion in 1996.

There are good reasons for this. Like Britain's SEAQ for which it provided a model, NASDAQ uses computers and telecommunications – the information age technologies – to bring securities firms together electronically, enabling them to compete with each other over the computer rather than on a trading floor in a single location. All the information needed for trading is in the open, on the NASDAQ computer screen, available at the press of the button.

This, to my mind, makes it more effective. Many of the world's leading information technology companies think so too, for they have chosen to list on NASDAQ. The fundamental difference is that a traditional floor-based exchange centralizes people in a single location where trading takes place face-to-face. NASDAQ centralizes the information, but then makes it available to those who need it wherever they are.

The central computer system for NASDAQ is in Trumbull, Connecticut, but there is a full back-up facility in Rockville, near Washington, in case of failure. Trumbull and Rockville are connected by 80,000 miles of leased telephone lines to 3,400 securities houses that use them to display prices at which they are willing to trade – as well as to report sales and purchases, and other market data. The NASDAQ system is always being refined and updated and is considerably superior to SEAQ. There is plenty of competition for a typical NASDAQ stock has 11 market-makers hungry for business.

NASDAQ market-makers, which include large national full-service firms, regional firms, local firms, and wholesale market-makers – are based in 38 states and in the city of Washington in which the organization has its headquarters. Securities dealers in over 6,000 offices have at their finger tips an exact, national, instantaneous wholesale price system, available in San Francisco, Chicago or Dallas at the same time as Wall Street. Indeed, it goes beyond that. There are over 8,500 quotation terminals outside the United States, most of them, about 5,000, in Europe, and NASDAQ plans to extend this.

The NASDAQ system is of benefit also to anyone else in the investment business, from brokers in San Antonio to the man on the stockbroker counter at the local shopping mall, and to those in London who want instant information about the American market. There is nothing to stop individual investors subscribing, and NASDAQ already has over 100,000 hooked up, including brokers who are members of the London Stock Exchange. Those who pay a small subscription have access to the system through a dumb terminal and a black and white monitor. By using a word code on the terminal keyboard, they can obtain on the screen a representative 'bid' and a representative 'ask' price on the stock; for example, if dealers or market-makers have quoted bids on a particular stock of 40, 40.25, 40.50, 40.75, and 41, the representative bid would be 40.5. If those with a terminal wish to buy or sell – or if their customer so wishes – all they have to do is to phone their broker and seek a real quote, asking that it should be close to the representative figure on the screen, and stipulating, if they wish, how far from the figure they are prepared to trade.

NASDAQ has a more sophisticated, and more expensive, service for professional traders. In this case, having obtained a representative quote, a user may then seek actual quotes from the firms making the market in the stock. This is what would happen if an individual using the basic service were to phone in. The screen would display all those offering a quote, together with their names and telephone numbers, ranked in order of best price. The final barter then takes place over the telephone, and the new quote is inputted on the screen, with the computer updating the representative or average price.

All deals in securities that are traded regularly and in large volume – a list of about 3,000 stocks – must be reported within 90 seconds of the trade taking place. There are safeguards built into the NASDAQ system to attempt to prevent malpractice, and to seek to provide the investor with the same security that he had under the London jobbing system. Once registered in a stock, a NASDAQ dealer must be prepared to buy or sell at any time, in much the same way as a jobber has been obliged to stand behind his price. There must be at least two market-makers for each stock quoted.

A market-maker whose spread – the difference between his 'buy' and 'sell' quotation – is more than double that of the representative or average spread, will be warned by the computer that his spread is excessive. The computer warning also finds its way into the directories of the National Association of Security Dealers, which will almost certainly call for an explanation, and may take disciplinary action.

Another safety measure is a provision in the NASDAQ rules that when a member dealer buys on his own account and not on behalf of a client, he should do so at a price which is 'fair' in relation to the prices being made by the market-makers. The factors which should be taken into account by both members and disciplinary committees in determining the fairness of such deals are set out in the Association's Rules of Fair Practice, and include the type of security and its availability in the market.

All members of NASDAQ must be members of the Securities Investor Protection Corporation, established by Congress in 1970; this means that those who buy and sell through the system have exactly the same protection as they would if they were dealing on the New York Stock Exchange. If an investor, or anyone else, feels he has been maltreated, or that there has been malpractice, the SIPC will contact the Association, which maintains a three-year computer file record of every price movement in a stock, and may trace the history of the stock second by second, identifying when changes took place, who initiated them, and what was the root cause. With such a complete audit trail, investigations are relatively easy to conduct.

5 Rough Winds in Tokyo

'We are rushing out into a wilderness where rough winds blow' – Juniche Ujiie, president of Nomura Securities.

On a busy day the stock market in Tokyo resembles a surging crowd on London's Waterloo station when the trains are all delayed. The dealers face the various display boards, indicating the latest prices, and at the slightest sign of action or excitement, surge forward together, their hands outstretched in unison in a kind of salute to capitalism. In mid-1997 Tokyo had a market valued at over $2,900 billion, and, on average, 330 million shares change hands every day.

Since the Second World War it has overtaken all the other exchanges in its volume of share trading, and is second only to New York in the value of stock moved. But for all this strength it is an erratic market, relatively open to manipulation. From time to time it also runs short of liquidity.

Even the Japanese government is not above managing the market when it suits it to do so, which damages Tokyo's credibility and makes it a place small investors should avoid. During the roaring bull market of the 1980s, the Japanese ruling Liberal Democrats privatized part of Nippon Telephone and Telegraph (NTT) at $7,100 per share. Further tranches were later sold off at even higher prices to enthusiastic private investors. But by mid-1992, after the steepest decline in share prices in post Second World War history, those NTT shareholders who had not taken their losses and got out were sitting on a decline in the value of their 'safe' investment of more than 80 per cent. With election pressures mounting, Kabun Muto, chairman of the Liberal Democrats' tax affairs council, told the government it had a 'duty' to small investors to get the share price back to its original offer price.

After leaks that the price of local phone calls would be increased, that optical fibre cable would be laid with the help of government investment, and that more than ¥10 million of public money would be spent in buying shares in good companies, the price of NTT stock moved back up to its previous levels. In other words all good dirty fun.

The Tokyo Stock Exchange, founded in 1878, combines the specialist system of New York with electronic trading. The shares of Japan's major corporations, and some overseas multinationals, are traded in what is called the First Section: dealing is broken up into a number of key industry groups, such as electronics, chemicals, utilities and so on.

In 1990, there were 1,200 corporate stocks listed in the First Section with a market capitalization of 404 trillion yen. Some of them are very large. NTT, for example, is the most heavily capitalized stock in the world, valued at more than the whole of the Italian stock market. The Second Section comprises smaller companies, and although some trading does take place on the floor, much of it is done through computers by a system known as CATS, Computer Assisted Trading System.

The criteria for a listing on the Tokyo First Section are onerous. A company must list 20 million shares or more, and the average monthly trading volume must be higher than 200,000 shares. The company must also demonstrate a dividend record of at least five yen per share for the previous three years, with the prospect also of being able to maintain that in future.

Dealing is handled by member brokers, including a number of overseas securities houses. Getting a licence in Japan is both expensive and time-consuming; the licences have only been made available to non-Japanese under substantial pressure from the United States and Europe. In the Pacific rim, Tokyo has become by far the most important financial centre, surpassing Hong Kong.

Tokyo's international role was not planned. It was a byproduct of the Japanese government's decision to liberalize the financial sector, mainly for domestic reasons. Japan is the largest exporter of capital in the world. The main source of this flow of yen outside the country is the huge pool of money saved by Japanese men and women. They save almost one-fifth of their incomes each year, putting money aside at four times the rate of Americans. This prudence generates roughly $3,500 billion a year. Another factor is the Japanese trade surplus created by successful exports. Although some of this money has found its way into industrial investment – such as Nissan's successful car assembly plant in the north of England, Toyota's venture in Derby and Sony's factory in Wales – much of it is invested in equities, bonds and real estate in the United States, Europe and Australia.

Another way this pool of wealth may be tapped is by securing a listing in Tokyo, so that the Japanese may invest in your corporation without moving their money outside the yen zone. But, unlike London, Tokyo has so far not promoted itself vigorously as a financial centre. One reason for this is that if it did so the Japanese government would find itself exposed to criticism that it was seeking to keep its financial surpluses at home. But despite this lack of promotion more and more international companies have been seeking to list their shares in Japan, despite the expense of doing so. Though costs vary, a multinational is unlikely to be able to obtain a listing through for less than $100,000, plus $75,000 a year running expenses.

Many companies do so in the hope of attracting Japanese shareholders to their registers. But I think a more compelling reason is that a listing ensures that the Japanese investment community, at all levels, gets to know about them, thereby providing immediate recognition and some long-term commercial benefits. Conducting business in Japan can be a complex and frustrating experience. A listing on the Tokyo Stock Exchange automatically bestows a Japanese status on foreign companies, making it easier for them to deal with both local and central government in Japan, Japanese industrialists and consumers.

Take, for example, Britain's leading trading bank and financial institution, Barclays. It has had representation in Japan for more than 20 years, was the first European bank to obtain privileged Japanese trust bank status, and decided it should list because, as a senior official put it to me: 'We are a global business, and therefore want to reflect that in the ownership of our shares. Secondly we have quite a big business in Japan, and we want to be able to use this share ownership as a way of increasing our picture, and we want to increase the number of owners of our shares.'

The reasoning was put the other way round by a senior staffer at Nomura Securities: 'The Japanese do not buy unfamiliar companies unless it's an exciting stock.' He said he thought a Tokyo listing useful for 'any company that has a consumer orientation and has identification at a retail level, and any company that has major operations in Japan or Asia. Heavy borrowers should also consider a TSE listing. If you've got all three it's a must.'

However obtaining and maintaining a listing in Japan carries with it considerably more work than achieving the same position in London or elsewhere. Applicants must be prepared for rigorous investigation by Japanese regulators. Once accepted, good investor relations become another substantial commitment. There is also another worry – the technical problem known in the jargon of stockbroking as 'flowback'. What happens is that if an investor in a company listed in London or New York cannot buy sufficient stock in those markets, he may simply instruct a Tokyo broker to purchase it in Japan. Thus the Tokyo equity may end up being largely held, not by Japanese or Asian investors, but by Americans or Europeans, thus largely defeating the purpose of a Japanese listing.

At the end of 1997 there were over 60 foreign companies listed on the Tokyo Stock Exchange, most of them from the United States, but with significant numbers from Europe and Australia.

From the United States they include financial institutions like Citicorp, Nations Bank, JP Morgan and Merrill Lynch; the automotive manufacturer, Chrysler; manufacturers like Boeing, Procter & Gamble, IBM, Apple and Motorola; and consumer giants McDonalds and PepsiCo. Also there are Mobil Corporation, Occidental, Dow Chemical, MIM, and GTE.

Two British banks, Barclays and Natwest, are on the list. Whereas no US telecoms company is listed, both British Telecom and Cable & Wireless from the UK are there. Other companies to note are BP, P & O, and BTR.

European representation includes all three major Swiss banks, food giant Nestlé, France's Alcatel, Sweden's Volvo, and Germany's Commerzbank, Dresdner Bank, Deutsche Bank, Hoechst, Daimler Benz, Volkswagen and Deutsche Telekom, the last mentioned as a result of its massive privatization in 1996, the biggest in European history.

A company needs to be of substance before a listing in Tokyo can be sought, but a recent relaxation in listing criteria opens the prospect up to a much wider group than before. The shareholders' equity required is now the yen equivalent to approximately 10 million US dollars, about a tenth of the previous required size.

Until recently annual profits had to be about 10 million US dollars, but this requirement has been reduced to $4 million in the last fiscal year, and an average of no less than $2 million over the past three years. That means that a company could have incurred a loss in one year, but still be considered for a listing.

It is inevitable, with the growth of Asian economies, that the Tokyo Stock Exchange will gain in both stature and size. Its members work long hours in a vigorous market. Ten years ago Japanese fund managers and market experts had a reputation for having no imagination and showing excessive caution. This is seldom the case today. 'We are stock-picking on an international scale – we intend to be number one,' the senior manager of one of Nomura Securities' divisions told me.

Until the collapse of Yamaichi in the autumn of 1997 over half of the business in Tokyo was handled by just four firms – Nomura, Yamaichi, Nikko and Daiwa. The big four accounted for three-quarters of all underwriting business in Japan, and half of all share broking. Nomura Securities is the world's largest securities house. Founded as a small money-changing shop in the back-streets of Osaka in 1872, it now makes more money than Japan's two auto giants, Honda and Toyota, and is one of the largest companies in the world.

In Japan it wields enormous power. Every Tuesday afternoon, at its headquarters in the Urbannet Otemachi Building, its senior stock-picker issues its selection. Nomura salesmen on the fifth floor telephone the prized information to selected clients and to the firm's extensive branch network, and within minutes the Tokyo stock market in Kabuto-cho is scrambling with buying orders. Nomura has sales shops right across Japan, mostly staffed by women who visit clients door-to-door, and who sell aggressively on the telephone. Their network was built on an old idea, adopted from the 1950's 'Man from the Pru' in Britain. The Japanese version has Nomura representatives lending wooden savings boxes to housewives, asking them to put all their 10-yen coins into a box.

Nomura provides a good example of Japanese aggression conducted with dignity and a certain amount of stealth. From its unpretentious headquarters in Tokyo it spreads its tentacles across every continent with offices in 28 cities in 19 countries. Its shareholders' equity is $14.3 billion, its assets total $126 billion, and it has 15,000 employees. It is by far the world's largest and richest securities house, earning more profits than Barclays Bank and JP Morgan combined. In 1986 it chose London as the location of one of two world regional centres – the other is in New York – and its declared aim is to become the dominant financial institution in every area of business. It is clear that, together with its domestic rivals, Daiwa and Nikko it poses as great a threat to the City as Sony and NEC have been in the electronics industry, and Toyota, Nissan and Honda to the motor industry. It will succeed by ruthlessly cutting prices to gain market shares – it has already done this in the bond markets. By 1996 it had become one of the top lead managers in the Eurobond market worldwide, managing $34.6 billion. In London it bought the vast old General Post Office building in St Martin's Le-Grand, and has preserved the façade while gutting the interior to provide one of the City's most impressive headquarters buildings. This is the Japanese technique – to operate behind the shelter of a local façade in just the same way that Nissan used a British company, Datsun UK, to build up a presence.

It seems improbable that Nomura will, in the short term, buy a British bank but more likely that it will be a wholesaler of finance and financial products, perhaps using a building society network at one end of the scale, and a sophisticated investment bank dealing with mergers and acquisitions at the other.

In recent years Nomura has been the largest single employer of Oxbridge graduates, ousting Unilever, BP, Shell and ICI from the top spots. These new recruits are each year flown to Tokyo for six months' training, and quickly become enthusiastic about their new employer.

Nomura and other Japanese securities houses showed remarkable prescience in hiring so many Oxbridge graduates, for as the end of the millennium approached it became clear that London's predominance as the most important international financial centre would be undiminished. In October 1997, Nikko Securities, Japan's third largest broker, moved responsibility for international operations away from its Tokyo base to London. At the same time it strengthened its collaboratioin with Barclays of Britain and Smith Barney of the US.

Masashi Kaneko, Nikko's president told the *Financial Times* why:

'With globalization we cannot manage our operations just by Japanese people. We want to learn from international investment bankers. Japanese investors are looking to diversify their portfolios more into international markets, so we have to strengthen our capability in that area.'

Recruits I met from Nomura seem to agree.

'I joined Nomura because I think their global expansion programme is absolutely phenomenal,' said Christopher. 'I am sure they are going to come up as number one ahead of the others.'

'They are going to be very, very big,' said Catherine. 'They are very ambitious, and the togetherness and the spirit really is obvious.'

'They really believe in team work,' said James, 'yet I am also amazed at the degree of responsibility that last year's graduates have been given.'

Didn't any of these young Britons feel uneasy that their country's own institutions might suffer as a result of the sheer force of Nomura's thrust? All scoffed at the suggestion. James held up a white Nomura carrier bag.

'I joined a Japanese institution for precisely that reason,' he said. 'I have brought this to show you because it sums up Nomura's attitude. It says: "Nomura makes money make money." Now a British institution would probably have had a Latin ode. Nomura knows what it is up to.'

He might have added that one of those Latin odes related

to honesty and propriety. Unfortunately Nomura failed to live up to the standards expected of it. On March 14 1997 Nomura's president, Hideo Sakamaki, was forced to resign after the company admitted making illegal payments totalling $50 million to *sokaiya*, mob gangsters who made a good living from threatening to disrupt companies' annual meetings. Nomura had been convicted of the same offence six years earlier, and it suffered the penalty of closure for a month of its equity sales and equity trading departments, which cost it $36 million in lost revenue.

This sent a shock-wave through the Tokyo markets, and Nomura began to lose major clients, like Tokyo Electric. The Ministry of Finance threatened to suspend the firm from trading for six months, which could effectively have put it out of business.

This threat was never carried out because Nomura appointed a new president, Junichi Ujiie, who promised to clean up Nomura's act. Ujiie had been out of the country when the offences took place so he was clean. Moreover he had served Nomura in the United States, where he developed an understanding of American ethics.

Ujiie got rid of 20 of Nomura's 43 directors, including everyone at the level of senior managing director and above, noting that this reduced the average age of members of the Nomura board from 55 to 48. It was the biggest purge in any Japanese company since the end of World War Two when the US military stripped many large corporations of their entire boards.

The move came not a moment too soon. The scandal led to customers deserting Nomura in droves. Big domestic borrowers on the bond market like Mitsubishi Motors, Tokyo Electric and the City of Yokohama dropped Nomura as an issuer. The firm's shares of business on the Tokyo Stock Exchange fell to just over six per cent, putting it in bottom place of the big four rather than top. It was also removed from the syndicate for Japanese government bonds.

Trouble at home was not the only problem. At the time of writing it was being prosecuted in Australia for allegedly manipulating the vulnerable local share market. In Britain it was suggested it had access to stolen documents in its support for an unsuccessful takeover bid for the Cooperative

Wholesale Society.

But as has been proved in London and elsewhere people have short memories of scandal, and it is probable that Nomura's fall from grace will be short. It is still a very large and powerful organization. A poll in *Diamond* magazine after the scandal emerged put Nomura favourite with chief financial officers. Ujiie not only changed the board, but he also changed the style of management: it became more open, less study. Outside directors were appointed, almost unheard of in Japanese corporations. The notorious 'recommended stock' list, issued to branches as administrative guidance, was abolished. And he made it clear that he would not tolerate malpractice and corruption. Nomura, he said, should be 'a company unable to act in anything other than a right-minded way in accordance with the spirit of the law'.

The spate of scandals affecting Japan's leading brokers had a substantial silver lining for British and American firms operating in Tokyo. They picked up a great deal of business. In the month of August 1997, the 21 foreign securities houses operating in Japan overtook the Japanese big four for the first time in history. As the year progressed, foreign brokers were busily expanding their staffs, while Japanese securities houses were cutting theirs.

6 Europe Takes to Shares

When, in the winter of 1990, the Berlin Wall came crashing down, symbolizing the end of the Cold War, there was an atmosphere of unrestrained euphoria. Germany, at last, could be reunited. New democracies in Czechoslovakia, as she then was, Hungary and Poland would take their rightful place in the European Community.

In February the following year I was staying in a small pension in a ski resort in Switzerland when a fleet of black cars turned up bearing Chancellor Helmut Kohl of Germany and the leaders of these emergent countries. Over lunch they talked bravely of the new dawn, how together they would help to rebuild Europe from the Atlantic to the Urals. At the World Economic Forum in nearby Davos they were besieged by businessmen anxious to take advantage of the new opportunities in the East.

One year later, at the 1992 Forum, the atmosphere was totally different. The faces of the East European government leaders showed the strains of office. There was not enough money to rebuild their shattered economies, production was falling, and unemployment was rising above 25 per cent. Chancellor Kohl was suffering politically because of the financial strain of supporting the East. Lester Thurow, professor of management at the Sloan School of Management at the Massachusetts Institute of Technology, said: 'What Europe needs is a Marshall Plan. If something is not done you will have a migration problem: the Poles will be in Paris.'

Having abandoned communism and embraced capitalism, the 'ossies', as they were called, found that the system that had paid dividends to the Germans, the French, the Dutch and the Italians appeared too cumbersome to do anything for them. The saner amongst them realized, of course, that the wrongs of 50 years would not be put right immediately. But capitalism was showing its cracks, and the biggest disappointment was that Europe's share markets failed to rise to the occasion. The buccaneering spirit that had seen the rise of Britain's first two public companies, the Muscovy Company and the East India Company, was not alive on Europe's bourses.

The cost of rebuilding the East was put at about one trillion dollars – and there are only three ways in which it can be found. The first is by taxing those who will benefit by an expanded market – West Europeans. This is political suicide. The second is through bank loans, but the banking system is overstretched and can only do so much. That leaves the bourses, which in Europe lack leadership and cohesion.

With the exception of London, which, in any case has a global rather than a European vision, the bourses in Europe have historically been narrow institutions, focused on the past, with little vision beyond the national boundaries of the countries in which they operate.

One reason for this, of course, is that they were shattered by the Nazi domination of Europe in the Second World War, when capital in many countries was devalued or destroyed. But that does not wholly explain their relatively insignificant role in capital formation. The real reason is the dominance of banks, both as a vehicle for individual savings and a source of finance for industry.

As Anthony Sampson explained in his book *The New Europeans*:

> The big continental banks evoke a much deeper dread than the British, partly because they have embraced industry with a closer hug. Their power goes back to the nineteenth century. The French Rothschilds helped to finance the railways in France and beyond, and their rivals the Pereires set a pattern for the 'universal bank', collecting savings from small-savers and deploying the capital for the development and control of industry, which was followed elsewhere in the continent. The French banks soon fell behind the German banks, who played a key part in the new industries, and used their deposits, and their customers' proxies, to establish controlling shares in the big companies. A German bank, as the saying went, accompanied an industrial enterprise from the cradle to the grave, from establishment to liquidation throughout all the vicissitudes of its existence.

Even a writer with Sampson's capacity for thoroughness could find no room for the bourses in his 450 pages. This is not surprising, given their low profile as Pan-European institutions, and the lack of a truly European stock exchange.

Still they are growing. In 1993 the combined market capitalization of all the European exchanges was little more than half that of London. By 1997 the size of Germany's market had risen from one tenth of the value of London to a third. France's Bourse was a quarter the size of London. But for the first time ever the total size of Europe's bourses exceeded London's market capitalization.

The European securities industry is on the move, fuelled by a wave of privatizations as large and as aggressive as those put through in Britain in the Thatcher years. The biggest of these, Deutsche Telekom, raised 20 billion DM in December 1996, with 690 million shares sold at 28.50 DM each.

Energizing the interest in Europe's stock markets has been a wave of mergers and acquisitions, a phenomenon little in evidence in the eighties and the early part of the nineties. The approach of European Monetary Union and the introduction of a single currency was probably the prime motivating force, but another equally powerful catalyst has been the trend towards globalization in business.

October 13 1997 was a particularly crazy day for the European markets, when news of six major cross-border mergers hit the screens involving capital in excess of $100 million. These were:

- a move by the Swiss Zurich Group to take over BAT's financial services company to create a new group worth $35.7 billion.
- a merger between Britain's Guinness and Grandmet, with France's LVMH having a 10 per cent stake in the new $39 billion entity.
- a merger between the Anglo-Dutch group Reed Elsevier and Holland's Wolters Kluwer to create the world's largest scientific and technical publisher worth $10.6 billion.
- a hostile $7 billion bid by Italy's Generali insurance company for AGF of France.
- a hostile $2.8 billion bid by Lafarge of France for Redland of Britain.

This kind of activity is a far cry from the decade earlier when most of European industry was financed and controlled by banks, and when most savers practised thrift by putting their surplus cash into interest-bearing deposit accounts or government bonds.

As in Britain a decade earlier the trigger for real interest in the equity markets came through privatization: and, in the case of the Germans, with the biggest privatization in history, the floating of Deutsche Telekom. Even if this did not turn Germany into a nation of shareholders overnight, it certainly raised awareness for the first time of the merits of stock market investment. Germany is now the largest telecoms market in Europe with a market volume in 1997 of DM 100 billion. By the year 2000 it will account for over seven per cent of GDP, ousting the automobile industry as the most important sector.

The other force for change was the onset of Economic and Monetary Union, due to be completed with the adoption of a single European currency, by the end of the century. This led to substantial interstate rationalization.

European countries also started creating hi-tech stock markets to match the new mood. The largest is the Deutsche Borse, which has both electronic and floor trading, and which replaced the federation of eight regional stock markets that used to comprise the German market. The regional pattern has, however, been retained as DB operates through a series of city exchanges of which the largest is the Frankfurt Wertpapierborse, or Frankfurt Stock Exchange, based in Germany's financial capital. It is the fourth largest exchange in the world, and can be accessed via the IBIS computer system or, electronically, on the floor.

The exchange is still controlled by the banks, who are very reluctant to loosen their grip on any aspect of the capital markets. It is run by a council of 24 members, elected for a three-year term. Besides bankers, council members include official exchange brokers, independent brokers, insurance companies and other issuers and investors.

The main German stock market index is the DAX, which is based on 30 most actively traded German blue-chip stocks. It represents over 60 per cent of the total equity capital of German exchange-listed companies, and trading in these

shares accounts for three-quarters of the market volume.
Another index, the FAZ, operated by the leading German
newspaper, *Frankfurter Algemeine*, is also an important
pointer, being more broadly based than the DAX.

For a long while Germany was slow to embrace the kind
of capital markets favoured in the Anglo-Saxon world. But
now tough rules are in place to fight corruption and encourage transparency. Based on the style of the US Securities
and Investment Board, a new Federal Securities Supervisory
Office is tasked with uncovering and prosecuting insider
traders and other miscreants as well as supervising disclosure
requirements.

Transparency has become a much favoured word amongst
stock market regulators, and is, of course, the opposite of
insider trading. As in Britain, insider trading used to be the
accepted way of doing things, but now companies who list
on the German exchanges are expected to be 'transparent',
which means they should let in as much light as possible on
their businesses. This, naturally, is often the opposite of the
inclinations of many senior executives and board members.

To its credit, the Deutsche Borse worked hard in the latter
part of the nineties to enhance transparency, even though, in
the Borse's own magazine *Vision and Money*, the head of
research at Commerzbank is quoted as saying that 'the
majority of businesses still have some catching up to do'.

One interesting initiative, which would also work well in
London, is the Germany Equity Forum. One of the services it
provides is to give enterprises seeking capital a low-cost
medium to profile themselves or to set out financing needs
and offer investment opportunities. The Borse does not act as
an adviser or mediator and does not take any responsibility
for the accuracy of the information. What it has done is to
run a Forum, the first of which was in Leipzig in September
1996. It now has an Internet site which enables companies
and investors to publish bids and offers.(htpp://www.
exchange.de). This is a useful way of putting venture
capitalists together with ventures, which, later in their
development, may wish to obtain a listing on the Borse.

Deutsche Borse also provides an Internet share market
database which provides on-line price and volume data for all
shares, bonds, indices, derivatives, and foreign exchange

instruments traded on German exchanges. This means that for the first time private investors will be able to access directly data that was previously available only to market professionals, including real-time prices. Thus Germany has avoided the class system that exists in Britain as described earlier.

Another initiative has been the Neuer Markt, which provides a framework for companies to meet disclosure requirements and gives investors direct access to company information. Members must agree to meet the most rigorous international standards of disclosure (as well as the German ones), must issue quarterly and annual reports in English as well as German, and provide regular events for analysts and investors.

Despite these strong advances in recent years, there is still much work to be done, particularly amongst the medium-sized companies that care little about their global financial image, and often disregard the regulations.

Mainland Europe's second largest exchange, the Paris Bourse, has also radically transformed itself in recent years. Its fine historical building on Rue de la Bourse belies the fact that, operationally, France now has one of the most modern and efficient stock exchanges in the world, with both screen and floor trading, a modern transactions system, known as Relit, and deregulated commissions for brokers. But it is still perceived to be over-regulated by the French government.

One interesting innovation from France has been the 'Nouveau Marché'. This was specially constructed for small but fast-growing companies in 1996. By its first anniversary in March 1997, it had 23 listed companies with a total market capitalization of almost nine billion French francs. In that time it raised 1.87 billion French francs of new capital.

The 'Nouveau Marché' has many similarities with the US NASDAQ discussed in Chapter 4. It requires the publication of quarterly results. Investors are obliged to retain their shares in the company after quotation, and cannot just sell out to make a quick profit.

The six million Swiss are perhaps the most heavily banked people on earth, and once had seven stock exchanges. But the big three banks – Union de Banque Suisse, Swiss Banking Corporation and Credit Suisse – decided to put a stop to this, and withdrew their support from the four smallest. In the end

Switzerland may well end up with only the Zürich Bourse, controlled by the banks. In Zürich there are no market-makers and no brokers: virtually all the work is done by the bankers' representatives, who only abolished fixed commissions because the Swiss Cartel Office forced them to do so. Institutional investors are not particularly active: Swiss pension funds have only about five per cent in local equities, though this is expected to increase. Despite its strong role as a banking centre, Zürich is not an important bourse. The 12 major Swiss stocks are also traded in London, which handles a fifth of total Swiss trading volume.

Eastern Europe

The video produced to celebrate the reopening of the Budapest Stock Exchange laid bare the wishful thinking of those pushing through economic reforms in Hungary. There were the usual images: dealers shouting at each other, their telephones wedged between ear and shoulder, one hand scribbling, the other operating a keyboard. Young women stared pensively at their screens; others swivelled in their chairs and scowled in a questioning manner at colleagues. The video showed the global markets in action: New York, Tokyo, London, Frankfurt, and, of course, Budapest.

Of course the Budapest Stock Exchange is not like that. Its venue – the baroque banking hall of the Bank of Budapest in Vorosmarty Square – owes more to the polished charm of the Austro-Hungarian empire than to the contemporary dealing room. The trading room has polished marble pillars and brown panelled walls, not false ceilings and smoked glass. But for the gilded brass chandeliers, dangling incongruously over a bank of computers, it might have been the old exchange closed by the communists in 1948 and now exhumed from a time warp.

When the exchange reopened, on Midsummer's Day 1990, after a 42-year break for the communist experiment, only three companies were listed.

One of the first international visitors to this limp, fledgling market was the then British prime minister, Margaret Thatcher. She congratulated Lajos Bokros, president of the exchange and a former communist, on being 'ahead of Moscow'. He replied that 'small is beautiful'.

That may well prove to be the case, sometime in the next century. For the moment investment in the share markets of the former Warsaw Pact countries has not produced the results expected or equivalent to those available elsewhere. In the five years following the break-up of the former Soviet Union, about $5 billion of private portfolio investment cash found its way into the equity markets of Eastern Europe, with Budapest, Prague and Warsaw the main recipients. This is a negligible amount compared with funding provided by the World Bank's lending arm, the International Finance Corporation, and by the London-based European Bank for Reconstruction and Development.

Of course many investors have put money into Eastern Europe without going anywhere near Budapest, Prague or Warsaw. Many went in through funds like the Merrill Lynch Austro-Hungary Fund, denominated in dollars and listed on the Amsterdam Bourse, or the First Hungary Fund, launched by Bear Sterns and Co with the help of financier George Soros, and the first institutional investment vehicle in the region. The fund was managed by the IFC and Bear Sterns. The First Hungary Fund pulled in $80 million. Seven years later it was valued at $180 million, not a brilliant return, and $100 million less than would have been achieved in other markets.

An investor would have done better to trade on the Budapest market. In 1997 it showed a 40 per cent gain in the first six months, and trading had risen to 2,000 transactions a day, with market capitalization of Ft420 million, ten times the level of 1992. Nearly 50 companies' stocks are traded, and, with private pension funds about to take off, this is set to grow.

By contrast, the largest of the region's stock markets, the Prague Stock Exchange, has fared less well. It should be the leader, but for a number of reasons has been a disappointment. In the months after trading began in 1993 it was the region's star performer. But it is owned by vested interests, mostly banks and other financial institutions, and has failed to provide adequate markets in popular privatizations, mostly because the government headed by Vaclav Klaus failed to establish clear ownership of assets.

7 The Share Buyers

'Have I made thee more profits than other princes can' – Prospero in *The Tempest*, Act I, Scene ii.

'Millions of the new investors have never traded a share, nor do they know how to do so. They only own one or two shares bought in the generously priced and heavily marketed privatization issues. They tend to see share ownership rather as a sophisticated gamble than as a long-term investment in the wealth-creating process' – Sir Peter Thompson, chairman of the CBI Wider Share Ownership Council.

Screen trading and deals by telephone have removed much of the lively atmosphere that used to be part of the daily life of stock exchanges. London, without a trading floor, offers little of interest to the casual visitor. But where exchanges still operate with an open-shout system, you will usually find 30 or 40 onlookers, most of them middle-aged. Some scan the boards with binoculars; others seem mesmerized by their own thoughts.

Most people who hold shares will never visit a stock exchange. They call their broker, and leave the rest to him. In America, where large national broking firms have branch offices in most towns, it is common for the private investor to drop by, look at the television screens bearing prices, and enjoy a cup of coffee and a chat with the local manager. It becomes a social occasion. Such share shops exist in shopping malls and in department stores. There are a few in Britain, mostly in the more affluent centres. Japan has investment shops in every town.

In Europe it is different. Investors prefer to conduct their business more discreetly, a throwback perhaps to higher personal taxation. On the Continent there is a tendency to favour fixed-interest securities, though that is now changing. And in Britain the number of people who actually own shares has risen significantly.

This stemmed from an objective of the Conservative government in the Thatcher years to turn Britain into a nation of shareholders. As an objective it was commendable. Individuals would be able to benefit from prosperity and economic growth, and would feel they had a stake in the country.

The instrument for carrying out this objective was privatization: the disposal of public assets for cash. Instead of the government holding all the shares in public corporations like British Gas, British Telecom or electric power generation and distribution, individuals were invited to become shareholders, and provided with valuable incentives to do so. Contrary to some expectations, Labour, when elected in 1977 continued the policy.

Unfortunately, however, the way most privatizations were carried out in Britain left much to be desired. The chief beneficiaries have been, not members of the British public, but the large institutions, domestic and international, who were given preferential treatment. Others who benefited were intermediaries such as merchant banks, large legal and accountancy firms, and public relations firms.

The great privatization sales in Britain led to one in four families in Britain owning shares. But almost two-thirds of the 10.5 million shareholders enfranchised by privatization held equity in only one company. The company tended to be the one they worked for, like British Telecom or British Gas. These small portfolio gains for private owners were dwarfed by the money pulled out of the share markets by institutional investors.

Could we ever return to the days when the private investor held a higher proportion of the British market? If individuals are to increase their stake from 20 per cent to say, 30 per cent, over the next ten years, they will have to invest at least £25 billion. This seems improbable, and it would require a change in savings habits by average families. The lion's share goes into building societies and banks, as well as pension schemes and life assurance policies. Many of these are compulsory, and so money could not automatically be diverted into equity plans even if the will was there to do so.

If the private investors' place in the market was considerably larger, the balance would be better. There would be a diverse body of investors with different timescales to the institutional manager, with different investment objectives in general, and a greater willingness to move in the opposite direction to the herd.

This would be a highly desirable scenario in any country, but it would not be achieved by mere numbers. Many small investors do not notice whether their shares go up or down. They look at long-term growth. Most private shareholders are traditionally passive. The classic case is of Aunt Maud, who inherited a handsome portfolio of shares from her father, and who will pass it on to her nephew in due course. In the meantime she takes little interest in the performance of her shares, and keeps the certificates, like a piece of valuable but unworn jewellery, in a bank vault.

What is needed is not the creation of tens of thousands more passive owners like Aunt Maud, but people who buy shares with the desire to pay attention to their investments. But that will require changes of policy and practice by the government, as well as a new attitude towards small investors in the City of London.

A move in this direction came with the launch of personal equity plans in the latter years of the Conservatives.

A PEP became one of the most useful vehicles available for reducing a tax burden. At the time of writing up to £6,000 a year can be invested in an approved plan, and, provided the plan is kept in place for five years, income from dividends is tax free. Capital gains are also exempt from taxation. The British scheme is one of the most innovative in the world, and, although complicated, provides a real incentive for wage earners to buy shares.

By 1997 there were millions of PEPs in issue. Among the rules are that at least half the investment has to be in the shares of companies incorporated in Britain, or in certain officially listed shares in other countries within the European Community or in unit trusts. By 1997 more than £30 billion was invested in unit trust PEPs alone. Most PEPs are managed professionally, by banks or by fund management groups, but there is nothing to prevent an individual from creating his own plan by investing in just one stock; in fact he is encouraged to do so. At the time of writing it is unclear what the Blair government will do about PEPs or whether it will keep them.

Those with an interest in equity markets should get a selection of literature from the many companies offering it, as well as keeping an eye on the rules, which are likely to change with every Budget. There are very few disadvantages for those who can afford to save regularly. One drawback is that they are of little benefit to the over-eighties, who may not want to tie up their savings for so long a period.

Attempts to increase direct share ownership took a while to win support from the institutions, and, in many cases, still have not done so. Many of those in the City of London have an antipathy towards small investors from the middle or working classes. Financial services institutions have conducted major advertising campaigns to persuade those who have bought shares through privatization to trade them in for collective investments like unit trusts, which, of course, bear high management charges which have to be paid by the unit holders. Many of these funds are not particularly well managed, and traditionally perform less well than the Financial Times-Stock Exchange 100 Share Index.

One of the most unpleasant features of the institutional fund management attitude towards private shareholders is their 'mother-knows-best' attitude. An example of this City arrogance occurred at the time of electricity privatization, when the BBC provided a free platform to one of the City's lively marketeers, in which he argued that most individuals were not suited to share ownership, and that their money was better invested in collective schemes. Like those run by him, of course.

There was a similar problem at the time of the privatization of British Airways, when many City pundits proclaimed to the media that because the airline had high risk potential it was not suitable for the small investor. As it happens BA shares have performed much better than most collective investments.

But distaste for dealing with those wearing boilersuits rather than pin-stripes is not the only problem. Many of the large share-broking firms claim that they cannot afford to handle transactions by private individuals involving sums under £5,000. This is true, but it is because of their high overheads and other costs, rather than for the technical reasons, such as settlement procedures, usually put forward.

Of course ordinary families do not normally deal in the City. After all, if you wish to pay your phone or credit card bill you go to your local bank or building society, not to a merchant bank. You may, of course, buy shares through a branch bank or building society. Some of the larger organizations have subsidiaries which provide a share dealing service. One of them, Barclayshare, makes it easy, providing several levels of service according to customers' requirements, as well as a place for certificates to be lodged, regular portfolio valuations, and an annual statement of dividends for the taxman. But few of the share-dealing services are well advertised, and the impression remains that the branch manager would rather sell you a life assurance policy or a personal loan.

The lowest cost solution for the private individual who wishes to conduct part of his or her investment through equities is to join a service like Barclayshare. A trade can be executed just as quickly through this system as through any London private broker. The investor has the choice of either discussing his portfolio with an investment manager – and paying for that service – or acting on intuition. If the latter is the choice, then it would pay to become a regular subscriber to an intelligent weekly publication such as *The Economist* or the *Investors Chronicle*. The serious Saturday newspapers also all provide a useful service.

Charles Schwab

An even better alternative could be Charles Schwab Europe, formerly known as ShareLink, a Birmingham-based service which grew out of the old established stockbroking firm of Albert Sharp. Its founder, entrepreneur David Jones, saw the advantages of using technology not only for the benefit of the brokers but for the consumer. Now Europe's largest share-dealing service with 10 per cent of the British markets, it is open seven days a week, and at hours when most other services or banks are shut. A few simple questions are asked and the trade is handled by the firm through SEAQ.

Because the service is open to all comers, rather than regular members or customers, Schwab quite rightly protects itself from those selling shares they do not own by insisting that if it does not receive certificates from customers within three weeks of the sale, then it will balance its books by buying the same number of shares on the market in the customer's name. It also imposes a penalty of £40. Those who are late in sending off share certificates could end up with a costly bill. One advantage of Schwab is that it is possible for members of the same family holding the same shares to amalgamate them, thereby incurring only one commission charge. This can be useful in the case of privatization or mutual sell-off issues. Another benefit is Schwab's Liberty service which allows customers to buy and sell US stocks when the markets are open at very reasonable commission charges and free of stamp duties or VAT. Over 12,000 leading stocks are covered, and investors enjoy American standards of protection, which, as we will discuss in a later chapter, are tougher than in Britain. Curiously, at the time of writing, Schwab had no plans for a similar scheme for those who wished to invest in Europe.

The basic Schwab service is what is called 'execution only', but as with Barclayshare, it is possible to seek advice if you are prepared to pay for it. This seems to me to be a much better arrangement than paying a financial adviser commission, as is the practice in the life assurance and unit trust industry (discussed later).

Schwab customers can subscribe to a number of services from its Schwab associate. There is a telephone service whereby investors may find out if the shares in which they are interested are rated 'buy', 'sell', or 'hold' by a consensus of investment specialists. A similar service is also available on a weekly basis in newsletter form. A company-reports service will give you the latest annual report and accounts of a listed company plus a summary of the views on a company by leading international research houses.

Those small investors who feel they would prefer something more personal may obtain a list of stockbrokers prepared to deal with small clients from the Stock Exchange in

London. Seekers of a 'dealing only' service should concentrate on the percentage commission and the minimum commission. It is likely to start at 1.5 per cent for small deals, but with a minimum charge. Those who require a regular supply of investment advice and analysis will have to pay substantially more, unless they are frequent traders in reasonably large blocks of stock. Then they will be offered additional services, such as the ability to buy nominee stock. Then there is portfolio management, for those prepared to entrust £50,000 or more to the broking firm to handle at its discretion. Apart from paying commission, the investor may also have to pay an annual fee. If the fee is high enough brokers may rebate all or part of the commission. In many cases it is better to pay a fee so as to avoid the incentive that commission-remuneration provides to brokers to churn stock.

Despite these opportunities, it is a sad fact that in Britain most people invest in the share markets indirectly – through the large institutions. These may be life assurance companies, investing the premiums that are placed with them, or pension funds, operated for large corporations or private individuals. Or they may be mutual funds or unit trusts, running collective investments for those who wish to see their savings spread among a number of equities or fixed interest securities.

Nowhere has this trend towards collective investment been more marked than in Britain. Here the percentage of the British stock market controlled by private investors has fallen from 28.2 per cent in 1981 to less than 20 per cent today. Thirty years earlier, two-thirds of the stock market was in private hands.

Whereas the political catch-cry of privatization across the world was that it would disperse wealth across the social spectrum – particularly allowing workers to take a stake in the enterprises by whom they were employed – in practice control of corporations is increasingly concentrated in fewer hands. Ownership and control by the state has been replaced by domination by fund managers.

Most fund managers have never scuffed their hands in manufacturing industry, or hustled for business in an overseas market, or designed a robot, a machine tool, or a new building. Whether based in London, New York, Tokyo or a handful of other financial centres, they wear grey pin-stripe suits and the introverted look of someone who has spent too long staring at spreadsheets and annual reports.

Because they can sack boards, determine the outcome of takeover bids, and make or break corporations, they are lobbied by a new breed of public relations consultant: the investor relations specialist who, in turn, is hired by corporate managers keen to keep their jobs intact. Gone is the Victorian-style capitalist, the owner-manager accountable only to himself.

The institutions take themselves, and their jobs, seriously. Hardly a working day goes by when they are not meeting with directors or managers of companies in which they have invested. Although they deny they have a day-to-day influence on managers, they do sometimes step in and exert their power when things go wrong.

Many believe that the investment institutions ought to be more interventionist. When in 1992 it was revealed that some of the management of British Airways had been involved in a shoddy dirty-tricks operation against competitor Virgin Atlantic, some fund-management groups complained to the airline's directors. But none of BA's institutional investors went so far as to call for changes in top management, even though there were strident calls in the media that senior directors should resign.

Whether in Europe or elsewhere, institutional investors differ in their objectives according to the sector in which they are. Pension funds – by far the most important by size of assets invested – invest the contributions of employees and their employers with the objective of maximum gain, so that the obligations of their various schemes may be fully and easily met. They are not above a bit of speculation, but generally their funds are directed towards meeting the pledges made to employees without necessitating an increase in employers' contributions. The better a pension fund is managed, the lower the employer's cost. So most pension funds, including those run exclusively for the benefit of trades union members, allocate their investments across a broad spectrum, preferring a diversified portfolio, as the jargon puts it, to excessive concentration in one or two stocks, or venturing into risky projects. Almost all pension funds have, in recent years, also diversified their portfolios to include investments in the United States, Western Europe, and the Far East and Pacific Basin.

Life Assurance Companies

Then there are life assurance companies, whose principal concern is to ensure that the premium incomes received are invested adequately to meet the eventual pay-out upon death or the end of a term. It is necessary for these huge investors to match their known obligations, calculated through actuarial tables, with investments maturing at the same time. For this reason assurance companies invest heavily in long-dated gilt-edged securities or bonds.

Some governments insist that institutions like life assurance companies and pension funds, which are often the recipients of generous tax treatment, allocate a substantial proportion of their investments to gilt-edged securities or semi-government bonds. There is, however, a trend away from such rules. Australia, for instance, abolished what was known as the 20/30 rule whereby for every $30 invested elsewhere, $20 had to be invested in government bonds. Japan, whose pension funds have colossal clout, has gradually been easing the restrictions which made it difficult for large sums of money to be invested elsewhere than in Japanese industry.

The absence of regulation does not stop critics of capitalism objecting strongly to privileged institutional investors failing, in their view, to use their funds in the national interest. The counter-argument, of course, is that it is the duty of pension funds and life assurance companies to do the best they can for those whose money they hold in trust – future pensioners and policy-holders – and therefore their fund managers should be unfettered by nationalistic controls.

Unit Trusts

The other set of powerful institutional investors are mutual funds, known in Britain as unit trusts, and investment trusts, and other managed funds. Trusts provide ways in which small and medium-sized investors can take an interest in equity markets without having to take the risk of buying shares in individual companies.

There are about 1,400 unit trust funds in Britain alone, managed by over 150 separate London groups for over 7 million unit holders. Total unit trust investment is around £120 billion. Some of the groups are very large. As advertisements in the Saturday papers show, there is a unit trust for everybody: trusts that offer the prospect of capital gain, and those that offer income; trusts that invest in blue-chip stocks, and those that specialize in high-risk, or 'recovery', shares. There are trusts for those who will only invest in ethical propositions. These eschew stakes in tobacco companies, for instance.

Some people believe that ethical investment will assume increasing importance as families become more concerned about health and the ecology of the planet. They are probably right, but then human nature historically has often put greed before public interest. It is very hard to gauge exactly how much money is placed into ethical investments, because not everybody who places such investment does so through an established ethical unit trust, preferring to use his or her own judgement as to what is right for them. But it does seem that the managed fund sector is growing. The Ethical Investment Research Service reports that there are at least 35 unit trusts, investment trusts or personal equity plans with ethical criteria that manage a total of £1.3 billion. That figure, for 1997, was 45 per cent up on the 1995 number.

Of course, even within the ethical funds industry, there is a debate as to what is ethical and what is not. Everyone would agree that to invest in a tobacco company or a company involved in animal testing should be avoided, but what about road building? Jupiter Asset Management, which runs two ethical funds, told the *Investors Chronicle* it would not; others were not so sure.

Almost all unit trust management companies, many of

them owned by banks, merchant banks, or insurance companies, have specialist country funds. The most popular are those with portfolios in Western Europe, the United States, Japan and Australia, and the more stable countries of southeast Asia – in other words stable economies.

A good idea of the range available can be seen by looking at the funds managed by just one average group, Montague Investment Management, headquartered in London. MIM Britannia Unit Trust Managers operates 40 trusts. Four of them are British specialist funds, seven are general funds, five are bond-related high income trusts, and the remainder are divided into sectors or countries. The specialist funds cover such fields as commodity stocks, gold, financial securities, property and international leisure.

Most unit trust managers also offer life or pension-linked funds, which in Britain allow the investor substantial tax advantages, in that the cost of units is permitted as a tax deduction so long as the investor does not sell the units or receive any dividends until retirement age.

Another form of unit trust investment which has become popular because of its tax efficiency is the umbrella fund, which allows investors to switch units between funds, without being liable for capital gains tax on any profit on the deal. This allows both fund managers and private investors to operate efficiently in the widely fluctuating foreign exchange markets.

One of the problems with unit trusts, from an investor's point of view, is that it costs rather too much to buy them. There is usually an up-front charge of five per cent, plus the burden of VAT, so that quite often it may be some time before the buyer can see any improvement in his portfolio. The spread between the bid and the offer price is also often large – six per cent or more, with some as high as 14 per cent – so your units will have to rise appreciably before you can sell them at profit. And the more you switch the more it costs, which may help the intermediary or discretionary portfolio adviser, but is no use to the investor at all.

There are widespread differences in the performances of the various funds, a fact which seems to escape much public notice.

The August issue of *Money Management* in 1997 showed

that over the previous five years, the Prolific Technology unit trust had outperformed everyone – £1,000 invested in it would have risen to £4,277. On the other hand £1,000 put into one of Govett's Bear funds would have been worth only just over £600. Of course these tables are about as useful as a league table in professional football. Just because you are top one month does not mean you will stay there. But just as Manchester United FC is usually to be found in the top tier of British Football clubs, so the best funds show a consistency. The truth is that if you have £10,000 to invest in a fixed-interest unit trust, you will have to pay around £750 in fees, plus annual management charges. Invest in a good income-producing blue-chip company or utility via a stockbroker, and the most you will be charged is £200, and there will be some upside capital gains prospects.

Investment Trusts

Often confused with unit trusts, but different in concept, are investment trusts. Like unit trusts, investment trusts allow the smaller private investor to benefit from having a stake in a large portfolio of widely spread shares, both by sector and by region. But there the similarity ends. Investment trusts are public companies like any other public company and their shares are traded on the Stock Exchange; instead of making motor cars, running hotels, or operating department stores, an investment trust company exists purely and simply to buy and sell shares in other companies, both for short-term speculative gain and long-term capital growth. Those who manage investment trusts, full-time executives responsible to a board of directors, buy and sell shares on the world's stock exchanges, exercising their judgement as to what will be a profitable investment. Just like any other public company, they make profits and incur losses, and pay dividends to shareholders. Because their companies have assets, investment trust executives can borrow against those assets, and are able to take both a long- and a short-term view of the money entrusted to them. Capital gains on share trading are not distributed in cash but used to build up portfolios and, through the generosity of the Treasury, escape taxation on capital gains. This means that the fund manager can realize the profits on the trust's investment at the most opportune time. Trusts can also offset their management charges against tax. Investment trusts have about £50 billion under management with 250,000 investors.

Investment trusts are cheaper to invest in than unit trusts. As stated earlier, for every £1,000 invested in unit trusts, it costs £50 in an initial management charge. The same amount used to purchase shares in an investment trust would incur less than £30 in stockbroker's commission and government stamp duty. Unit trust managers also charge an annual fee of between 0.75 to 1.0 per cent for looking after their trusts; investment trust management charges are much lower.

So why do average investors not flock to investment trusts? The answer is hype. Unit trusts are prolific advertisers in the financial press, and therefore get much more than their fair share of space in the editorial columns. By contrast, investment trusts are restricted by law in their advertising, and get comparatively little press attention. The serious newspapers provide free space to unit trusts to publicize their prices, acknowledging it a public service to do so, but provide only limited price information on investment trusts.

Moreover unit trusts are, like most life assurance products, sold by middle-men – insurance brokers, financial advisers, even accountants and solicitors. They receive a handsome commission from this form of activity, most of it up-front. With the exception of investment trust savings schemes, there is no commission for intermediaries on investment trusts, so, for the most part, they do not recommend them. This, of course, makes a nonsense of the idea that the average insurance broker is a genuine financial adviser. The 350 or so investment trusts in Britain deserve a place in everyone's savings portfolio, and, in many cases, offer a better return than the average with-profits policy.

Another important difference, seldom understood, between investment trusts and unit trusts is that the latter are priced according to their net asset value, known as NAV. Investment trusts, like other equities, are valued according to what the market thinks they are worth, which is more often than not below the value of their assets. The discount to NAV at the time of writing was ten per cent, and reflects a recognition that disposing of assets costs real money, but it also reflects the market's perception of the business and the economic environment. The result is that something can be built into an investment trust's share price for future prospects. This can never happen for a unit trust.

Managed Funds

The final group of large institutional investors is different again. These are professional fund management groups, which manage, at their own discretion, the money of others, both individuals and companies. Here again there are similarities with previous groups.

At one end of the scale, there are large stockbroking companies, which take in funds from individuals who either cannot be bothered or feel they lack the expertise to watch the market. These individuals, which range from pensioners in Worthing or Westchester County to wealthy Arabs in Dubai, entrust sums of money – the minimum is usually at least £20,000 – to fund managers within broking houses who manage their portfolio, and keep them posted, through a quarterly or half yearly report, as to what they have done with it. Only rarely would a fund manager consult a client about the purchase or sale of an investment, though most of them are receptive to suggestions. Many broking firms' fund management teams invest in unit trusts and investment trusts, and some have portfolios that stipulate such a limitation.

Some broking houses charge for this service; others rely for income on the commission obtained through sale and purchase of shares, or from a percentage paid to them by unit trusts. This itself can lead to conflict of interest. Those brokers that leave an investment undisturbed are obviously going to benefit less than those that are constantly trading their customer's portfolio, and on many occasions there is much to be said for sticking with the status quo.

At the other end of the scale are the large fund management groups, often a major branch or department of a well-known merchant bank. The principle is the same as with small portfolio management by brokers, but their clients are usually rich individuals, and other very large clients for whom they also act as investment bankers.

The funds under their stewardship are usually measured in billions. For instance, in 1985 Baring Brothers and Co. Ltd managed funds of more than £2,500m, just over half of it in Britain, with clients as diverse as Bowater Corporation, London Transport and London University. More than twice as large, in fund management terms, is Robert Fleming Investment Management Ltd, with £5,800m of clients' money to invest, including some of the funds of the Royal National Lifeboat Institution, IBM, Dow Chemical, and Whitbread. Recently Flemings have pushed hard with some success to manage the vast pool of money in the Japanese pension funds.

Other big fund managers include GT Management, with the BBC as a client, Hambros Investment Management, Hill Samuel, Lazard Securities, Montague Investment Management, UBS, J. Henry Schroder Wagg and Co., N. M. Rothschild Asset Management Ltd, and Mercury Asset Management.

For all of these groups fund management means a lot more than sitting in a City office, reading research reports, and studying the prices on the electronic monitors. The good fund manager needs to have excellent judgement, the speed of decision-making of a track bookmaker, an ability to size up a balance sheet in minutes, the nose for news of a good newspaper editor, and an eye on the main chance.

With intense competition, both to sell and to perform, and round-the-world trading, the active fund manager can only grow old in the job if he or she is prepared to put work above everything. It is a long way from the days when the investment manager of the Pru would make his way back to his office from a lunch at the club to place an investment of £1m in the British Motor Corporation.

The Fund of Funds

Another concept is the fund of funds, designed to minimize risk for the small investor and to remove him one further stage away from direct purchases of shares. Instead of having to pick and choose between many hundreds of unit trusts, the investor could buy units in a master fund, which in turn would buy units in one or more of its subsidiary funds. From the point of view of someone with a small amount of capital to invest – but no clear idea if and when to move out of a British equity trust and into a Japanese, German or American one – the fund of funds seems no bad idea. Let someone else do the worrying and save yourself the expense of having a stockbroker to manage a portfolio of unit trusts.

Like most bright ideas, the notion was not a new one. The fund of funds first obtained notoriety as a promotion in 1962 of the international investment swindler Bernie Cornfeld, whose misdeeds are well spelt out in a brilliant book *Do You Sincerely Want To Be Rich?* by Charles Raw, Bruce Page and Godfrey Hodgson. This cautionary tale should be required reading both for investors and all those involved in the financial services industry. As the authors say:

> The salesman's rationale for the Fund of Funds was an unusually owlish piece of nonsense – one of those things that sounds impressive until you really think it through. Mutual funds, and all investment concerns, are sold on the proposition that the ordinary man needs investment advisers to make choices for him. The Fund of Funds went further and suggested that the ordinary man now needed professionals to choose the professionals who would make the choices. The Fund of Funds would take your money, and invest it in other mutual funds – but only in those whose values were rising most rapidly.

A lawyer from the US Securities and Exchange Commission exploded the Fund of Funds argument succinctly:

> If funds of funds are permitted to proliferate, how would an investor decide among the many companies seeking his investment dollar? Would he not need a fund of funds of funds to make this decision?

Cornfeld's Fund of Funds run by his Investors Overseas Services and given the hard-sell by thousands of salesmen calling themselves 'financial counsellors', gathered in $100m of people's savings within two years of its launch. The customer's money was transferred immediately into separate proprietary funds, for a brokerage fee which was pocketed by IOS. For the privilege of investing at all, the customer had to pay what has become known as a 'front-end load', much of which was used to pay a commission to the salesman who persuaded him to part with his money in the first place. For every $3,000 invested in Cornfeld's Fund of Funds, $540 vanished immediately in fees. A further 10 per cent of any income generated also went in fees, as did 10 per cent of any capital gain. According to Raw, Page and Hodgson an investor had to wait six years before he could even get his money out without loss. An investigation found that money which was supposed to be held on trust for customers was being used for the benefit of IOS itself, its directors, employees and friends; and that the IOS sales force engaged in illegal currency transactions on a major scale, and constantly misrepresented the investment performance of its largest fund.

Whitehall Relaxes the Rules

The shockwaves that surrounded the fall of IOS were such that the Department of Trade and Industry put a stop on the establishment of any other funds of funds. So adamant were the men in Whitehall that the concept was fraught with danger that few financial institutions bothered to apply for approval of schemes they preferred to call 'managed funds'.

But there were good arguments in favour of them. A fund of funds saves small investors from the perils of switching. It also saves a small problem over capital gains, for an investor transferring from one unit trust to another and making sufficient profit in the process could be liable for capital gains, even though he is only being prudent in transferring an investment to a different sector. A fund of funds is not liable for capital gains.

But strict rules were introduced. An approved fund of funds is restricted in its investments to its manager's own unit trusts, in total contrast with the United States where master funds may invest in anything but their own in-house trusts. A new fund of funds must also be in a group holding at least four subsidiary trusts and not more than 50 per cent of assets can be invested in any one of them. It is allowed to make an initial charge to investors, but cannot charge unit holders a further front-end load when buying into a subsidiary fund. It may also charge double annual management fees.

8 And Now for Something Riskier

*'Risks are explicit, and well priced. The skills of the
bookmaker have proved more reliable than those of
the banker'* – Anthony Harris, economist and
columnist, *The Times.*

*'If you are very good at market timing, you can
make out like a bandit'* – Donald Mesler, author of
Stock Market Options.

Anyone unlucky enough to get on to mailing lists for financial services will have received an invitation to attend a
'three-day up-to-the-minute workshop' on 'advanced exotic
options'. Many end up none the wiser about the new and
sometimes rewarding opportunities offered by the markets in
such areas as derivatives and options.

Many people find it difficult to come to terms with investments that are less tangible than a share in a corporation or
a well-defined unit trust. Some of the new financial products
that have been conceived in recent years are exotic, and many
of them carry a greater degree of risk than more straightforward investments. But that is not always true. Some of the
new concepts are designed to reduce, even minimize, risk.

One such concept is that of tracker funds, a portfolio of
investments that aims to track accurately the performance of
a stock market index. This involves the buying and holding
of equities in proportions designed to equal precisely the performance of selected indices of the stock market. In America
the most common of these is the Standard and Poor's 500, a
selection of mostly large stocks in blue-chip companies. In
Britain the FTSE 100 Index of top industrial companies is
used for the same purpose. The attraction of indexation is
that it allows fund managers to show that, by mirroring the
market, their investments have performed at least as well as

the market. Since most equity fund managers fail to match the FT-SE index, this is a goal which would content most long-term investors.

Constructing an equity portfolio to track any given index is not as easy as it sounds. The obvious way of doing it is to invest in all the stocks in the index at the same weightings as the index, and then adjust the portfolio whenever it changes. This is known as full-replication. But the constant adjustments that have to be made involve considerable cost, and such a scheme is expensive to administer. A number of computer programs have been generated which will achieve roughly the same result, however. Once purchased, these will allow fund managers to sleep soundly confident that they have not made major errors of judgement. This technique is called optimization, and creates a sample portfolio from a stock market index which bears the characteristics of the index itself. Developed by a number of academics at Berkeley University in California while they were investigating the components of risk in equity portfolios, the Barra program is used extensively by the Bankers Trust in the United States, and has been adapted for use with the FT-SE index in London by Barclays, County Natwest, and the United Bank of Kuwait. It is estimated that an optimized portfolio will track an index accurately at a value as low as £500,000, and therefore is a considerable attraction to institutions and pension fund trustees.

It is, of course, possible for an individual investor to put money into a tracker or indexed fund, but he faces the same kind of additional charges imposed for unit trusts. The more sophisticated private investor can buy computer programs to guide him in establishing his own indexed portfolio, but this has two disadvantages. Firstly, you need to be prepared to invest a substantial amount of your capital in a variety of stocks in order to make it financially worthwhile. Secondly, it removes most of the fun from investing. Like the punter slipping £50 on a horse in the Grand National, the small investor aims to *beat* the performance of market indices, not match them.

Options

Options are as old as history itself, and mean exactly what the name implies. Phoenician merchants bidding for the opportunity to buy the cargoes of the first ships to arrive in port used to purchase an option to acquire a vessel's contents – in other words the right to be first in the queue. If the cargo turned out to contain little of any interest or value, the merchant would not exercise the option. Today a family interested in a new house being built but unable to sell their own property might advance a small sum of money as a three-month option to buy at an agreed value. This would both prevent the developer from selling to anyone else during that period, and also assure the price. But if the option was not exercised, the purchaser would lose the cost of the option.

Options are now highly developed on global stock markets and for those prepared to risk a little money on speculation, they offer an attractive prospect. Many people have been heard to say: 'I would like to be able to buy shares in BP, ICI, or Microsoft, but their prices are so high I could not possibly afford them.' Leaving aside the loose logic of that statement – for an individual can always buy 50 or even 25 shares if he wishes – it is true that the chances of a major capital gain on one of the large and better known shares are slim.

Options increase opportunity, but at a known cost and defined risk. For example let us say that just before Christmas an individual thinks that a retail group is going to achieve record Christmas sales, and that the margins on this extra volume will be such as to generate handsome profits for the full year. He fancies risking £5000 on his theory that the shares will rise. But at 642 pence each his £5000 will only buy him 778 shares. Even if the shares rise by £1 to 742 pence, he will only have made a profit of £778, less the broker's commission on both the sale and purchase, which would bring the profit down to about £650.

By using his £5000 to buy options he would have done much better. At a cost of 30p each his £5000 would have bought him 16,666 three-month call options – giving him the right to buy the shares at any time during the next three months for the original 642 pence price. If the shares do not go up he does not exercise the option – and loses his £5000.

That's the risk. But if they did in fact rise by £1 as in this example he will have made a capital gain of £11,666, less broker's commission (£16,666 less the £5000 spent for the options).

If the stock is one in which the Stock Exchange runs a traded options market, then the investor has another possibility open to him, and that is to sell the option to another investor. The price of a traded option is decided by two factors: the underlying price of the share itself, and the market's expectations as to which way it will move in the weeks or months ahead. Obviously those operating in the traded options market expect to make a profit, so there is a premium to be paid for selling the unexpired portion of an option rather than sitting it out. But where an investor fears he has made a major misjudgement he can, to some extent, cover a big position by using the traded options market.

Another form of option is the 'put' option, which is the opposite of a 'call' option. A put option is taken out in anticipation of a fall in the value of the relevant share, and gives the owner the option to sell a quantity of shares at a given price. A put option can act as insurance against an investment in ordinary shares falling in value. The profit on a put option could offset any loss in the value of the underlying share.

Information about the prices at which you can buy or sell both call and put options is readily available in the daily newspapers that take investment seriously, such as the *Daily Telegraph* or the *Financial Times* in Britain, or the *Wall Street Journal*. Reproduced below is part of a table from the *FT* of October 22, 1997. The underlying share is the company for whose stock an option is available, and the underlying share price is the price at the previous night's close. The exercise price is the price at which an option contract gives the holder the right to buy or sell the underlying security. The expiry date signifies when the option contract runs out, which means that if the option is not exercised by then it is invalid. And the premium is the amount per single share at which a contract may be available.

Option		CALLS			PUTS		
		Jan	Apr	Jul	Jan	Apr	Jul
ASDA	160	10	15½	19	7	10	12½
(*161)	180	4½	7⅓	11	20	22½	24½
Abbey National	900	90½	113½	135½	35	56½	70
(*946)	950	63½	88	111	57½	81	94
Alliance & Leicester	700	37	53	67½	25½	40	47½
(*702½)	750	18½	33½	46	55½	69	75½
Allied Domecq	500	52	64	72	9	19½	24
(*535½)	550	25	35	45	29	41½	46½
BAA	460	47	60½	70½	11½	17½	25½
(*487½)	500	24½	39	50	38½	35	44
BAT Industries	500	54½	70½	78½	17	33	31
(*534)	550	27	47	54	39½	59	56
Barclays	1400	122½	157½	197½	71	98	119
(*1442½)	1450	98½	132½	173	96½	122½	144
Bass	850	45½	75½	80½	37	56	51
(*868½)	900	22½	52½	57½	65½	83½	78
Boots	850	59½	86	101½	29	41½	51½
(*870½)	900	35½	60	74	54	66	75½
British Airways	500	66½	81	92	11	19½	27
(*549½)	550	37	54½	64	30	40	47½
BP	850	60½	89½	104½	38½	55	64½
(*865½)	900	38	65½	79½	61	78½	89½
British Steel	40	8	14½	18	9	11½	16
(*140½)	160	2½	7	11	23½	25	29½

Taking the example of British Airways, the chart shows that a call option to buy 1,000 shares at 500 pence in the airline any time between 22 October 1997 and April 1998 may be bought for 81p per share. If a longer call option period were required to buy BA at the same price, the option cost per share would be 92p. A put option for the same dates would, however, cost less – 19.5p and 27p per share respectively. These figures indicate that those writing the option – in other words taking the risk – expect BA shares to rise marginally rather than fall.

Writing an option contract – as distinct from buying traded options – is a job for the professionals. It reverses the risk of buying or selling an option. Essentially the writer is gambling that the option will expire worthless, and that he will have received the put or call money for taking the risk. The job is akin to that of an insurance underwriter: he charges you a premium but hopes you will never claim. And, just like the underwriter, the person writing the risk in return for a premium needs to have a thorough knowledge of the markets and companies concerned. Those that do write options are required to deposit a sum of money, called margin money, with their broker as security for the performance of their obligations.

In Britain the concept of investing in options has been slow to catch on among general investors, although it plays a major part in the lives of the professionals. There is no reason for this, other than lack of education about the markets. In the United States, where attitudes are very different, options are booming.

The Chicago Board Options Exchange is the third largest securities market in the United States, after the New York Stock Exchange and NASDAQ, and more than two-thirds of those who use it are private investors. It is helped by the attitude of the US regulatory authorities, who are strong supporters of options trading, with the Securities and Exchange Commission arguing that it significantly enhances liquidity and makes for better and more accurate markets.

Europe is catching up, though options markets are still used mostly by professional investors. In 1978 there were only two equity options markets in Europe, one in Britain and the other in Holland. Today they are either established or being set up in every advanced country.

In Britain options are traded at the only exchange with a floor, the London International Financial Futures Exchange (LIFFE), which is based under the arches of Cannon Street station, having moved there from the more august but less appropriate surroundings of the Royal Exchange, close to the famous Change Alley. LIFFE calls its trading floor area a pit, in the manner of its Chicago contemporary, and dealers work under the auction system of open outcry. It is the size of a football pitch, and those who stray into it are in danger of being kicked down.

At LIFFE they trade in options in 75 major companies – mostly Alpha stocks on SEAQ – and in the future movement of the Financial Times 100 Index. Orders are phoned through to the LIFFE building to operators who wear sweatshirts identifying their firms. More than 200 firms are members, and the exchange is a hive of activity between 8.35hrs and 16.10hrs each weekday. Outside these hours the dealers, mostly young with Cockney accents, can be found in local cafés or in an adjoining health club.

But if you imagine that by buying options you are sure to win a fortune, be warned by the following remark from Stephen Figlewski, the Associate Professor of Finance at New York University:

> Small investors lose because they believe their information is better than it really is. They take positions that aren't any better than their beliefs, and their beliefs aren't any better than throwing darts.

There are other forms of share options that are much more familiar to members of the public, those that are available to employees of public companies. These are often, though not exclusively, reserved for executives, and usually allow the employee the right to buy a limited number of shares in the company for which he works once he has completed five years' service. These options are available for nothing, and the price is normally set at a discount of the price at the start of the option period. Some far-sighted employers in Britain encourage all employees to join a government-backed scheme which gives tax incentives to companies who promote a long-term saving plan with a building society where the final amount saved is used to buy shares at a low-cost pre-set option price. Unless you work for a company that is on the slide, these are the best form of savings plan available, combining the benefit of regular commitments via a building society with the chance of cashing in on long-term capital appreciation. It is perhaps the only risk-free route to the stock markets. Unfortunately many companies fail to explain these schemes properly to their workforces; if they did there would be a much higher percentage of the workforce owning shares.

Futures

If trading in options sounds a little like a casino, it is dull by comparison with the activities on the futures markets. There are futures in everything – commodities like cocoa, coffee, wheat, lead, zinc and gold; meats like cattle and pork; currencies like the dollar, the yen, the Deutschemark, and the pound; and of course, shares.

Buying futures is speculation, and some people make and lose millions by doing it. It requires knowledge of changing circumstances, as well as intuition as to the way events will turn out. If you think that there will be a severe frost in Brazil – or are prepared to bet that this will be so – you may buy 6-month coffee futures, in the belief that by the time your coffee is delivered at the end of the period, it will be worth a lot more. Of course, there is no need for you to take delivery of the coffee at all; if the frost comes, the price of your futures contract will rise sharply, and you may sell out.

There is, of course, good reason for buying futures other than speculation. If you are a coffee wholesaler and you fear a cold snap in Brazil, you will buy futures to protect yourself, regarding the extra cost of the contract as an insurance premium. The same is true of the manufacturing industry. If you have ordered an expensive set of machine tools from Germany, due to be delivered in six months' time, you will not want to pay for them until delivery. But supposing the pound falls against the mark in the meantime? You cover yourself by buying the required amount of Deutschemark futures. This process is called 'hedging'.

There are futures markets in all the major financial centres, while Chicago has assumed pre-eminence in the trading of commodities.

There has been considerable growth in bond markets, for the increase in the number of gilt-edged market-makers has placed a premium on hedging contracts. For instance, a fund manager may know that in three months he will receive cash for investment in gilts, and he has picked long gilts – those maturing in 15 years' time. Rather than waiting to see what the interest rate will be at that time, he can lock into today's rate by buying LIFFE's long gilts futures contracts for delivery in three months' time. If gilt yields then decline, the investor will have to pay a higher price, but the price of the long gilts futures contracts will have risen, and the fund manager's profits will reduce the effective cost of buying the stock.

The FT-SE 100 futures contract is priced by taking one-tenth of the value of the FT-SE 100 Share Index published

throughout each business day. It may be used by an investment manager concerned that the market will rise before he
can place funds becoming available to him.

Dabbling in futures is much more risky for private
investors than options. This is because of the greater leverage
involved. Investing in commodity futures, in particular, has
proved a fatal attraction for many speculators who have
wrongly assumed that they can pit their wits against the
experts: I do not recommend it. Let me give you an example
of how a commodity futures contract works. Suppose coffee
for delivery three months from now is trading in London at
$900 per tonne. A speculator buying ten tonnes will have
coffee worth $9,000, but will have to pay only a ten per cent
deposit for a contract providing for delivery at the end of the
quarter. The speculator does not, of course, take delivery. If
the price goes up to $1,000 a tonne, he sells the contract and
takes a handsome profit of $1,000. Although the coffee price
has gone up only a little over 10 per cent, his return on
capital is well over 100 per cent. But if coffee goes down to
$810, he will be obliged to buy the coffee at the agreed price
of $900, and then sell it again before delivery at its lower
market rate. The loss would probably more than wipe out his
deposit; in other words he would have lost his bet.

Many people imagine that they can follow stories in newspapers and on the wires and second guess what tropical
storms or frost will do to coffee prices. They are much mistaken. The professional buyers, working for companies like
Nestlé, Kenco or Maxwell House, have agents on the plan-
tations and know exactly what the crop will be. My guess is
that anyone seriously interested in trading futures will probably not be reading this book; for the newcomer or non-
professional, trading options is probably as risky as one will
want to get.

Emerging Markets

While there are exceptions to every rule, it is often the case
that the less you know about a country, or a company in that
country, the riskier the investment. It follows that sometimes
the rewards can also be great. As stock market investments

have proliferated, and new exchanges opened or old ones revitalized, a sector that has become of considerable interest to investors prepared to take risks are the emerging markets. There are now stock markets operating in at least 60 countries worldwide.

Emerging markets split into several groups. There are those in southeast Asia, which have attracted considerable interest as the Asian 'tiger' economies have grown. Separated from this group, but reflecting the extraordinary size of the Indian economy, is the Bombay Stock Exchange, which in 1995 was the best performing global stock market. Indian shares have been particularly popular amongst the large Indian communities working in the Gulf.

Then there are a variety of Middle East markets. In many liquidity and lack of adequate regulation is a problem, but stock markets as varied as Beirut, Muscat and Bahrain have begun to arouse considerable interest amongst nationals, and a small amount of participation elsewhere.

Central and Eastern Europe is another emerging market sector, where investment has been stimulated by the many privatizations that have taken place, although, all too often, with the result that the old communists who controlled businesses before the collapse of Comecon are the new capitalists of today.

Latin America is following the pattern of southeast Asia, and a special case is South Africa. Although the Johannesburg Stock Exchange is one of the oldest in the world, there is no doubt that the new South Africa is an emerging market with its fair share of risk and reward. So far it has chosen to go down the route of democratic capitalism. President Nelson Mandela, upon release from 27 years of incarceration, initially embraced socialism, and, upon election, opposed privatization. His team of African National Congress ministers, including the able Trevor Manuel, his minister for finance, and Thabo Mbeke, the deputy president, persuaded him to change his mind, and South Africa, despite numerous setbacks, now offers opportunities to those prepared to take some risks.

Not everybody agrees that the expansion of stock markets in developing countries will expand their economies and eradicate poverty. In the *Economic Journal* of May 1997,

Ajit Singh of the University of Cambridge argued that they were more of a hindrance. Many of Singh's arguments are well worn – that stock markets are short-termist, that swings in share prices can be too volatile, and that those in emerging markets are little more than a casino. It is true that in many markets there can be a boom and bust mentality, which, at one level, raises investors' expectations beyond what is reasonable, and, at the other end of the equation, provides for despair which has little relation to the facts. Similar concerns have been raised by the billionaire investor George Soros, who has repeatedly warned that unexpected and chaotic movements of financial markets might destroy society. 'We are creating global financial markets without understanding their true nature,' warned Soros in May 1997. 'We have this false theory that markets, left to their own devices, tend towards equilibrium.'

Another argument mustered against paper wealth is that it encourages a consumer boom, which then has to be choked off by higher interest rates, depressing economic growth. This seemed to be the case with the windfall gains provided in Britain by the demutualization of some building societies and life assurers in 1996-98. So much cash was released into the market as members sold their shares that interest rates went up. In an emerging market like South Africa the same process created considerable disquiet amongst the majority black community who, of course, were not the beneficiary of windfall gains.

In a letter to the *Natal Mercury* complaining that the £3.5 billion windfall from the demutualization of South African Mutual was a 'sad reflection of society's greed', Terry Crawford-Browne wrote:

'Demutualization is a ploy to enrich the financial status quo, so that the rich (whites) get richer and the poor (blacks) get poorer. It is a recipe for revolution. The long-term implications for the country are disastrous. Our cities are housing time bombs, ringed by shantytowns and blighted by crime. The shacks of 7 million South Africans are a disgrace to a financial instituion like South Africa Mutual. Cape Town urgently needs 120,000 houses. At 50,000 rand a house (about £6,500) the cost would be 6 billion rand. That is almost petty cash for the 235 billion rand institution which is so cash flush that it proposes both to pay its policyholders 29.3 billion demutualization profit and to transfer 50 billion rand out of South Africa.'

These fierce words show why, in an emerging market like South Africa, share ownership and capital markets may have gathered a bad name. Against that the equity markets have financed ventures too risky for the staid commercial banks to consider.   Mr Singh's own study showed that in many developing countries equity finance take a greater share of company finance than in a mature economy like Britain's. It also exceeded bank finance. Countries where this was the case included Brazil, Jordan, Korea, Malaysia, Mexico, Turkey and Zimbabwe.

9 Getting Rid of Paper

'This draconian cancellation is a shock' – Michael Lawrence, chairman of the 100 Group of leading finance directors, on the collapse of the London Stock Exchange's Taurus project.

'Don't intrude on private grief. This is a shock. Certainly no one suspected it' – Judith Vincent, head of company and commercial law at the Confederation of British Industry.

'We will be the laughing stock of Europe. We have a Third-World settlement system in a first-rank financial centre' – Robert Binney, Chase Manhattan Bank.

'There is a discrepancy in London between the efficacy of the trading system and the efficiency of settlement operations. Some back offices are still in the Victorian age' – Annual report of the Frankfurt Stock Exchange, 1989.

Buying and selling shares is a brief transaction, often no more than two phone calls. But, unlike a family purchasing a kilo of apples from a market stall, the sharebuyer has nothing physically to show for it, other than a debit on his bank account after he has written out a cheque to his stockbroker. In order to be able to sell his shares again at a later date, he or she requires proof of ownership.

Traditionally this has been the share certificate, a legal document issued by the registrar of the company that issued the shares in the first place. With millions of shares changing hands each day – many of them in large blocks – settlement has been a cumbersome paper chase, employing thousands of people and costing investors, companies, and brokers millions of dollars to operate.

When London had a trading floor the details of all transactions recorded in the broker's dealing book were entered in ledgers, or computer programs, back at the office. The client was sent a contract note and a share registration form, which he had to return, together with an account. In London there are 22 accounting periods during the year, and statements were normally sent out after each one. Anyone who bought and then sold their shares during an accounting period – a short-term speculator, for instance – would not have to pay for them.

The jobber's dealing record was also committed to ledgers back in his office, and it was here that the paper chain began. If he had bought shares in the market, say 1,000 ICI, he would expect to be able to find someone to take them over before the end of the account period, relieving him of the necessity to chase up the scrip. If he sold 500 BP shares, things might have been more difficult. Within the accounting period he would expect to come across a seller of BP shares, hopefully prepared to sell at less than he had sold the earlier lot for, to enable him to cover his position and to make a profit.

But where he was a seller of shares, he faced the task of producing the scrip; in other words, of ensuring that the share certificates were passed to the broker acting for the purchaser. With small parcels this was relatively easy, but where large trades occur, he might encounter some difficulty. In any event it is unlikely that he would be able to match the sale exactly, so to obtain the scrip for any one parcel sold, he might have to go to several sellers for shares, thereby necessitating several contract notes to complete the transaction.

Back in the broker's office, clerks had to enter details of all these transactions into several other ledgers. There was the client ledger, dealing with each customer's transactions, which formed the basis of client billing. There was a list book, classified under the names of shares, to keep track of all trades. Each day clerks from broking houses would meet in the settlement room at the Stock Exchange to check the bargains reported by their dealers. Sometimes, in the mêlée of a busy day, errors occurred. Where the error was not the obvious fault of any one party, losses would be divided.

Once clients buying shares had returned their registration documents and settled their accounts, the broker had to make sure the relevant share certificates were provided to them. Share certificates were delivered by the selling brokers to the Central Stock Payment Office of the Stock Exchange, sorted into correct destinations, and collected by messengers of the buying brokers. For the reason explained earlier, in many cases there was more than one certificate, often from more than one individual. In the case of someone buying 1,000 ICI shares, for example, the certificates would come in odd lots, perhaps from different parts of the country. Details of the names and addresses of the former owners of the certificates would have to be recorded in yet another ledger, before the certificates were scrutinized by clerks for authenticity, and then sent off, together with the transfer authority, to the share registry of the company concerned. Very few listed companies, whether large or small, maintain their own share registry, preferring to pay for the services of specialist registrars, often operated by bank departments scattered around the country. Lloyd's Bank's Registry department at Goring-on-Sea is one such registrar, and has become one of the largest employers in West Sussex; during the height of the British Telecom flotation it was handling more than one million pieces of mail a day.

The system barely changed for two centuries, and by sheer weight of numbers it had become costly and grindingly slow. With up to half a million tickets and transfer forms passing round the market at the end of each account period, it was often many weeks before the purchaser of shares received the evidence of his purchase, by which time he might well have sold them again. By 1980 it was costing registrars £75m a year to maintain the share registers for just 9,000 securities.

Then the London Stock Exchange introduced the Talisman system. The definition of the Talisman system given in its brochure highlighted an almost effusive enthusiasm for new technology:

'Talisman, tal'is-man, or-iz-n. Transfer Accounting Lodgement for Investors, Stock Management for jobbers: Gr. payment, certificate, later completion; or an object induced with magical powers through which extraordinary results are achieved.'

Under Talisman the title of each share changing hands was transferred from its registered owner to Sepon Ltd, a Stock Exchange nominee company formed to hold shares in trust on behalf of the underlying new owner, whose interests are at all times fully protected. Sepon Ltd then transferred the shares on to the buying client.

Talisman was logical but cumbersome. When the selling broker received the share certificate and the returned signed transfer form from his client, he deposited them at the nearest Talisman centre, either in London or at one of eight other centres. At the Talisman centre the documents were checked for accuracy, and the transfer information – the names and addresses of the sellers and the contract price – entered into the central computer system.

The documents were then passed from the Talisman centre to the company's registrar for registration out of the client's name and into that of Sepon Ltd, although control of the stock stayed with the selling client until payment was made and delivery effected. When that happened ownership was transferred within the Talisman computer to the buying job-ber's – or market-maker's – account. Individual items of stock lost their identity, and simply became a pool of shares with which to satisfy buyers. The buying broker simply called up Talisman, the purchase information was entered into the computer, authorizing the removal of shares from the Sepon account into the name of the buying client, who then received a new share certificate.

The Talisman system also generated accounts for over 200 member firms of the Stock Exchange located in 65 cities and towns. By belonging to the network, each firm had only to write (or bank) one cheque in each accounting period. The system acted as a clearing-house between all the member firms, apportioning debits and credits, and providing them with a detailed statement, which they use to check their own records. Talisman also calculated payments due to the Inland Revenue for stamp duty, paid them regularly in bulk, and debited brokers' accounts.

While Talisman was a major advance over the cumbersome old systems, it did not offer anything like all electronic settlement. The back offices of London's stockbroking firms continued to be inundated with paper. So the LSE decided it would have to reduce, perhaps even abolish, paper share certificates, and announced its intention to launch a computerized share directory, in which transfer of shares would take place simply by moving the shares from the seller's directory in the computer to the buyer's. The directory was to be known as TAURUS, which stood for Transfer and Automated Registration of Uncertified Stock.

Taurus was to have been the vehicle for paperless settlement, whereby all records of share holdings were held on a central computer operated by the London Stock Exchange. But the large registrars that maintain the share registers of major companies objected to the idea. This was not surprising; they would have been put out of business. So the Stock Exchange committee driving the development of Taurus came up with a much more complex and expensive solution – a series of distributed databases at 400 different locations, some of them far flung, with a different combination of hardware and software on each site.

To most intelligent observers this was a non-starter. The *Investors Chronicle* published an article headed 'Cock and Bull Taurus' claiming that investors were confused, brokers were ill prepared, and the securities industry plagued by doubts. It coined a new word 'Taurophobia'. But the London Stock Exchange pressed gamely on, until 11 March 1993 when it announced that Taurus was being abandoned, at a cost of £75 million and at least 350 jobs. The Chief Executive of the Stock Exchange, Peter Rawlins, who had been brought in to modernize the organization and revamp its computer systems, resigned.

As the *Financial Times* commented at the time: 'The Taurus project was blighted by misjudgement, mismanagement, and neglect.'

The real trouble was that Taurus was unnecessarily complicated yet lacked a logical design, and suffered also from Whitehall intervention. The Department of Trade and Industry was responsible for drafting the legislative and regulatory framework for Taurus, which, as you might expect from civil servants, was both slow and voluminous. The project team also bought in a high-priced and much-respected global custody software system from the United States, but then made extensive alterations to it.

With Taurus abandoned, the LSE had to stick with Talisman, while seeking a new solution. This time it decided against developing its own operation, and opted for CREST, a proprietary system run by a subsidiary of British Telecom.

In theory all United Kingdom and Irish shares are now held on CREST's computers. When ownership changes, the details are simply amended in the computer upon proof of a transaction. Those that want the assurance of a paper certificate can get one.

The basic principle behind CREST is that it will prove much more efficient than Talisman, as well as considerably cheaper. Unfortunately this proved not to be the case. One study, by the private client stockbroker, Capel-Cure Meyers, found that although the cost of settlement of a typical share trade had been halved by CREST, communications costs to and from the system had wiped out the savings. Of course these costs are much lower for large securities houses, which feel the benefit, but it is clear that the LSE is still far from solving one of its most pressing problems.

It is particularly ironic that London, the global pioneer in share trading, should have so much trouble in an essentially simple matter, especially when major international equity transactions are settled highly efficiently by a global corporation based only 200 or so miles away in Brussels.

Euroclear

When global deals involving many millions of dollars are concluded within seconds, it obviously does not make sense for settlement to become a slow and almost unending paper chase. Two telephone conversations in dealing rooms in London and Frankfurt repeated below show how casually dealers approach settlement.

The phone rings in London.
London dealer: Jenkins. Dealers.
New York dealer: Hallo, Bill. I'm ready to do that ICI deal.
London: Great.
New York: We'll take four million at 680.
London: Fine, settle through Euroclear.

New York: Settle through Euroclear.

Or in Frankfurt.
Person 1: We're looking for some ten million marks out of this.
Person 2: Deutsche Bank is the book runner?
Person 1: Yes, and we'll issue through Euroclear.

Euroclear is, by turnover, the most high-value office in the world. It is by far the largest settlement system for internationally traded securities. In 1993 it was processing more than $65 billion worth of transactions every working day, quietly, calmly, almost seamlessly. On some days the daily transactions rose to $100m. About 2,700 participants from 29 countries use Euroclear's computers for settlement – working in 35 different currencies, the most important of them being US dollars, German marks, French francs, Dutch guilders, British pounds, Japanese yen, Spanish pesetas and, of course, the European Currency Unit, or ECU. Altogether over 85,000 different securities are settled through the system.

Despite its high-value business and the huge numbers of securities passing through it, the activities of Euroclear are little known to members of the public. Its global headquarters, in a brand new building, adjoin the red-light district of Brussels, close to one of the main railway stations. But it is much more discreet about its business than the girls who decorate the adjoining bars and brasseries or who ply their trade by pouncing on passers-by as they seek this global hi-tech hub of international settlement.

Euroclear keeps a very low profile. There are no markings or nameplates on its office building to identify it. If you do not know where it is, you may never find it. Brussels taxi drivers appear never to have heard of Euroclear, and usually try to divert you to the headquarters of the European Commission a short distance away. The building itself is remarkably similar to those used by intelligence services in London and other parts of Europe – bland, understated and very well protected.

It is not like a bank or a stockbroking firm, with courteous doormen; polite, well-dressed receptionists; comfortable waiting chairs; and plenty of high-quality brochures to read. The entrance hall is spartan and unattended, apart from a lone security man who sits inside a glass box, and issues pre-booked passes to those who line up and identify themselves before him. A visitor is then escorted through turnstiles by the person he has come to see, usually after a spell in a waiting room completely devoid of any reading material.

This is entirely logical. Euroclear does not deal with the general public, or with paper. It works entirely with information technology. Because it provides the location for the settlement of many trillions of dollars of global assets, it needs to be protected by maximum security. Any disruption to its operations would be harmful. To guard against fire its fabric is specially reinforced. It has back-up generators for its power systems and air conditioning. And just in case it is hit by a thunderbolt, its computer systems and databases are replicated in another building elsewhere in Europe.

Today's global traders want settlement arranged with speed and accuracy at low cost. Key information provided by the buyer's securities house is tapped into a template in a program called Euclid 90, which is the Euroclear proprietary operating system. Ninety-five per cent of the global firms that use Euroclear are directly on-line; the remainder use fax or telex. The buyer's details are matched with the seller's template, which also tells Euroclear in which safe deposit the paper certificates are located.

These safe depositories could be anywhere in the world. Euroclear works with blue-chip depositories the world over, and guarantees the safety of its participants' documents. The documents are seldom, if ever, moved from their original depositories; when ownership changes the details of the new owner are merely recorded in the Euroclear system.

Actual settlement takes place on the same original principle used in the famous Jonathan's coffee shop in London's Change Alley – full delivery versus payment. Everyone using Euroclear has two accounts, one for cash and the other for the securities they hold. On the eve of the day set down for settlement – usually five days after a deal is struck but it could be much less – Euroclear checks that the seller actually possesses the securities sold, and that the buyer has the cash. If the answer is 'yes', then settlement is by simple book entry. If not, a buyer can switch to Euroclear's electronic funds transfer system, and effortlessly call up a loan to replenish his account. Equally a seller without enough stock can borrow the shortfall from other participants in the Euroclear network. Funds available from within the system total several trillion dollars; it is quite normal at the close of business each day for up to $4 billion of loans to be outstanding.

Of course Euroclear's huge investment in computers – with 170 specialist engineers to manage and maintain them – enables the operation to provide other services, which bring it into competition with domestic settlement systems. One of these is to act as custodian for those owning large batches of stock or bonds. Those who use Euroclear's custody services can instruct it to act as mailbox for the circulars and entitlement letters sent to security holders; to collect and bank dividends and payouts; to vote as proxy holder; and to inform them of corporate events such as annual meetings and special celebrations. Euroclear will also deal with legal administration, evaluate portfolios and offer international tax advice.

Euroclear is owned by its participants: over 2,000 users are shareholders. Some of them are major banks, but no shareholder has more than a 3.5 per cent stake. The system is operated under contract by the New York bank Morgan Guaranty, which provides all the staff and technical services. Morgan also guarantees the loan of any shares under its custody. But policy is decided by an independent board, which meets monthly.

It is not without competition; another global settlements system is run by the Luxembourg-based Cedel. But in recent years Euroclear has been steadily increasing its dominance of the market.

10 Raising Money

Almost every entrepreneur has a dream that he will be able to build up his own business as a private company, and then, because of its success and opportunity for further growth, be able to sell it to the market. For many the happiest solution is to find large numbers of individuals prepared to buy a total stake, of say, 47 per cent, so that the original founder and his family may retain control, while pocketing the cash generated by the sale. The lucky ones who do this become instant multi-millionaires, and are still able to hold on to the businesses they started and to run them in much the same way as before.

So how can an entrepreneur use the stock markets for his own benefit? The cardinal rule is that there should be some other reason for turning a private company into a listed one rather than just to obtain a personal fortune. It would not be easy to bring a company to the markets if that were seen by the markets as the prime purpose.

The most obvious attraction of going public is that obtaining a listing on any major stock exchange improves the standing of the concern and its products. There are very few manufacturers of branded products or household names that are not public companies or corporations.

Apart from obtaining a better image, becoming listed on a stock exchange also makes it easier, in normal times, to raise finance for expansion and development. Both investors and lenders have a distinct preference for an enterprise that is not the plaything of an individual, or a group of individuals. Even though it is still possible for one man to hold the reins of a large public company, there are many more checks and balances than on private companies, where clever accountants can play interesting games with the balance sheet. The accounts, and other indicators of performance, of public companies are closely scrutinized by meticulous analysts, who are always prepared to publish adverse comment where they believe it to be merited. Thus most public companies are assessed with one objective – are they good investments? By contrast, the potential of private companies is not easy, even when they are open to scrutiny; private company accounts are freely available only at Companies' House, and then usually one year in arrears. This alone explains why both institutional and private investors are reluctant to commit large sums to unquoted companies. What happens when the leading figures in a private company die? Their heirs may be hopeless businessmen, or may be forced to sell up part of their holding at an inopportune time in order to pay capital transfer tax. Father may drop dead just as the next recession is approaching: subsequent family feuding and a forced sale could leave the outside investors with little to show for their years of support to the old concern.

Another strong advantage to an expanding business in being publicly listed on an exchange is that it helps in takeovers. Instead of paying cash for an acquisition, a company can often provide at least one part of the cost by offering a share swap, as in the summer of 1985 when Guinness offered shareholders in Bell, the whisky distiller, paper worth considerably more than the market price of their own scrip. When an efficient company is taking over a dull one, shareholders of the latter are often only too glad of the chance of just such an easy escape route.

A further advantage of obtaining a listing is that the company attracts unsolicited funds. If they think you are doing well, any number of investors will buy your shares. Regular mention in the financial pages is useful publicity and, in the case of well-run companies, makes for easier relations with customers and helps when attempting to attract executive staff.

Going Public

When a company decides it would like to go public, it normally approaches a firm of stockbrokers through its accountants or bankers. There is then usually a lunch or dinner, a getting-to-know-you session at which little more will be achieved than a general understanding of the nature of the business, and its goals and aspirations. The directors of the company considering a listing will also obtain some idea of how the operation, which is almost certainly a lengthy one, is to be planned.

Once contact has been established, and a decision made in principle, a partner in the firm of brokers will seek a total brief on the company – particularly its management structure, strengths and weaknesses, labour force, present shareholders, competitors, and, of course, a detailed study of full sets of accounts for the previous five years. Quite often this study will show that a listing quote is out of the question. In Britain investors and fund managers are spoilt for choice, and with governments the world over off-loading billions of pounds' worth of assets in state enterprises, any company that does not offer first-class prospects will not attract support. To go down the road towards a listing, and to issue a prospectus, and then have to withdraw it, would be a costly mistake.

Assuming, however, that the feasibility study shows a good prospect of success, the next stage for the stockbroker is to visit the company and its major plants or operations and to see it at work. This will usually be carried out by a senior member of the firm, under the supervision of a partner. The staff member will also try to visit competitors of the company, to seek another assessment, although the need for strict confidentiality makes this aspect of the study difficult. A firm of accountants, not the company's own auditors, will also be commissioned to carry out a thorough investigation.

All this will have to be done within three months, if a reasonable target for a listing is to be achieved. The next step is for the brokers to prepare a detailed proposal for the flotation, which will, in effect, form the blueprint for the day-by-day progress towards the listing. The broker will suggest a price band within which shares might be offered – the decision on a firm price will come much later. He will set out a list of financial requirements which will have to be met and propose underwriters, who, at a substantial discount on price, will agree to purchase any shares if the float is undersubscribed. The company will usually be asked to pay off all major loans – for no investor is keen on picking up a load of debt – and to revalue all its properties.

This stage completed, the next step is to decide how the capital of the company is to be made available to the public. In most cases, this will be through the issue of a prospectus, offering the shares at a price expected to be lower than the price at which the company will start its life on the exchanges. In the main European markets such a prospectus is published in full in the *Financial Times*, and, occasionally, other newspapers. The prospectus is, in fact, an offer for sale. It will detail the price at which shares will be available, and name any proposed restrictions on voting rights. The terms of sale will be set out, as well as the names and addresses of the auditors, stockbrokers, bankers, solicitors and directors. There will be a full description of its products or services.

Isotron, a company providing the only independent gamma radiation service in Britain, published just such a prospectus. It devoted thousands of words to an extremely detailed description of its technological processes, and its business prospects. A large part of the prospectus was devoted to the curricula vitae of the directors and senior employees, right down to site managers. There was a chapter on safety procedures, while over a page of closely-spaced print was devoted to publication of the independent report by accountants KPMG Peat Marwick. The reader was spared no detail, and the prospectus constituted an extremely thorough insight into the company.

Once the prospectus has been written, usually by the merchant bankers advising the company in association with the stockbrokers, the approval of the local exchange where the shares are to be listed must be sought. This is much more than a formality, and it is quite normal for questions to be raised on matters of detail. For instance in London the most pressing concern of the LSE's quotations department is to see that the prospectus gives as full and accurate a picture as possible of the company and its prospects, and it is unlikely that a document will pass through unamended.

The terms of sale vary widely. Sometimes an underwriting firm of brokers will agree to buy all the share capital to be offered for sale on a given day, and then do their best to dispose of the shares to investors at a sufficiently higher price to offer them a profit. Sometimes the shares will be offered directly to the public by advertisement; where this happens the underwriters will only have to take on the shares left unsold, and if the issue is a success, may end up with no commitment and a useful underwriting fee.

Finding an underwriter is usually not a major problem, for all brokers have a list of those they can call upon, whether institutions, investment banks or other financial groups. Underwriters do count, however, on the integrity and accuracy of a broker's recommendation. No securities house can consider accepting the job of arranging a flotation unless it is convinced it is a sound investment.

An increasingly popular way of raising the cash is through public tender – used by bankers J. Henry Schroder Wagg and Co. in the Isotron case mentioned earlier. Here 3,290,088 ordinary 25p shares were offered at a minimum tender price of 120p a share, the principle being that those prepared to offer a higher rate would receive the biggest allocation. Having received all the applications, Schroder's were left with the task of setting a 'striking price', not exceeding the highest price at which sufficient applications were received to cover the total number of shares offered. A public tender was also used by Schroder's and UBS Phillips and Drew in bringing Andrew Lloyd Webber's Really Useful Group to a full London listing.

Obviously public tender is a system favoured by highly successful, confident and relatively well-known companies. It is not to be recommended if oversubscription is thought unlikely. It also avoids 'stagging' – a stag being the individual who buys new issues in the confident belief that oversubscription will lead to the price rising sharply on the day of listing.

Whether stagging occurs in the majority of cases when the tender system is not used depends, of course, very much upon the price at which the shares are fixed for sale. Pricing can be the key to the whole issue. If prices are pitched too low, there will be a huge oversubscription, involving vast amounts of extra paperwork, the return of cheques, and the difficult job of selecting the lucky applicants to receive shares. The stags will reap rich rewards. If, at the other extreme, the price is pitched too high, the issue will be a disaster, and months, even years, of work will be wasted. There have been examples of both, and where there is oversubscription, those applicants left out, or as happened in some privatizations, awarded derisory holdings, feel aggrieved, even bitter.

Fixing the price is not easy, however, because most companies are the prisoners of current events. A series of air crashes could damage the price of the shares of a manufacturer of jet engines, for instance. Inevitably setting the price is left to the last possible moment, with brokers and bankers using their experience to judge market conditions as D-Day approaches. The 40 days and 40 nights before and after the day of flotation are the busiest, especially in the offices of those directly participating. It is not unusual for the major people involved to camp in their offices during much of this period, and certainly holidays are out of the question. While the final offer documents are away at the printers, they just hope that they have got it right.

Whether a company goes public through a full float or sale by tender, it is a costly business. The experts needed – lawyers, investment bankers, accountants, brokers, and financial public relations men – do not come cheap, especially in the City of London. There are few ways of doing it cheaper, but one of them is to arrange what is called a placement. In this case, the stockbroking firm buys all the shares and sells them direct to its clients, avoiding the cost of dealing. This method is used in small new issues in London or where there is unlikely to be much public interest. But even here, the Stock Exchange regulations stipulate that at least 35 per cent of the company's issued capital must be in the placement, thereby preventing directors from using the system as a ploy to pick up some useful cash while still totally dominating the company. At least one-quarter of the shares must also be sold to the public on the stock markets, which helps when open dealings start. A placement is considerably cheaper because the costs of advertising, printing and professional services will be much less, and there is no need for underwriters.

There is also the alternative of arranging an introduction, but this way of obtaining a quotation in London is only available to those companies that already have a wide distribution of shareholders, and where there is no immediate intention of anyone selling out. No capital is offered prior to listing, and it is therefore not necessary for the company to go through the procedures described earlier, or to issue a prospectus, although it is required to take an advertisement to publicize the move. This method is most commonly used when a large foreign company decides to have its shares listed in London as well as on its home exchange.

Raising More Money

The stock markets were founded to raise money for industry and to provide finance for great national projects such as railways and canals. They raised money with great success until the Second World War, and in the early post-war years it was the place where companies went for extra funds if they wanted to expand. Borrowing from the banks was, in Britain at least, considered expedient only for short-term finance. Borrowing from overseas – through instruments such as eurobonds, and more recently eurobonds and euronotes – was not even in the minds of those few City types who supported Jean Monnet's vision of an integrated European Economic Community. Raising money was the job of the Stock Exchange. Why go further than Throgmorton Street?

Things began to go badly wrong with the capital-raising function of the Stock Exchange when successive governments in the middle years of this century decided that the best way of paying for expensive public programmes was to tax the rich, which, to them, included almost everyone who did not belong to a trade union and pick up his wages in a brown envelope once a week. Income from share ownership was 'unearned income', and somehow thought of as less decent than interest obtained from a building society. Making a capital gain by selling one's own shares at a profit in order to pay for old age, school fees, or even a trip to the Bahamas, was regarded as sinful, and therefore had to be discouraged through extra taxation. Company taxes were raised, making it harder for businesses to fund expansion. And, in order to justify an ill-judged attempt to curb a free market for wages, 'dividend restraint' was imposed. With little point in investing either for capital growth or for income, investors followed the example of the trade union movement, and went on strike. In other words, they ceased buying shares.

The political effect of the onslaught on the investor in the 1960s and 1970s was to bring to an almost complete halt a stock exchange system which allowed development capital to be raised, pluralistically, by a large number of individuals and institutions, and to replace it by a more costly system of finance through banks. It seems unlikely that the trend will ever be completely reversed, but in recent years there has been an encouraging revival of capital-raising on stock exchanges, to the benefit of both saver and entrepreneur.

Today business school studies by Nobel Prize winners Professor Franco Modigliani and Professor Merton Miller show that the costs of debt and equity financing are comparable. The cost of debt – of course – is easiest to measure: it is the interest paid by the company on its bank loan or bond. Assuming the company is a highly credible and successful one, known as a blue-chip, it will pay a premium of about two per cent over a bond issued by a credit-worthy country like Britain or Germany.

The cost of equity is the dividend yield, which should be cheaper, but often is not. Dividends often depend on taxation policy. Raising money through the share markets from rights issues also strengthens balance sheets and prevents the kind of over-borrowing that has forced many large companies into difficulty.

Sometimes companies will want to use both methods. For instance a British company may use a rights issue to fund a UK acquisition, but, if seeking to take over a European company, could use a foreign currency bond to match the currency of the target company's country.

What happens with a rights issue is that the holders of ordinary shares in a company are offered further shares at a discount, usually substantial enough to make it attractive. Under British rules, such new shares must be offered to existing stockholders in quantities proportionate to their holdings. This is known as a pre-emption right, which has been abandoned in the United States. A lively debate has been taking place in Britain over whether this rule is sensible. In many cases not all shareholders are willing, or even able, to take up the rights offer. So, under the present system, underwriters have to be found who will. As with new issues, pitching the price right is crucial. If a rights issue is undersubscribed there is a danger that the share price will fall, even if underwriters have been appointed, and this would defeat part of the objective of the exercise, which is to raise more capital.

The most important question for a company making a rights issue is to decide on the terms at which it will offer new shares. Normally this is done by offering the shareholders the right to buy a number of shares at a special price for each share they own. So, for example, in 1990 the British brewing group Bass sought to raise £558 million by giving its equity holders the right to buy one new share for every five they already owned. This is known as a one-for-five issue. In order to persuade shareholders to subscribe to a rights issue, the price has to be a worthwhile discount to the prevailing market price. But this does not mean that rights issues present shareholders with a bargain – an offer they cannot refuse. As soon as a rights issue has been completed, the price of the existing shares usually falls to reflect their dilution as a result of new stock on the register.

The small shareholder offered a rights issue is often in a Catch-22 situation. If he takes up the offer he has to dip into his savings and increase his risk exposure to the company concerned; in other words an additional investment is forced upon him. If he does not take up his rights he may sell them to a stockbroker for the difference between the rights price and the market price, but unless there is a substantial volume of shares involved the commission is likely to be prohibitive. If, as often is the case, you do nothing at all, the company will automatically sell your rights for you, and pay you the proceeds.

Rights offers are usually contained in a long and arcane document preceded with the suggestion that if you do not understand it you should see a stockbroker. Many people, particularly those who have not paid close attention to their investments or who have inherited equities, mistakenly throw these documents into the rubbish bin, and lose out.

After the deregulation of Britain's financial markets at the time of Big Bang in 1986, many people believed that companies would move across to the American system of placements, described earlier. They reckoned without the big pension funds and life assurance companies, which dominate the British markets and who were jealous of their automatic right to get a slice of anything new going. These institutional investors formed a cosy cartel, which called itself the 'Pre-emption Group', and set itself the goal to protect at all costs the right of existing shareholders to get first refusal of any new shares. At the time this group was established, the British government was supporting a change in the rules, which would have allowed companies to raise additional capital directly from new shareholders. The Pre-emption Group frustrated this change by introducing a rule book binding on all its members. One of the guidelines was that in any issue of more than five per cent of a company's capital, the existing shareholders had to be given first call. Of course, as long as the institutions stuck to their own rules, their dominance in the market was such that nobody would be able to change matters. And, in Britain at least, so it has proved.

A rights issue is not cheap, which is one of the main arguments against this form of raising additional capital. First there are underwriting fees, paid by the company seeking to raise the money to the merchant bank or securities house managing the issue, and to those who have undertaken to buy any unwanted shares. These fees come to about two per cent of the amount of money raised. Then there is the paperwork – fees to lawyers, accountants and public relations consultants, plus the actual cost of printing and distributing the substantial amount of documentation necessary. Add to this the discount which must be offered to make the rights issue attractive – a figure of around 20 per cent is common practice – and it is easy to see why many a corporate financial director would rather go to see the company's bankers or, if it were possible, to arrange a placement.

An alternative to a rights issue is loan capital, which may be raised on the Stock Exchange either through unsecured loan stock or convertible stock. Loan stock is usually issued only by blue-chip companies. A company without a top rating would not find investors ready to buy it even at very high interest rates, and might offer the inducement of convertibility to enable the holder to convert all or some of the shares at a later stage to equities.

If a company is planning to modernize its plant to increase

output and productivity, loan capital can be a particularly attractive vehicle. The interest paid is deductible before corporation tax is payable, so the company's tax bill is reduced. And as output rises, and hopefully profits, so does the company's share price, making it beneficial for the shareholders to make the conversion.

As with new issues, there are several ways in which a stockbroker can obtain loan capital for his clients. He can arrange for a full prospectus detailing the offer to be prepared, published and advertised, and wait for the response, usually stipulating preferential treatment to existing shareholders. He may, if he chooses, place the loan stock with institutions direct – unlike placements with new issues, where a proportion has to be offered on the Stock Exchange. Or he may limit the offer to existing shareholders, an unlikely course because especially attractive terms are usually necessary to get full support. A placement is usually much more efficient.

Then there is the bond market, of which the eurobond market is the best known. Not long ago, only governments of stable and prosperous democracies and large international institutions such as the World Bank and the European Investment Bank would go to the bond market for funds, by issuing securities at good interest rates with maturity dates 10 to 20 years away. Mostly denominated in dollars, these securities offered large institutional investors an attractive hedge against the fall of sterling and against inflation.

Taking AIM

Money can, in theory, be raised for small and medium-sized go-ahead businesses through the junior stock exchange, better known as AIM, which replaced the Unlisted Securities Market, its predecessor. Similar markets have evolved in the United States and France, and the idea has widespread political support because small businesses are seen as major sources of job creation, technological innovation and entrepreneurship. The high-interest rate environment of the past few years has compounded the financing problems of the growing company, but AIM does offer those who have a case and can present it well the chance not only of raising capital for their expansion, but also of becoming rich in the process.

AIM offers all the benefits of a stock market, such as the opportunity for a higher public profile, and access to new capital and investors, with a much simpler entry structure than going for a full listing. For instance, there are no restrictions on the size of companies who join, the percentage of shares to be placed in public hands or how long they have been operating.

The key to AIM, and what distinguishes it from its predecessor, the Unlisted Securities Market, is the compulsory appointment to AIM-listed companies of two key people – the nominated adviser and the nominated broker, each drawn from specialist corporate finance companies which have been approved by the LSE.

The *nominated adviser*, who could be a stockbroker, accountant or banker drawn from a list of about 70 people, has the responsibility for deciding whether a company is suitable for the market, and for making sure it conforms to the AIM rules. Once listed the company must retain the adviser to keep it on track and to make sure it fulfils its obligations, which include disclosing all material information to investors. The *nominated adviser* has to undertake to be available at all times to advise and guide the company's directors on the AIM rules. The *nominated broker* has to be a member of the exchange, and, in the absence of a market maker, provides a means for investors to buy and sell the company's shares.

AIM is clearly designed for professional, rather than amateur investors, and is for the risk-taker who accepts that not all young and growing companies succeed. It is of particular appeal to the large number of fund management groups that specialize in investing in smaller companies.

AIM companies do not have to be British, nor of a certain size, nor do they have to prove a lengthy trading history. But they must be public companies, registered under the laws of their country, and have published accounts which conform to proper internationally-accepted accounting standards.

Before being admitted to AIM, the company has to publish a prospectus not very different from that required for a full listing; this is required whether or not the company intends to raise funds. The prospectus has to include a description of the securities to be traded, a full description of the company and its principal activities, the company's financial history and performance, details of the management, full details of all directors and their personal business histories, and the names of substantial shareholders.

AIM shares are traded on what is called SEATS PLUS, which enables buyers and sellers to trade with each other through the LSE. They can do this either through a market-maker, if there is enough of a market to justify one, or by an order board, which displays publicly orders to buy and sell shares, and allows trades to be executed automatically.

The service also allows financial information about each company to be entered by the nominated broker, thus helping investors to evaluate the shares. By March 1997 the AIM exchange had raised a total of £1.15 billion pounds with its listed companies having a market capitalization of £5.9 billion. Of the 271 companies on AIM, all but 18 were British. Those listed included several football clubs – Birmingham City, Charlton and West Bromwich to name but three – leisure companies, Internet firms, recruitment consultants, wine importers and even one rail privatization.

A comparable operation exists across the Channel in France, where the 'Nouveau Marché' was set up in 1996 to cater for small and fast-growing businesses. This also has relaxed joining rules so that, for example, new companies do not have to provide three-year financial projections, but must provide quarterly results. At the time of writing the number of companies listed on the 'Nouveau Marché' was measured in tens rather than hundreds, but since its launch the index has grown by more than 50 per cent.

The problems of raising money for small companies in Britain are not confined to the equity sector; banks have also had difficulty in providing adequate funds at a reasonable price and on reasonable conditions. Despite attention-grabbing advertisements proclaiming their support for small business, the banks have failed to win many friends in this area. Under pressure to improve their margins and the quality of their loans following the mistakes of the 1980s, the High Street banks have demanded interest rate margins and levels of security that make it very difficult for a small business to establish itself. Midland Bank as good as admitted this when its chief executive suggested that the best way for the small business sector to move forward would be if there were some kind of government support or guarantee for small business loans. He has a point, but the British government had its fingers badly burnt with the ill-fated Business Expansion Scheme which was largely used for property-backed ventures, many of which collapsed in the early 1990s.

Across the Atlantic, the NASDAQ market discussed earlier has provided the capital support for some of the most dynamic and innovative companies in the United States – Microsoft was founded in this way. Of the 100 best performing companies, 75 have had their first public offerings in the past 15 years. NASDAQ listings contain hundreds of quality young companies whose securities trade in large volumes. NASDAQ has recognized that small companies are in the forefront of economic opportunity: small to medium-sized companies have created most new jobs in the United States in the past ten years.

The number of companies traded on NASDAQ expanded rapidly in the 1980s, from 2,894 in 1980 to 4,132 in 1990. This 43 per cent rise in the number of companies generated a rise in market capitalization of 155 per cent to $311 billion. Most of these have come to the exchange after an IPO (initial public offering).

A company seeking an IPO in America will normally be advised by its investment bankers to offer its stock at 10 to 15 per cent below trading expectation in order to attract suitable support. The bankers will produce a highly detailed prospectus, with considerable attention paid to competitive advantages compared with other listed companies operating in the same field. The Securities and Exchange Commission has a complex set of rules governing the issue of a prospectus, the foundation stone of which is full disclosure of anything likely to be relevant to an investor. But this rigorous attitude pays off; it gives the investor more confidence. In the United States a prospectus must include information about products and services, manufacturing facilities, competition, and possible risks – apart from full financials – and omission of information, or inclusion of misleading information, can provide a valid cause for a class action lawsuit. Once a prospectus has been filed with the SEC, the officials review it, and come back with comments, suggestions and criticisms.

Once a public offering has been made and the IPO company is trading, it is subject to strict rules on corporate governance and the provision of information. There must be a minimum of two independent directors on its board. There is a total ban on the issuing of any preferential shares, or taking any action that would restrict or reduce the voting rights of ordinary shareholders. The company must also complete SEC documents 10-Q and 10-K which require disclosure of a wide range of information, including executive compensation, and security ownership of certain beneficial owners and managers.

There is also the NASDAQ Small-Cap Market, which has about 1,200 smaller companies listed. The requirements for listing on this market are substantially less than those for NASDAQ itself, and it is used as a conduit to the main exchange.

11 Selling the Family Silver

'It's like selling the family silver' – Harold
Macmillan, speaking in the House of Commons.

*'I am not able to say myself whether it will be worth
all the labour involved in privatization. I do not know.
I think we shall find out only a lot later on'* – Sir Denis
Rooke, chairman of British Gas.

'Get it out . . . get it sold' – Kenneth Baker, when
chairman of the Conservative Party.

*'Privat: Middle English proverb from Latin,
privatus, not belonging to the State, not in public life,
deprived of office, from the past participle of private,
to deprive, release'* – American Heritage Dictionary.

Privatization – pioneered in Britain by Margaret Thatcher's
Conservative government on the idea of the management
guru Peter Drucker – is a philosophy which has swept the
world. One by one governments have been divesting themselves of great state-owned corporations. Britain led the way
in ridding the taxpayer of the burden – and the public servant
of the responsibility – of huge utility businesses like power
and gas supply, telecommunications and airlines. Five years
after people queued in the streets of London to buy shares in
British Telecom, the Poles and the Czechs were forming their
own lines to buy assets once controlled by the communists.
Now privatization has reached Africa, Asia and Latin
America.

Alas, in Britain a brilliant idea has been poorly executed
with the result that very few members of the public have
ended up with more than a handful of shares. Instead of
encouraging saving, privatization bred stagging – making a
capital gain by selling equity at a profit immediately upon

acquisition. The issues were priced too cheaply, and the City made huge profits, leaving a nasty taste in the mouths of ordinary families who came to believe that share-trading was not for them.

It did not start off that way. I remember spending one wintry evening in the Conservative Club at West Houghton, an unpretentious Lancashire village in the drab industrial belt between Liverpool and Manchester. A group of women, two of them the wives of packers at a nearby baked-bean factory, were discussing the price of British Telecom shares. All had small holdings, following the government's decision to sell off three billion shares in British Telecommunications plc to the public, in what had been the world's largest-ever share sale. The women agreed that they planned to hold on to their shares, even though they could sell out at a tidy profit. And they had become addicted to share ownership. Since the British Telecom issue three of them had bought other shares. Said one: 'I have bought Marks & Spencer; I bought Rank Organisation and sold them again, and I am buying Dobson Park, because I think that will benefit from the end of the miners' strike.' 'I watch the prices every morning in the *Daily Mail*,' said another, 'and sometimes I keep a watch on them through the day on teletext.' Neither the women nor their families had ever had shares before. 'I did not really know how to go about it; I did not know a reputable stockbroker, or how to go about finding one, and I certainly did not know the bank would do it. It was a matter of ignorance, really.'

The experience of West Houghton confirmed that a vein of popular capitalism existed to be tapped in Britain. Some stockbrokers argue that, even without privatization of great state monopolies at the initiative of the government, new conditions had come about to make share ownership attractive to the individual. For the first time for over a quarter of a century, it was possible to generate a better return on capital invested in equities and other financial instruments than from that great middle-class – and heavily subsidized – bolthole, the family home. It was also true that some alleviation in death duties and other capital taxes had resulted in many couples in their late forties and early fifties inheriting a useful sum of money, which they chose to invest rather than spend on material possessions. When a City firm of stockbrokers conducted two investment seminars to canvass new business, one in London and the other in Preston, they obtained a significantly better response in the North.

Yet it is unlikely that the burst of interest in share ownership, particularly among the working classes, would have come about if the British Telecom float had not taken place, with its hype, touring road shows, television campaign and gimmicks like bonus shares and vouchers to help pay the phone bills.

Even more hype went into the sale in December 1986 of over four billion shares in British Gas, with the introduction to the nation's television screens nightly of an ubiquitous but enigmatic character called Sid. Clever if unsubtle advertisements by the Young and Rubicam agency urged viewers to 'tell Sid' about the opportunities for the public to buy shares in British Gas. One even had a pigeon fancier releasing his bird and saying 'there y'are my darlin', just go and tell Sid'. Right to the end of the campaign, Sid was never to be spotted; in the very latest advertisement a near-demented potential shareholder was seen climbing a mountain peak and peering through the mist crying 'Sid' at a shape that turned out to be nothing more than a startled sheep.

The British public gratefully accepted the offer – and why not? As with British Telecom, the government had priced British Gas attractively and with a forthcoming election in mind – those who sold quickly were rewarded with a capital gain in excess of 20 per cent, and those who held the stock could look forward to cheaper fuel bills with the prospect of gas vouchers in addition to normal dividends. For every 100 shares bought, investors received a voucher worth £10 payable over a two-year period.

Once British Gas was safely out of the way, the government set about another major sale, that of British Airways. This was followed by British Steel, the nation's electricity industry, and the water authorities. *The Economist* saw it as 'the largest transfer of property since the dissolution of the monasteries under Henry VIII'.

Russian roulette

Twelve Russians waited patiently in line for what, to them, was the sale of the century. This was not the type of queue so familiar in the 1960s and 1970s for bread, meat, or items of everyday clothing. The Muscovites had come to buy shares in one of the country's best-loved concerns – the BBC, or Bolshevik Biscuit Corporation, which, in earlier times, had held 12 per cent of the Soviet market for cookies.

Each of them held a voucher worth 10,000 roubles, issued by the Russian government, entitling the holder to exchange it for shares of equivalent value in any enterprise offered for sale by the Ministry for Privatization. Advising the ministry were dark-suited experts from two Western financial institutions, Credit Suisse First Boston, and the European Bank for Reconstruction and Development. As they advanced to bid for their shares, the shabbily dressed men and women paid scant attention to the documentation set out on the tables before them. But their questions showed their relish for their proposed investment, as they asked: 'What will the return on capital be?', 'What are your profits?', 'What are your marketing plans?'

That day was the first time in Russian history that ordinary men and women had been able to bid for shares. Though the sale was not reported on television news bulletins in Europe or America, history was being made. Three years earlier, confounding Lenin's predictions, communism as practised in the Soviet Union and its Warsaw Pact allies had collapsed, leaving an economic shambles as serious as that faced in Germany at the end of the Second World War. New, democratically elected leaders sought to rekindle their economies by resorting to privatization: putting the ownership of enterprises into the hands of individuals and private institutions rather than under the control of the state.

From Warsaw to Washington workers now own shares, but there is a considerable debate on the effectiveness of employee ownership. So far there is little evidence to suggest that employees use their position as shareholders to influence boards, although in some cases workers have delegated their voting rights to trades unions. Even in companies where generous workers' participation exists, their collective holding seldom rises above five per cent. There is also an argument that workers should behave in exactly the same way as prudent investment managers, and spread a share portfolio over a number of stocks to minimize risk. Certainly an *employee* with shares in his employer's company should be wide awake to the downside possibilities – in other words that he may lose all or most of his investment.

Another complication comes when employee share ownership is mistakenly seen as a form of performance-related pay. Share ownership is not, and should not, be seen as an alternative to incentives. Share ownership gives employees a stake in the capital of a company, regardless of whether individually or collectively they have made a positive contribution. Profit-related pay and bonus schemes, which may be based on meeting budget or on the return of capital, however desirable, are quite separate.

Privatization: Privileges for the Workers

Few employees have fared so well as those working for privatized concerns in Britain, for in almost all cases they were offered privileged treatment both on price and allocations.

Let us look at just one example: the employees of Northumbrian Water, the most over-subscribed of the ten new water companies. Those who did not live in Northumbria were restricted to just 100 shares each, and even the customers were allocated only 200: hardly worth the bother, and almost a waste of time. Those who worked for the company, however, had every reason to smile, for they were entitled to apply for and get up to 5,000 shares. Workers at the other companies received the same preferential treatment.

The Northumbrian shares were priced at 240p, payable in instalments, but water employees were able to invest at a 10 per cent discount. When trading started on the share-markets, the opening price showed a premium of 60p a share. A worker taking his full allocation would have shown a paper profit of about 84p per share.

The water workers – along with other employees of privatized concerns – have also enjoyed other special privileges denied to others, the most significant of which is exemption from the punitive taxation imposed on their counterparts who work for other companies seeking extra capital through rights issues. Although companies offering rights issues normally allocate employees' shares – through the distribution of the so-called pink forms signifying a priority offer – those workers who take advantage of this have to pay tax as PAYE on the premium to the issue price when the share starts trading, as if it was income. Indeed so unfair is this rule that most employees end up having this tax deducted from their wages before they are able to dispose of the shares. The workers of privatized companies face no such intolerable burden.

The 90,000 workers of British Gas were also given generous treatment, which cost the taxpayer a total of £54 million. Each employee was awarded £70 worth of shares, plus a further £2 worth for each year of service. Those able to invest their own money were given two free shares for each one bought, up to a limit of £300 of free shares. Those inclined to dig deeper into their savings could buy up to £2,000 worth at a ten per cent discount. Pensioners were also each given about £75 of free shares. This was in sharp contrast to the parsimony of British Telecom, whose employee shareholders missed out.

In all the major privatizations so far, the majority of employees have taken up their entitlements, though many later sold or reduced their holdings. Foolishly perhaps, most employees sold their holdings on the market, rather than to work colleagues or trade unions, for had they adopted this latter course they could have wielded more influence in their companies. To some extent this happened in the case of British Airways where 5,000 employees gave their union a proxy vote over their shares.

The system used in Britain to enable workers and members of the public to buy shares was not suitable for former command economies like Russia and Eastern Europe, for two reasons. First, the public did not have the cash to buy privatization issues. Second, it proved difficult, sometimes impossible, to put a value on the former state enterprises being sold, especially as a large number of them were technically bankrupt. Many governments overcame the first hurdle by giving their citizens vouchers whose only value was as an instrument to be exchanged for shares. If, in so doing, the citizens found themselves in possession of shares that were worthless, at least they had not lost their own savings.

Sale by mutual consent

Just when the flow of British privatization bargains had dried up another trend emerged. It was called – in another massacre of the English language – demutualization. For year s many of Britain's most established institutions, building societies which competed with each other to occupy prime space in the High Streets, and old established life assurance societies had been operating, literally, for the mutual benefit of their members.

Building societies were created to enable people to buy houses. At its simplest, the concept of the building society movement was that some members lent their savings to the societies at one rate of interest, and those buying borrowed money to purchase their homes at a higher rate. The money accumulated because of the difference between the two rates, both of which moved up and down more or less in line with market forces, went to pay for expenses, or to boost reserves. While the societies noisily defended the level of management costs and the need to establish visibility in the High Street through branch networks, many felt there were inefficiencies in the system. (Actually the relative efficiency of many building societies pointed up the inefficiencies of the High Street trading banks.)

This principle of mutuality also extended to a large number of life assurance companies. Their difference between income and expenditure also went towards building up lavish reserves, generous staff benefits for employees, especially senior management, and bonuses for policyholders possessing 'with-profits' endowment policies. Quite often building societies worked alongside the assurance mutuals, encouraging individuals to purchase homes on an interest-only basis with the capital repaid on the maturity of the endowment policy. This inefficient form of home purchase was for many years encouraged by the government, which made both the interest charges and endowment assurance premiums tax deductible, thus conferring a substantial benefit to the higher-paid at the expense of those who could not afford to buy property.

As successive governments stripped away most of these tax benefits both building societies and life assurance mutuals found they had to compete in the real world, and many of them did so very well. The Conservative government also introduced legislation to encourage competition in the financial sector, and many organizations from both groups felt they would be able to hold their own against public liability companies.

Many, but not all, also felt they would be best able to compete by being on level terms, and becoming a fully listed public liability company with the ability to raise funds on the stock market. One of these came from the East Anglian city of Norwich, where not only is it the biggest source of employment but in 1995 surprised the local community by offering a job to every school leaver in the county of Norfolk with A levels.

For all its humble origins the Norwich Union, at the time of its flotation, was a global business with branches worldwide. Its approach to 'demutualization' was even bolder, because not only did it offer its members, those holding 'with-profits' policies, a free windfall of shares worth between £800 and £4,000, depending on the size of policy, but also raised about £1.8 billion of new money with an additional offer to policyholders. By the time it had joined the Stock Exchange and its shares were trading on June 16 1977, it was one of Britain's top 50 companies, worth around £5.5 billion.

Many of those receiving the windfall shares – for unlike privatization issues they did not have to pay anything for them – sold them shortly after June 16, pocketing the cash in time for the family summer holiday. However those who did not sell received an added bonus: under a government dispensation they were able to transfer the shares into a personal equity plan which guaranteed they would pay no tax either on the capital gain when sold or on any income from dividends.

12 The Takeover Trail

'That's what a dawn raid is – you hit at dawn' –
Robert Holmes à Court.

Hardly a day goes by when the news headlines do not contain a major story about a takeover. Usually it is one large company bidding a billion dollar sum for another. Often the bid is unwelcome: that is, the directors and management of the targeted company would rather be left alone. And what normally happens is that the investment bankers or stockbrokers to the predator company send a pre-printed letter, known as an offer document, to the shareholders of the target company, proposing to purchase their shares for cash or for stock in their own corporation, or a mixture of the two.

This inevitably raises the biggest question that arises with any takeover – value. How do you value a public company? One simple answer is market capitalization: the price of each share on the stock markets on a given day multiplied by the number of shares issued. Then all a bidder has to do is to pitch his offer sufficiently higher than the current price in order to persuade shareholders to give up their long-term prospects with the existing board of directors.

But is the stock market price the right one? The prices of shares are fixed not by any measure of assets or even current profits, but by the market's perception of value based on all the information that might affect a company's future cash flow. All the company's financial statements are digested and assessed against competitive forces by scores of analysts. Their collective wisdom is pitted with the judgement of those who make markets and distilled into a share price. This sounds entirely plausible, but how can you then account for the fact that the world stock market as a whole on 19 October 1987 was worth only four-fifths of what it had been the previous day? Or that on the same day ten years later the

FTSE index was three times higher? Share prices can only really be the best guess at a value. An acquirer is not really buying the buildings, machinery and the workforce – he is getting what he thinks these are capable of producing.

As the Wall Street arbitrageur, Ivan Boesky, later to be gaoled for insider trading, put it in 1985:

> An analyst may fully understand a company he is following, may even be able to forecast its future earnings with unmatched precision. Does that mean he can forecast its future stock price with any precision at all? Of course not. Price-earnings multiples averaged as high as 25 or so in the heyday of stock trading in the 1960s. In the mid-seventies these multiples had fallen to 6 and 7. Any stock market price is buffeted by sweeping market forces that are virtually impossible to predict with any reliability. These forces are often important: the growth rate of the economy, the course of interest rates, the international value of the dollar, the inflation rate, an overseas war, a presidential election. They also can be distressingly unimportant: this week's change in money supply, the Federal Reserve Board's sale of securities, its reversal of that sale the next day.

Nevertheless many large and significant public corporations have changed hands on the simple basis of share values. The predators have got what they wanted. The shareholders, presumably, were satisfied because they were able to take a profit and re-invest their money in other investments. But the companies and their staffs that found themselves with new owners were not necessarily better companies for the transformation. In some cases new blood made them more efficient, and more effective use was made of their assets. 'Making assets sweat' is one of the main justifications for takeovers. In many others the acquired company, its costs swollen by the expense of its own acquisition, has fallen apart.

I doubt whether there is any better example of this than what happened to Australia's three main television networks in the late eighties. The Nine Network was controlled by Kerry Packer, a single-minded entrepreneur with a reputation for seeking value in his investments and businesses. Run by a New Zealander, Sam Chisholm, later to become managing director of British Sky Broadcasting, it topped viewer ratings year after year. The Seven Network was owned by leading newspaper interests, including the Fairfax dynasty, proprietors of the influential *Sydney Morning Herald* and the *Melbourne Age*. And Network Ten was owned by Rupert Murdoch's family company.

Just before the Great Crash of 1987, Packer sold his network to the ambitious Alan Bond for $1.1 billion – a figure which represented a premium on its market worth, and was much more than its true value. Another eager entrepreneur with Hollywood ambitions, former financial journalist Christopher Skase, paid $780m – well over the odds – for Seven. And, as Australian law prohibits foreign interests controlling the electronic media, Murdoch was forced to sell Network Ten when he took American citizenship. He did so, at a handsome price, to some would-be media moguls who thought commercial television was, as Lord Thomson of Fleet had once put it, 'a licence to print money'.

All three newcomers crashed, their networks flattened not so much by an advertising recession as by the crippling interest rate burden of acquisition. In 1990 Packer bought back his Nine Network for one half of what he had been paid for it. The other two networks went into receivership, and for years were run by banks and firms of accountants. In each case the aspirants had made miscalculations about their future cash flows.

Not all of those carrying out takeovers continue to run the businesses they have bought. In many cases they sell the assets for cash. Asset-stripping became fashionable in the eighties and is a popular occupation of those who believe that the stock markets often underestimate the true value of companies, and they put their beliefs to the test by acquiring businesses and then breaking them up. This has frequently happened in the past when a company has a number of assets in its books – particularly real estate – which have not been written up with inflation. By disposing of the property, or by coming to a lease-back arrangement with a finance company, an asset-stripper can acquire huge sums of cash. By the 1990s the activities of two generations of asset-strippers had sharpened up directors to the risk, though there is still a hard core of professionals on every continent who make money by spotting companies that are under-valued.

Despite the asset strippers and the ordinary everyday risks in mergers, such evidence as there is shows that takeovers often succeed in their objective of achieving real growth for the acquiring company. A study published by McKinsey, the management consultancy, found that even cross-border acquisitions had achieved a high rate of success compared with other forms of corporate expansion.

McKinsey reviewed the overseas acquisition programmes of the top 50 companies in Europe, Japan and the United States – and found that 57 per cent were judged a success. However almost all the success stories related to a company merging with another in the same business. Most of those involving moving into non-core businesses failed.

Takeover Rules

In each country there are rules that govern takeovers. In some cases these rules are enshrined in legislation, in others they form part of a code, written or unwritten. In Britain the rules do not have statutory backing and have been rewritten several times since they first appeared as the City Takeover Code in March 1968. Their observation is supervised by the City Takeover Panel, a group of twelve City elders whose modest secretariat is based on the twentieth floor of the Stock Exchange building. There is a director-general, two deputies, a secretary, and a few other executives. The permanent staff provide interpretations of the Code, but contested rulings and disciplinary cases are considered by the Panel itself, with the right of appeal to the Appeals Committee, which sits under the chairmanship of a retired Lord of Appeal. The Panel operates under the watchful eye of the Bank of England; it is usual for the majority of its staff to be on secondment from the Bank, providing a constant flow of fresh ideas.

The most important rule is that you may bid for up to 29.9 per cent of a company's shares before launching a full bid, but after that you must make a full offer for all the remaining shares, at the highest price you have paid for the purchases so far. This is to prevent a predator buying a company on the cheap, especially where there is a wide spread of share ownership.

Another fundamental principle is that shareholders must be treated evenly. 'All shareholders of the same class of an offeree company must be treated similarly.' Another rule provides that before an offer is announced, no one privy to the preliminary takeover or merger discussions is allowed to deal in the shares of either the bidding or target company. Once an offer is announced, the share transactions in all the companies involved must be reported by all parties to the City Takeover Panel, the Stock Exchange, and the press. Companies defending a bid must not do anything without shareholder approval 'which could effectively result in any bona fide offer being frustrated, or in the shareholders of the offeree company being denied an opportunity to decide on its merits'.

The City Takeover Panel's executive staff are available throughout a takeover to advise whether the rules are in danger of being broken, as all bids for public companies, listed or unlisted, are strictly monitored. The staff work closely with the surveillance unit at the Stock Exchange to investigate dealings in advance of publication of bid proposals, the aim being to establish whether there has been any breach of the rules governing secrecy and abuse of privileged information.

If there appears to have been a breach of the code, the Panel staff invite the chairman of the company involved, or other individuals, to appear before the Panel. He or she is informed by letter of the nature of the alleged breach, and of the matters which the director-general will present to the hearing. These hearings are informal, there are no rules of evidence, and, although notes are taken, no permanent records are kept. The principal against whom the complaint has been made is expected to appear in person, although he may bring his lawyer with him. At the hearing he is expected to set out his reply, normally based on a document which should already have been produced in reply to the director-general's letter. If the Panel finds there has been a breach, the offender may be reprimanded there and then, or may be subjected to public censure with a press release distributed to the media, setting out the Panel's conclusions and its reasons for them. In a bad case, where the Panel feels that the offender should no longer be able to use the Stock Exchange temporarily or permanently, the case may be referred to a professional association, the Stock Exchange, the Department of Trade and Industry, or the City Fraud Squad.

The Panel is considered to be a legal entity, and the Court of Appeal has ruled that its decisions may, if need be, be reviewed by the Courts.

Making an Acquisition

Before considering how a takeover works, it is perhaps worth analysing some of the many and varied reasons for making an acquisition. The most obvious is that it is often much easier and cheaper than starting a new business, except in the case of a product or service that is exclusive enough to depend for its success on the professional drive and energy of the entrepreneur and his team. If you have a product that will put your rivals out of business, you will usually be best served by building up the business yourself.

But if you wish to expand a business, a takeover is a useful route. Apart from anything else, it often enables you to use other people's money to achieve your ambition. A takeover can be a way of swallowing up the competition, and thereby increasing profit margins.

This was the case with many of the large takeovers in the early part of this century, when the first wave of mergers took place. Many of these were designed to set up large monopolies that could raise prices in basic industries such as steel, power and transport. Some of them were brought about by the legendary New York financier, J. Pierpont Morgan. His biggest deal, in 1901, brought together 11 companies that accounted for half of America's steel industry to form US Steel.

These days there are regulations to prevent monopolies through merger. In the United States there are strong anti-trust laws, and the European Commission is also vigilant against the development of new monopolies. New European rules effective September 1990 gave the Brussels-based Commission control over not just the major mergers and acquisitions, but also over small purchases made by mega companies. Mergers are subjected to Commission scrutiny where the combined worldwide turnover of the undertakings involved is more than 5 billion ECU, and where the Community-wide turnover of at least two of the undertakings is above 250 million ECU. Additionally Britain has a Monopolies and Mergers Commission.

In many cases, a takeover may appear to be the only way to fulfil ambitions of growth. Sometimes a takeover may be the result of egomania on the part of the chairman or controlling shareholder; there is never a shortage of new owners for Britain's national newspapers, for instance, or for prestigious department stores, and breweries also seem popular. Sometimes the thrust of a takeover effort is to achieve a lifetime ambition, such as the fruitless attempt by Lord Forte and his son Rocco to gain control of the Savoy Hotel in London.

Whatever the reason, there are usually only two forms of takeover: those that are uncontested, and those that involve a fight. But it is never as simple as that. There have been many occasions when a board of directors has decided to open merger discussions with a potential target rather than to proceed by stealth, only to find that the opposition is so great that all they have achieved is to give the other side advance warning to prepare for an assault. And there have been occasions when a contested battle has been so fierce and the cost of the operation so high that it might have been better to attempt to achieve the same result through negotiation.

Some takeovers are solicited. Many a company, for lack of progress or good management, feels that it would be better served if it were to be incorporated in a better run, and perhaps larger, business. I was once a non-executive director of a small public company in the retail motor trade. It had garages as far-flung as South Wales, Southampton, Birmingham and Lincolnshire, with different franchises in each. In one period of three months the Thatcher government lifted interest rates three percentage points, thereby forcing the sale of used cars in stock at giveaway prices; an oil company decided not to renew the lease on the premises with the best showroom because they wanted a larger forecourt for petrol sales; and a strike at Vauxhall Motors dried up the supply of new cars for valuable orders at the main dealership. The directors, rightly I believe, sought to merge our company with a larger group better able to sit out what was to become a four-year crisis for the motor trade, and entered into discussions with a number of potential buyers. At one stage we were close to a deal. But then our shares slipped in the market; our creditors, seeing our market capitalization falling and rightly assuming that interest bills were rising, pressed harder, and the banks called in the receivers. The irony is that had it been a private company, without a listing, the company could well have weathered the storm, for the shareholders would have been obliged to stick with it through the bad times. Directors, of course, were not allowed to sell out, nor could they tell those friends who had supported the company, because that would have been classed as insider trading, punishable by heavy fines or imprisonment. So those that had risked their savings lost their investment. It seemed rough justice at the time, but does illustrate an important point made earlier: the shareholders in a public company are much better protected than those in a private one.

There may also be hidden hazards in a solicited takeover. Take the case of Sinclair Research, a company built up by a technological wizard, Sir Clive Sinclair, credited with building the world's smallest portable television set, and the designer of an all-British range of microcomputers. Sinclair's drive and technological brilliance were not matched, however, by management skills, and many of his investments, such as his battery-operated vehicle, were less than successful.

In 1983, four years after it was founded, Sinclair Research had a market capitalization of £136m. In 1983 and 1984 the company was turning in profits of about £14m, and in 1985, although market conditions turned down due to a slump in the personal computer market, it was still looking to a useful profit. But in May of that year, serious cash flow problems became evident as stocks of £35m of unsold goods built up, with suppliers demanding payment of their bills. For a while the main creditors, Thorn EMI and Timex of Dundee, agreed to hold off, and Sinclair's bankers, Barclays and Citicorp, increased the company's borrowing facilities. But, almost inevitably, the crunch came, and Sinclair turned to the bear-like clutches of Robert Maxwell, publisher of Mirror Group Newspapers, who, for reasons which have never been made very clear, made a £12m rescue bid for Sinclair Research.

Two months later, on 9 August 1985, it was all off. Maxwell announced that he was pulling out, saying the deal 'just did not gel', though he had no doubt that Sinclair computers were a 'fine product appreciated by millions'. Sir Clive Sinclair put a brave face on it, smiled wanly, and went off to see his creditors. It is a salutary lesson for those who see a takeover as salvation: you have to be sure you are really wanted, or that your saviour is really genuine.

With any takeover there are two stages: the preliminaries, which may take weeks and even months, and the active stage, when the bid is made and the offer digested and voted upon by the shareholders. Very few takeovers are the result of a whim, but are usually considered only after painstaking research, involving the company's solicitors, accountants and merchant banks, or other financial advisers.

Takeover specialists are at a premium in the City, and are paid enormous salaries. A senior director in the corporate finance department of one of the better known British merchant banks may expect to earn about £350,000 a year in salary and bonuses, while a junior director, who could be in his late twenties or early thirties, might receive £100,000 upwards. American companies pay more, but offer marginally less job security. For this, the specialists advise those either making or subject to a takeover on strategy and tactics, capital-raising where necessary, and public relations, often calling in outside specialists to assist. When the pressure is on, most advisers would expect to work 14 hours a day, as well as attending meetings at weekends. If their homes are outside central London, they would be lucky to see their families except at the weekend, and would almost certainly have to have a flat close to the City. One merchant bank maintains an apartment for its directors above an expensive West End restaurant. However, if you are seen dining with a new client, word soon gets out. Takeover advisers have to work under conditions of great secrecy, for an essential part of the takeover game is to anticipate your opponent's next move, and to outwit him.

However, for the merchant bank that can grab the lion's share of the business, the rewards are great, with takeovers and operations in the European markets earning the greatest portion of its income.

Growth Through Acquisition

In planning a takeover, it is essential to work out a strategy before going public. This usually means weeks closeted with financial advisers, and is a time when security is all-important. A stray document left in a photocopying machine, a loose word dropped to a friend in a bar, or even a minor indiscretion at lunch can lead to a leak. One paragraph in a newspaper can be enough to set the takeover target's shares racing ahead on the Stock Exchange, which could rule out a bid, or alert rivals to the possibility.

Furthermore, takeover strategy these days is not confined merely to obtaining enough shares in the targeted concern. In almost every situation, politics and public relations come to the fore.

The predator in a takeover enjoys one major advantage: it can always count on the full support of its management team, which usually has much to gain from taking charge of a larger organization. By contrast the management of a target company often finds itself in a difficult, even ambivalent, position; its loyalties are to its present board of directors, but its future, as likely as not, will lie elsewhere. It also has the burden of dealing with a worried staff, not to mention suppliers, distributors, and others with whom the company has close connections. And it has to continue to run the business. It used to be the case that shareholders tended to stand by a business that has done well by them, unless those making the bid make an irrefutable case. But, in 1996, when Rocco Forte tried to persuade shareholders to stick with him, they rejected his pleas and fell for the Irish charm of Gerry Robinson and his Granada group.

It is also true that the best defence against a takeover is to act before a bid, rather than afterwards – in other words, take action which will deter a predator from striking, such as selling off subsidiaries which do not fit the core of the business, or explain the company's strategy to analysts in such a way that the share price rises to reflect an accurate, rather than an undervalued, view of its stock. Once a bid is made, it is hard to do this, because any disposals or other capital restructuring have to be approved by shareholders.

When it is clear that a takeover bid is going to fail, what

does the bidder do? There are occasions when a predator can come badly unstuck. Almost certainly he will have built up a parcel of shares in the company in which he is interested, although his bid will be conditional on sufficient acceptances to give him control. No one is expected to make an unconditional bid, but, once the fever is over, it can be difficult to recover the price paid for a block of shares on a rising market, and the bidder may be forced to take a loss. In such cases it is normal to arrange a placement through his brokers, in much the same way as when raising capital for his own concern. It is not unusual for the shares to be picked up by forces sympathetic to the company that has successfully defended itself against takeover, for the last thing directors want is an unstable market, especially if some of the allegations made in the heat of the moment seem likely to have stuck in the minds of the market.

A more interesting development occurs when an unsuccessful bidder actually walks away from the event with a large profit – not uncommon. Sometimes this can be achieved through barefaced cheek, especially if the subject of a bid has a group of directors and a large shareholder determined to hold on to their property at all costs.

This is what happened as a result of a visit on 20 November 1979 by the publisher Rupert Murdoch to his father's old office at the *Herald and Weekly Times* newspaper group in Melbourne, Australia, where he cheerfully greeted Sir Keith Macpherson, the chairman and chief executive, with the glad tidings that his News Group was about to present the Stock Exchange with the terms of a $A126m bid for just over half of the company. Since the offer valued *Herald and Weekly Times*, the country's largest newspaper group, at $A100m more than News Group, Macpherson suggested that the whole idea was ridiculous.

Perhaps it was; one newspaper later suggested it was like a snake trying to swallow a sheep, and similar metaphors were used when five years later, the entrepreneur, Robert Holmes à Court, made an unsuccessful bid for Australia's largest company, BHP, and was described, colourfully, as 'trying to rape an elephant'. Murdoch, however, knew what he was up to. He wanted the *Herald and Weekly Times* desperately – ever since his father, whose genius had built up the paper, had died, he had set his sights on it – but he suspected that he would not get it, even though News Group offered $4 a share, a premium of $1.26 on the market price.

His suspicions were correct. His bid caused panic at the headquarters of another newspaper group 400 miles away in Sydney. John Fairfax Ltd, a conservative family concern, had a minority stake in *Herald and Weekly Times*, and its newspapers were bitter rivals of Murdoch's. Apart from the extra power Murdoch would gain if he controlled HWT, he would become a partner of Fairfax in two other major enterprises, Australian Newsprint Mills, the country's only newsprint manufacturer, and Australian Associated Press, the national news agency, both controlled jointly by Fairfax and HWT. Fairfax instructed its brokers to buy all the HWT shares it could muster to thwart Murdoch, and the price rose quickly to well above the $4 that Murdoch had offered. Within two days Fairfax had laid out over $A50m and had acquired 15 per cent of HWT. The shares stood at $5.52. Murdoch knew that he was beaten, but he saw a lucrative way out. Instead of conceding defeat, he instructed his brokers, J. B. Were and Co., to continue buying shares but on a much more limited scale. At the same time he commissioned another broker, May and Mellor, to unload the 3,500,000 shares he had already purchased. The Fairfax people, convinced that Murdoch was still a buyer, snapped up the lot, paying top prices, only to face the humiliation of hearing that they had been outwitted and that Murdoch had quit, using one of his own newspapers to condemn the Fairfax 'rescue' of HWT as 'two incompetent managements throwing themselves into each other's arms at the expense of their shareholders'. Maybe, but the real point was that Fairfax was determined to stop Murdoch at any price, and paid dearly for it – for when the shares settled back down at a lower price, it had lost over $20m, plus the interest on the $50m laid out to acquire the stock.

Ironically several years later Murdoch got his prize, as a result of some spectacular blunders by Warwick Fairfax, a junior member of the Fairfax family, whose dealings in the junk bond market lost him the empire his grandfather had built. Junk bonds are discussed on page 144.

The trick is that your opponent has to hate the idea of

losing his beloved company so much that he will pay almost anything to keep it. It is not a ploy that is encouraged by some of the more conservative bodies in the City of London, but it is fair game, and the best defence, if you are sure that the predator does not have the nerve or the money to go ahead with a bid, is to call his bluff, let him face the test of the market, and then take large advertisements in the financial press to deliver a wounding riposte.

In most contested takeovers the issue of who wins is decided by institutional investors, as the major shareholders. In Britain they are not quite as fickle as in the United States, on which more later, but increasingly the institutions are under pressure to perform. Stanley Kalms, whose Dixons electronics group won control of the electrical goods retailer Currys in 1984, accurately reflected the current attitude: 'Companies can only expect loyalty when their shares are performing well, and the market has confidence in the management.'

The New Takeover Game

'Speculators may do no harm as bubbles on a steady stream of enterprise. But the position is serious when enterprise becomes the bubble on a whirlpool of speculation. When the capital development of a country becomes a by-product of the activities of a casino, the job is likely to be ill done,' wrote John Maynard Keynes in 1936. 'What kind of society isn't structured on greed? The problem of social organization is how to set up an arrangement under which greed will do the least harm,' said Milton Friedman, in 1973.

Those who promote takeovers – or believe that there should be no restriction other than a prohibition on monopoly – argue their case by saying that shareholders benefit by the maximization of share values. They also suggest that business is made more efficient, and necessary rationalization brought about, because large and indolent managements are forced to promote change, in order to survive. Be that as it may, the real reason for the frenzy of takeover activity in Britain and elsewhere is the desire of large numbers of corporate raiders to get rich.

As is usually the case, the Americans are well ahead when

it comes to exploiting the possibilities available to the corporate raider. Indeed, so sophisticated have US financial markets become that individuals are able to use an array of new financial instruments to play the same old games. One game, popular in the mid-nineties, was called appropriately 'Copycat', involves studying the moves of renowned old style raiders like T. Boone Pickens, and emulating them. You will be 24 hours behind, of course, but those who have followed this course in a bull market have seldom fared badly. Nor is there any need to use much of your own money; you can buy stock options for a fraction of the real cost, exercise the option when the price rises, and then sell out for a large capital gain.

It sounds like, and is, the stuff on which the 1929 Wall Street crash was founded, but now there are record numbers of people playing the share markets, and using sophisticated methods to do so. Scores of computer programs became available for individuals to analyse their portfolio performances, and to carry out 'what if?' analyses. Some programs are highly advanced, and can detect prices of related stocks that get out of step with each other. Armed with his personal computer and a copy of the *Financial Times*, the personal investor found he was almost as well informed as many professional investment advisers. There was no need to accept the low returns offered by his neighbourhood bank, or savings institution. Why should he not get the kind of interest, or strike the kind of deals, organized by the big boys? He wanted to climb on to the gravy train.

In 1980 only 49 million shares changed hands daily on the New York Stock Exchange. By 1991 this had more than tripled to 156 million shares. In this period prices rose sharply. Two-thirds of the rise is credited by analysts as being due to a feverish increase in takeover activity.

Much of this American activity was fuelled by borrowed money, in which the leveraged takeover has been a favourite technique. A corporate raider would take a modest position in a large company, wait a short while, and then offer to buy the entire stock by making a takeover bid. Where would the corporate raider's small company raise these billions of dollars from, you may well ask. Simple. He would approach a broker specializing in the art of raising junk bonds for worthwhile causes.

Where There's Junk There's Money

The man in the street might suppose that those proposing to take over a company have the wherewithal to do so. After all takeover merchants have always been painted as piranhas swallowing the small fry. This is not necessarily the case.

In the late 1980s many takeovers were achieved with borrowed money, and in some instances this money was borrowed, indirectly, from the company that the predator was targeting.

Let me explain. Company X wishes to buy company Y, but has insufficient spare cash on its balance sheet to do so. Nor does it have enough security to offer its bankers, and it does not believe it can raise cash from its shareholders in a rights issue.

So instead it issues junk bonds, which are no different from any other interest-bearing security except that they carry a substantially higher than average interest rate. These bonds raise the capital required to finance a bid, and are normally secured against the shares of the company targeted. An investor in a junk bond normally does so on the basis that his money is only committed if the takeover bid succeeds. If it is successful the corporate raider issuing the bond can afford to pay the higher interest rates because he will have the assets of the newly-acquired company at his disposal. In other words the strength of the victim company's balance sheet is its own downfall. If the corporate raider fails and is unable to get enough shares in his target, it is a fair bet they will have risen in the market, and he will have made a sizeable capital gain.

The use of junk bonds was championed most heavily in the 1980s by the Wall Street broking firm Drexel Burnham Lambert, where its greatest advocate was Michael Milken. By 1985 $27 billion worth of junk bonds had been issued, most of them through Drexels. In 1970 there had been only $7 billion worth of high-yield bonds outstanding, and most of that was for quality offerings. By 1989, at the peak of the junk bond craze, the amount of junk that had been unloaded was $201 billion.

Many people imagine that the holders of junk were avaricious investors, dissatisfied with the more prosaic returns available on ordinary investments. They were not. At the beginning of 1989, 30 per cent of junk bonds outstanding in the United States were held by insurance companies, 30 per cent by mutual funds, and 15 per cent by pension funds. Many of them lost their money as the companies in which the junk was secured turned down. Drexels went bankrupt, and Michael Milken went to gaol. Junk bonds went out of fashion.

Poison Pills

There were other forces at work in the leveraged takeover game which have caused grave disquiet, particularly for those who subscribe to the old-fashioned view that since a public company is owned by its shareholders it is reasonable to assume that their interests take precedence. The truth, of course, is a little different.

One of the victims in a court battle which was to become known as the 'poison pills' case was Lord Hanson. In its hey-day more than half of Hanson Trust's income came from businesses in the United States. In August 1985, Hanson identified a major American company as a suitable case for takeover. The SCM Corporation was a solid if dreary con-glomerate which manufactured outmoded typewriters, processed food, pigments and an assortment of other products. On 21 August, Hanson Trust offered $60 a share cash for SCM Corporation, valuing the company at $755m, well below its market capitalization. Robert Morton, an analyst with brokers de Zoete and Bevan, told me at the time that this was 'in the mould of Hanson acquisitions: SCM is exactly the kind of company he goes for, a company which has already undergone a great deal of rationalization and sorting out, which perhaps has not been fully realized by the shareholders.'

The SCM management was horrified. Here was this lord from England buying their company at rock-bottom value. By all the precedents, it was clear that, before they knew where they were, they would be looking for new jobs. Fortunately for them the board saw matters the same way, rejected the Hanson bid, and refused even to talk to Hanson's US chief Sir Gordon White, despite several invitations to do so. It hastily called in its financial advisers, the New York firm of Goldman Sachs.

Curiously, however, it was not Goldman Sachs that came to the rescue of SCM's beleaguered management, but Wall Street's largest broking house, the New York financial conglomerate Merrill Lynch. Merrill Lynch's capital markets division, headed by a young go-getter, Ken Miller, was hungry for new business, and skilful in organizing what has become known as leveraged management buyouts. Within a few days, Miller and his team had come up with a means whereby, at the stroke of a pen, Hanson could be thwarted, the SCM management could save their jobs, and Merrill Lynch would receive a large fee.

So it was that on 30 August, only nine days after Hanson's bid, a new company was announced – legally a partnership between the SCM Corporation's management and Merrill Lynch, but funded by the Prudential Assurance Company of America. It offered $70 a share – $10 more than Hanson – for 85 per cent of the SCM shares, and promised to buy the rest out of SCM profits at some future date, through the issue of junk bonds, which, it was hoped, would trade at about $70. A confidential Merrill Lynch paper described the deal as representing 'one of the most asset-rich LBO opportunities we have ever encountered'.

The wily Merrill Lynch team hoped that Lord Hanson would withdraw, but they took sensible steps to protect themselves, and their fees, if he did not. If Miller pulled this one off it would be the first time that a leveraged management buyout had been successful against a tender offer for cash. But there was a risk, so a clause was written into the contract providing for a $9m fee should the bid be topped and the arrangement terminated, in addition to the basic fee of £1.5m for fixing the deal in the first place.

Lord Hanson proved their fears justified. On 3 September, Hanson Trust increased its offer to $72 a share. Unlike the first offer, which valued SCM at a bargain basement price, this was a much more attractive offer for shareholders. For a start it was all in cash, with no waiting around for junk bonds and future profits which might or might not appear. For the SCM management, however, it presented the same problem, the prospect of losses, made even more certain as a result of their tactics in signing up with Merrill Lynch, and handing over $9m. of the company's money in fees. Sir Gordon White did, however, hold out an olive branch. On 10 September, after several failed attempts by telephone to contact SCM's chairman or board, he sent them one further invitation: 'We believe it is in our mutual interests, including those of your stockholders, management and employees, that we should meet promptly.'

There was no reply, for, behind the scenes, Miller and his team had again been hard at work, advancing another, much more ruthless, way of frustrating Hanson's ambitions. Meanwhile the $9m fee had already been placed in escrow. The new plan was to strip out of SCM Corporation its two most potentially profitable businesses, in the belief that the Englishman would either lose interest or be left with a crippled business.

This tactic has become known as the use of the 'poisoned pill', although a more appropriate metaphor might be that of a scorched earth policy. In this instance, the SCM management and Merrill Lynch increased their leveraged buyout offer to $74 a share, but subjected it to a new condition: if Hanson or another party got more than a third of SCM shares, Merrill would have the right to purchase the two most thriving parts of the SCM Corporation – the pigments and processed food businesses – at knockdown prices. The business would then be run by the same SCM management. These two businesses were to become known as the 'crown jewels', for Merrill Lynch obtained the options for a total of $430m against the SCM board's own valuation of $400m for the pigments business and $90m for the foods division. For organizing this neat new arrangement, Merrill Lynch took a retention fee of $6m, investment banking fees of $8m., and dealer-manager fees of $2.75m, in addition, of course, to the $11.5m already paid.

The next morning Hanson Trust withdrew its $72 a share offer, and spent $200m buying SCM shares on the New York market; within a few hours it had acquired 25 per cent of the company. But on 16 September Merrill Lynch acted again. With the Manufacturers Hanover Bank working as agent, it put the shares of the crown jewel subsidiaries in escrow, and apparently beyond Hanson's reach. At this point the lawyers took over, with the action moving to the New York District Court in Lower Manhattan. In the end Hanson Trust lost the case, but the verdict was reversed in the subsequent appeal.

Discussion in the United States has ranged over whether the law courts are really the place to decide such matters, as well as whether the frenzy of takeover activity wastes scarce investment capital, inhibits innovation, and forces managers to sacrifice long-term goals to the next quarterly profits sheet. Kathryn Rudie Harrigan, Professor of Strategic Management at the Columbia University Business School, talked to me about the increasingly common tendency for stock market takeovers to be decided in courts of law:

> It is just one more in a string of devices that managers and their investments bankers have come up with to avoid being taken over when they do not want to be.

Is this new trend likely to be damaging to shareholders? Professor Harrigan thinks perhaps not, in that values are often forced up by what is essentially a game:

> It is a game, and it is a game that is played with great ritual, and is being played in many, many companies these days. It is often cheaper to acquire something than it is to build it from the ground up.

But she does believe that business will suffer in the end.

> I think it is damaging to the long-term health of the business, because when you are so busy satisfying these short-term requests of the financial community, who are looking for instant gratification from their investment, you often cripple the long-term ability of the company to be able to reposition itself to remain competitive in a changing environment.

Professor Harrigan also believes that the concepts of poison pills and crown jewels could be exported to Britain:

> The two capital markets are becoming very similar in the way that people operate within them, and the kinds of expectations they have of the companies whose equities they hold. And more and more of the equities are held by institutional investors, who

have this kind of short-term expectation, and they want to see this quick pay-off on their investment. I think the kind of behaviour we see here, with these leveraged buyouts, will undoubtedly be appearing also in your stock markets.

'Abuses by some banks and financiers are feeding a take-over frenzy that strikes at the economic well-being of this country,' one potential victim of a leveraged takeover wrote to Paul Volcker, then the chairman of the Federal Reserve. 'They are engaging in stock and bond and credit schemes reminiscent of those of the 1920s – but on a multi-billion dollar scale.' By extending the 50 per cent rule to shell companies, Volcker did not rule out using such tactics. He just made them less attractive – 50 per cent less attractive, in fact. For those that have the stamina to engage in it, it is still potentially a high risk strategy, so long as you can stay ahead of the game.

13 Fast Money

Within microseconds of the price of a major company changing on any of the major markets, investors anywhere in the wired-up world will hear of it. Financial news travels faster than anything else.

For the full-time dealer in a broking firm or institution there are on-line services which provide prices in real-time. These, of course, are expensive, but for market-makers competing with each other they are an essential tool of the trade. The professional investor normally makes do with less expensive electronic services, which none the less provide essential figures and information within five minutes of their release. Dow Jones, founded by Charles Dow, a self-effacing reporter on Wall Street who became the first editor of the *Wall Street Journal*, is one of the world's leading information providers, rivalled by Reuters, the British news agency started in 1851 by Paul Julius Reuter using a flock of carrier pigeons. A more recent and significant player is Bloomberg, founded by Michael Bloomberg.

The basic Reuter source contains about 2,500 pages of information, which are regularly updated by some 400 contributors. Instruments covered include straight and convertible bonds, stock market indices, government and domestic bonds, warrants, swaps, euronotes and commercial paper. Reuter also maintains an accessible database, which covers almost 5,000 eurobond issues, in all major currencies.

Another service, Reuter 3000, provides a complete and continuous overview of market movements and relevant factors affecting currency futures and options, interest rate instruments and stock index futures and options. A real-time quotes service covers equities, options and futures fed from stock exchanges around the world.

Some of the Reuter news services have become interactive

– all or some of those who subscribe may use the terminals that are provided to trade on the information made available. Reuter currency services, for instance, link via satellite and high-speed cable foreign exchange dealers in more than 110 countries – and have become the world's de facto foreign exchange market. Money dealers may access real-time information on currency and deposit rates, employ a range of graphs and other analytical aids to help their decision-making, and then use the Reuter network to complete their transactions with counterparties. Regardless of location, a dealer can contact any other in the world in no more than four seconds. The average connection time is two to three seconds. To contact a counterparty in Tokyo, a dealer in London or New York simply presses a four-letter code, or a single-key macro code stored in an address abbreviation facility. This facility also stores frequently used phrases or sentences, and can instruct the system to find the first free counterparty on a list and send a prepared message. An automatic print-out records details of every transaction for both dealing parties. The network is secure and private.

Roughly a third of the world's foreign exchange is done through Reuter dealing screens, and another third is transacted by telephone after consulting a Reuter monitor. Clients, who include most of the world's banks, pay a rent for the screen and a fee.

Reuters continues to develop a number of other interactive services to meet the needs of international capital markets, and constitutes a major challenge to stock markets that do not move swiftly to offer electronic on-screen dealing. Already its wholly-owned Instinet trading service in the United States is used by professional investors to trade 8,000 American equities. Instinet is legitimized because its subsidiaries hold membership of seven major United States securities exchanges, as well as the International Stock Exchange in London. The network has more than 750 terminals connected, and in 1977 transacted 1.44 billion shares, with each transaction executed in seconds. Most of these services are of interest or use only to the major professional investor or institution.

Reuter is moving fast to take advantage of new technology. In 1992 it bought the television news company,

Visnews, renaming it Reuters Television, and buying for it a significant stake in Independent Television News, which supplies news programmes to Britain's three commercial channels. It includes video clips in its main news services, and positions miniature cameras above the computer terminals used by specialist correspondents and leading market analysts so that it can include commentaries by them on major news developments.

Then there are a host of telephone services. These range from the relatively unsophisticated, which enable you to make a phone call and hear a recording of the latest major share prices, to several well-developed schemes where once you are connected to the database, you key in a code from your telephone handset and hear the latest price of the share or unit trust identified by the code. Subscribers are given a free directory listing the codes.

Competitors to Reuter include Telekurs, a Swiss-based news service, owned by the banks, with terminals that are very user friendly, and Bloomberg News Service, started in the United States with a strong focus on integrating financial information across all forms of media – the printed word, electronic publishing, and broadcasting. Bloomberg is aggressive and entrepreneurial in the market-place, and in the United States is the market leader. In the next few years it is likely to provide a fierce challenge to the older-established financial services in other countries.

Television has also become a significant source of information on financial and business news, particularly in the United States, where there is a full-time financial network, CNBC, owned by General Electric. From modest headquarters on two floors of an office block in New Jersey, it broadcasts over American cable networks to over 40 million television sets. During stock market trading hours, it positions a camera permanently on the ticker of the New York Stock Exchange, so investors at home or in their offices can get the latest pricing information in real-time. Throughout the business day it runs a programme sequence called *Money Wheel*, where breaking stories are discussed and analysed by experts and, in some cases, the principals. Out of market hours it maintains a series of other financial and business programmes, some concerned with personal investment, some with management and some with boardroom styles and practices. CNBC launched a European network in 1996, and covers all the markets thoroughly. Competing with CNBC is Ted Turner's Cable News Network (CNN) which, although a general news channel, devotes a substantial proportion of its programming to business, and has brief hourly market updates. In 1996 it launched CNNFN (CNN Financial News) in direct competition with CNBC.

Europe's traditional broadcasters have been slower to develop financial programming, and much of it is not very good. Channel Four, the network set up to cater for minority interests, abandoned its *Business Daily* programme in 1992 even though it drew good audiences . Following the new franchise round, the ITV companies dropped *The City Programme*, which Thames had successfully launched several years earlier. The BBC has *Business Breakfast* early each weekday morning, but the emphasis tends to be on stories about industry and the economy, rather than on the markets. BBC Radio pays some attention to the markets in its late-night Radio 5 programme, *Financial World Tonight*.

Taking the media as a whole, there has been an explosive growth in the financial information industry, which has increased the pool of knowledge about the financial markets and the companies traded there to the point where it is now well beyond the capability of one person to digest it all. Gone are the days when a stockbroker would sit in his first-class rail carriage from Sevenoaks to Charing Cross and comb through the pages of the *Financial Times*, working out his share tip of the day. Once at the office, he would telephone his friends and relations, and they would all be on to a good thing. A former City Editor of the *Daily Express* once told me that he had bought a house in the stockbroker belt and always travelled in a first-class compartment so as to be able to pick up juicy tips from those who were habitually on the same train. The journey home would usually be spent in the buffet-car where, over a beer or two or three, the successes of the day and the tips for tomorrow would be discussed.

In the late 1950s, the City Editor was a man of great authority, with an arrogance that could come only from having a considerable following of small investors. I remember Patrick Sergeant of the *Daily Mail* informing readers, just before leaving for his annual holiday one August, that they should not buy or sell any shares until after he got back. Patrick was not amused when he returned to find an anonymous telegram saying: 'Now that you are back, can we buy? – signed Pru and Pearl.'

City Editors also conducted their business with a certain panache. They would arrive in the office after a long lunch, smelling of port and accompanied by a cloud of cigar smoke. Even today, several Fleet Street City Editors are provided with dining rooms, at which they entertain City bankers and brokers and government economic ministers. One or two others have a regular table provided for them at the Savoy Grill.

But nowadays most broadsheet newspapers have an army of financial journalists reporting on the markets.

Then there are specialist publications, which include the *Financial Times, Wall Street Journal, The Economist, Investors Chronicle,* and *Financial Adviser.*

In the printed word the *Financial Times* is the best guide for the share investor in Europe, while the *Wall Street Journal* leads in the United States. Those serious about the markets should take both, or read them on the Internet, where FT.com is one of the leading sites, and is a highly efficient way of keeping up with all the major stories at no cost.

But if the press has made great strides in the last decade in the spread and depth of its financial coverage, it is no longer the only, or even the major, source of information. The real explosive growth in the financial information industry has come from stockbrokers themselves, with almost all the major broking houses running their own publishing operations. These brokers pride themselves on being able to get their publication out fast. On Budget day, for instance, some broking firms, as well as a few firms of accountants, will have their analysis of the Chancellor's measures in the hands of important clients long before the newspapers arrive.

Brokers' publications fall into two categories. There are regular weeklies or monthlies which contain a detailed review of the major economies and their financial markets, and offer a number of recommendations. Their forecasts have a high reputation for accuracy, usually better than the Treasury's. Amongst the regulars are Morgan Stanley's and

Merrill Lynch's monthly outlooks, which are always good reading. There are regular specialist publications also, such as Salomon Brothers' *Financial Futures*, and *Options Analysis*. Then there are sector or subject reports, which look at either a company or an industry in great detail, and come up with recommendations.

In contrast with these worthwhile publications are the tip-sheets. All you need to be a tip-sheet publisher is a word processor, a jobbing printer, some stamps, and a bit of flair. You also need to be licensed. Some of these tip-sheets tend to be a little self-indulgent, but there must be a market for them, otherwise they would not exist.

Investor Relations Managers

The rise of the specialist broking press has been such that the financial directors of large companies, and their public relations men, often spend more time wooing brokers' analysts than talking to financial journalists. Many companies employ an investor relations manager, whose job it is to keep both institutional investors and analysts informed of the more favourable aspects of the company. They now have their own body, the Investor Relations Society. Many of its members have lavish expense accounts, and jet in and out of two or more European capitals a day, expending great energy and charm on their subjects. Things can, however, go wrong. I remember the investor relations executive at Olivetti wringing his hands at an unfavourable broker's circular on his company written by a very presentable woman analyst, and crooning down the phone: 'How can you do this kind of thing to me?'

In recent years increasing attention has been paid by the major European companies to soliciting investment in the United States, and those who have neglected this aspect of financial public relations have done so at their cost.

An example is provided by ICI, which maintains a full-time investor relations executive in New York to keep analysts at both institutions and broking firms up to date with the company's financial affairs. Some of the information is printed material, but another aspect of the job is to organize an annual road show to five American cities. There are also quarterly meetings allowing all major US analysts to meet the company's finance director and other top members of staff, and visits are arranged for those who wish to tour ICI's operations in Britain.

The Analysts

Once the analyst was the office introvert, who spent his day hidden from view in a corner behind a pile of dusty papers, fretting over obscure charts while his broking colleagues got on with the business of trading shares.

Securities analysts have now formed an industry in their own right, and have their own professional body. It is a highly competitive business, and one in which the rewards can be considerable. There are even annual contests for best analysts, and broking firms, sector by sector. The best known survey, now the annual Extel Ranking of UK Investment Analysts, was started in 1973 by Continental Illinois, and is based on a detailed questionnaire sent to investment managers of the major institutions. Only four out of ten bother to reply in detail, but this still makes almost 100, with over £600 billion. of funds in their care, and the survey is self-perpetuating, as the winners can count on many a new job offer and a stream of telephone calls from journalists, merchant bankers, accountants and others also anxious to tap their expertise.

A similar analysts' Oscar awards takes place in New York, under the aegis of Institutional Investor magazine. Across the Atlantic it seems much more of a one-horse race. Merrill Lynch, the world's largest broking firm once nicknamed 'the thundering herd' has won the award for each of the past three years, and for 16 of the 26 years the contest has been going. The US survey is the result of 1,500 interviews with professional investors.

The top ten broking firms in London together employ over 650 analysts, of which about a third cover European and overseas sectors.

The Extel surveys also reveal how specialist analysts have become. The typical analyst covers three or four sectors of the market, and studies 38 companies. Their average age is thirty-three, and the typical member of the fraternity will have spent six and a quarter years in the business, and three and a half years with his or her firm. Fundamental research and field trips take up to two thirds of their time – and they spend a surprising amount of time on marketing activities, frequently talking to the media. This partly explains why analysts, especially those who appear often on radio and television, are not universally admired, particularly by the chairmen of companies upon whose operations they comment.

The world of the analyst starts with the fundamentals – the numbers that are used to measure a company and to compare it with another. An analyst will work through these looking at the EPS, the PE ratio, the yield, the NAV, and the DE ratio. It is worth explaining each of these terms, because they have significance for the serious personal investor.

EPS, or earnings per share, measures the amount of profit after tax. It is sometimes confused with the dividend, but it is not the same. The dividend is the payout to shareholders which usually consists of only a portion of the profits, the rest having been ploughed back into the business. Some companies pay higher dividends than they should in order to retain the support of shareholders, and neglect re-financing their businesses. Earnings per share is a more accurate measure of a company's success, and a good EPS may be an indication of a company that is growing sharply. However be cautious, for there are many successful companies that are parsimonious with dividends, and which may well be of less interest to those seeking income rather than long-term growth. EPS figures can sometimes be deceiving when a company has sold assets during a trading year and added the amount that has been raised to profits. To avoid confusion the Institute of Investment Management and Research has devised a new standard for EPS which excludes both profit from asset sales and the tax thereon.

The PE ratio is one of the most widely quoted measurements. It gives you the earnings per share as it relates to the price of the share. A PE of 12 means that the share price is 12 times the earnings per share.

Yield is a key indicator for those whose priority is income from their investments. It expresses the actual dividend as a proportion of the share price. A yield of 4 means that the dividend provided 4 pence or cents for every pound or dollar of a share's listed price. As a share price rises, yields go down to the point where an investor will probably be deterred from buying the stock.

NAV is the net asset value, and is particularly useful as a measurement when takeovers are being considered. It is an estimate of what each share would be worth if the company were liquidated, all its assets sold, and all liabilities settled, leaving a residue to be distributed to shareholders.

Net debt or gearing measures the company's borrowings as a percentage of total assets, and comes into importance at times when interest rates are high. A highly geared company is often of concern to investors, because it has to trade profitably in order to meet interest bills.

The job of an analyst is part office-based, part on the road. He or she – and there are an increasing number of women in the business – has access to high technology, particularly numerous computer programs designed to make the postulation of future trends easier. An analyst will also spend a lot of time on the telephone asking questions, as well as attending briefings and seminars. In recent years it has become customary for companies, particularly large companies, to make life as comfortable as possible for analysts, transporting them en bloc or individually to expensive country hotels, where it is possible for them to socialize with directors and senior management as well as to talk shop. A thorough briefing of analysts immediately after a company's results are published can be crucial in getting a good press, for increasingly newspapers are dependent on the views of analysts for comment. Expectations can be lowered, if profits are going to be bad, and vice versa. Some companies choose an exceptionally attractive venue for six-monthly or yearly meetings with analysts. Carlo de Benedetti, when chairman of Olivetti, favoured Florence, where the men and women from broking houses across Europe could sample art and Tuscan wine. British Airways sometimes flies opinion-makers in the City to a variety of exotic overseas locations in the old but not mistaken belief that the further away from home the closer the mind might be concentrated on the subject in hand.

Often it is the City public relations firm which oils the

wheels of the information industry function. Financial public relations companies like to think that they are a cut above their contemporaries in the West End who deal with products and services, and they probably are. Their senior people certainly exude more style, and maintain larger expense accounts. Their role is also much more important. There are legal obligations on companies who make financial changes to inform the press, and someone has to ensure that announcements are hand-delivered or sent electronically round the City at the right time, usually before market trading starts or in late afternoon. There can be no question of sending out details of an acquisition, or a rights issue, on an embargoed basis.

But City PR advisers are no mere messenger boys. In many cases they are the eyes and ears of a company chairman and, occasionally, his voice. Some company chairmen are gregarious and well-connected individuals, able both to project a positive image and to be sensitive to public opinions. The majority are not. A good PR person will be able to keep the chairman and directors informed of shareholders' opinion, what the newspapers are saying and, increasingly important, an assessment of political, Whitehall and Brussels opinion. If needed, he will be able to lobby politicians on the company's behalf. In major takeover activity, or in rights issues, the public relations man will also become a valuable aide to merchant bankers and stockbrokers.

The Chartists

Unlike the 'health warning' advertisements, chartists believe that past performance really is a guide to the future of share price movements, and go out of their way to prove that this is the case. Chartism goes in and out of fashion, and some of the best chartists – or technical analysts as they are sometimes called – command respect and a large audience whenever they make a presentation.

The chartist is particularly interested in market peaks and troughs, and believes that these high and low points can be predicted with a reasonable degree of certainty. Expressions like 'points of resistance' are important. Just as it is possible to foresee that house prices cannot rise beyond a certain point (because the ratio of borrowings to average incomes becomes too high) or that prices can fall no further (because demand will rise from those on lower earnings) so stock market chartists are convinced that it is possible to assess a share's intrinsic value.

By carefully plotting price movements over a period of time – an easy process with high-speed personal computers – a chartist can spot a trend, and recommend a time to buy or sell. That is the theory; in fact chartism is fallible. The chartists failed to predict the great stock market crash of 1987, but then so did most other so-called experts.

Those who wish to learn more about the charms of chartism would do well to go to their nearest business book shop, and browse through some of the many titles available. An easier option might be to use the *Financial Times* to plot the performance of the main indices, and to look at shares that, year after year, appear to better it. If you have a PC there are some interesting and inexpensive computer programs that enable you to do this.

Financial Advisers

With such a wealth of information available, to whom do today's investors turn for knowledge, and from whom can they obtain the most reliable advice? It is an obvious question, and it is perhaps the one that is most frequently asked by those with more than a few pounds to invest. It is also one of the hardest questions to answer.

One quite correct answer is no one. In the end the investor, whether the chief investment manager of a large insurance company or a widow in Worthing, has to make the decision as to which is the best vehicle for improving the value of his or her savings. It is possible, even for those who do not consider themselves financially literate, to have cheap access to a great deal of information, and even that is sometimes of less use than a hunch or an everyday observation. For instance, anyone who has watched the development of Britain's High Streets over the past ten years will have noted the rise of Tesco or Marks & Spencer. Shopping at Marks is not cheap, but its goods are of high quality, and its stores are full. Goods are seldom discounted, not even when adjoining stores are holding cut-price sales. Anyone reading the details of the M&S credit card, and its very high interest rate, and reading in the press of the large number of cardholders, will see that profits from this source will grow. You may not make a quick profit on M&S shares, but they will grow, along with British Telecom, Tesco, British Airways, and smaller concerns like Forte.

But this is to avoid the real question. To whom can one turn? A bank manager, stockbroker, accountant, building society manager, perhaps. All have their place and purpose, but none of them is necessarily a good investment adviser. Today's bank managers prefer to lend money than to give investment advice, steering customers in the direction of in-house unit trusts, which have not been the best performers. Accountants are useful tax advisers, and usually save you the cost of their fee, but when one seeks investment advice from them, they can start talking about complicated accountant-run pension schemes for the self-employed, and property trusts. Building society managers live or die by the balances on deposit in their branches, so it is not easy to accept their views as impartial. This leaves stockbrokers, who can be either good or bad advisers, but mostly are a mixture of both.

Regrettably very few large stockbrokers seem to want to service individual investors, and an increasing number of firms will not deal with them at all, unless the clients are very rich. This short-sighted approach is in contrast to the interest shown in small investors in the US, where share shops are common. But it is typical of the patronising attitude of many in the City towards the average member of the public.

It may well be that Britain will follow the example of the United States. There, sharebrokers take their business to the public, and in almost every prosperous suburb there will be one or more open-plan broking offices, laid out rather like a large travel or estate agent, where members of the public may call, enjoy a cup of coffee, and discuss their investments with a consultant. There is plenty of literature available, including both brochures and financial magazines; Wall Street prices run continuously on television monitors, and there is a friendly and unpressurized atmosphere.

It is a pity that one of the few equivalent places in Britain's High Streets appears to be the betting shop. The emergence of independent financial advisers should have led to the development of money shops, but not very many exist. For the most part the advisers stick to insurance broking, leaving share dealing to the banks and big securities houses.

14 Policing the Markets

*'The financial planning industry is in many ways
still in the days of the Wild West. The marshal hasn't
ridden into town, there's mayhem in the streets, a lot
of random shooting'* – Scott Stapf of the North
American Securities Administrators' Association.

At four o'clock in the morning of 23 October 1812, three men
called at the Popincourt Barracks in Paris with the devastating
news that the Emperor Napoleon had died beneath the walls
of Moscow. It was a plausible story – news from the campaign
front took three weeks to get back and the French armies had
just achieved a great victory at the Battle of Borodino that had
opened the gates to the Russian capital. The men also said that
the Senate had abolished the Empire and appointed a
Provisional Government, and was calling on the 10th Cohort
of the National Guard for support. Within hours a huge conspiracy against Napoleon was under way, and the Emperor's
leading supporters were thrown into prison.

This story, told in more recent times by Italian author,
Guido Artom, in his book *Napoleon is Dead in Russia*, was
the inspiration for one of Britain's most notorious examples
of share market rigging. In the early nineteenth century only
major news moved the fledgling stock market, and it took
headlines like 'Napoleon Set to Invade', or, better still,
'Napoleon Dead' to move the market.

Since, even in the days before the telegraph, old news was
no news, so stockbrokers often placed faithful retainers in
the port of Dover to listen to the rumour mill, watch the sea,
talk to fishermen, and report back regularly. So, when on 21
February 1814, Colonel de Burgh, alias Charles Random de
Bérenger, turned up in Dover in a red uniform, saying he was
aide de camp to General Lord Cathcart, and reported the
death of Napoleon and the fall of Paris, the news flashed to

London at the speed of a pony and trap. Although foreign reporting was severely limited in those days, along with share ownership, there were those in London who had heard of the earlier, unsuccessful conspiracy against Napoleon, and the subsequent execution, not only of the plotters, but also of the soldiers who unwittingly carried the message. They were therefore very much on their guard against such stories. But 'Colonel de Burgh' had an elaborate story, a detailed account of how Napoleon had been butchered by the Cossacks. He had also made a point of going directly to the headquarters of the Port Admiral in Dover to apprise him of the facts. Surely, said brokers, it must be true.

Prices on the Stock Exchange shot up, as the wealthy clients of brokers received the news, apparently confirmed by hand bills distributed in the streets of London. They were not to know that these had also been handed out by de Bérenger who had himself taken a coach to the capital, to collect his gains, estimated at about £10,000. It was, of course, all pure fiction, but note that those who lost out were those who had been contacted by brokers, those who, themselves, were often privileged possessors of inside information, which, in this case, turned out to be false.

Not much changed in the following 175 years. Until recently it was those 'in the know' who stood to make rich pickings from speculative trading on the Stock Exchange. Latter-day frauds on similar lines to that perpetrated by de Bérenger were common in the early 1970s, during the so-called Australian mining boom. Reports of a nickel 'strike' by an obscure, barely known and usually recently listed mining company would reach Sydney as a result of a tip from Kalgoorlie, a remote dusty gold town in Western Australia. Confirmation was impossible, but the word flashed round, and the price of the stock shot up. I once worked on a magazine where the financial editor would return from lunch, very excited, and shout something like 'Bosom's Creek has struck nickel,' and rush to the phone to buy shares. Some brokers made a point of reserving shares for journalists, who could be counted upon to write favourably about a mining prospect, which, more often than not, when the geologists' report arrived, turned out to be nothing more than a hole in the ground or a stick marking a spot in the desert. Fortunes were made and lost.

Much of the activity was 12,000 miles from the geologists' trowels. Each day, as soon as the London Stock Exchange opened there was feverish activity as investors sought to cash in. Many had their fingers badly burned, and the two-year 'boom' earned Australian brokers a bad reputation which took years to live down. As one merchant banker, who frequently visits Sydney, put it: 'The Aussies saw it as a way of getting their own back on the Poms.'

Ramping stocks was not confined to those on the fringe of share markets. Writing in the *Observer* on 5 September 1971, under the headline 'Digging up the Dirt', I reported how an Australian Senate Committee investigation into the series of mining collapses and false claims in that country had severely shaken investors' confidence.

One thoroughly dishonest practice disclosed to the Committee was the purchase of huge blocks of shares in early trading by certain brokers, using their house accounts. By lunchtime, word would be round the markets that a particular share was on the move, and the broking house would unload its newly acquired holding at a substantial profit. Those shares that remained unsold would be allocated to clients for whom the firm held discretionary accounts, at a substantially higher price than the firm had paid for them, thereby enabling it to take a profit at its clients' expense. To add insult to injury, the clients would be charged brokerage, but usually would be none the wiser, for they would see from the *Australian Financial Review* that they had apparently obtained the shares at the 'market price'.

The Committee's report makes interesting reading, even years after the inquiry. It scrutinized in detail the accounts of one sharebroking firm that had gone into liquidation, only to find that about 80 per cent of the firm's trading was on its own account, and that its income from commission amounted to only a minor proportion of turnover.

Another prominent Sydney stockbroker, who was also a director of two major mining companies, was exposed for trying to have one of the companies taken over by a joint venture operation, in which his stockbroking firm's affiliated investment house had a stake. Evidence to the Senate Committee revealed that the stockbroker planned the takeover without informing the company chairman or his fellow directors, and that an associate company of his firm was to act as the underwriters.

Let us move back to London, and to 13 June 1985. It was a typical summer Thursday on the Stock Exchange. Trading was languid, as is so often the case at this time of the year. Then came a sudden burst of activity, much to the curiosity of a party from a Norfolk Women's Institute that was visiting the public gallery that day. Someone was buying large blocks of shares in Arthur Bell and Sons plc, and their prices rose by 14 per cent.

The visitors had to wait until reading their Saturday edition of the *Eastern Daily Press* to find out why. Guinness plc had made a bid for Bell on Friday the 14th, and on the eve of that takeover offer, someone had got wind of what was going on, and had been buying Bell's shares furiously in the hope of a quick profit. Yet 'insider trading' is strictly forbidden both by the law, which since 1980 has made it a criminal offence, and by the rules of the Stock Exchange. Despite that, as a practice, it is still widespread.

According to the magazine *Acquisitions Monthly*, the share prices of takeover targets rise on average between 20 and 30 per cent in the month before a bid. Over 90 per cent of prices move before a bid. One reason for this may well be that astute investors have spotted, from their own research, likely targets for takeover. Passing insider information is more likely.

To combat this the Stock Exchange maintains a special squad of men and women at its Throgmorton Street offices to try to track down insider traders. This means questioning those suspected of using inside knowledge to make money, and putting the evidence before the Exchange's Disciplinary Committee.

New and powerful computers allow the squad to spot erratic price movements in London and on other major international markets, and they have the authority to question anyone who works for a member of the Stock Exchange, which, of course, includes a large number of international banks and other financial conglomerates. Their computers have instant access to all Stock Exchange transactions over the previous six months, and they may manipulate the database by asking over 100 questions.

But just like detectives from the regular police forces, they rely more on hot tips from informants than from the craftsmanship of a Sherlock Holmes. The number of tips runs at about ten a week. Many of them come from market-makers spotting something suspicious. Since market-makers can lose thousands of pounds by incorrect pricing, they are very aware of phoney figures.

The Stock Exchange also has the backing of compliance officers employed in securities houses. These men and women make sure that both the Stock Exchange rules and their own house rules on share trading are strictly observed, and if they spot an irregularity in a transaction involving another firm, they usually report it to their opposite number.

Some companies are stricter than others in observing the code of conduct they insist staff must obey when buying and selling stock on their own account. Chase Securities insists that all transactions are placed through the company, and that compliance staff are notified. At most securities houses the phone transactions of all dealing staff are logged, so that investigators could, if they wished, find out who telephoned whom and when. Some firms have taken this a stage further and record the telephone calls of all staff.

A mixture of recorded conversations and the alertness of the London Stock Exchange's surveillance unit has already been responsible for trapping several insider traders. Just before the Mecca group bid for Pleasurama, the casinos and restaurant company, the members of the unit spotted that there had been an increasing amount of trading in Pleasurama. Their suspicions were further aroused when they received calls from market-makers in some leading broking firms drawing their attention to the fact that something irregular must be going on. Compliance officers at several houses were phoned, and after a tape at Morgan Grenfell had been played, it was discovered that a tip had been passed on by a female member of Samuel Montagu's corporate finance team. This was the department involved in advising Mecca on its offer. The other banks then listened to their own tape recordings, and the woman plus two others who had used the information were unceremoniously sacked. The three stood to have made a useful sum of money from trading on inside information. That they were caught owes much to their own greed and the vigilance of the surveillance squad. If they had been more cautious and less avaricious their dealings might well have passed unnoticed.

Even so, many insider traders escape detection. One particular problem is the use of nominee companies in offshore tax havens as the trading vehicle. The Stock Exchange team of former policemen, computer consultants, stockbrokers and accountants, say they often follow good leads only to come up against obstacles when a block of shares is purchased by a nominee company. 'There is no way we can see at the moment of busting offshore companies without international cooperation,' I was told. 'All the old names are always there – the Cayman Isles and so on. But it is not only in the Caribbean or in Liberia that this problem exists – much closer to home, in the Channel Islands or the Isle of Man we have just no hope of getting behind the nominee thing.

The Securities and Exchange Commission

Policing the markets is conducted in two ways: through self-regulation by quasi-official bodies set up by stock exchanges in consultation with governments, or by official agencies staffed by professionals. For many years there have been arguments about which is the more effective way of protecting the investor and preventing fraud and corruption. The debate continues, but, with time and experience, the weight of opinion seems to be moving in favour of a regulatory system run by full-time professionals with no vested interest in any company within the securities industry.

The most important regulatory body in the world is the United States Securities and Exchange Commission (SEC), which protects the interests of America's estimated 50 million investors. Although its authority is technically limited to policing the securities industry in the United States, its tentacles are spread much wider, extending, for example, to the conduct of American investment institutions in their operations outside the country.

The SEC, with a staff of 1,800, was established in July 1935, some years after the Wall Street crash of 1929. A

Congressional investigation found that there had been stock manipulation on a huge scale, blatant dishonesty and insider trading, and the SEC was established with sweeping powers over the securities industry.

Now all corporations have to file quarterly financial returns, and much more detailed annual ones, with the SEC, as well as informing it promptly of any facts or important events which might affect the market for the company's stock. Federal laws require companies intending to raise money by selling their own securities to file with the Commission true facts about their operations. The Commission has power to prevent or punish fraud in the sale of securities, and is authorized to regulate stock exchanges. The law under which it operates lays down precise boundaries within which directors, officers and large shareholders may deal in the stock of their companies.

In its time the SEC has notched up some notable successes in prosecuting corporate crime. In August 1968, it filed charges of securities fraud against 14 Merrill Lynch officers and employees. In the end Merrill Lynch publicly consented to an SEC finding that it had used advance inside information from the Douglas Aircraft Company for the advantage of pre-ferred institutional clients, defrauding the investing public of an estimated $4.5m in the process – no mean sum at the time. The Securities and Exchange Commission is a mecca for bright young lawyers who wish to make their name as determined investigators, and then, as often as not, get out into lucrative private practice with the SEC name on their credentials.

However, while the SEC has a reputation as a vigorous force, and has claimed many scalps, it is severely constrained in its activities by a shortage of funds. Although the SEC collects fees from registered investment advisers, it has to hand over a large share of the proceeds to the United States Treasury. It has only about 300 enforcement officers to cover the whole of the United States, and the section which deals with the investment management and mutual funds industry has an inspectorate of only about 60 people.

Although this group undertakes about 1,500 spot checks each year on investment advisers, it is not surprising that many confidence tricksters escape unscathed. Officially there are about 17,000 registered investment advisers in the United States, so on average each gets a spot check once a decade, during which time many will have sold their businesses on. But these figures include only the registered advisers. The Consumer Federation of America (CFA) believes that there could be about half a million people acting as unofficial financial advisers, while even the Securities Administrators Association accepts that there are 250,000. Many of these not only claim to offer investment advice; some of them actually manage clients' money.

The SEC also depends greatly on a number of self-regulatory bodies to fulfil its task. For the most part stock exchanges police the activities of their members, and each has an investigations branch. The New York Stock Exchange, the American Stock Exchange and the National Association of Securities Dealers (NASDAQ) all work in close cooperation with the SEC.

The SEC has much wider powers than Britain's Department of Trade, and has much more inclination to use them. The DTI so far has been reluctant to use its power to force open bank accounts and to demand documents, though this may change. But the SEC may subpoena individuals and companies in the US, and demand sight of their bank accounts. Outside America it has agreements with the British, Japanese, Swiss, Cayman Isles and other governments to gather information, and it can also call for sanctions to be imposed on the US branches of un-cooperative foreign banks. Offenders may not only be prosecuted, with penalties as high as three times the illicit profits, but the SEC will turn over all the evidence it has gained to civil litigants who have been disadvantaged as a result of someone's insider trading.

Even these powers are inadequate when one considers the definition of the modus operandi of an insider trader provided by the *Financial Times*:

The would-be insider trader gets a job with the corporate finance department of a merchant bank active in mergers and acquisitions. Always travelling via a third country, he visits two tax havens, Panama and Liechtenstein, which have resisted foreign pressure on their secrecy laws. In each country he sets up a trading company, and opens bank accounts in two or three banks in their names. He only uses banks with no operations or assets in Britain or the United States. He never tells the banks his real name, but arranges for them to deal through a large London broking firm whenever they receive coded instructions over the telephone.

When he picks up inside information, he always trades alone using a call box. He never trades in large amounts, but may break up a transaction into a series of deals from different accounts. He avoids the mistake of trading just before a bid announcement – it makes the market makers vengeful.

As the *Financial Times* pointed out, the SEC's achievements highlighted 'the passivity of the DTI'.

Curiously, though, it was the SEC's biggest coup, catching Boesky, the self-styled 'king of the arbs', that provided the DTI with some of their best leads into City fraud this side of the Atlantic.

Boesky was brought to book because of the Levine case. Levine pleaded guilty, paid back $12.6m in illegal profits, and talked to the SEC, implicating Boesky. Boesky was charged with making a personal killing on insider information provided by Levine, fined $100m, barred for life from working on Wall Street, and ordered to dismantle his $2 billion firm.

Boesky was one of the biggest and best-known speculators in the feverish takeover business in America, using a phenomenal network of contacts to make huge profits through arbitraging. Like Levine, he also 'cooperated with the authorities', which is a euphemism for becoming a supergrass in order to keep out of jail.

The Securities and Investment Board

The foundations for the present regulation of Britain's security markets were laid by the Financial Services Act of 1986. Many of the statutory powers are held by the Securities and Investment Board (SIB), which is a dedicated agency established by the British government with many but by no means all of the powers accorded the US Securities and Exchange Commission.

Some important aspects of regulation have been devolved to the Stock Exchange. It is tasked with regulating those who use its markets, and to make sure that there is proper protection for investors. It also has the job of regulating the companies that are listed on the Exchange, or who wish to do so.

The LSE achieves this through dedicated teams. The Listing Department assesses the suitability of companies seeking to join the Exchange and reviews their activities. It has the power to approve, suspend or cancel listings.

The Market Regulation Department monitors trading on the LSE by examining market-makers' quotes and the prices at which trades are done, and looks for irregularities. It is within this group that the surveillance team discussed earlier fits. All the time this group seeks to make sure that the Exchange's dealing rules are being respected.

The Continuing Obligations Department regulates the flow of information from listed companies to ensure that all users of the market have simultaneous and equal access to information. Listed companies have to make a variety of regular announcements to the market, and to inform it of any development which could have an effect on its shares.

The City has grown up on the principle that those in key position could be trusted. 'My Word is My Bond' was the Stock Exchange motto, and although insider trading was rife, it was true that a handshake sealed a deal. But as the financial markets became more sophisticated, there was concern at two levels – that consumers were being sold products and services that either they did not want or which were unsuited to their financial needs, and that City insiders were making unreasonable profits from their inside information.

An inquiry under Professor Jim Gower was appointed to investigate the need for regulating and policing financial services, and did an extremely thorough job. It found much in the American Securities and Exchange Commission to its liking, and made a series of complicated recommendtions.

The British government's response to the Gower report and all the lobbying that accompanied it was a classic British fudge which was to remain in place for more than 15 years. The Conservatives led by Margaret Thatcher were ideologically opposed to the creation of a new bureaucracy but also knew that the dictum of 'my word is my bond' was no longer enough to stop people being cheated.

The government wanted the City to police itself – and, in spite of Professor Gower's misgivings, believed it could. But it decided an umbrella organization was needed to oversee this self-policing, so it established the Securities and

Investment Board, staffed by professionals and headed by a former civil servant, Sir Kenneth Berrill. The SIB sat on top of a plethora of self-regulatory bodies – one of which was the Stock Exchange – and tried to make sure they drew up rule books and made their members stick to these rules.

The result was an octopus with tentacles that touched every aspect of the financial services industry, and a set of regulations that were so complex that even the regulators were thoroughly confused. Many of the self-regulatory bodies had names based on hideous acronyms, such as LAUTRO (Life Assurance and Unit Trust Regulatory Organization), IMRO (Investment Management Regulatory Organization), and FIMBRA (Financial Intermediaries, Managers and Brokers Regulatory Organization). The Securities Association was created to take over the regulatory role of the Stock Exchange.

The Securities and Investment Board and these bodies had to follow a number of guidelines laid down by the Financial Services Act. For example, approved investment businesses had to be 'competent, financially sound and to offer best advice' after 'getting to know' the customer.

Berrill could have chosen to leave the definitions vague, and trust the self-regulatory bodies to interpret the law in a reasonable way. Instead, rather in the manner of an American contracts lawyer who anticipates everything in a deal will go wrong, he drew up very detailed rules, so that there could be no ambiguity about what was permissible.

The result was that practitioners had to face some of the most extensive, expensive and taxing conditions imposed on any sector of industry. Whereas the American Declaration of Independence ran to only 1,337 words, and the ten commandments to a mere 333 words, the SIB and SRO rule books ran to more than a million words.

It was not long before this panoply of regulation was severely tested, and found wanting, in what became known as the Barlow Clowes affair. In the summer of 1988, thousands of investors reading their daily newspapers were startled to discover that the money they had set aside for pensions or other long-term savings had vanished. Barlow Clowes, the company to which it had been entrusted, was being liquidated. This might, in the history of personal investment, be a familiar story, but what made matters worse was that most of the funds lost were commuted lump sums from life savings or redundancy payments. A majority of the investors were elderly.

What was also particularly interesting about this scandal was that it embroiled both financial advisers and the government. It was not just a question of investors losing their savings as a result of sharp practice by a fund management group. Many of the 11,000 who lost a major part of their life savings did so after being advised to invest in the Barlow Clowes fund by professional independent financial advisers who should have known better. Their defence was that Barlow Clowes had been licensed by the Department of Trade and Industry after suspicions had been raised about the firm's activities.

Barlow Clowes was built up as a low-cost management group. Its funds were not designed to attract the reckless, but the cautious investor seeking a better return than a deposit account in a bank or building society. The attraction was that expert managers would consolidate investors' cash into interest bearing deposits, principally British gilt-edged securities. That indeed was the intention of the fund's chairman, Peter Clowes, but, alas, he succumbed to the temptation of using some of the cash along the way for sumptuous living, including yachts and fast cars. The sorry tale finally ended in the criminal courts, Peter Clowes spent a number of years in one of Her Majesty's prisons, and the regulators had learned the lesson that even the thickest of rule books do not prevent investors being fleeced.

Widespread concern about the complexity of the regulatory system led to Sir Kenneth Berrill being replaced by David Walker, a former executive of the Bank of England, who simplified structures, and while relaxing some aspects of regulation, toughened up others. Even so there continued to be continuous concern about the efficiency of self-regulation, and in 1996 and 1997 a series of pensions scandals came to light. These scandals were not, like Barlow Clowes, examples of blatant fraud, but the product of the uncaring and greedy salesmen from well-known life assurance companies. Incentivized by large commissions, these salesmen persuaded middle-aged people to relinquish their income-based pensions for money value schemes, where the total worth varies according to the price of the securities that make up the portfolio. Many people were persuaded to make the change, with the result that most of them could expect a large downturn in their potential pension incomes. This led to many of the companies being fined, and forced to retrain salesforces, as indicated earlier with the example of the Prudential.

When Tony Blair's revitalized Labour Party was elected to government in 1997 one of the first acts was to announce the establishment of an American-style SEC to be known as the Financial Services Authority and intended to be a 'world class regulator'. Headed by a former deputy governor of the Bank of England, Howard Davies, the FSA took over banking regulation from the Bank of England, and integrated the work of the Securities and Investments Board and all its subsidiary self-regulatory organizations. When Davies met the former chairman of the American Federal Reserve Board, Paul Volcker, the big American greeted him with a laugh and the comment: 'Big job, I just hope you can retain your sense of humour.'

Unfortunately this process of merger and reorganization was not being carried out swiftly, and it will be beyond the year 2000 before all the SROs are wound up and put to sleep, with the new regime due to come into full operation by the autumn of 1999.

Unlike the previous system, the aims of the FSA are clear cut:

1. First and foremost, to protect consumers of financial services. It says it will 'set, promote, monitor, and enforce high standards of integrity, financial soundness, fair dealing and competence for those it regulates in order to protect and secure fair treatment for investors, depositors and policyholders'. This is by no means an easy task, but the FSA has added an even sterner obligation 'to aim to ensure that consumers receive clear and adequate information about services, products and risks'. This of course means making a subjective judgement about the vast amount of financial services marketing that comes through people's letter-boxes, and could become a very

onerous obligation. Undertaken to the letter it would mean making contact with every customer, or, at least, allowing free access for customers to FSA staff, which might become a substantial burden. We shall have to see what happens in reality. But if it can ensure, as it puts it, that although customers are responsible for their own decisions, they are not exposed to unreasonable risks, it will have done a good job.

2. Promote clean and orderly markets. Here the FSA says it 'will promote fairness, transparency and orderly conduct in financial markets, looking in the first instance to the markets and market participants to set and enforce high standards', but taking action itself when these standards are inadequate or are inefficiently enforced.

3. To maintain confidence in the financial system. This in essence is the 'feel good factor', restoring consumer confidence in the City and financial institutions. It promises to make sure, in cooperation with the Bank of England, that the 'failure of individual financial institutions does ot undermine the overall stability and soundness of the financial system'.

The FSA says it will pursue these aims in an efficient way that will aim to ensure that the costs of regulation are proportionate to the benefits. One important aspect of the new regime is that it undertakes to differentiate between the regulation of wholesale and retail business, reflecting the varying needs to consumers and the degree of protection required. In other words highly paid dealers in a major securities house are expected to be a great deal more risk aware than the elderly widow living alone in an apartment on the South Coast.

As this book went to press it is too soon to make a judgement on whether the new system is as great an improvement on the old as it is expected to be. The process of change is moving slower than many believe should be the case, but if the result is a significant improvement in protection without losing the driving force of the free market that will be a net gain.

15 Prudence, the Motley Fool, and the World Wide Web

'The Wise would have you believe that "A Fool and His Money are soon Parted". But in a world where three quarters of all professional money managers lose to the market averages, year in and year out, how Wise should one aspire to be' . . . from the Motley Fool Investment Guide.

When I was a child in post-war Britain, each fortnight there was a knock on the door from the Man from the Pru. Many households in suburban London put aside a shilling or two for this frequent visitor, who dutifully jotted down this contribution to a life assurance fund in a large black book, and pedalled off on his bicycle to the next house. Rather like a football pools addict, we all looked forward to the day when these small contributions would turn into a deposit large enough for a down payment on a car, or as Man from the Pru put it 'small acorns would turn into mighty oak trees'.

It was only years later, after a short spell working in the insurance industry, that I realized what an inefficient form of saving industrial life assurance, as it was called, actually was. But to many living on modest incomes it was their only form of saving. The prospect of buying shares was beyond contemplation, although somehow we always heard of elderly aunts who uncovered some tattered certificates in an old chest in a loft only to find they were worthless.

Half a century later the Man from the Pru is no more, having long been replaced by the tacky salesman with a glib tongue and an overpowered but small company car. Unlike his trusted predecessor, today's life assurance and financial product salesman has developed a reputation for selling relatively hard-up families financial services that they do not want, do not suit them, and are beyond their financial reach.

Unlike the purchase of a set of encyclopaedias, or double glazing of doubtful quality, payment for these schemes lasted a lot longer than a couple of years. In many cases families found they had taken on burdens that were to last for two decades. They could not get out of them without losing most of their money.

It is sad to see, in the late nineties, that the Prudential, as well as some other household brand names, is in the list of those corporations who have been heavily censured by the authorities for its practices. The Pru was in the forefront of those pensions groups who persuaded families to give up contributing to their company pension schemes and to start their own private pensions plan. What this often meant was that those in company schemes, where the pension to be paid was to be based on a percentage of final salary, took out plans where the payout depended on the value of the fund, in other words on the performance of the fund's investments. Under the latter there was no guaranteed pay out.

The regulators found that there were more than half a million people in Britain who were 'mis-sold' a personal pension in the 1980s and early 1990s, and companies were ordered to review all complaints and to offer compensation. Some of them did so with alacrity, discovering that in order to achieve a sensible review it was necessary to hire much better qualified staff, and to retrain large groups within their workforces.

The Prudential, the country's largest pensions group, was one of those that dragged its feet. The Securities and Investment Board found in late 1997 that the Pru had more cases of 'mis-selling' than any other provider, and had done less about it; by the September deadline it had only dealt with less than a third of the 70,000 cases. The Securities and Investment Board accused the Prudential of 'serious shortcomings', and said the Pru had 'failed to exercise the requisite due skill, care and diligence in its conduct of the pensions review – it has placed too much faith in its line managers and their reassurances'.

The old Man from the Pru would have turned in his grave.

Politicians, regulators and most of us would prefer that these incidents could be avoided. The only real solution is for consumers to be better informed and more knowledgeable about the financial markets, and therefore able to involve themselves more deeply in their own investment decisions.

Despite the fact that one family in four are now shareholders – and with many more householders having an interest in the stock markets because of their employment or pension plans – the truth is that people find buying and selling shares a discomfiting experience. Trading shares should be no more fearsome than buying a vacuum cleaner or a television set, or booking a holiday at the travel agent. Yet many small investors have told me that they feel very inhibited about contacting a stockbroker. They suspect, probably correctly, that the better known brokers will not be interested in their business.

They tend to the view that many High Street financial advisers know and care little about the equity markets, and that if they enter their premises they will be subjected to high pressure salesmanship to buy endowment assurance or unit trusts. The bank manager, if you can find one, will also discourage equity investment, and try to sell you one of his company's collective personal equity plans, the charges for which are often excessive. If you deal through a bank you will almost certainly pay too high a rate of commission.

Companies like Barclayshare and Schwab Europe are more approachable and user friendly, but the huge market success of the latter has meant that you can sit on the telephone for a long time waiting to place an order. Once through, Schwab is not allowed to offer advice, so conversations can be stilted, and while there is no obligation to buy or sell, many feel subconsciously obligated to do so.

The World Wide Web

One solution is the World Wide Web of the Internet. The Web is easy and inexpensive to use, and provides investors with tools and information that allow them to play the markets at leisure with real pleasure, effecting personal decisions at home free from the pressures of commission-hungry salesmen. Unfortunately trading via the Internet is not as straightforward and available in Britain and Europe as it is in the United States, but it is only a matter of time before we catch up. But there is no shortage of information on this side of the Atlantic; arguably there is too much of it.

The kit needed to access the Web can be obtained, new, for £500 or less. This sum will buy a PC with a Pentium chip, and a modem to connect to the Web through a normal telephone line. It is important to buy a modem capable of speeds of at least 28,000 baud, for otherwise downloading information will be irksome and use too much telephone time. The only other requirement will be a subscription to an Internet service provider, who will charge a monthly fee. There are dozens of service providers competing for business, but my preference is for a well known, branded service like America On Line or Netcom. They offer unlimited access for a fee of £15 or less per month, and offer subscribers the benefit of being able to dial in as a local call from almost every major city in the world. Both these services offer excellent free electronic mail, and a wide range of financial information.

It would be quite easy to fill a whole book on investment and the Web, but by the time the manuscript reached the printers much of the copy would be out of date, and readers would be exposed to information overload. I will confine myself here to the three most relevant aspects - software that helps to make the Web a wonderful investment tool; information providers that offer real value; and ways of executing your own low-cost on-screen trading.

The pennywise investor can use the Web without any software beyond the browser provided free by America On Line, Microsoft or Netscape. These browsers will enable you to download and save as much data and reading matter as you wish. Common proprietary programs in use such as Microsoft Excel and Access, Corel Word Perfect and Lotus Smart Suite allow users to manipulate and store material from the Internet easily and inexpensively.

But there are a number of additional programs easily available which offer additional benefits to investors. The best known of these is Quicken, produced by Intuit. Quicken's prime purpose is to let you control your family finances, but it contains a very useful portfolio section, which enables you to keep your log of shares and other investments up to date with consummate ease, including downloading prices from Quicken's own web site. The United States version of Quicken is richer in features, and I have found it more useful than the British one, so long as you do not mind substituting a dollar sign for pounds.

For example the US Quicken integrates with another Intuit product, Investor Insight, which allows you to track, analyse and manage your investments from the desktop. You can download stories from the Dow Jones News Service, and get five years of price histories for any company or mutual fund listed on the New York Stock Exchange, the American Stock Exchange or NASDAQ. You can display charts and reports that show the performance of each investment, including comparisons with other companies, and order in-depth company reports.

Another program is Microsoft Money which is plain and straightforward, and very simple and easy to use. It lacks some of the character and complexity of Quicken, but it is easier to adapt it to your own requirements.

Then there are programs which use 'push' technology, which means that they are pro-active and while you are connected to the Internet go in search of the information you want, using so called 'agents'. The best known of these is Pointcast, which allows you to select the information you wish brought to your screen on a regular basis, and displays it as a screen saver whenever you cease working for a period of, say, two minutes or more.

For example, you can ask PointCast to bring to you the latest share price of each stock in your portfolio, as well as any article or comment that comes up on the Web. This can be a very effective way of tracking information, as well as saving hours on your computer hacking through databases. If, for instance, you want anything on British Telecom, it will bring you the share price in near real-time, as well as articles about BT that have appeared on open Web sites, such as Bloomberg, Reuters, Sky News or CNN. The beauty about PointCast is that it works and is free to those who are prepared to download it from the Web. Those who value a CD-ROM and a manual can obtain them from any good computer store for about £25.

There are many thousands of sites of interest to the stock market investor, and those with the inclination to do so could spend an interesting wet winter afternoon browsing through them. What I will try to do here is to list a handful of the most useful and user-friendly: sufficient to provide the reader with a core amount of solid information.

First stop for the European investor should be FT.com and the related sites of the Financial Times group. Access to the site requires registration – filling in a coupon on-screen – but at the time of writing is free. Once on the site you can read the content of the newspaper, the scripts of its eight hours of television programming each day, and download articles from back numbers. You can get the major breaking business news and listen to voice reports on market activity.

A step up from this is Financial Times Briefing, which, like Point Cast mentioned earlier, is a push service. This provides four bulletins on global news, business news, emerging markets and economic news; a three-part background briefing on the main news story of the day, with comment and analysis by *Financial Times* journalists, and a two-deck ticker that scrolls the news summaries and the latest global market numbers across your desktop. Two other useful sites are those provided by Bloomberg and Reuters.

There are many other web sites of interest. Some of the best are provided by big investment houses like Merrill Lynch, Fidelity or Cazenove, the last-mentioned being of particular interest because it is one of the most blue-blooded brokers in London. But, like Buckingham Palace, which is also on the Web, it is up with the times.

The Motley Fool

The browser should also not miss the Motley Fool site on Motleyfool.com. This was one of the first and most original web sites in the financial area, and contains a mixture of amusing and sound advice. When in 1993 the big information providers and stockbrokers were trying to come to terms with the Web, three young people, David Gardner, Tom Gardner and Erik Rydholm conceived a site that would actually help investors with a mixture of statistics and wry commonsense comments.

This extract gives a good sense of what the Motley Fool is about:

Conventional wisdom: 'You should just let "experts" invest your money for you by putting your money in mutual funds.'
Foolish response: 'Hmmm. Well, if you really have NO time or interest in managing your own money, this may be true. But did you know that more than 75 per cent of all mutual funds underperform the stock market's average every year? In other words, most of the Wise "professionals" out there are losing to market average year in and year out. They'll try to convince you to invest in their funds, of course, by using jargon designed to confuse or intimidate you, and by putting up colourful graphs of their performance. Unfortunately, this hoopla dissolves away very quickly underneath the Foolish lens which compares the actual performances to the market averages.'

Why is such a sensible site called Motley Fool? The name comes from Shakespeare's *As You Like It*, in which Jacques says 'A fool, a fool, I see a fool in the forest, a motley fool', going on to say he was 'ambitious for a motley coat'. Motley was the multicoloured garment worn by Elizabethan court jesters, while Fools were paid to entertain royalty, and were the only people who could poke fun at the monarch without having their heads chopped off.

For readers who have endured an overdose of bank managers, financial advisers, insurance salesmen, accountants and all the other hustlers in the financial services industry an afternoon spent on-line with the Motley Fool is worth the time and the telephone charges.

Trading on the Web

The Web is a wonderful source of information for investors, but what is its capacity for trading? Here the differences between the United States and the rest of the world become truly apparent. In America there are numerous inexpensive services offering on-screen Internet trading. One of the best known is the Main Street broker Charles Schwab which will provide its Street Smart software to clients enabling them to track their portfolios, to check the latest prices on-line, and then to buy and sell on their accounts.

Very little specialist knowledge is needed to trade on-line, but it is as well to familiarize yourself with some of the vocabulary of the trading world. You may want to put a 'limit' on a trade, which means that you specify a price above or below which you will not trade. Or you may indicate you will trade 'at best', which means, as it suggests, at the most attractive price currently being offered.

In Britain the protectionist policies of the London Stock Exchange inhibited early attempts to get Internet trading off the ground. It was not so much that the London exchange objected to electronic trading *per se*, but it objected to providing share prices to on-line services at anything close to real-time. In the end, after threats of legal action by on-line traders, the exchange was forced to change its ways.

Electronic Share Information, founded by Herman Hauser on the Cambridge Technology Park, offers straightforward on-screen trading, and its Silver service, at a cost of £20 per month, offers unlimited access to real-time prices. Another slightly more expensive service is Infotrade, which provides a great deal more information, including a company's share history over three years, directors' dealings, broker forecasts and a charting model. At the time of writing several companies were planning on-line electronic trading services.

As the World Wide Web develops there will be even more opportunities for families to follow their fortunes from their living rooms, independent of the salesman knocking on the door.

16 Things That Go Bang in the Night

'*It's paper anyway. It was paper when we started, and its paper now*' – Sam Moore Walton.

'*When stocks go down, shoe shines go down. It's rough*' – Wall Street shoe cleaner.

'*The greatest London stock market crash was like the bursting of an over-inflated balloon. It came without warning, and with a speed and totality that was frightening*' – The *Financial Times*.

'*History is bunk*' – Henry Ford.

During the early hours of Friday October 16 1987, the sleep of most people living in south-east England was interrupted by a tearing sound, like sheets of yarn being ripped apart. Outside gusts of 120 miles an hour were scything through pristine suburban gardens and across rolling farmlands, lifting up everything from grotesque ornamental gnomes to horse boxes and family caravans, and smashing them to the ground. The tearing sound was that of wood splintering, as trees felled by the gales crashed downwards.

Not since World War Two had suburbanites experienced anything comparable. Tornadoes and hurricanes were not part of British life. But scores of people died or were seriously injured, and tens of millions of pounds' worth of damage was done to homes and gardens, offices and shops, factories and warehouses.

More than a million people were left without electricity for almost a week. Commuter road and rail routes into London were blocked by fallen timber; more than 300 trees were blown across just one line, between Tunbridge Wells and Battle. At the south coast resort of Brighton, the sea front was laid to waste. Shingle had been hurled across the marine parade and into doorways. Fleets of boats lay, shipwrecked, in the sodden streets. The windows of dingy boarding houses and smart hotels were caved in. In London's fashionable squares, telephone lines and the branches of fallen plane trees tangled across the streets.

Not surprisingly the BBC's news programmes were dominated by the devastation. Only about one in five of those working on the financial markets made it to the City of London. Even so, at noon on Friday October 17, the Channel Four *Business Daily* was able to report that shares were still being traded despite the fact that very few market-makers had made it to their dealing rooms.

Shortly after lunch I received a call from my son's school in Sussex asking me to fetch him home because the building was without heat, light, or power. The journey south was like finding a route through a maze, as main roads were blocked, forcing frequent retreats and detours. I turned on the radio. The news announcer advised people to stay at home. Then, right at the end of the bulletin, almost as a casual throwaway remark, came a one-line report that made me grip the steering wheel in disbelief. In the first few hours of trading on Wall Street the Dow Jones Industrial Average had dropped by over 100 points, its biggest-ever one day fall.

The BBC continued to major on the hurricane, its editors seemingly unaware that the losses caused to one corner of England by the hurricane were insignificant compared with the devastation being caused to families' savings, pensions and investments by the crash of the world's stock markets. But, over the next few days, we witnessed a drop in share values as large as during the Great Crash of 1929, when bankrupt brokers leapt to their deaths from the tower blocks of Wall Street. This time no one jumped, and one man took his pain, a loss of £308 million, with phlegm. 'It's only paper,' he said. 'It was paper when we started and it is paper now.'

Initially, because of the dislocation to business and financial activity caused by the storm, London was spared what New Yorkers described as a 'financial meltdown'. But by the evening of Monday October 19, now remembered as 'Black Monday', panic selling had swept through the British financial community, and share prices had fallen by one eighth, with the Financial Times 100 Share Index recording its largest ever one day fall. Across the Atlantic the Dow crashed again, recording an astonishing drop of 508 points, 23 per cent of its value. By the following night, Tuesday October 20, the FTSE index had tumbled by more than a fifth.

The fall might have been greater had all those who wanted to sell managed to get through to their brokers. Switchboards were jammed, and there were accusations that many market-makers had left their phones off the hook, reluctant to trade even at the low prices to which they had marked down stocks, for fear that these were nowhere near low enough.

No popular shares escaped the crash. More than 39 million shares in British Petroleum, Britain's largest company, changed hands, with the price at one stage falling as low as 271p, compared with the 410p it had been only a few weeks earlier. For the Conservative government, which had been heavily advertising BP shares on television, urging investors to 'be part of it', the fall had special significance. It had set the public privatization price at 330p, thereby ensuring that the sell-off of the last segment of BP shares would become a dismal failure. It also proved to be a major burden for the professional underwriters who were called to soak up the shares the public did not want.

Amongst those who suffered the most were pensioners and families who had much of their life savings tied up in unit trusts and other collective investments. Many small investors and their advisers found that the 'buy-back' promises of the fund management companies were hollow indeed. Many unit trust managers refused to quote prices on the telephone, advising customers to write in. I met one angry investor who had tried to contact seven companies, but managed to get through to only two. 'I think it is totally unacceptable and unethical that they will not quote me a price', he said. Of course these same managers were themselves struggling to raise cash in the market to meet the demands of those who had the presence of mind to send written instructions to sell.

In all tens of thousands of investors saw their precious capital ebb away, and learnt the lesson that buying shares is not a one-way street. A worm breeder in Scotland who had been playing the options market on the advice of his broker ended up owing Natwest Bank over £3 million. Many cautious investors, particularly the elderly, were much worse off as a result of responding to offerings that were grossly over-hyped. Perhaps the most blatant of these came from Royal Life, an insurance group, which promoted a series of new unit trusts, labelling its £6 million marketing campaign a 'Royal Event'. It netted almost a quarter billion pounds, but it was late on the Wednesday afternoon of October 21 before anyone trying to sell could get a price quote.

Across the world politicians bewailed the crash. The United States Treasury Secretary, James Baker, said the Reagan administration saw no cause for panic. 'We see it for what it is', he said, 'a very, very major correction to a market that is driven by inflationary fears that are unjustified'.

In London the Chancellor of the Exchequer also urged investors to stay cool, describing the market panic as a 'gross over-reaction'. Nigel Lawson said: 'My advice to millions of investors would be to stay calm. There is absolutely no reason not to do so.'

This turned out to be sound advice, but as he spoke institutions the world over were unloading stock. In Hong Kong the stock exchange was shut down for a week, a measure which triggered a major upset throughout the area. The Asia Pacific region felt the impact of the Crash of '87 more than anywhere else. In Sydney share prices fell by a quarter; in Tokyo they fell by one fifth. One person who followed Lawson's advice was Sir John Templeton, founder of the fund management group bearing his name. Asked by panicky fund managers what to sell, he barked back at them. 'Sell? You buy!'

The effects of the crash were felt for months, and it was not until the end of the following year that markets made a partial recovery. Only Tokyo managed to regain its pre-cash values within the year. But by the end of 1989, just over two years from Black Monday, the FTSE 100 index had passed its pre-crash peak of 2300.

Viewed from a ten-year perspective the Crash of 1987 looks more like an uncomfortable blip rather than an event of historic importance. The *Daily Telegraph* called it an 'amusing historical interlude'. True to form, the BBC forgot about it, but devoted an hour-long special to the 1987 storm damage. In general the tenth anniversary of the crash passed without much comment or interest. On the equivalent Monday in October 1997, the FTSE 100 index closed near to an all time record high of 5300.

As I am writing this there has been another period of turmoil on the markets. The word 'crash' was back in the headlines throughout the autumn of 1997. But what happened this time felt more like a correction of overbloated markets than a crash. In the critical last week of October 1997, the Dow Jones Industrial Average dropped a mere 3.5 per cent, the FTSE 100 2.6 per cent, the Nikkei 5.2 per cent, and the Hang Seng in Hong Kong only 4.7 per cent. Emerging markets suffered worse. Hardly enough to hurt investors who had gained more than 25 per cent over the previous year. Within three months the markets were on the rise again.

The lesson from all this is that in the long run crashes do not matter all that much, except to those who need to cash in their equities in the short term. It could be argued, of course, that if that is a serious possibility, you should not be in equities in the first place. But on a medium- or long-term basis, shares outperform all other assets, including property. BZW's redoubtable Michael Hughes worked out that if you had put £100 into shares at the end of the First World War, and reinvested all your dividends, you would have a capital gain of £710, 456. Had the same amount been invested in gilts the gain would have been £8,817. And on deposit at a High Street bank your £100 would be worth a measly £6,101.

Another lesson from 1987 is that big setbacks are inevitable. The doomsayers believe that well before the millennium there will be another crash. Others argue that the markets have entered a new golden age, powered by a heady mixture of the collapse of communism, the arrival of an information society, and the potential for growth created by the convergence of three of today's top technologies – computing, telecommunications and broadcasting.

The sensible investor, like the Motley Fool described earlier, will listen to the philosophy, the psephology, and the kidology, but pay more attention to basic principles. One major reason why the Crash of 1987 occurred was because dividend yields had fallen to a record low of three per cent, making it clear shares were overvalued.

But with two substantial crashes this century, when can we expect a third? It could be a long time coming. With the collapse of communism and much of the public sector now in private enterprise, the world is capitalist and a very different place. From time to time there will be setbacks. When these run for a long period we will have a bear market. But a crash of the size of 1929 or 1987 is less probable.

There are thousands who claim to be able to predict when markets will fall. Some are chartists with some knowledge of statistics and a sense of historical perspective. Others are mere astrologists. There is no reason to believe the astrologists will be any less accurate than the experts.

Inevitably there are academics with sound theories. One, Robert Shiller, an economist from Yale University, has made detailed studies of investors' behaviour, and accepts the argument that share prices are governed by price earnings ratios. Investors make money when share prices trade at between six and twenty times a 30-year average of earnings per share, he says. Above that level, and people have a two-thirds chance of losing money over the next ten years.

This seems convincing, but for the fact that stocks have outperformed all other investments in the long run. Concentrating on earnings per share may also be highly misleading. Because, in many countries dividends are taxed twice, many large companies are paying lower dividends and trying to concentrate on improving shareholder value by getting the price up. Jeremy Siegel, author of the book *Stocks for the Long Run*, believes that when you take this into account share prices in the late nineties were not overrated.

I leave you with a comment from John Kay, director of the new Said Business School of Oxford University. Writing in the *Financial Times* he said that investors should not worry unduly about stock market gyrations. Since the First World War, wrote Kay, the equity premium in both Britain and the United States has averaged an astonishing 8 per cent. The equity premium is the difference between the average return on investments in major shares over the return on 'safe' investments, like gilts and bonds.

Henry Ford once said 'history is bunk', but if you believe in history then the stock markets will remain at the heart of sensible investment.

Index

SOMMAIRE

France ■ ■

LE PAYS

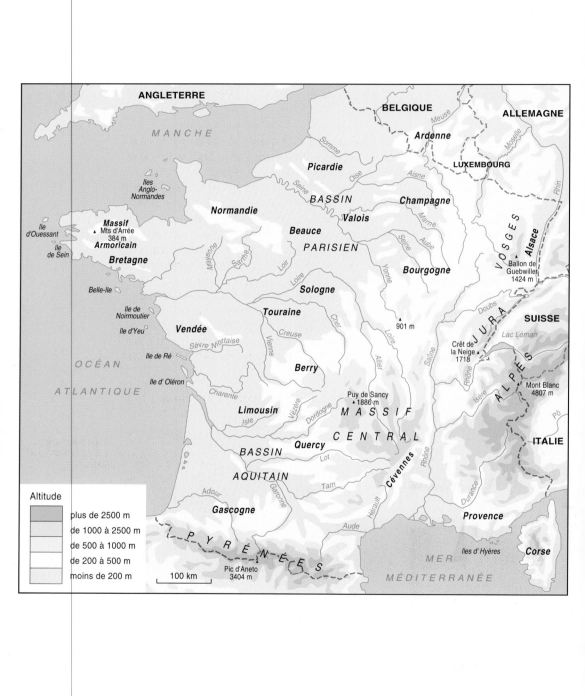

ANGLETERRE

BELGIQUE

ALLEMAGNE

MANCHE

Meuse

Ardenne

LUXEMBOURG

Picardie

Somme

Oise

Aisne

Moselle

Iles Anglo-Normandes

Normandie

Seine

BASSIN

Valois

Champagne

Marne

VOSGES

Alsace

Ile d'Ouessant

Massif
Mts d'Arrée
384 m

Armoricain

Beauce

PARISIEN

Aube

Ballon de Guebwiller
1424 m

Rhin

Ile de Sein

Bretagne

Mayenne

Sarthe

Loir

Loire

Yonne

Seine

Bourgogne

Belle-Ile

Sologne

Doubs

JURA

SUISSE

Ile de Noirmoutier

Touraine

Cher

Loire

901 m

Saône

Lac Léman

Ile d'Yeu

Vendée

Creuse

Vienne

Allier

Crêt de la Neige
1718

Sèvre Niortaise

ALPES

Ile de Ré

Berry

Mont Blanc
4807 m

OCÉAN

Charente

Ile d'Oléron

Isle

Vézère

Dordogne

Puy de Sancy
1886 m

MASSIF

Isère

Pô

ATLANTIQUE

Limousin

CENTRAL

ITALIE

BASSIN

Quercy

Lot

Rhône

Cévennes

AQUITAIN

Tarn

Rhône

Durance

Adour

Garonne

Hérault

Gascogne

Provence

Aude

Iles d'Hyères

Corse

PYRÉNÉES

MER

Pic d'Aneto
3404 m

MÉDITERRANÉE

Altitude

plus de 2500 m
de 1000 à 2500 m
de 500 à 1000 m
de 200 à 500 m
moins de 200 m

100 km

1

Le cadre naturel

La France s'étend sur 550 000 km², ce qui en fait le plus vaste pays d'Europe devant l'Espagne, l'Allemagne et la Suède. Située à l'ouest du continent européen, elle a pour voisins six États : la Belgique et le Luxembourg au nord, l'Allemagne et la Suisse à l'est, l'Italie au sud-est et l'Espagne au sud-ouest. Sa situation géographique lui confère deux atouts essentiels. Placée au cœur de l'Union européenne, elle bénéficie d'abord d'une position de carrefour valorisée par d'excellents réseaux de communications. Par ses régions orientales, la France est liée au vaste espace industriel et urbain qui s'étend de l'embouchure du Rhin à la plaine du Pô. Au nord-ouest, elle est proche des pôles industriels du Royaume-Uni et, au sud, elle s'intègre dans l'arc méditerranéen qui va de la Catalogne à l'Italie centrale. Elle dispose par ailleurs d'une double ouverture maritime, d'une part sur la mer du Nord et la Manche, d'autre part sur l'océan Atlantique et la mer Méditerranée, qui figurent parmi les mers les plus fréquentées du globe. Ces étendues maritimes facilitent les relations avec l'Europe du Nord, l'Amérique et l'Afrique.

Le territoire français, de forme ramassée, s'inscrit dans un hexagone dont les dimensions ne dépassent pas 1 000 km de côté

Le canal de Bourgogne
à La Bussière-sur-Ouche
(Côte-d'Or)

Une grande diversité de paysages

Les falaises d'Étretat
(Seine-Maritime)

Le Cirque de Salazie,
dans l'Ile de la Réunion

Le confluent de la Vienne
et de la Loire
à Candes-Saint-Martin
(Indre-et-Loire)

mais qui offre une exceptionnelle diversité de paysages ; cette situation contribue largement au développement touristique, d'autant que s'y ajoute un riche patrimoine culturel.

Un relief diversifié

À l'ouest d'une diagonale Bayonne-Sedan, les altitudes sont peu élevées, le plus souvent inférieures à 200 mètres. Les plaines et les bas plateaux du Bassin parisien et du Bassin aquitain couvrent la majeure partie du territoire. Ils présentent des altitudes faibles mais des paysages contrastés, en partie liés à leur origine variée. Certaines plaines littorales, comme celles de Flandres, ont été gagnées sur la mer à la suite de leur remblaiement par des dépôts d'origine fluviale ou maritime. Des bas plateaux, comme ceux de Beauce, de Brie et de Picardie, sont d'origine sédimentaire. Ils ont été façonnés dans les calcaires et les argiles déposés au fond des mers lors des ères secondaires et tertiaires. S'ajoutent à cela de belles plaines alluviales comme celles de la Seine et de la Loire. À la périphérie du Bassin parisien, les altitudes se relèvent. C'est le cas au nord, dans les Ardennes, vieux massif hercynien raboté par une longue érosion, au nord-est sur le versant lorrain des Vosges, au sud en bordure du Massif central et à l'ouest dans le Massif armoricain. Il en est de même pour les bordures du Bassin aquitain, au contact du Massif central à l'est et des Pyrénées au sud.

Les terres cultivées
du Lauragais
(Aude)

La moitié sud-est du pays présente des modelés plus accidentés. Les moyennes montagnes présentent des altitudes comprises entre 500 et 1 700 mètres. Certaines d'entre elles sont constituées de vieux massifs hercyniens. C'est le cas des Vosges et du Massif central, basculés lors du soulèvement des chaînes alpines. Ils présentent des sommets aux formes lourdes et des vallées encaissées qui constituent de rudes obstacles aux communications. Le Massif central porte en outre de nombreux volcans aujourd'hui éteints, comme le Cantal et le Puy de Dôme. D'autres massifs anciens moins étendus, comme les Maures et l'Estérel, ravinés par les averses méditerranéennes, offrent des formes plus spectaculaires bien que les sommets ne dépassent pas 900 m. Le Jura constitue aussi, par ses altitudes, une moyenne montagne, mais il s'agit d'un massif récent, formé à l'ère tertiaire. Constitué de roches sédimentaires plissées au sein desquelles abondent les calcaires, il présente des reliefs plus accidentés, marqués par l'alternance de monts et de vaux et par des crêts parfois vertigineux. Les plis sont souvent traversés par des vallées étroites, les cluses, qui constituent des axes de communications privilégiés. Ces paysages de moyenne montagne se retrouvent dans les Préalpes du Nord et du Sud qui offrent des altitudes souvent supérieures à 2 000 m. Les plissements plus violents et l'érosion plus active y ont façonné des reliefs escarpés qui prennent localement l'allure de la haute montagne.

Cette dernière est surtout bien représentée dans les parties centrales des Pyrénées et des Alpes, chaînes dont la formation a commencé il y a plus de 50 millions d'années, à l'ère tertiaire, dans la zone où les plaques de l'écorce terrestre qui portent d'une part l'Europe et d'autre part l'Afrique sont entrées en collision. Ces massifs, qui débordent les limites du territoire national, culminent à de hautes altitudes : les Alpes à 4 807 m au Mont Blanc, les Pyrénées à 3 298 m au Vignemale (3 404 m au pic d'Aneto en Espagne). Ils offrent des reliefs majestueux, en grande partie hérités de l'érosion glaciaire : sommets escarpés, lignes de crêtes déchiquetées et vallées profondes façonnées en auge. Dans la moitié sud-est du pays, toutes ces montagnes, anciennes ou récentes, ne laissent que peu de place aux plaines. Celles-ci s'allongent le long des littoraux comme celles du Languedoc et de Corse orientale, d'autres s'étirent entre les montagnes, comme dans les vallées de la Saône et du Rhône.

La chaîne des Pyrénées
vue des abords
d'Aurignac
(Haute-Garonne)

Quatre fleuves importants drainent le territoire et constituent des axes privilégiés de développement industriel et urbain. La Loire (1 012 km) et la Garonne (575 km) ont un régime assez irrégulier qui les rend inaptes à la navigation moderne, mais leur estuaire abrite des ports actifs comme Nantes-Saint-Nazaire et Bordeaux. Les autres fleuves, bien aménagés et au régime plus régulier, sont de grands axes de circulation. C'est le cas de la Seine (776 km) qui fait de Rouen et du Havre les grands ports de la région parisienne. C'est aussi le fait du Rhône (522 km en France), bien aménagé de Lyon à la mer. Quant au Rhin, qui forme sur 190 km de son cours la frontière franco-allemande, il constitue l'une des principales artères navigables du monde.

La diversité du relief se retrouve sur le littoral. Long de 5 500 km, celui-ci offre des paysages très diversifiés. Les côtes à falaises, souvent rectilignes, bordent la Manche dans les régions de l'Artois, de la Picardie et de la Haute-Normandie. Échancrées de quelques estuaires comme ceux de la Somme et de la Seine, elles reculent sous les effets de l'érosion marine et continentale. Les côtes rocheuses, qui ourlent les massifs anciens et les montagnes jeunes, présentent un tracé plus complexe. La mer y a sculpté des caps et des baies, parfois frangés d'écueils comme en Bretagne, en Provence et à l'ouest de la Corse. Il en résulte un tracé très irrégulier du littoral, favorable à l'implantation des ports mais rendant la navigation délicate. Les plages de sable, quant à elles, bordent les plaines et les bas plateaux, comme en Flandre, dans les Landes, le Languedoc et en Corse orientale. Favorables au tourisme balnéaire, ces côtes rendent difficile la construction de ports. Enfin, les côtes marécageuses, comme en Camargue ou dans le marais poitevin, longtemps hostiles à l'implantation humaine, constituent aujourd'hui des espaces touristiques souvent intégrés dans des parcs naturels.

Des climats tempérés

Située entre 41° et 52° de latitude nord, sur la façade occidentale du continent eurasiatique, la France appartient à la zone tempérée. Elle est le plus souvent placée sous l'influence des vents d'ouest qui apportent des masses d'air maritimes adoucissant le climat des régions littorales et intérieures. Cependant, en hiver, les anticyclones continentaux peuvent faire souffler sur la France des vents froids comme la bise. Au total, le jeu combiné des influences maritimes, de la latitude et de l'altitude contribuent à la diversité climatique du pays.

À l'ouest, le climat océanique domine. Il est marqué par des précipitations régulières et abondantes, apportées par les dépressions atlantiques et qui prennent souvent la forme de fines averses. Ce climat offre des hivers doux, surtout au sud, et des étés frais. Le temps perturbé est le plus fréquent, avec une alternance de ciels nuageux, de pluies et d'éclaircies lumineuses. Vers l'intérieur du pays, ce climat se dégrade. En Lorraine et en Alsace, il revêt des nuances continentales, avec des étés chauds et orageux, des hivers plus froids et des précipitations moins abondantes, en partie concentrées en été sous forme d'orages. Dans les régions du sud-ouest, le climat océanique est marqué par des étés plus chauds et des automnes plus lumineux.

Le littoral breton : le cap de la Chèvre (Finistère)

Le climat méditerranéen domine dans le sud-est du pays et en Corse. Il est marqué par un ciel limpide, des étés chauds et secs et des hivers doux. L'ensoleillement est souvent supérieur à 2 500 heures par an. Les précipitations, concentrées sur le printemps et l'automne, prennent souvent la forme d'averses violentes qui accélèrent l'érosion et provoquent parfois de redoutables inondations. Les vents sont forts, comme le mistral, qui descend la vallée du Rhône, ou la tramontane qui souffle sur le Languedoc. Les gelées comme les chutes de neige sont rares dans les plaines littorales mais le climat se dégrade rapidement sur les montagnes de l'arrière-pays. Le climat méditerranéen est favorable aux cultures délicates comme la vigne et les fruits et surtout au tourisme estival, d'autant que la mer Méditerranée atteint 23 à 25 °C en été le long des côtes.

Enfin, le climat de montagne caractérise les régions élevées. Il est marqué par des températures plus fraîches et des précipitations plus abondantes. En haute montagne, le nombre de jours de gel peut
dépasser 150 par an et le manteau neigeux peut persister durant 6 mois.
Les variations climatiques liées à l'altitude entraînent un étagement de la
végétation. Ainsi, les feuillus laissent progressivement la place aux conifères qui s'effacent à leur tour au profit de la pelouse alpine au-dessus de
2 000 m. De grandes différences apparaissent cependant entre les versants en fonction de leur exposition. Les adrets exposés au sud constituent un cadre privilégié pour l'implantation des villages et des cultures
alors que les ubacs, tournés vers le nord, restent souvent boisés.

Les ressources naturelles

La forêt

Le relief, la géologie et le climat confèrent à la France d'excellentes potentialités agricoles. Les bons sols abondent dans la plupart
des régions, à l'image des terres à limons du Bassin parisien, des sols
bruns des forêts atlantiques ou de la terra rossa des régions méditerranéennes. La France dispose par ailleurs de la première superficie boisée
d'Europe. Celle-ci s'étend sur 16 millions d'hectares, soit 29 % du territoire
national. Bois et forêts ont presque doublé depuis un siècle et ils continuent à progresser depuis la fin de la seconde guerre mondiale, à la
faveur des opérations de reboisement et de la déprise agricole. Les forêts
de feuillus dominent dans les régions de climat océanique. Les chênes privilégient les régions bien ensoleillées alors que les
hêtres préfèrent les régions plus humides et plus
fraîches. Dans les régions méditerranéennes, l'adaptation à la sécheresse estivale favorise les espèces à
feuilles persistantes. Parmi les feuillus, le chêne-vert
se développe sur les sols calcaires et le chêne-liège
sur les sols siliceux. Les conifères sont surtout représentés par le pin maritime, le pin d'Alep et le pin lari-
cio. Dans les forêts de montagne, les feuillus
occupent les vallées et les bas versants. Ils cèdent
progressivement la place aux conifères, plus résistants au froid hivernal, dès que l'altitude augmente.
Parmi ces conifères, le sapin et l'épicéa dominent
dans les montagnes humides comme les Vosges, le
Jura et les Alpes du Nord. Dans les régions sèches
comme les Alpes du Sud, en revanche, les mélèzes,
qui perdent leurs aiguilles en hiver, constituent l'essentiel de la couverture forestière. En dépit de son
étendue, la forêt française ne livre que 33 millions de
m³ de bois par an. Cette production ne suffit pas aux
besoins du pays et la balance commerciale du bois

**Forêt de hêtres
dans les Vosges**

et des produits dérivés enregistre un déficit annuel de plus de 16 milliards de francs (2,6 milliards de dollars). Cette déficience s'explique en partie par l'extrême morcellement des forêts. En effet, l'État et les communes ne contrôlent que 4 millions d'hectares, surtout situés dans le Bassin parisien, la vallée de la Loire et le nord-est du pays. Ces forêts sont gérées par l'Office national des forêts et remarquablement exploitées. Il n'en est pas de même des 11 millions d'hectares restants, qui sont entre les mains de 3,7 millions de propriétaires privés dont les deux tiers possèdent moins d'un hectare. Ces petites propriétés sont souvent peu productives.

La pêche

Avec des livraisons annuelles d'environ 850 000 tonnes, la France se place au quatrième rang de l'Union européenne derrière le Danemark, l'Espagne et le Royaume-Uni. La pêche artisanale rassemble la majeure partie des effectifs. Pratiquée sur des bateaux de petite taille à proximité des côtes, elle est très active en Bretagne et en Méditerranée. Livrant des poissons frais, cette pêche connaît un regain d'activité depuis quelques années. La pêche industrielle, qui mobilise des bateaux de gros tonnage dotés d'équipements sophistiqués pour la recherche du poisson et sa conservation, anime les grands ports spécialisés comme Boulogne, Lorient et Concarneau. Ces navires effectuent le plus souvent des sorties d'une ou deux semaines, mais certaines campagnes, pratiquées au large de l'Afrique ou de l'Amérique tropicale, peuvent durer plusieurs mois.

La pêche française connaît depuis deux décennies de graves difficultés. Les prises stagnent et le déficit commercial se creuse, dépassant désormais les 11 milliards de francs annuels (1,8 milliard de dollars). L'effectif des marins-pêcheurs, aujourd'hui de 16 500, a été divisé par deux depuis 1970 et il en a été de même pour la flotte qui ne compte plus que 6 500 unités. Les problèmes tiennent à l'épuisement des ressources, à la pollution de certaines eaux littorales et à une concurrence accrue émanant des pays industriels comme de ceux du tiers monde. Par ailleurs, la mise en place de la zone économique exclusive de 200 milles a privé les navires français de certains champs de pêche traditionnels, ce qui les a conduits à se diriger vers les eaux froides de l'océan Arctique et de l'Atlantique Nord et vers les eaux tropicales de l'Atlantique. L'adoption en 1983 d'une politique européenne de la pêche a permis de mettre en place un certain nombre de mécanismes visant à éviter l'épuisement des champs de pêche communautaires, à régulariser le marché du poisson, à financer la restructuration des flottes et à conclure des accords avec des pays tiers. L'État lui-même a adopté des mesures financières pour atténuer la crise sociale qui a

**Le port de Binic
(Côtes-d'Armor)**

touché les ports bretons en 1993 et 1994. Par ailleurs, l'aquaculture connaît un essor remarquable. Les huîtres sont surtout produites sur les littoraux charentais, bretons et normands, ainsi que dans le bassin d'Arcachon. Les moules proviennent de la baie de l'Aiguillon, de la rade de Brest et la baie du Mont Saint-Michel. Les productions se diversifient depuis deux décennies avec la mise en place de nombreux élevages, comme ceux de saumons et de truites de mer en Bretagne ou de bars dans l'étang de Thau, sur la côte languedocienne.

Les ressources énergétiques et minérales

Si le sous-sol français fournit en abondance des matériaux de construction (gravier, sable, calcaire pour les cimenteries) et des matières premières (kaolin, talc, soufre, sel, potasse), il est pauvre en produits énergétiques et en minerais. La production de houille est en recul constant (8 millions de tonnes en 1997) et toutes les mines doivent fermer avant 2005. Les ressources en hydrocarbures sont encore plus limitées (2,1 millions de tonnes de pétrole et 2,9 millions de m^3 de gaz naturel) et couvrent moins de 5 % des besoins nationaux. Le pays est mieux pourvu en uranium, avec une production annuelle de près de 1 000 tonnes. La France dispose aussi d'un bon potentiel hydroélectrique, mais l'équipement du pays est achevé. Quant aux énergies d'appoint, elles n'assurent encore que 1,8 % de la consommation nationale. En ce qui concerne les minerais métalliques, seul le nickel de Nouvelle-Calédonie est abondant. Le minerai de fer lorrain a vu son exploitation cesser, faute d'une rentabilité suffisante, et tous les autres minerais doivent être importés.

Les terres lointaines

Outre ses quatre-vingt-seize départements métropolitains, la France compte quelques terres dispersées dans toutes les régions de la planète. Héritées de son passé colonial et des périples accomplis par ses explorateurs, ces régions couvrent environ 120 000 km^2. Si elles ne rassemblent que 1,5 million d'habitants, elles contribuent à la présence de la France sur tous les océans, fournissent des boissons et des fruits tropicaux ainsi que des minerais. Elles offrent aussi un potentiel touristique remarquable et confèrent à la métropole un vaste espace maritime. En effet, dans le cadre de la « zone économique exclusive » définie par le nouveau droit de la mer, dont la Convention a été signée en 1982, elles représentent le troisième domaine maritime du monde, après ceux des États-Unis et du Royaume-Uni. Il s'étend sur 10,2 millions de km^2 et offre des ressources biologiques variées, mais aussi des réserves énergétiques et minérales, à l'image des nodules polymétalliques qui tapissent certaines parties du plateau continental bordant ces îles.

Ces France lointaines sont d'abord constituées par quatre départements d'outre-mer, ou DOM, situés dans des régions tropicales. Trois d'entre eux, la Guadeloupe et la Martinique dans les Antilles, et la

Réunion dans l'océan Indien, sont des îles montagneuses. Les volcans, éteints comme la Montagne Pelée à la Martinique, ou encore actifs comme la Soufrière à la Guadeloupe ou la Fournaise à la Réunion, accaparent une large partie du territoire. Ils ne laissent aux plaines que de modestes superficies. Les côtes sont souvent très découpées. Elles sont constituées de falaises, de plages de sable noir d'origine volcanique ou de sable blanc dans les zones alluviales. Quelques-unes sont frangées de récifs coralliens. Dans ces îles le climat tropical, marqué par des températures toujours supérieures à 20 °C, est surtout caractérisé par l'alternance entre une saison humide d'été et une saison sèche d'hiver. Les versants « au vent » exposés au souffle des alizés enregistrent d'abondantes précipitations alors que les versants « sous le vent », abrités derrière les hauteurs, apparaissent plus secs et plus favorables au tourisme. Ces îles sont parfois soumises en fin d'été au passage de redoutables tempêtes tropicales ou de cyclones qui occasionnent de graves dégâts.

La Guyane, en Amérique du Sud, est un département d'outre-mer ponctué de collines de moins de 600 m d'altitude et presque totalement recouvertes par la dense forêt amazonienne dont la croissance est favorisée par la chaleur constante et la forte humidité. Cette forêt, qui abrite un grand nombre d'essences, reste difficilement pénétrable et exploitable et peu peuplée. Près de la côte, bordée de mangrove, se dresse le site spatial de Kourou utilisé pour le lancement des fusées Ariane.

La France compte aussi quatre territoires d'outre-mer, ou TOM. Parmi ces derniers, trois sont situés dans le Pacifique. La Nouvelle-Calédonie est une longue île montagneuse entourée d'une barrière de corail et bordée des îles Loyauté, petites îles basses. Le climat d'alizé est favorable à la végétation, très diversifiée, et au développement du tourisme. La Polynésie française rassemble plus de 150 îles ou îlots volcaniques et atolls coralliens. Wallis et Futuna sont également deux îles volcaniques, tout comme les Terres australes, situées dans l'océan Antarctique. Constituées par les îles de Crozet, de la Nouvelle-Amsterdam, de Saint-Paul et de Kerguelen, elles sont soumises à de violentes tempêtes et servent surtout de bases scientifiques. Il en est de même de la terre Adélie, portion de l'inlandsis antarctique. S'ajoutent à cela les collectivités territoriales de Mayotte, dans l'océan Indien et de Saint-Pierre-et-Miquelon, dans l'océan Atlantique, au large du Canada. Ce dernier archipel vit avant tout de la pêche.

Pour en savoir plus :

R. Brunet, F. Auriac (sous la dir. de), *Atlas de France* (14 vol.), tome 6 : *Milieux et ressources*, Reclus-La Documentation française, 1995.

F. Damette, J. Scheibling, *La France, permanences et mutations*, Hachette, collection Carré géographie, 1995.

J. Martin, L. Pernet et al., *Géographie*, Hachette, 1991.

Ph. Pinchemel, *La France*, 2 vol., A. Colin, 1992.

D. Pumain, Th. Saint-Julien, *La France*, Géographie universelle Belin-Reclus, tome 2, 1990.

La métropole, les départements d'outre-mer (DOM), les territoires d'outre-mer (TOM) et les collectivités territoriales à statut particulier : des terrres réparties sous toutes les latitudes

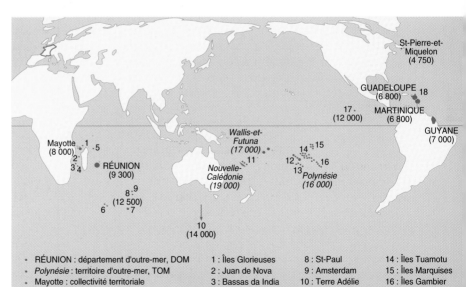

St-Pierre-et-Miquelon (4 750)

GUADELOUPE (6 800) 18

MARTINIQUE (6 800)

17 (12 000)

GUYANE (7 000)

Mayotte (8 000) 1 5

2 3 4

RÉUNION (9 300)

Wallis-et-Futuna (17 000)

Nouvelle-Calédonie (19 000)

11

14 15 12 16 13 Polynésie (16 000)

8 9 (12 500) 6 7

10 (14 000)

- RÉUNION : département d'outre-mer, DOM
- *Polynésie* : territoire d'outre-mer, TOM
- Mayotte : collectivité territoriale

(12 000) : distance de Paris, en km

1 : Îles Glorieuses
2 : Juan de Nova
3 : Bassas da India
4 : Europa
5 : Tromelin
6 : Îles Crozet
7 : Îles Kerguelen

8 : St-Paul
9 : Amsterdam
10 : Terre Adélie
11 : Îles Loyauté
12 : Tahiti et Îles de la Société
13 : Îles Tubuai

14 : Îles Tuamotu
15 : Îles Marquises
16 : Îles Gambier
17 : Clipperton
18 : St-Martin et St-Barthélémy

La protection de l'environnement

En France, comme dans la plupart des pays développés, une véritable politique de l'environnement ne s'est développée que depuis un quart de siècle. La France est cependant l'un des premiers pays à avoir créé, le 27 janvier 1971, un ministère de la Protection de la nature et de l'Environnement, simplement chargé alors de coordonner les efforts des autres ministères. Auparavant, quelques mesures avaient témoigné de l'intérêt porté à ces questions, comme le montrent la loi de 1960 créant les parcs nationaux et la loi sur l'eau de 1964, très en avance sur son temps, comportant des mécanismes d'incitation financière fondés sur le principe pollueur-payeur.

De 1970 à 1990, la politique française en matière d'environnement a surtout consisté à mettre en place une réglementation et des institutions spécialisées concernant la récupération et l'élimination des déchets (1976), la qualité de l'air (1981) et la maîtrise de l'énergie (1982), institutions regroupées depuis 1990 au sein de l'Agence de l'environnement et de la maîtrise de l'énergie (ADEME). À l'issue de ces vingt années, un Plan national pour l'environnement a été débattu par le Parlement et approuvé par le gouvernement à la fin de l'année 1990.

Des crédits en essor

En 1999, le ministère de l'Environnement et de l'Aménagement du Territoire compte près de 2 550 agents répartis entre une administration centrale et des services déconcentrés. Son budget approche les 4 milliards de francs (666 millions de dollars), soit une remarquable progression de 110 % par rapport à 1998. Une dotation nouvelle de 500 millions de francs (83,3 millions de dollars) est affectée à l'ADEME, chargée de relancer la politique de maîtrise de l'énergie et de développement des énergies renouvelables. Le budget alloué à la protection de l'environnement bénéficie également de la création de la taxe générale sur les activités polluantes ; en revanche, il n'inclut pas les crédits consacrés à l'environnement par les autres administrations, les établissements publics et les collectivités locales, qui dépassent 80 milliards de francs (13,3 milliards de dollars). La part la plus importante (plus de 65 milliards de francs) de cette dépense publique provient des collectivités locales, notamment des communes qui constituent, à côté de l'État, le niveau essentiel quant à la gestion des problèmes d'environnement en France. Si l'on ajoute les dépenses des industries et des ménages, la dépense nationale consacrée à l'environnement dépasse 150 milliards de francs (25 milliards de dollars). L'arsenal législatif et réglementaire dont dispose le pays est relativement complet. La création, en mars 1993, du Comité interministériel pour l'environnement permet de faire valoir davantage le souci de la protection de l'environnement dans tous les services de l'État. Une autre avancée est liée à la création, en 1991, de vingt-six directions régionales de l'environnement (DIREN), dont quatre dans les départements d'outre-mer, qui servent d'interlocuteurs aux acteurs locaux de l'environnement.

Le ministère de l'Environnement et de l'Aménagement du territoire privilégie la concertation plutôt que la répression et met plus l'accent sur la prévention que sur la réparation des dommages. Les collectivités locales ont un rôle fondamental à jouer depuis la loi de 1983 sur la décentralisation des compétences en matière d'urbanisme. Alimentation en eau potable, assainissement, occupation des sols, ramassage et traitement des déchets ménagers, circulation des véhicules, sont ainsi placés sous la responsabilité du maire. De plus en plus de villes se sont dotées de services spécialisés : plus d'une centaine d'entre elles ont élaboré un plan municipal d'environnement ou ont conclu une charte pour l'environnement afin de parvenir à une gestion globale, s'inscrivant dans le cadre d'un développement durable. Quant aux citoyens, ils se sont également mobilisés. Environ 40 000 associations ont été créées ces quinze dernières années (1 500 semblent réellement actives) pour défendre le cadre de vie, la nature et le patrimoine. Grâce au décret du 7 juillet 1977, les associations reconnues par les autorités sont considérées comme des partenaires officiels de la politique de l'État, qui leur attribue des subventions. En vingt ans, leur position s'est plutôt assouplie. D'une position défensive, elles se sont orientées vers une politique de dialogue.

L'action internationale de la France

Au cours des dernières années, la protection de l'environnement est apparue comme une nécessité qui dépasse les frontières d'un État pour atteindre, parfois, une dimension planétaire. Cette prise de conscience a donné lieu à de nombreux traités, directives et conventions. La France est engagée dans plus d'une centaine de ces textes conclus dans le cadre européen et dans une trentaine à l'échelle mondiale. De plus, elle a joué un rôle moteur dans bien des négociations. C'est notamment le cas pour l'adoption par 24 États, le 11 mars 1989, de la déclaration de La Haye sur la protection de l'atmosphère et pour la création, en 1990, d'un Fonds pour l'environnement mondial, destiné à aider les pays moins favorisés. La France a aussi proposé que l'Antarctique soit considéré comme une réserve naturelle et une terre à vocation scientifique et que, en outre, un sanctuaire pour les baleines soit créé autour de l'Antarctique. Par ailleurs, Paris a accueilli, le 16 juillet 1989, le quinzième Sommet des pays industrialisés accordant à l'environnement une place primordiale et la France a participé active-

ment à la deuxième Confé-
rence des Nations unies sur
l'environnement et le développement de Rio de Janeiro, en
juin 1992. Elle a ratifié les deux
conventions sur le climat et sur
la biodiversité, respectivement
en janvier et juin 1994, et signé
la Convention sur la désertification adoptée à l'issue de négociations qui se sont déroulées à
Paris, en octobre 1994. La
France a lancé un programme
en faveur des énergies renouvelables en Afrique, afin de
réduire l'impact de la déforestation. En mars 1998, une conférence inter-
nationale consacrée à l'eau et au développement durable a accueilli à Paris les représentants de 84 pays. Au cours des sommets internatio-naux de Rio (1992), New York (1997) et Kyoto (1997), la France s'est engagée à promouvoir le développement durable.

En organisant à Paris la conférence « Eau et développement durable », la France entend mobiliser la communauté internationale sur la gestion des ressources en eau, Unesco, mars 1998

Par ailleurs, la prise en compte à moyen et long terme d'un modèle de croissance économisant les ressources naturelles et protégeant la qualité de l'environnement et de la santé est élevée au rang des politiques communes (comme la politique agricole) par le Traité d'Amsterdam, dont l'article 6 souligne la nécessité afin de préser-ver l'avenir des générations futures.

La protection de l'atmosphère

Le tramway de Strasbourg (Bas-Rhin) : un mode de transport en commun non polluant

Afin d'apporter sa contribution à l'effort de mobilisation mondiale, la France a mis en place, dès 1990, une Mission interministérielle de l'effet de serre. Ne disposant pas de res-sources appréciables en éner-gie fossile, la France a fondé sa politique de l'énergie sur un important programme électro-nucléaire, qui soulève notam-ment la question des déchets mais qui lui a permis de réduire d'un tiers ses émissions de gaz carbonique entre 1980 et 1988. Depuis lors, le développement

des transports a contrarié ce processus de réduction mais, avec 1,9 tonne par an et par habitant, la France reste, parmi les pays industrialisés, celui qui rejette le moins de dioxyde de carbone (CO_2). En ce qui concerne la protection de la couche d'ozone, la France a participé activement aux négociations du protocole de Montréal, ratifié en janvier 1989, qui prévoyait initialement d'éliminer totalement les chlorofluorocarbures (CFC) d'ici le 1er janvier 2000. Depuis lors, la France et ses partenaires européens ont surenchéri en optant pour le 1er janvier 1995. S'agissant de la pollution locale, on note une diminution des émissions de dioxyde de soufre (SO_2) et une stabilisation de la pollution par le plomb, mais une augmentation ponctuelle de la concentration en oxydes d'azote, liée à la circulation automobile. Le contrôle plus strict des véhicules anciens, l'encouragement du gouvernement à éliminer les plus vieux d'entre eux par une prime à la casse et l'usage du pot catalytique, obligatoire sur les voitures neuves depuis le 1er janvier 1993, associé à l'usage d'essence sans plomb, n'ont pas suffi. C'est pourquoi des recherches sont en cours pour trouver des carburants de substitution moins polluants, tel le gaz naturel ou liquéfié. Par ailleurs, le développement de la voiture électrique a été relancé. Sur le territoire français, environ 1 500 établissements sont soumis à une taxe spécifique et proportionnelle aux quantités de polluants atmosphériques rejetés, les fonds collectés servant à mettre au point des techniques de dépollution et de réduction des rejets ainsi qu'à financer la surveillance de la qualité de l'air. Pour contrôler la pollution de l'air dans les villes, la France a, en effet, mis en place un système original. Gérés par des associations regroupant l'ensemble des partenaires locaux impliqués, une trentaine de réseaux de mesures automatiques sont implantés sur le territoire, prêts à donner l'alerte en cas de dépassement des normes.

Borne de recharge des voitures électriques à La Rochelle (Charente-Maritime). En l'an 2000, il y aura environ 100 000 véhicules électriques immatriculés en France

La lutte contre la pollution de l'air

Les usines ayant été modernisées et les chauffages utilisant de plus en plus le gaz naturel, la pollution de l'air résulte essentiellement des émissions de gaz des véhicules et de l'augmentation du trafic automobile. Pour lutter contre ces émanations, les pouvoirs publics ont multiplié les initiatives. La loi du 30 décembre 1996 sur la qualité de l'air et l'utilisation rationnelle de l'énergie fixe un certain nombre de mesures pour que tout habitant du pays puisse « respirer un air qui ne nuise pas à sa santé ». Lorsque le seuil d'alerte est atteint, le public en est informé et des mesures de restriction de la circulation et de l'activité industrielle sont prises. Elles peuvent aller jusqu'à l'interdiction de circuler pour les véhicules non munis d'une pastille verte. Cette dernière est réservée aux véhicules peu polluants fonctionnant à l'électricité ou au gaz, ou encore munis d'un pot catalytique. Le réseau de surveillance de l'air, actuellement surtout implanté dans les principales agglomérations, à l'image d'Airparif qui dispose d'une trentaine de stations de surveillance dans la capitale, sera étendu à tout le territoire.

L'eau : une ressource à préserver

Comparée à bien d'autres pays, la France est favorisée par l'abondance de ses ressources en eau. Cependant ces dernières, inégalement réparties sur le territoire, sont fragiles. Pour gérer ce patrimoine, évalué à 1 000 milliards de m³, une organisation originale a été mise en place il y a une trentaine d'années : les Agences de l'eau. Au nombre de six pour couvrir chacun des grands bassins hydrographiques, ces organismes publics, placés sous le contrôle du ministère de l'Environnement et de l'Aménagement du territoire, sont financièrement autonomes. Ils perçoivent une redevance auprès des usagers, proportionnelle aux quantités d'eau prélevées ou à la pollution rejetée. Ces fonds sont ensuite redistribués sous forme de prêts ou de subventions pour aider, par exemple, un industriel à construire ou à améliorer une station de traitement d'effluents. Bien que cette politique soit fondée sur le principe pollueur-payeur,

Le « Silure », le bateau-nettoyeur de la Seine, à Paris

les Agences de l'eau ont toujours privilégié la concertation, grâce notamment à l'existence d'un Comité de bassin. Celui-ci joue, au sein de chaque agence, le rôle d'un Parlement de l'eau où tous les acteurs concernés peuvent s'exprimer. La loi sur l'eau de 1964 a été revue en janvier 1992 ; elle renforce le rôle des collectivités locales, notamment pour entretenir les cours d'eau, et affirme un principe essentiel : l'eau fait désormais partie du patrimoine commun de la nation. Le but poursuivi est de restaurer la qualité des cours d'eau, soit 277 000 km de ruisseaux, fleuves et rivières. Grâce au rôle actif des Agences de l'eau, des progrès réels ont été accomplis par les industriels ; en vingt ans, ils ont réduit leurs rejets de plus de 70 %. L'un des objectifs visé par le gouvernement consiste à supprimer totalement les rejets toxiques avant la fin du siècle.

Les nappes d'eau souterraines ne sont pas épargnées par la pollution dans les régions d'agriculture intensive. Un programme national vise à mobiliser les agriculteurs, remettant en cause certaines pratiques comme l'épandage inconsidéré de lisier de porc ou l'apport surabondant d'engrais dans les champs. Quant à la pollution domestique, la France s'est engagée, dans le cadre de la directive européenne de 1991, à achever la collecte et le traitement des eaux usées d'ici 2005 au plus tard. La relance de la politique de l'eau est une priorité pour la France. Depuis 1992, les aides et les investissements ont été considérablement augmentés.

Les eaux maritimes sont également concernées par la lutte contre la pollution, qu'elle soit d'origine agricole, urbaine, industrielle ou qu'elle résulte d'une catastrophe maritime. Chaque année, les plages situées le long des 5 500 km du littoral français attirent des millions de touristes. La surveillance des eaux de baignade est effective dans plus de 700 communes balnéaires. Tout au long de l'année,

Le Conservatoire de l'espace littoral et des rivages lacustres, un acteur efficace

Fleuron méconnu du ministère de l'Environnement et de l'Aménagement du territoire, le Conservatoire de l'espace littoral et des rivages lacustres est un établissement public administratif. Créé en 1975, il a réussi, en une vingtaine d'années d'existence, à préserver de l'urbanisation, de l'industrialisation et de l'agriculture intensive 10 % du littoral national. Ceci, sans pour autant transformer en musée figé les 360 sites ainsi protégés, qui représentent près de 50 000 hectares, sur 650 km de côtes. Parmi les grands lacs concernés figurent les lacs d'Annecy, de Grandlieu, de la forêt d'Orient... et le Léman. Car une fois acquis par le Conservatoire, les terrains sont confiés aux communes ou aux départements afin que ces paysages préservés profitent au plus grand nombre. Le Conservatoire fonctionne depuis ses origines comme une agence foncière : ses délégués régionaux sillonnent leur territoire, localisent des terrains intéressants pour leurs qualités écologiques ou paysagères, les préemptent, font des offres d'achat, s'efforcent de convaincre les élus locaux de l'intérêt de «geler» ces espaces naturels, enfin négocient avec des mécènes pour boucler leur budget.

L'établissement public est habilité à recevoir des dons et des legs, mais trouve l'essentiel de ses ressources auprès de l'État. Le budget d'investissement est d'environ 130 millions de francs (28 millions de dollars), dont une partie est consacrée aux travaux d'aménagement et de remise en état des sites acquis : ouverture de sentiers, fixation des dunes et reboisement. Le Conservatoire vise, à terme, la protection de 25 % du littoral français. La marque laissée sur les paysages par les générations précédentes est inestimable. Certains d'entre eux figurent au patrimoine mondial de l'Unesco. C'est le cas d'une vingtaine de sites dont le Mont Saint-Michel.

plus de 20 000 prélèvements effectués en mer sont analysés pour vérifier que les normes édictées par une directive européenne ne soient pas dépassées, chaque campagne annuelle donnant lieu à la publication d'un palmarès avant la saison estivale. Parallèlement au développement des stations d'épuration des villes côtières, les bilans de santé des plages se sont considérablement améliorés puisque plus de 85 % des points de surveillance répondent aux normes. Par ailleurs, le Conservatoire de l'espace littoral et des rivages lacustres a pour vocation de protéger le patrimoine inestimable que constituent les paysages des côtes françaises. L'action de cet établissement public, dont la création remonte à 1975, consiste à acquérir des terrains situés en bord de mer ou autour des grands lacs et plans d'eau afin de préserver le caractère naturel de ces sites dans leur intégrité et leur diversité. S'il n'était pas envisageable de figer les paysages et les activités sur tout le littoral français, des mesures de protection particulières ont été prises. Ainsi, la loi sur le littoral du 3 janvier 1986, renforcée en 1989, a pour but de freiner ou d'empêcher les aménagements dans les espaces définis comme remarquables au sein de plus de 1 100 communes.

La protection de la nature et des paysages

La diversité des milieux naturels se traduit par une grande richesse de la flore et de la faune sauvage. La France a adopté une loi sur la protection de la nature dès 1976. Depuis 1982, plus de 14 000 espaces, répertoriés sous le nom de Zones naturelles d'intérêt écologique faunistique et floristique (ZNIEFF), ont été identifiés et étudiés, la majeure partie se situant dans des zones humides ou dans des forêts. Pour répondre à la nouvelle directive européenne (directive Habitat), adoptée le 21 mai 1992, sur la conservation des habitats naturels, de la faune et de la flore sauvages, la France complète ce premier recueil de données. D'ici à 2004, le réseau Natura 2000 regroupera tous les sites intéressants et assurera la conservation de la biodiversité au sein de l'Europe. Certaines espèces menacées demandent des mesures de protection particulières. Ainsi le saumon atlantique, qui avait totalement disparu de la plupart des rivières, réapparaît grâce à la restauration des zones de reproduction, à la construction de passes à poissons et à la réintroduction d'alevins. Une charte a été signée en 1994 par le ministre de l'Environnement et les maires des communes concernées pour tenter de protéger les derniers ours des Pyrénées. Leur réintroduction progressive est également prévue. La nouvelle loi du 8 janvier 1993 sur la protection et la mise en valeur des paysages permettra, notamment, de revoir les abords des villes, souvent défigurés par la disposition anarchique de panneaux d'affichage, d'usines ou de supermarchés, ou encore d'enfouir dans un certain nombre de sites les lignes électriques et, d'une façon plus générale, de prendre en compte le paysage dans sa globalité. Le problème le plus crucial pour l'avenir est celui des campagnes. Une agriculture de plus en plus industrialisée et un exode rural continu ont des conséquences dommageables sur l'entretien des paysages ruraux traditionnels. Il faut donc trouver rapidement des solutions pour sauver ce patrimoine.

Les parcs nationaux, dont la partie centrale est inhabitée, restent les fleurons du dispositif de protection des espaces naturels. Il en existe six en France métropolitaine et un en Guadeloupe. Six autres sont à l'état de projet, notamment dans le massif du Mont-Blanc, en Corse, en Bretagne et en Guyane. Ces parcs couvrent au total 992 000 hectares, dont 371 000 de zone dite centrale, sous haute protection. Alors que les parcs nationaux, à l'exception de l'île de Port-Cros, sont situés dans des massifs montagneux, les parcs naturels régionaux, au nombre d'une trentaine, sont répartis sur l'ensemble du territoire : monts d'Arrée, ballons d'Alsace, Camargue, Brenne, Lubéron... Ils couvrent 5 020 000 hectares et concernent 2 600 communes et près de 2 millions d'habitants, et plus d'une dizaine d'autres sont en projet. Dotés d'une législation plus souple que celle des parcs nationaux, ces parcs régionaux sont certes voués à la protection de l'environnement, mais aussi au développement équilibré des différentes activités économiques. Il existe enfin de nombreuses réserves naturelles qui appartiennent à l'État, aux communes ou encore à des propriétaires privés. Elles constituent parfois le dernier refuge d'espèces menacées. Il existe aujourd'hui 132 réserves naturelles et une quarantaine sont à l'état de projet. Parmi les plus connues figurent celles des Aiguilles Rouges dans les Alpes et du Banc d'Arguin dans le bassin d'Arcachon.

La politique des déchets

Dans tous les pays industrialisés, la quantité de déchets, ordures ménagères ou déchets industriels, ne cesse d'augmenter. Chaque année, la France produit plus de 24 millions de tonnes d'ordures ménagères. La production globale a plus que doublé en trente ans pour atteindre aujourd'hui 416 kilos en moyenne par personne et par an. La part des grosses agglomérations est beaucoup plus lourde que celle des communes rurales. La majeure partie de ces ordures aboutit, après compactage dans la plupart des cas, dans des décharges. Depuis le 1er juillet 1992, celles-ci n'acceptent que les résidus ultimes qui n'auront pu être valorisés ou recyclés par les usines d'incinération : cendres volantes et résidus d'épuration des fumées, très chargés en métaux lourds et polluants divers. En moyenne, 30 000 tonnes par jour d'ordures ménagères sont brûlées dans près de trois cents incinérateurs dispersés sur le territoire français. Dans les plus grosses usines d'incinération, le potentiel énergétique est récupéré sous forme de chaleur et d'électricité, dans le cadre de la cogénération. Le but est de produire moins de déchets à la source et de valoriser ou de recycler ceux qui subsistent. Le tri des ordures domestiques par les ménages devient une priorité. Un grand nombre de communes a adopté des poubelles spécifiques ou de gros conteneurs qui servent à séparer papier, verre, voire aluminium, fer blanc, plastiques et huiles de vidange usagées, des autres déchets. Outre le plastique, c'est le recyclage du verre qui a obtenu, en France, les meilleurs résultats. La quantité de verre récupéré a plus que doublé en l'espace de quinze ans, atteignant 35 % aujourd'hui. Depuis le 1er janvier 1993, les industriels sont obligés de contribuer à financer ou d'assurer l'élimination des emballages qu'ils lancent sur le marché. L'objectif consiste à en recycler 75 % d'ici à 2002. La loi du 13 juillet 1992 qui contraint, à compter de 1996, chaque département à élaborer un plan d'élimination des déchets ménagers, concerne aussi les déchets de l'industrie. Ces derniers représentent quelque 150 millions de tonnes. 100 millions de tonnes peuvent servir de remblais, 40 autres sont considérés comme des résidus banals assi-milables aux ordures ména-gères et le reste contient des polluants toxiques ou dange-reux. Les déchets spéciaux suivent différentes filières d'éli-mination. Ils sont incinérés ou subissent des traitements phy-sico-chimiques de détoxication ou sont, c'est le cas pour la moi-tié d'entre eux, enfouis dans une des onze décharges contrôlées qui leur sont réservées. À partir de 2002, seuls les déchets ultimes pourront y être stockés. La nouvelle réglemen-tation a prévu la création, sur chaque site de traitement ou de stockage de déchets, d'une commission locale d'information et de surveillance, à laquelle participent riverains et associations. Malgré ces dispositions, il existe encore d'anciens dépôts clandestins. La nouvelle réglementa-tion condamne ces pratiques, ainsi que les importations d'ordures ménagères destinées à la mise en décharge. Le contrôle des transferts transfrontaliers de déchets a d'ailleurs été sérieusement renforcé. Enfin, le 1er avril 1993, une taxe sur la mise en décharge des produits ména-gers et assimilés a été imposée et la loi du 2 février 1995 instaure une autre taxe sur les traitements ou la mise en décharge des déchets industriels spéciaux.

Chaque personne en France produit annuellement, en moyenne, 416 kilos d'ordures ménagères, ce qui rend nécessaire le tri des ordures comme ici, à Clermont-Ferrand (Puy-de-Dôme)

La lutte constante contre la pollution des sols

La pollution des sols est provoquée par des agents très variés, qu'il s'agisse d'éléments-traces, constitués de métaux, de métal-loïdes ou de micropolluants organiques, ou bien de produits phytosani-taires, d'hydrocarbures ou de produits radioactifs. Les métaux les plus dangereux à terme sont le mercure, le plomb, le cadmium, le nickel et le chrome. Les insecticides, les herbicides, les fongicides et les bactéri-cides, dont l'emploi s'est généralisé dans l'agriculture, occasionnent aussi de graves dégâts. La présence de polluants dans les sols entraîne des dommages à la végétation et une concentration d'éléments toxiques dans les végétaux ; c'est la bio-accumulation, redoutable pour l'homme. Les produits chimiques peuvent aussi entraîner dans les sols la corrosion de structures enterrées.

Les régions minières, les régions d'agriculture intensive, les prés et les terres labourées proches des autoroutes, ainsi que les terrains d'épandage des effluents agro-industriels ou des composts urbains figurent parmi les sites les plus touchés. En 1998, l'inventaire du ministère de l'Environnement et de l'Aménagement du territoire recense 896 sites pollués. Depuis 1994, 123 sites ont été traités et 226 nouveaux autres ont été identifiés. Les grandes régions industrielles, notamment le Nord-Pas-de-Calais, l'Ile-de-France et Rhône-Alpes, recensent la majeure partie des espaces concernés.

Les sites pollués par des activités industrielles ont donné lieu au développement de procédés spécifiques de dépollution. Certains conduisent à la mise en sécurité des substances polluantes par confinement à l'intérieur de barrières étanches. Cette technique ne supprime par les déchets, mais empêche leur migration dans le milieu naturel. La véritable dépollution conduit, quant à elle, à l'élimination des substances polluantes. Les produits toxiques sont traités sur le site ou transportés dans des centres spécialisés. *In situ*, le traitement se fait selon des procédés variés : par incinération pour les hydrocarbures, par lavage des sols pollués par des substances minérales, par volatilisation des déchets ou encore par voie biologique pour des pollutions dues à des produits organiques. L'Agence de l'environnement et de la maîtrise de l'énergie (ADEME) est acteur dans tous ces domaines.

Économie, recherche et développement

Le rôle de l'environnement vient d'être pris en compte dans le plan de relance de l'activité du pays. La France consacre globalement plus de 1 % de son produit intérieur brut à la protection de l'environnement. Les industriels ont été conduits à intégrer des plans environnement dans leur stratégie. Le véritable progrès ne consiste pas seulement à dépolluer, c'est-à-dire à installer des filtres, des dépoussiéreurs ou des stations d'épuration, mais à adopter une technologie propre. L'ADEME, qui dispose d'un budget de 1,1 milliard de francs pour ses interventions, a consacré à cet objectif une partie de ses crédits. Les produits eux-mêmes doivent devenir des éco-produits ne polluant ni durant leur production, ni durant leur utilisation, ni au moment de leur destruction. Créé en 1991, le label français NF Environnement englobe jusqu'à la matière première et exige un écobilan préalable, sorte d'inventaire des conséquences du produit sur l'environnement. Le chiffre d'affaires annuel des éco-industries dépasse les 110 milliards de francs (18 milliards de dollars). Les secteurs de l'eau et des déchets en sont les principaux bénéficiaires.

Près de 400 000 personnes sont employées dans la protection de l'environnement, dont plus de 60 % dans la lutte contre les pollutions. La désertification progressive des campagnes françaises tend à accroître les besoins : l'entretien des rivières ou des chemins de randonnée, la préservation du patrimoine exigent de la main-d'œuvre. Le gouvernement participe d'ailleurs à la création de nouveaux emplois verts dans le cadre de la lutte contre le chômage.

Une politique efficace de l'environnement doit aussi s'appuyer sur une recherche de haut niveau. La France y consacre 4,5 % de la dépense publique de recherche, mobilisant près de 4 000 chercheurs et ingénieurs au sein d'équipes de renommée mondiale, notamment dans le domaine des climats, de l'atmosphère, de la sécurité et de l'hydrogéologie. Mais contrairement à d'autres pays, comme les États-Unis ou le Japon, la France ne possède pas de grand organisme de recherche spécifique à l'environnement. Les travaux sont dispersés dans plusieurs centaines de laboratoires universitaires et dans des établissements scientifiques comme le Centre national de la recherche scientifique (CNRS), le Muséum national d'histoire naturelle, l'Institut national de la santé et de la recherche médicale (INSERM), l'Institut national de la recherche agronomique (INRA), le Bureau de recherches géologiques et minières (BRGM), l'Institut français de recherche scientifique pour le développement en coopération (ORSTOM), l'Institut français de recherche sur la mer (IFREMER), le Centre national du machinisme agricole du génie rural, des eaux et des forêts (CEMAGREF), Météo-France ou encore le Centre national d'études spatiales (CNES)... Seule exception à cette règle, l'Institut national de recherche sur l'environnement industriel et les risques (INERIS) est spécialisé dans l'analyse et la mesure des risques, le développement de procédés permettant de limiter les émissions polluantes et l'aide à l'élaboration des normes. L'Institut français de l'environnement (IFEN), créé le 18 novembre 1991, est également un outil essentiel de la politique d'environnement. Chargé d'observer, de surveiller, d'évaluer et d'informer, il collecte et traite toutes les données relatives à l'environnement, en liaison avec tous les organismes concernés. L'IFEN est le correspondant de l'Agence européenne de l'environnement qui siège à Copenhague.

Une nouvelle vision

Le réel progrès, en dehors de cette démarche globale, tient à l'esprit de concertation qui régit de plus en plus l'aménagement du territoire. D'ailleurs, l'environnement et l'aménagement du territoire sont actuellement regroupés au sein d'un même ministère. Désormais, les grands projets d'infrastructures, qu'il s'agisse d'autoroutes ou de lignes de train à grande vitesse (TGV), donnent lieu à un débat démocratique. Sur les 6 000 études d'impact réalisées chaque année en France, 300 concernent des projets d'infrastructures, y compris les réseaux de lignes à haute tension. Le décret du 25 février 1993 élargit le champ de l'étude d'impact et la rend plus accessible au public. L'enquête publique, obligatoire avant la réalisation d'une route, d'une portion d'autoroute ou d'un tronçon de TGV, fait également l'objet d'une réforme qui doit assurer une meilleure transparence et une concertation en amont. Par ailleurs, toutes sortes d'initiatives voient le jour pour susciter une nouvelle valeur civique, l'éco-citoyenneté. Ainsi, l'opération « mille défis pour ma planète », lancée en 1993, a mobilisé plus de 120 000 jeunes. C'est à ce titre également que 250 appelés volontaires ont effectué, dès 1994, leur service militaire dans l'environnement, service devenu civil en 1995. L'environnement devient, en France, l'affaire de tous les citoyens.

Pour en savoir plus :

Ministère de l'Environnement et de l'Aménagement du territoire, *Données économiques de l'environnement, édition 1997*, La Documentation française-Économica, 1997.

Ministère de l'Environnement - Institut français de l'environnement, *L'environnement en France*, Dunod, 1994-1995.

Ministère de l'Environnement, *Éthique et environnement*, Actes du colloque du 13 décembre 1996, La Documentation française, 1997.

P.-H. Bourrelier, Commissariat général du Plan, *La prévention des risques naturels : rapport d'évaluation*, La Documentation française, 1997.

R. Brunet, F. Auriac (sous la dir. de), *Atlas de France*, tome 6, *Milieux et ressources*, Reclus-La Documentation française, 1995.

3

La population

La population de la France métropolitaine s'élève à 58,7 millions d'habitants au 1ᵉʳ janvier 1998, ce qui la place au vingt et unième rang mondial et au troisième rang de l'Union européenne. En ajoutant les effectifs des DOM-TOM, qui dépassent 2 millions d'habitants, la population française approche 61 millions de personnes.

Densités : de forts contrastes

Avec 107 habitants au km², la France apparaît comme l'un des territoires bien peuplés de la planète (45 h/km² pour le monde, 29 pour les États-Unis), mais moyennement peuplé en Europe : elle se situe au neuvième rang de l'Union européenne, loin derrière des États comme les Pays-Bas (460 h/km²), le Royaume-Uni (240 h/km²), l'Allemagne (235 h/km²), l'Italie (195 h/km²). Cependant la densité moyenne a

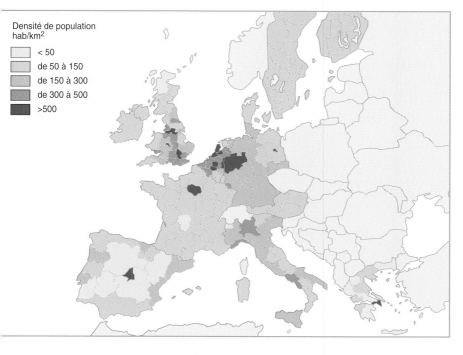

Densité de population hab/km²

- < 50
- de 50 à 150
- de 150 à 300
- de 300 à 500
- >500

Les densités en Europe : au contact de la diagonale européenne des fortes densités, la France fait figure d'oasis, faiblement peuplée à l'exception de la région parisienne

peu de sens car la répartition de la population présente de forts contrastes. La moitié des Français vit sur un peu plus de 10 % du territoire : région parisienne et basse Seine, carrefour lyonnais, vallée du Rhône et littoral méditerranéen, axes de la Loire, de la Garonne et du Rhin, façade maritime armoricaine, régions industrielles du Nord et de Lorraine. On trouve là les arrondissements les plus peuplés du pays, celui de Paris détenant le record avec 20 000 h/km^2. À l'inverse, de vastes zones sont faiblement peuplées, avec des densités moyennes parfois inférieures à 20 h/km^2 ; outre les montagnes, Alpes, Massif Central, Pyrénées, Corse, ces vides humains correspondent aux grands massifs forestiers, Landes, Sologne, est du Bassin Parisien, Ardennes. Ces faibles densités prennent en écharpe le territoire, du piémont pyrénéen au massif ardennais : dans cette «diagonale du vide», on trouve des arrondissements qui comptent moins de 10 h/km^2 (comme Castellane, Florac ou Barcelonnette).

La France s'est urbanisée plus lentement que d'autres puissances européennes comme l'Angleterre et l'Allemagne et il a fallu attendre 1930 pour que la population urbaine dépasse la population rurale. À partir des années cinquante, le rattrapage a été rapide et, en 1996, 76,4 % de la population vit dans les 361 aires urbaines définies par l'INSEE (Institut national de la statistique et des études économiques). Dans un premier temps, la croissance urbaine a profité à la fois aux villes-centres et aux banlieues ; un retournement s'est opéré dans les années soixante-dix et la plupart des villes-centres et des proches banlieues des grandes agglomérations ont vu leur population diminuer. Les banlieues plus lointaines et les communes rurales qui entourent les villes, en revanche, ont connu un fort accroissement de leurs effectifs : ces zones périurbaines groupent aujourd'hui 9 millions d'habitants et leur population a augmenté de près de 800 000 personnes entre les recensements de 1982 et 1990, alors que celle des villes-centres diminuait de plus de 700 000.

En 40 ans, la France a gagné près de 15 millions d'habitants, autant que de 1810 à 1959, mais le rythme de croissance tend à s'essouffler

Évolution de la population de la France

Vers 1150	15 millions
Vers 1680	20 millions
1750	25 millions
1810	30 millions
1841	35 millions
1924	40 millions
1959	45 millions
1968	50 millions
1985	55 millions
1999	59 millions

La première des aires urbaines est celle de Paris, avec 10,3 millions d'habitants, soit plus de 20 % des citadins du pays. Les aires urbaines du Nord (3,7 millions), de Marseille et du bas-Rhône (2,8 millions) et de la région lyonnaise (2,8 millions) arrivent assez loin derrière la capitale, seul pôle urbain capable de rivaliser avec les grandes métropoles comme New York, Tokyo ou Londres. La direction de la Population et des Migrations (du ministère de l'Emploi et de la Solidarité) estime

Un territoire d'une densité de peuplement contrastée

Toulouse et ses ponts
sur la Garonne
(Haute-Garonne)

Un village de Bourgogne,
Monthélie (Côte-d'Or)

Le boulevard
de Villefontaine
à L'Isle-d'Abeau (Isère)

d'ailleurs que, de 1990 à 2020, la population de l'Ile-de-France devrait s'accroître de 16 %, atteignant ainsi 12 millions d'habitants. Cette croissance à venir sera encore plus marquée en Languedoc-Roussillon (+ 37 %) et en Provence-Alpes-Côte d'Azur (+ 30 %), régions déjà les plus dynamiques du pays au cours des deux dernières décennies, ainsi qu'en Rhône-Alpes, dans la région Centre et en Aquitaine. Les régions précocement urbanisées et industrialisées comme le Nord-Pas-de-Calais, la Lorraine, Champagne-Ardenne et les régions essentiellement rurales comme le Limousin et l'Auvergne, en revanche, devraient enregistrer une stagnation voire une diminution de leur nombre d'habitants. La tendance à la redistribution de la population sur le territoire national, amorcée depuis près d'un quart de siècle, se confirme ainsi dans ses grandes lignes.

La fin de l'élan démographique

La France a longtemps eu un comportement démographique original par rapport à ses voisins ; elle fut l'un des premiers pays du monde à connaître une baisse significative de la mortalité, au XVIIIe siècle, et à entrer dans une phase de croissance forte de sa population. Mais cet essor ne dura pas et, du début du XIXe siècle à la seconde guerre mondiale, l'accroissement fut modeste en raison d'une baisse précoce de la fécondité : 30 millions d'habitants en 1800, 41 millions en 1940. Pendant la même période, la population de l'Allemagne et celle du Royaume-Uni étaient multipliées par quatre environ ; une évolution du même ordre aurait donné à la France 120 millions d'habitants en 1940 et peut-être 150 aujourd'hui. À l'inverse, la croissance démographique de l'après-guerre a été plus importante en France qu'ailleurs : les effectifs ont augmenté de 18 millions en cinquante ans, soit une croissance totale de 44 %. La reprise durable de la fécondité pendant le *baby boom* (elle oscille entre 2,9 et 2,3 enfants par femme entre 1946 et 1973), la baisse continue de la mortalité, et de la mortalité infantile en particulier (le taux de mortalité infantile était de 52 pour 1 000 en 1950, contre moins de 5 pour 1 000 aujourd'hui), ainsi qu'une forte immigration qui a représenté le quart de la croissance en moyenne, expliquent cet important rattrapage qui a mis la France au niveau démographique de ses grands voisins européens.

Avec l'espérance de vie qui augmente chaque année, grands-parents et petits-enfants partagent les mêmes loisirs, ici le vélo tout terrain

Actuellement, la démographie de la France se porte un peu mieux que celle des autres États d'Europe ; avec une croissance naturelle de 3,3 pour 1 000 en 1997 (natalité : 12,4 pour 1 000, mortalité : 9,1 pour 1 000), elle se situe au troisième rang des quinze pays de l'Union, derrière l'Irlande et le Luxembourg. Ce taux est cependant très faible et, si la France n'a pas encore rejoint l'Allemagne, l'Italie et l'Espagne dont le solde naturel est nul ou négatif, elle devrait, à terme, s'aligner sur ces pays. En effet, la démographie française bénéficie encore des effets positifs de sa croissance passée : les femmes en âge de procréer sont nombreuses car nées dans des périodes où la natalité était encore forte (l'âge moyen de la maternité est de 29 ans) et la mortalité se maintient en dessous de 10 pour 1 000, en raison d'une structure de population relativement jeune. Il n'en sera pas de même lorsque les générations moins nombreuses de ces vingt dernières années arriveront en âge de procréation : le nombre de naissances, de l'ordre de 740 000 par an actuellement, pourrait alors se réduire de 200 000 si la fécondité se maintient au niveau actuel de 1,7 enfant par femme. Dans le même temps, le nombre de décès ne reculera pas et pourrait même augmenter en raison du vieillissement de la population. La longévité s'accroît en effet, avec une espérance de vie de 74 ans pour les hommes et de 82 ans pour les femmes, ce qui, combiné à une faible fécondité, entraîne un vieillissement inéluctable de la population. Compte tenu de ces facteurs et en l'absence d'une immigration capable de compenser les déficits, la population de la France pourrait diminuer dans un quart de siècle environ.

Une vieille terre d'immigration

La France accueille des immigrés depuis bientôt 150 ans. Dans la deuxième moitié du XIXe siècle, alors que la majorité des migrants européens se dirigeait vers les pays neufs en cours de

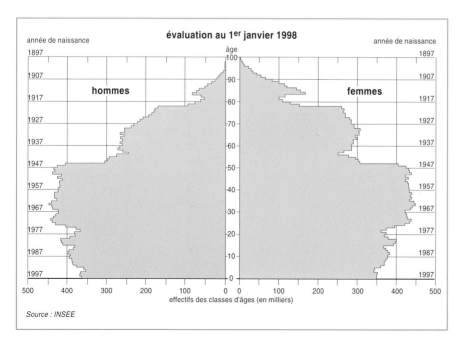

Source : INSEE

La baisse de la natalité rétrécit la base de la pyramide des âges, alors que l'augmentation de la durée de vie renforce les étages supérieurs

peuplement (États-Unis, Canada, Argentine, Australie, Brésil...), la France était la seule des vieilles nations à compter sur son sol un contingent important d'étrangers : ils étaient plus d'un million au moment du centenaire de la Révolution, en 1889, et beaucoup ont été naturalisés à cette occasion. Jusqu'à l'entre-deux-guerres, le pays manque d'hommes et de bras, compte tenu de sa faible croissance démographique d'alors, et à l'immigration de travail (Italiens et Polonais surtout) s'ajoute l'accueil de réfugiés : Grecs, Arméniens, Russes, Espagnols...

L'immigration reprend vigoureusement après la seconde guerre, surtout à la fin des années cinquante ; les enfants du *baby boom* ne sont pas encore en âge de travailler alors que le pays entre dans un cycle de forte croissance, les Trente Glorieuses. Les immigrants sont alors de jeunes travailleurs venus d'Italie et d'Espagne au départ, puis du Maghreb et du Portugal, d'Afrique Noire, du Proche-Orient et d'Asie un peu plus tard. À partir du milieu des années soixante-dix, la crise économique et l'arrivée de générations nombreuses sur le marché du travail s'accompagnent d'une montée rapide du chômage. En 1974, des dispositions restreignent l'immigration de travail. Les entrées se ralentissent alors ; elles étaient en moyenne de 220 000 par an entre 1974 et 1982, contre 100 000 entre 1982 et 1990, les flux annuels étant estimés à 120 000 en moyenne entre 1990 et 1995 et à 74 000 en 1997. L'immigration change aussi de nature ; le regroupement familial devient sa composante principale, les entrées de femmes et d'enfants rem-

Un Français sur quatre a des racines étrangères ; l'immigration récente, plus jeune et plus féminine qu'autrefois, provient de pays très divers

plaçant celles des hommes jeunes. Les origines se diversifient aussi, avec une montée importante des flux venus d'Asie et d'Amérique latine ainsi que, plus récemment, des pays d'Europe de l'Est et de Russie. Enfin, l'immigration clandestine touche la France comme de nombreux pays de l'Union européenne ; elle est, par nature, impossible à mesurer, ce qui donne lieu à de nombreuses spéculations. On sait cependant qu'elle est constituée de jeunes travailleurs attirés par la possibilité de gagner leur vie en travaillant « au noir ».

En temps de crise, l'immigration suscite de vifs débats et il en a toujours été ainsi dans les périodes difficiles. On observe cependant que les flux anciens d'immigration se sont toujours intégrés, non sans difficultés parfois. Les évolutions récentes montrent d'ailleurs que les immigrés de la deuxième ou de la troisième génération alignent leur comportement et leurs habitudes de vie sur ceux des Français. Si l'on ajoute aux Français ayant au moins un de leurs parents ou grands-parents d'origine étrangère les étrangers actuellement présents sur le territoire (environ 4 millions), on aboutit à un total de plus de 12 millions de personnes issues d'une immigration assez récente. En tenant compte des apports de l'immigration depuis le XIXe siècle, on peut raisonnablement estimer qu'un Français sur quatre a des racines étrangères. Par ailleurs, l'accroissement naturel se tarissant progressivement, seul l'apport migratoire pourrait, à terme, permettre à la population de se maintenir, voire d'augmenter.

La population active

La population active totale, qui comprend les personnes ayant un emploi, les demandeurs d'emploi et les préretraités, s'élève à 26,6 millions de personnes en 1997, soit 45,3 % de la population. Elle a fortement augmenté depuis quarante ans (19,5 millions en 1954), en raison du *baby boom*, de l'essor de l'immigration et de l'extension du travail féminin. Le nombre de femmes actives a doublé depuis 1954 et elles représentent aujourd'hui 47 % de la main-d'œuvre du pays.

Dans le même temps, la structure de l'activité a changé. L'emploi agricole achève un long recul et ne représente plus qu'un million de personnes, soit 4 % de la population occupée, contre 30 % en 1954. Les agriculteurs sont devenus très minoritaires dans la plupart des campagnes : un rural sur cinq seulement vit dans une famille agricole. La part de l'industrie et du bâtiment diminue depuis plus de 20 ans. Ce secteur employait 38 % des actifs au début des années soixante-dix et 26 % seulement en 1996. Cette diminution s'est accompagnée d'une forte hausse des qualifications : alors que le nombre d'ouvriers non qualifiés diminuait de près de 2 millions entre 1975 et 1996, celui des ouvriers qualifiés et des techniciens augmentait de 700 000. Enfin, les activités commerciales et de services du secteur tertiaire ont renforcé leur domination sur

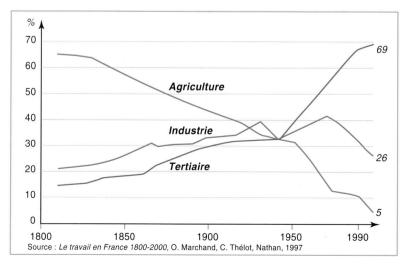

Effondrement de l'emploi agricole depuis un siècle, baisse de l'emploi industriel depuis 25 ans et envolée des emplois tertiaires marquent les profondes mutations de la société et de l'économie du pays

Source : *Le travail en France 1800-2000*, O. Marchand, C. Thélot, Nathan, 1997

l'économie. Elles occupent aujourd'hui près de 16 millions de personnes, soit 69 % de l'effectif employé (contre 40 % en 1954) et ont créé plus de 5 millions d'emplois depuis 1970. Là aussi le nombre des postes peu qualifiés diminue, en raison, en particulier, de la généralisation des équipements informatiques. Si des branches comme les transports, la santé, le tourisme et les loisirs, l'environnement, créent encore de l'activité, d'autres comme le petit commerce de détail ou la banque réduisent leurs effectifs.

La France compte 3,1 millions de chômeurs en 1997, soit 12,4 % de la population active. Jusqu'en 1974, le taux de chômage était inférieur à 3 % et le million de chômeurs n'a été dépassé qu'en 1977 : en vingt ans, le chômage est devenu le problème social majeur du pays. L'augmentation du nombre des actifs dans un contexte de crise durable explique ce phénomène : les générations présentes sur le marché du travail sont celles du *baby boom* et celles qui arrivent en âge d'activité sont encore nombreuses, alors que la

Techniciennes de laboratoire au centre de Mirabel (Puy-de-Dôme) : les femmes représentent 47 % de la main-d'œuvre du pays

progression du travail féminin se poursuit. Face à cette situation, on assiste à un fort recul des emplois industriels et à une stagnation voire une diminution de l'emploi tertiaire de masse. Ce sont de plus en plus des postes qualifiés qui sont offerts et souvent en petit nombre. La création d'emplois à temps partiel, qui concernent 16 % des actifs, n'est qu'une réponse insuffisante à cette situation qui pèse lourdement sur la collectivité nationale : plus de 300 milliards de francs (50 milliards de dollars) sont dépensés chaque année pour l'indemnisation du chômage et les différentes politiques pour l'emploi. Des solutions durables comme la réduction du temps de travail (semaine de 35 heures) sont recherchées mais un allégement réel interviendra à partir de 2006, lorsque les génération du *baby boom* commenceront à partir à la retraite et seront remplacées par les classes d'âge plus restreintes nées depuis la fin des années soixante-dix.

Pour en savoir plus :

R. Brunet, F. Auriac (sous la dir. de), *Atlas de France* (14 vol.), tome 6 : *Milieux et ressources*, tome 2 : *L'espace des villes*, Reclus-La Documentation française, 1995.

D. Noin, *L'espace français*, A. Colin, 1995.

J.-L. Mathieu, *La France en Europe et dans le monde*, Géographie Première, Bordas, 1997.

P. Merienne, *Le petit atlas de la France, départements et territoires d'outre-mer*, Édition Ouest-France, 1997.

L'état de la France 98-99, La Découverte, 1998.

Données sociales 1997, INSEE, 1997.

L'HISTOIRE

4

De l'Antiquité à la Ve République

La France est souvent citée comme l'exemple type de l'État-nation, aboutissement historique et géographique assez rare dans le monde et qui correspond à une situation où les trois composantes principales qui font l'identité d'un pays – le territoire, l'État et le peuple – se confondent en un tout. Il faut en effet que les citoyens s'identifient à un espace et à un système politique suffisamment stable et continu, en l'occurrence la République, pour en arriver à ce stade. Cet état de fait est le fruit d'une longue construction dont on peut considérer qu'elle se poursuit et se perfectionne jusqu'à la Ve République.

La France avant la Révolution : une lente gestation

Il est bien difficile d'attribuer à la France une date de naissance ; faut-il choisir 496 et le baptême de Clovis, roi des Francs, 987 et le sacre d'Hugues Capet, fondateur de la dynastie qui régna pendant neuf siècles sur le pays, ou 1789 et la Révolution, quand la France s'affirme comme une nation dans un État déjà constitué ? Historiens et citoyens sont partagés sur ces origines. La communauté nationale a d'ailleurs fêté récemment les trois anniversaires : les 1 500 ans de la conversion de Clovis au christianisme, le millénaire du sacre d'Hugues Capet et le bicentenaire de la Révolution. La pluralité des choix possibles montre, en tout cas, que la France, comme un être vivant, s'est lentement constituée, intégrant des apports multiples à partir desquels elle a construit son identité.

L'Antiquité et le Moyen Âge n'ont certes pas produit une France à l'image de celle que nous connaissons et, à la fin du XVe siècle, le domaine capétien ressemble davantage à un

La vie en France au XVe siècle – moissons et baignades au mois d'août –, illustrée par Pol de Limbourg dans les « Très riches heures du Duc de Berry », œuvre conservée au musée Condé de Chantilly

archipel composite qu'à l'Hexagone actuel. Ces longues périodes sont cependant essentielles, car elles établissent les trames du peuplement et jettent les bases de l'organisation du territoire, en fixant l'emplacement de la plupart des villes et des réseaux de communication. C'est à partir de ces pôles et de ces axes que les solidarités territoriales vont fonctionner et que l'espace français va se construire, à travers des guerres, des annexions, des cessions, des héritages, des mariages. Quelques phases sont essentielles dans ce long processus : la domination romaine d'abord, qui maille la Gaule de villes et de routes et qui établit un embryon d'unité linguistique en répandant l'usage du latin ; l'expansion médiévale, aussi, qui voit renaître les villes, se multiplier les villages et se développer les échanges du XIᵉ au XIIIᵉ siècle.

De cette lente émergence il faut aussi retenir les brassages humains. Aux noyaux de peuplement préhistoriques attestés par de nombreux sites, dont quelques-uns comme Lascaux ont une renommée mondiale, se sont ajoutés les apports celtes, ceux des peuples de la Méditerranée, Grecs et Romains, ceux des nomades guerriers venus de steppes, comme les Huns, ceux des peuples nordiques et germaniques, Vandales, Suèves, Burgondes, Alamans, Wisigoths, Francs et, plus tard, Arabes et Vikings... Ces peuples ont en partie déterminé les souches de population de certaines régions mais, surtout, ils se sont fondus dans le creuset qui deviendra la France. C'est également au cours de cette période, sous l'autorité des Capétiens, que se construit progressivement le territoire et que se mettent en place les institutions et l'administration qui le gèrent et l'organisent. Le choix de Paris comme capitale est à cet égard décisif : le territoire et l'État qui en émane trouvent là un centre à partir duquel l'unité de la France se réalise.

Le legs de la Révolution et de l'Empire

La France s'affirme comme nation avec la Révolution de 1789. Le 14 juillet 1790, lors de la fête de la Fédération, des délégués venus de tout le pays proclament leur appartenance à la même communauté nationale. L'idéal affiché alors est celui de la liberté de chacun dans le respect de tous, du droit des peuples à disposer d'eux-mêmes, d'institutions faites pour garantir le bien-être social... Ces aspirations, formulées dans la Déclaration des Droits de l'homme et du citoyen du 26 août 1789, sont héritières de la « philosophie des Lumières » du XVIIIᵉ siècle et fortement imprégnées de la pensée d'auteurs comme Montesquieu, qui a posé le principe de la séparation des pouvoirs exécutif, législatif et judiciaire dans *L'Esprit des lois* (1748), ou comme Jean-Jacques Rousseau qui développe les notions d'égalité politique et de souveraineté du peuple dans *Du contrat social* (1762). Ces textes ont d'ailleurs beaucoup inspiré les rédacteurs de la Constitution des États-Unis d'Amérique en 1787. Les valeurs qui sont ainsi mises en avant se veulent universelles et peuvent être considérées comme fondatrices de la démocratie moderne. Elles auront d'ailleurs un grand retentissement et guideront les mouvements de libération nationale au XIXᵉ siècle, avant d'être largement reprises dans la Déclaration universelle des Droits de l'homme, adoptée le 10 décembre 1948 par les Nations unies.

Ces principes ne seront cependant pas immédiatement acquis. S'ils sont inscrits en grande partie dans la première Constitution, dont la France s'est dotée en 1791, et encore plus largement dans celle de 1793, il faudra du temps, de nombreux combats politiques et des luttes sociales avant qu'ils ne deviennent des droits inaliénables. La Première République est proclamée le 22 septembre 1792 mais la Constitution démocratique à laquelle elle donne naissance en 1793 ne sera jamais appliquée. La guerre civile à l'intérieur, les combats qu'il faut mener sur tous les fronts contre les États européens coalisés contre la France aboutissent à la mise en place de la Terreur, bien éloignée des nobles principes de 1789. Après l'exécution de Robespierre en juillet 1794, la Convention thermidorienne (1794-1795) et le Directoire (1795-1799) conduisent à la prise du pouvoir par Bonaparte, consul de 1799 à 1804 puis empereur des Français. La monarchie, abolie en 1792, cède la place à l'Empire, bien différent dans ses structures et son organisation mais où les Français se retrouvent sujets, comme par le passé, après avoir été d'éphémères citoyens.

Montesquieu (1689-1755) publie en 1748 *L'Esprit des lois*, ouvrage politique majeur qui définit les principes de l'État démocratique et la séparation des pouvoirs exécutif, législatif et judiciaire

Pendant les guerres de la Révolution et de l'Empire, la France a tenté d'imposer son modèle et ses institutions à une partie importante de l'Europe ; mais la volonté initiale d'apporter la liberté aux « peuples opprimés » s'est vite muée en conquêtes et en annexions, le « droit des peuples à disposer d'eux-mêmes » apparaissant alors comme une formule bien vaine... La France perd son Empire en 1815 mais ne recouvre pas pour autant liberté et démocratie. La monarchie est restaurée avec Louis XVIII. Charles X lui succède en 1824 puis, à la suite des journées révolutionnaires de juillet 1830, Louis-Philippe entame un règne de 18 ans. La Révolution de 1848 met en place la Seconde République qui, comme la Première, débouche sur un coup d'État, celui de Louis-Napoléon Bonaparte en 1851 et l'instauration du second Empire (1852-1870). Sous ces différents régimes, le recours aux citoyens n'a guère été pratiqué : jusqu'en 1848, le vote se fait au suffrage censitaire, donc limité à une minorité, et l'expression politique du plus grand nombre passe en fait par quelques épisodes insurrectionnels vite réprimés.

Cependant, derrière l'instabilité politique s'opèrent des changements de fond à travers lesquels se construit la France moderne. Ils sont d'abord d'ordre territorial et administratif. En 1789, l'unité administrative de la France était inachevée. La France était divisée en circonscriptions diverses, apparues à des périodes différentes et qui se chevauchaient : baillages, gouvernements, généralités, États provinciaux, pays. Une telle complexité entraînait des lenteurs et des conflits de compétence et limitait une gestion efficace du pays. Sur ce plan, la Révolution et l'Empire vont perfectionner l'œuvre centralisatrice entreprise sous l'Ancien Régime. En 1790, le territoire est divisé en départements, eux-mêmes divisés en cantons découpés en communes, qui constituent encore aujourd'hui les entités locales stables de l'espace de vie des Français. Bonaparte complète le dispositif et lui donne cohérence et efficacité par la loi du 28 Pluviôse an VIII (17 février 1800), qui institue les préfets et les maires, ces derniers aujourd'hui élus étant alors nommés. Les circonscriptions administratives sont donc homogénéisées sur une base égalitaire et le recrutement des personnels par concours substitue le mérite aux anciens privilèges. C'est au cours des mêmes périodes que l'on assiste à la naissance de véritables services publics, au renforcement du rôle de l'État dans l'aménagement du territoire, la création d'infrastructures, l'urbanisme. La volonté unificatrice passe aussi par le souci de créer des normes et des repères communs partout valides, ce qui se traduit aussi bien par l'institution du Code civil que par le cadastrage systématique de la propriété ou encore par le choix du système métrique et l'unification des poids et mesures, cette dernière décision étant aujourd'hui devenue universelle.

La période qui va de la Révolution au Second Empire est aussi marquée par une profonde transformation de l'économie et de la société. Même si les bouleversements que la France a connus entre 1789 et 1815 ont permis à l'Angleterre de prendre une avance économique certaine, la France entre, elle aussi, dans l'âge industriel, celui des charbonnages, de la machine à vapeur, des forges modernes, des grandes manufactures textiles et du chemin de fer. Le second Empire apparaît à cet égard comme une période décisive, surtout après 1860 : la démocratie a été confisquée, l'affairisme bat son plein, l'aventure coloniale entreprise en 1830 avec la conquête de l'Algérie se poursuit, mais le pays enregistre des transformations profondes et rapides qui vont en faire une puissance moderne : développement de l'industrie, création de banques et de grands magasins qui inaugurent le système de distribution moderne, remodelage urbain, extension importante du réseau de chemins de fer, politique de reboisement et de lutte contre l'érosion... Cependant, si l'essor économique est incontestable, le progrès social reste à la traîne et, dans cette première moitié du XIXᵉ siècle, les conditions de vie sont dures et la misère aiguë pour le prolétariat qui s'entasse dans les villes industrielles.

1870-1914 : la France républicaine, crises et consolidation

Après la défaite de la France devant l'Allemagne en 1870, la Troisième République apparaît, en dépit des turbulences internes qu'elle doit surmonter et de la première guerre mondiale qui meurtrira profondément le pays, comme une période de stabilisation et de consolidation. La République a été proclamée le 4 septembre

1870 et Adolphe Thiers en devient le premier Président le 31 août 1871, alors que l'insurrection de la Commune de Paris s'est achevée par une répression sanglante à la fin du mois de mai 1871. Les débuts du régime sont difficiles et pourtant cette République sera la plus durable de toutes puisqu'elle se maintient jusqu'en 1940. D'abord monarchiste, Thiers se rallie progressivement à l'idée républicaine et les textes législatifs qui définissent l'organisation et le fonctionnement des pouvoirs sont adoptés entre février et juillet 1875. Mais il faut attendre les élections des 14 et 28 octobre 1877, qui donnent une majorité républicaine à la Chambre des députés, pour que le régime soit légitimé.

Le « Triomphe de la République », œuvre allégorique du scupteur Jules Dalou réalisée entre 1879 et 1899, place de la Nation à Paris

Jusqu'à la guerre de 1914, la République doit faire face à deux crises graves qui menacent son existence même : le boulangisme (1886-1889), qui rallie des mécontentements de toutes origines et menace les fondements parlementaires du régime, et l'affaire Dreyfus (1894-1899), qui révèle l'ampleur de l'antisémitisme en France et les divisions profondes qui partagent le corps social et les courants politiques. Ces crises sont d'autant plus menaçantes pour la République qu'elles se déroulent sur un fond de tensions sociales et politiques vives : luttes ouvrières, actions violentes des ligues et factions politiques, affrontements entre cléricaux et anticléricaux qui aboutissent en 1905 à la séparation de l'Église et de l'État. Par ailleurs, des scandales politiques et financiers et des actes terroristes (assassinat du président Sadi Carnot en 1894) viennent exacerber les tensions. Cependant, les acquis de cette période sont importants sur le plan institutionnel et social et dans le domaine des libertés publiques. Aux lois de 1882 et 1885 instituant l'école primaire obligatoire et gratuite, s'ajoutent les lois sur la liberté de la presse (1881), la liberté syndicale (1884), la réglementation du travail des femmes

En instituant l'enseignement primaire gratuit et obligatoire, la IIIᵉ République a fait de l'éducation de tous une de ses priorités ; cantine scolaire de l'école primaire de Bellevue (Orne), 1889

et des enfants (1892), la liberté d'association (1901). La modernisation économique se poursuit en dépit de crises conjoncturelles et la France est l'un des principaux berceaux des innovations scientifiques et techniques qui sont à l'origine de la deuxième révolution industrielle. Pendant la Belle Époque qui précède la Grande guerre, le rayonnement international de la France est grand : elle dis-

pose du deuxième empire colonial du monde, joue un rôle diplomatique de premier plan et s'impose comme le pays phare de l'art et de la culture.

1914-1945 : d'une guerre à l'autre

Les premières années du XXe siècle voient la montée des tensions internationales en Europe ; les rivalités politiques, commerciales et coloniales entre les puissances s'inscrivent sur un fond de nationalisme croissant exacerbé par des crises régionales comme celles du Maroc et des Balkans. La France a constitué une Triple-Entente avec la Russie (accords de 1893), elle-même alliée à la Serbie et à la Grande-Bretagne (par l'Entente cordiale, signée en 1904). Face à ce bloc s'est formée la Triple-Alliance des «empires centraux» qui comprend l'Allemagne, l'Autriche-Hongrie et le royaume d'Italie, soutenus par l'Empire ottoman. L'assassinat du prince héritier d'Autriche-Hongrie par un Serbe de Bosnie, le 28 juin 1914 à Sarajevo, alors sous domination autrichienne, est l'étincelle qui met le feu aux poudres : le système d'alliance patiemment constitué fonctionne et conduit au déclenchement de la première guerre mondiale.

Le 3 août 1914, la France entre en guerre contre l'Allemagne et l'Autriche-Hongrie aux côtés de l'Angleterre et de la Russie, rejointes plus tard par l'Italie et les États-Unis. Les Français sortent victorieux de ce conflit long de quatre années mais le bilan est lourd pour le pays comme pour les autres États d'Europe qui ont participé à la guerre. Le Nord et l'Est du territoire ont été dévastés, l'effort de guerre a épuisé les finances et l'économie nationale et interrompu les progrès sociaux engagés ; mais surtout, la guerre se solde par un véritable désastre humain : près d'1,5 million d'hommes jeunes ont été tués et près de 3 millions blessés, alors que le nombre des naissances s'effondrait, hémorragie démographique d'autant plus grave qu'elle touchait un pays dont la croissance de la population était déjà très affaiblie.

La guerre avait permis de réaliser l'Union sacrée des partis politiques autour de la défense de la nation, union symbolisée par la forte personnalité de Clemenceau, le « Père la Victoire », au pouvoir jusqu'en janvier 1920. La vie politique des années vingt est ensuite dominée par des coalitions de droite, à l'exception de la période 1924-1926 où le Cartel des gauches, unissant socialistes et radicaux, est au pouvoir. Depuis décembre 1920 et la création du parti communiste, la gauche socialiste s'est divisée. La crise économique des années trente, les difficultés financières et sociales, la détérioration de la situation inter-

Une des mesures sociales importantes du Front populaire, en 1936, est l'instauration des premiers congés annuels payés.
Photo Willy Ronis

nationale avec l'arrivée au pouvoir du fascisme en Italie et du nazisme en Allemagne, aggravent les divisions dans le pays et favorisent la montée de nombreux mouvements antiparlementaires, conservateurs nationalistes et d'extrême droite qui s'organisent en « ligues ». Ces organisations multiplient les manifestations violentes, comme celle du 6 février 1934 qui suscite en réaction une alliance antifasciste rassemblant les socialistes, les communistes et les radicaux et donne naissance au Front populaire. La gauche réunie triomphe aux élections de 1936 et le gouvernement de Front populaire, avec Léon Blum à sa tête, réalise d'importantes réformes : semaine de travail de quarante heures, conventions collectives, congés payés, premières nationalisations, modification du statut de la Banque de France. Toutefois, les divisions intérieures et surtout les difficultés extérieures ne sont pas réglées. Après avoir cru échapper aux hostilités par les concessions faites à Hitler à Munich, en 1938, le nouveau président du Conseil, Édouard Daladier, engage le pays, aux côtés des Britanniques, dans la seconde guerre mondiale (3 septembre 1939).

La guerre laissera une France doublement traumatisée, par la défaite rapide et inattendue devant les armées allemandes, d'une part, mais aussi par la politique de collaboration avec l'ennemi qui est mise en œuvre par le gouvernement de Vichy, d'autre part. La débâcle de l'armée devant l'invasion nazie, en mai 1940, jette des millions de civils sur les routes de l'exode. L'armistice est signé le 22 juin 1940. La France est divisée en deux zones, l'une occupée et l'autre libre. La Troisième République s'effondre ; le 10 juillet 1940, le Parlement donne tout pouvoir au maréchal Pétain, héros de la première guerre mondiale, qui met en place à Vichy, capitale provisoire, un régime nouveau, l'État français : régime à caractère personnel, autoritaire, corporatiste et discriminatoire à l'égard des Juifs, qui sont soumis dès 1941 à un statut spécial. La collaboration avec l'Allemagne nazie est engagée le 24 octobre 1940 par l'entrevue de Montoire entre Pétain et Hitler. Elle conduit le régime de Vichy à apporter son appui aux vainqueurs en soutenant l'effort de guerre allemand, en traquant les opposants au nazisme et en livrant les Juifs à la déportation. La Légion des volontaires français contre le bolchevisme combat même aux côtés des divisions allemandes sur le front de l'Est.

Cependant, la Résistance qui s'est manifestée dès les premiers jours de l'Occupation sera le ferment d'une France nouvelle qui prend les rênes du pays après la guerre. On peut dresser son acte de naissance au 18 juin 1940, quand le général de Gaulle appelle de Londres les Français à poursuivre le combat aux côtés des Alliés. Une Résistance extérieure, composée des Forces françaises libres (FFL) et d'un Comité français de libération nationale, se forme autour de lui. Des territoires coloniaux se rallient. En France

L'appel du 18 juin 1940 : « J'espérais qu'allaient venir me rejoindre les têtes des grandes administrations, des Églises, des états-majors. Et j'ai vu arriver les sans-grades, les marins de Dunkerque et les pêcheurs de l'Île-de-Sein. Finalement j'ai pu bâtir la France libre avec eux, avec le peuple. » **Charles de Gaulle, Mémoires de Guerre, tome 1, Plon**

A TOUS LES FRANÇAIS

La France a perdu une bataille!
Mais la France n'a pas perdu la guerre!

Des gouvernants de rencontre ont pu capituler, cédant à la panique, oubliant l'honneur, livrant le pays à la servitude. Cependant, rien n'est perdu!

Rien n'est perdu, parce que cette guerre est une guerre mondiale. Dans l'univers libre, des forces immenses n'ont pas encore donné. Un jour, ces forces écraseront l'ennemi. Il faut que la France, ce jour-là, soit présente à la victoire. Alors, elle retrouvera sa liberté et sa grandeur. Tel est mon but, mon seul but!

Voilà pourquoi je convie tous les Français, où qu'ils se trouvent, à s'unir à moi dans l'action, dans le sacrifice et dans l'espérance.

Notre patrie est en péril de mort.
Luttons tous pour la sauver!

VIVE LA FRANCE !

18 JUIN 1940

GENERAL DE GAULLE

la Résistance intérieure, d'abord très limitée, s'organise et se renforce, constituant de véritables réseaux qui, outre les actions conduites dans le pays, apporteront un appui précieux aux Alliés par leur travail de renseignement et leur aide militaire lors du débarquement. En Afrique du Nord, libérée par les Alliés dès novembre 1942, une nouvelle armée française se constitue et participe aux combats. Au printemps 1943, sous l'impulsion de Jean Moulin, délégué du général de Gaulle en France occupée, le Conseil national de la résistance (CNR) unit les principales organisations de résistants ; de Gaulle, alors installé à Alger, met sur pied le Gouvernement provisoire de la République française, issu du CNR. Si le rôle de ce combat ne fut pas décisif dans la victoire alliée sur le nazisme, il a été essentiel pour la France car il a convaincu les Anglais, les Américains et les Soviétiques plus tardivement, qu'il fallait faire à la France une place dans le camp des vainqueurs, plutôt que de l'occuper à la Libération, comme on l'aurait fait d'un territoire ennemi. La France sera ainsi présente comme un acteur à part entière de la victoire, lors de l'acte de capitulation de l'Allemagne le 8 mai 1945. En ce sens, on peut affirmer que la Résistance, personnifiée par de Gaulle, a permis à la France pourtant militairement vaincue de conserver son rang sur la scène internationale.

La reconstruction : 1945-1958

Deux guerres en trente ans ont représenté pour la France une période d'épreuves. Les pertes humaines ont été moindres pendant la Seconde guerre (600 000 morts environ) que pendant le premier conflit mondial. En revanche, les pertes matérielles sont beaucoup plus lourdes. Combats et bombardements ont détruit villes, usines, ponts, gares et voies ferrées. S'y ajoutent les pertes causées par l'exploitation intensive, par l'occupant, d'une économie asservie. Cependant, on peut parler de véritable élan dans la remise sur pied du pays ; les temps sont difficiles mais la paix restaure la confiance en l'avenir, comme en témoigne la vigoureuse reprise démographique du *baby boom*, et l'aide américaine du plan Marshall permet de parer au plus pressé.

Dès 1945 et bien que la situation soit difficile, des mesures d'urgence sont prises : nationalisations de secteurs-clés de l'économie (énergie, transport aérien, banques de dépôt, assurances) et de grandes entreprises (Renault), création de la Sécurité sociale, des comités d'entreprise et mise en œuvre d'une planification économique dont la responsabilité est confiée à Jean Monnet. Mais les forces politiques issues de la Résistance, communistes, démocrates-chrétiens et socialistes, qui soutiennent le gouvernement provisoire du général de Gaulle, se divisent rapidement sur le choix des institutions et sur les grandes options économiques. Le chef de la France libre finit d'ailleurs par quitter le gouvernement en janvier 1946 et fonde un nouveau parti politique, le Rassemblement du peuple français (RPF), en 1947. Il faut deux assemblées constituantes élues au suffrage universel (le vote des femmes a été instauré en 1944) et trois référendums pour que soit enfin adoptée la Constitution de la IVᵉ République, promulguée le 27 octobre 1946, qui institue une Assemblée nationale toute-puissante et un Président aux pouvoirs limités. En janvier 1947, Vincent Auriol est élu président de la République par le Parlement.

Aux divisions politiques internes s'ajoutent bientôt celles nées de la guerre froide et de la décolonisation. Malgré l'opposition des communistes, la France affirme son atlantisme et se range résolument dans le camp occidental. Elle intègre l'Organisation européenne de coopération économique (OECE), créée en avril 1948 pour répartir l'aide américaine, et adhère à l'Alliance atlantique (OTAN) en avril 1949. Par ailleurs, après la division de l'Allemagne, la France opte pour une politique d'entente avec la RFA qui sera à la base de la construction européenne. Jean Monnet, Robert Schuman et le chancelier Konrad Adenauer sont les principaux artisans de ce rapprochement qui aboutit en 1951 à la création de la Communauté européenne du charbon et de l'acier (CECA), première structure autour de laquelle va se construire l'Europe unie. Si la France repousse la création d'une Communauté européenne de défense (CED), gaullistes et communistes s'opposant à ce qu'ils jugent être un abandon de la souveraineté nationale, elle joue un rôle actif dans l'institution de la Communauté économique européenne (ou Marché commun), qui voit le jour avec le traité de Rome, le 25 mars 1957.

La IVᵉ République doit alors faire face à une grave crise engendrée par la décolonisation. Celle-ci commence en Indochine, d'où la France doit se retirer après huit années d'une guerre difficile. Pierre Mendès France, président du Conseil, met fin au conflit (accords de Genève, le 20 juillet 1954). Le Maroc et la Tunisie deviennent indépendants en 1956, tandis qu'une décolonisation pacifique s'amorce en Afrique noire. La décolonisation de l'Algérie, en revanche, donne lieu à un conflit qui durera de 1954 à 1962 et sera fatal à la IVᵉ République.

Jean Monnet (1888-1979) fut un grand partisan du rapprochement européen ; commissaire général du Plan en 1946, il est à l'origine de la déclaration du 9 mai 1950 qui jette les bases de la Communauté européenne du charbon et de l'acier (CECA), dont il devient le premier président de la Haute Autorité (1952-1955)

Pour en savoir plus :

Histoire de la France en 3 volumes, sous la dir. de G. Duby, Larousse, 1971.

Histoire de France en 5 volumes, Hachette, 1990.

C. Ambrosi, A. Ambrosi, B. Galloux, *La France de 1870 à nos jours*, A. Colin, collection U, 1997.

J.-C. Caron, *La nation, l'État et la démocratie en France de 1789 à 1914*, A. Colin, collection U, 1995.

X. de Planhol, *Géographie historique de la France*, Fayard, 1988.

5

La France
depuis 1958

La France gaullienne

À la suite d'émeutes de Français d'Algérie, le 13 mai 1958 à Alger, le dernier gouvernement de la IVᵉ République, dirigé par Pierre Pflimlin, tombe. Quittant sa retraite de Colombey-les-Deux-Églises, le général de Gaulle est appelé par le président de la République, René Coty, à assumer la direction du gouvernement. Il est investi par les députés le Iᵉʳ juin 1958 et met en chantier l'élaboration du texte constitutionnel qui va organiser le nouveau mode de fonctionnement des institutions. La Constitution de la Vᵉ République est adoptée par référendum le 28 septembre 1958. Elle accorde une place éminente au président de la République. De Gaulle est investi de cette fonction suprême par un collège de députés, sénateurs et élus locaux, le 21 décembre 1958.

Le général de Gaulle lors d'une visite à Villefranche-de-Rouergue (Aveyron), septembre 1961

À partir de 1960, les pays de l'Afrique française accèdent peu à peu à l'indépendance tout en gardant avec la France des liens privilégiés. Mais la guerre qui se poursuit en Algérie constitue l'abcès principal hérité de la République précédente. Des troubles graves, en métropole et en Algérie, ainsi que le putsch des généraux, qui s'emparent du pouvoir à Alger le 22 avril 1961, conduisent à accélérer les négociations avec le Gouvernement provisoire de la République algérienne et aboutissent aux accords d'Évian, approuvés massivement par référendum le 8 avril 1962. Un million de rapatriés doivent quitter l'Algérie indépendante et se réinsérer en France. Par le référendum du 28 octobre 1962, de Gaulle fait adopter l'élection du chef de l'État au suffrage universel direct. Il est lui-même élu à ce poste au deuxième tour de scrutin, le 19 décembre 1965, contre François Mitterrand, candidat de l'opposition de gauche.

Le mode de scrutin majoritaire assure au courant politique dominant une majorité durable et garantit donc une stabilité politique et parlementaire que la France n'avait pas connue depuis longtemps. La prospérité économique et l'assainissement monétaire, symbolisé par la création du nouveau franc en 1960, permettent au général de Gaulle de mener une politique extérieure très active. Son but est d'affirmer l'indépendance et le rôle mondial de la France. Il s'appuie, pour y parvenir, sur la capacité de dissuasion dont dispose le pays depuis qu'il maîtrise l'arme nucléaire. Le 13 février 1960, la première bombe atomique française a été testée à Reggane, au Sahara. La France se dotera ensuite de l'arme thermonucléaire (premier essai en 1968) et de toute la panoplie moderne de vecteurs : missiles terrestres, bombardiers de la force aérienne stratégique et sous-marins lanceurs d'engins. Elle devient ainsi la troisième puissance nucléaire derrière les États-Unis et l'URSS, avec cependant une capacité de feu très éloignée de celle des deux grands. Afin de bien marquer la nouvelle indépendance acquise, de Gaulle décide de retirer la France du commandement militaire intégré de l'OTAN, tout en restant membre de l'Alliance atlantique.

L'Europe se construit et la France se transforme

La politique européenne de la France se développe dans deux directions : mener à bien ce que de Gaulle baptise « la détente, l'entente et la coopération » avec les pays de l'Est pour mettre un terme à la guerre froide et préparer la construction d'une Europe de l'Atlantique à l'Oural ; mettre en œuvre le traité de Rome, tout en défendant très fermement la souveraineté des États et leurs intérêts fondamentaux. Ainsi la France, estimant que la Commission européenne a outrepassé ses attributions, s'abstient pendant six mois (en 1965) de participer aux instances européennes (politique de la chaise vide). Cette crise aboutit au compromis de Luxembourg : lorsqu'un État membre juge ses intérêts fondamentaux menacés, une décision ne peut être prise qu'à l'unanimité. Par ailleurs, les projets d'union politique (plan Fouchet) proposés par la France échouent, et de Gaulle s'oppose par deux fois à la candidature britannique à la CEE, qu'il juge prématurée.

Mais le plus important reste l'établissement d'une étroite coopération franco-allemande mise en œuvre par les relations personnelles entre le chancelier Adenauer et le général de Gaulle. Le voyage officiel du chancelier en France et celui du général en Allemagne, la création de l'Office franco-allemand pour la jeunesse, la signature du traité de l'Élysée, en 1963, couronnent ce rapprochement. Le couple franco-allemand devient l'un des « moteurs » de la construction européenne et le restera jusqu'à la période actuelle.

De grands projets économiques, favorisés par le dynamisme technique et démographique de la Ve République, voient le jour : lancement du paquebot France en janvier 1962, de l'avion supersonique Concorde (dont le prototype vole pour la première fois en 1969), début de l'exploration spatiale (1965), soutien à l'innovation technologique et aux industries de pointe – aéronautique, informatique, télécommunications –, ces actions s'inscrivant dans une politique active d'aménagement du territoire. Cependant, au cours des années soixante, les profondes mutations de l'économie française, ainsi que les changements sociologiques importants qu'enregistre le pays, en liaison avec le rajeunissement de la population et la hausse continue du niveau de vie, suscitent des inquiétudes et des aspirations sociales nouvelles. La multiplication de nouveaux médias (radio à transistor, télévision) contribue à donner un écho national à ces revendications que les événements de mai-juin 1968 vont catalyser.

La rupture de 1968 et la succession du général de Gaulle

La révolte étudiante du printemps 1968 touche de nombreux pays industrialisés mais prend en France une ampleur particulière car la revendication s'étend aux salariés, gagne la province et finit par paralyser l'ensemble du pays ; celui-ci compte, dans les derniers jours de mai, mois qui a connu des affrontements à caractère insurrectionnel, environ 9 millions de grévistes. Les divisions profondes du mouvement contestataire, le fait que les appareils politiques et syndicaux établis craignent des dérives incontrôlables, permettent une reprise en main de la situation par le pouvoir, après deux semaines d'atermoiements. Un discours ferme du général de Gaulle, la mobilisation de ses partisans et l'appel aux électeurs, après la dissolution de l'Assemblée nationale, rétablissent la situation en juin 1968. Moins d'un an plus tard cependant, de Gaulle quitte

définitivement le pouvoir après l'échec d'un référendum sur la régionalisation et la réforme du Sénat, le 28 avril 1969. Il meurt le 9 novembre 1970. Un de ses anciens Premiers ministres, Georges Pompidou, lui succède (élection du 15 juin 1969) ; après la mort prématurée de ce dernier, Valéry Giscard d'Estaing, son ministre des Finances, est élu le 19 mai 1974.

À la fin du mois de mai 1968, la France compte près de 9 millions de grévistes ; manifestation de la CGT à Paris, 24 mai 1968

Il n'y a pas de coupure brutale dans la manière de gouverner la France, après le départ de De Gaulle, mais plutôt des infléchissements progressifs. Sous Georges Pompidou, la tradition gaullienne est largement préservée et les grands axes de la politique intérieure et extérieure sont maintenus. Dans le cadre du projet de « nouvelle société » du Premier ministre Jacques Chaban-Delmas (1969-1972), des avancées sociales significatives sont adoptées en matière de formation profession-nelle, de protection des démunis et des personnes âgées. Au plan euro-péen, un pas décisif est accompli : la France lève son veto à l'entrée de la Grande-Bretagne dans la CEE, étendue à l'Irlande et au Danemark, et l'Europe passe à neuf membres en 1973.

Le septennat de Valéry Giscard d'Estaing marque plus nettement la volonté d'instituer un libéralisme moderne (« Société libé-rale avancée ») et de moderniser les rapports sociaux, d'autant plus qu'il s'inscrit sur fond de changement économique radical. Au milieu des années soixante-dix, en effet, la forte croissance des « Trente glo-rieuses » s'achève et la France entre dans une crise durable. D'impor-tantes réformes sont cependant accomplies : majorité à 18 ans, autorisation de l'IVG (interruption volontaire de grossesse), fin de la censure au cinéma et dans l'audiovisuel... Valéry Giscard d'Estaing est, par ailleurs, l'initiateur des réunions du G7 (Groupe des sept pays les plus industrialisés) et, avec le chancelier allemand Helmut Schmidt, il est à l'origine de l'organisation du Système monétaire euro-péen (SME) et de l'élection au suffrage universel des députés au Par-lement européen.

Avec l'élection de François Mitterrand à la présidence de la République le 10 mai 1981, la gauche accède au pouvoir pour la première fois sous la Ve République ; la cérémonie d'investiture au Panthéon, à Paris, 21 mai 1981

L'alternance de gauche

Alors que la majorité au pouvoir connaît des dissensions politiques croissantes entre l'Union pour la démocratie française (UDF), qui regroupe giscardiens et centristes, et le Rassemblement pour la République (RPR), parti créé par Jacques Chirac en décembre 1976 et

qui se veut héritier du gaullisme, l'opposition met en place, dans les années soixante-dix, une straté-gie de conquête du pouvoir sous la direction de François Mitterrand. Le Parti socialiste, rénové au congrès d'Épinay (juin 1971) par François Mitter-rand, le Parti communiste et les Radicaux de gauche forment, avant les élections législatives de 1973, l'Union de la gauche et adoptent un Pro-gramme commun de gouvernement. Malgré de sourdes tensions, des ruptures passagères puis l'abandon du Programme commun en 1978, cette union se reforme au deuxième tour de l'élection présidentielle d'avril-mai 1981, que François Mitter-rand gagne contre le Président sortant Valéry Gis-card d'Estaing. Pour la première fois sous la Ve République, la gauche accède au pouvoir. Cette alternance montre que la Constitution de 1958, qu'on disait taillée pour le général de Gaulle, per-met un changement démocratique de majorité poli-tique tout en garantissant la stabilité des institutions.

Le gouvernement de Pierre Mauroy (juin 1981) comprend quatre ministres communistes et décide d'un important train de réformes : retraite à soixante ans, réduction du temps de travail à trente-neuf heures hebdomadaires, cinquième semaine de congés payés, recrutement de fonctionnaires, nationalisation de groupes bancaires et industriels, impôt sur la fortune, décentralisation des pouvoirs vers les collectivités territoriales, abolition de la peine de mort, fin du monopole d'État sur la radio puis sur la télévision... Mais le déficit commercial s'accroît dangereusement, la dette s'alourdit alors que l'inflation persiste et que le franc perd de sa valeur par rapport aux grandes monnaies rivales. La contrainte économique est lourde et, après trois dévaluations successives, une politique de rigueur, plus réaliste à l'égard du marché et que l'engagement européen de la France rend inéluctable, se met en place. Le ministre des Finances, Jacques Delors, en est l'artisan ; il met fin à l'indexation des salaires sur les prix et engage une politique de contrôle des déficits publics, de lutte contre l'inflation et de défense de la monnaie. La nomination de Laurent Fabius comme Premier ministre en juillet 1984 et le départ des ministres communistes du gouvernement consacrent la prépondérance au sein de la gauche d'un courant réaliste, de plus en plus ouvertement social-démocrate.

Le temps des cohabitations : 1986-1998

La cohabitation est, sans conteste, la grande nouveauté politique de la période récente. Elle intervient quand le président de la République et le gouvernement issu de la majorité parlementaire appartiennent chacun à l'un des camps qui se partagent la vie politique en France et qu'on désigne par les termes de droite et de gauche, bien que ce classement soit aujourd'hui réducteur. Personne n'avait vraiment prévu une telle éventualité, sans doute ni les rédacteurs de la Constitution ni le général de Gaulle. En effet, pendant longtemps, le corps électoral élisait un Président et une Assemblée nationale appartenant à la même majorité, tradition confirmée lors des dissolutions de l'Assemblée prononcées par de Gaulle en 1968 et par Mitterrand en 1981, dissolutions suivies d'élections législatives qui avaient donné aux deux Présidents une confortable majorité.

Les choses changent en 1986, lorsque les électeurs donnent au président de la République, François Mitterrand, une Assemblée où les deux formations RPR et UDF sont majoritaires ; cette situation donne naissance à la première cohabitation qui durera jusqu'en 1988, avec Jacques Chirac pour Premier ministre. L'élection de François Mitterrand pour un deuxième septennat en 1988 marque la fin de la première cohabitation. La dissolution que prononce le chef de l'État amène à l'Assemblée nationale, en juin 1988, une majorité socialiste ; Michel Rocard devient Premier ministre, puis cède sa place à Édith Cresson en mai 1991, laquelle est remplacée par Pierre Bérégovoy en avril 1992.

La seconde cohabitation intervient en mars 1993 quand le Président Mitterrand choisit pour Premier ministre Édouard Balladur, à la suite des élections législatives qui ont dégagé une forte majorité RPR-UDF. L'élection de Jacques Chirac à la présidence de la République en 1995 met fin à cette cohabitation. Les pouvoirs exécutif et législatif appartiennent à nouveau à la même majorité et Alain Juppé est désigné comme Premier ministre. La troisième cohabitation commence en juin 1997 ; les élections législatives qui suivent la dissolution de l'Assemblée prononcée par Jacques Chirac, en avril 1997, désignent une majorité de députés de gauche et Lionel Jospin, chef de file du Parti socialiste, est nommé Premier ministre par le Président. Les termes de la troisième cohabitation sont inversés par rapport aux deux précédentes mais il semble bien que ce nouveau mode de fonctionnement satisfasse de plus en plus un corps électoral devenu versatile. Dans l'ensemble, les trois cohabitations montrent que les institutions de la Ve République fonctionnent de façon satisfaisante et assurent à la France une certaine stabilité politique.

La cohabitation en politique étrangère : le Président de la République, Jacques Chirac, et le Premier ministre, Lionel Jospin, avec Tony Blair, Premier ministre britannique, lors du sommet franco-britannique à Londres, 6 novembre 1997

Les constantes de la politique intérieure et extérieure

La fréquence des changements de coalitions politiques, ces dernières années, pourrait donner à penser que la France est gérée de manière discontinue. Les forces qui se succèdent au pouvoir gardent certes leur spécificité, marquée par des orientations et des choix particuliers. S'agissant de la coalition RPR-UDF, elle a pris l'initiative des privatisations de grandes entreprises du secteur public comme Saint-Gobain, la Société Générale, TF1, Rhône-Poulenc, etc. Les majorités de droite prônent une réduction du rôle de l'État et ont engagé, quand elles étaient au pouvoir, la baisse des impôts et des prélèvements obligatoires. À l'inverse, les socialistes et les majorités de gauche ont opté pour le *statu quo* en matière de nationalisations et de privatisations, favorisé le recrutement de fonctionnaires et maintenu, autant que faire se peut, les contrôles de l'État et de l'administration sur la vie économique du pays.

Cependant, on retrouve des permanences fondamentales, quelle que soit la couleur politique des gouvernements au pouvoir. Elles touchent à la politique de l'emploi et à la lutte contre le chômage, qui font l'objet d'un traitement social qui consiste à indemniser les chômeurs, à assurer des revenus minimaux aux plus démunis (revenu minimum d'insertion ou « RMI », minimum vieillesse), à développer la formation et à favoriser l'insertion sur le marché du travail (stages, contrats-emploi-solidarité, emplois-jeunes...). Elles concernent aussi la construction européenne, dont tous les Présidents et les Premiers ministres ont été des artisans convaincus, mobilisant leur majorité pour ce projet. Les clivages ont d'ailleurs transcendé les oppositions traditionnelles en ce domaine et on a vu, lors du référendum sur le traité de Maastricht le 20 septembre 1992, la droite et la gauche se diviser en partisans du oui ou du non, à l'image d'ailleurs de toute la France puisque le oui ne l'a emporté qu'avec 51 % des voix. Depuis, le camp des pro-européens a progressé et le consensus est plus large sur le passage à la monnaie unique, même si de vives oppositions se manifestent encore. Enfin, tous les pouvoirs successifs ont concouru à maintenir la France dans la compétition économique mondiale, en encadrant le repli des activités en difficulté (pêche, sidérurgie, textile...) et en favorisant le développement de branches nouvelles (aérospatiale, télécommunications, biotechnologies, activités liées à l'environnement, etc.).

On constate, au total, que les cadres et les organisations qui ont structuré la vie politique depuis les années soixante n'évoluent que lentement mais que les comportements et les idéologies ont changé en profondeur. Un réel consensus s'est dégagé sur les options fondamentales et la France évolue vers un modèle proche de celui des social-démocraties d'Europe du Nord.

Pour en savoir plus :

J.-J. Becker, *Crises et alternances 1974-1995*, Le Seuil, collection Points histoire, Nouvelle histoire de la France contemporaine, 1998.

D. Borne, *Histoire de la société française depuis 1945*, A. Colin, collection Cursus, 1992.

D. Chagnollaud et J.-L. Quermonne, *Le gouvernement de la France sous la Ve République*, nouvelle édition, Fayard, 1996.

J.-F. Sirinelli, *Dictionnaire historique de la vie politique française au XXe siècle*, PUF, 1995.

C. Ysmal, *Les partis politiques sous la Ve République*, Montchrestien, Domat politique, 1989.

Les présidents de la République française

L.-N. Bonaparte (1848-1852) - A. Thiers (1871-1873) - Mac-Mahon (1873-1879) - J. Grévy (1879-1887) - S. Carnot (1887-1894)
J. Casimir-Périer (1894-1895) - F. Faure (1895-1899) - É. Loubet (1899-1906) - A. Fallières (1906-1913) - R. Poincaré (1913-1920)
P. Deschanel (1920-1920) - A. Millerand (1920-1924) - G. Doumergue (1924-1931) - P. Doumer (1931-1932) - A. Lebrun (1932-1940)
V. Auriol (1947-1953) - R. Coty (1953-1959) - C. de Gaulle (1959-1969) - G. Pompidou (1969-1974) - V. Giscard d'Estaing (1974-1981)
F. Mitterrand (1981-1995) - J. Chirac (1995-...)

L'ÉTAT
ET LA
VIE POLITIQUE

Schéma de la Constitution de 1958

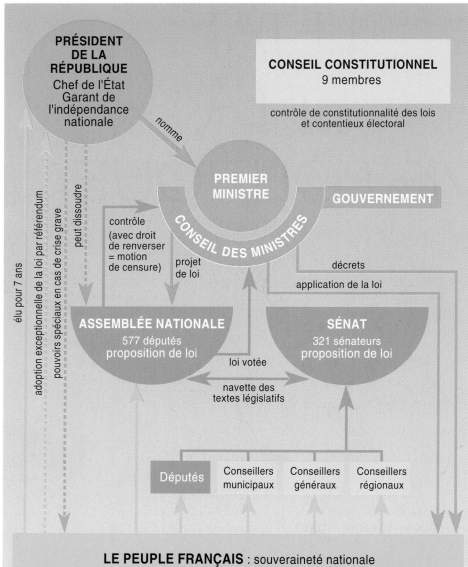

PRÉSIDENT
DE LA
RÉPUBLIQUE
Chef de l'État
Garant de
l'indépendance
nationale

CONSEIL CONSTITUTIONNEL
9 membres

contrôle de constitutionnalité des lois
et contentieux électoral

nomme

PREMIER
MINISTRE

GOUVERNEMENT

CONSEIL DES MINISTRES

élu pour 7 ans

adoption exceptionnelle de la loi par référendum

pouvoirs spéciaux en cas de crise grave

peut dissoudre

contrôle
(avec droit
de renverser
= motion
de censure)

projet
de loi

décrets

application de la loi

ASSEMBLÉE NATIONALE
577 députés
proposition de loi

SÉNAT
321 sénateurs
proposition de loi

loi votée

navette des
textes législatifs

Députés

Conseillers
municipaux

Conseillers
généraux

Conseillers
régionaux

LE PEUPLE FRANÇAIS : souveraineté nationale
suffrage universel : tous les citoyens de plus de 18 ans votent

pouvoir législatif   pouvoir exécutif

6

Les institutions

Un pouvoir exécutif fort

La Vᵉ République, mise en place par la Constitution de 1958, a renforcé le rôle du pouvoir exécutif (président de la République et gouvernement) et a permis de dégager une majorité politique nette à chaque législature, ce qui a mis fin à l'instabilité parlementaire qui prévalait auparavant. Après qu'elle ait suscité, à ses débuts, une vive opposition de gauche, la Constitution de 1958 a fini par faire l'objet d'un consensus assez large, en liaison sans doute avec le fait qu'elle ait permis, depuis 1981, l'alternance politique et les cohabitations. Si les institutions ont fonctionné de manière satisfaisante, c'est peut-être parce que le gaullisme qui les inspire est, plus qu'une idéologie politique, une méthode d'action fondée sur quelques principes clairs : grandeur de la France, rôle central de l'État, prédominance de l'intérêt de la nation sur les idéologies, nécessité que le chef de l'État soit «au-dessus des partis» et tire sa légitimité de la souveraineté populaire. C'est ce dernier point qui a conduit le général de Gaulle à proposer une réforme essentielle du texte de 1958 : l'élection du président de la République au suffrage universel direct, instaurée par la révision constitutionnelle de 1962.

Prépondérance du président de la République

La Constitution du 4 octobre 1958 instituait l'élection du président de la République au suffrage universel indirect par un collège électoral comprenant les membres du Parlement et divers représentants des élus locaux. Élu par ce collège en 1958, le général de Gaulle le fut au suffrage universel direct à l'élection de 1965. Ce mode de désignation fait du Président la clef de voûte des nouvelles institutions et rompt avec le régime de la IIIᵉ et de la IVᵉ Répu-

Le Palais de l'Élysée, situé rue du Faubourg-Saint-Honoré à Paris, est le siège de la présidence de la République et de ses services depuis 1873

blique qui donnait la primauté au Parlement élu et lui attribuait le pouvoir de désigner le Président. Par ailleurs, la pratique constitutionnelle, dominée par la forte personnalité du général de Gaulle, va renforcer cette prépondérance du pouvoir exécutif.

La Constitution définit les attributions du président de la République :

• le Président est élu pour sept ans - le mandat le plus long des régimes parlementaires - et indéfiniment rééligible ;

• chef des armées (art. 15), le Président est également le garant de l'indépendance nationale, de l'intégrité du territoire et du respect des traités (art. 5). À ce titre, il joue un rôle essentiel en matière de politique étrangère, un domaine qu'il partage avec le gouvernement ;

• le Président veille au respect de la Constitution. Il assure, par son arbitrage, le fonctionnement régulier des pouvoirs publics ainsi que la continuité de l'État (art. 5). Il nomme le Premier ministre et préside le Conseil des ministres ;

• le Président promulgue les lois (art. 10), signe les ordonnances et les décrets délibérés en Conseil des ministres (art. 13) ;

• le Président est garant de l'indépendance de l'autorité judiciaire (art. 64) et préside le Conseil supérieur de la magistrature ;

• il nomme aux emplois civils et militaires les plus importants (art. 13). Il dispose du droit de grâce (art. 17) et peut être investi de pouvoirs exceptionnels en période de crise grave (art. 16). Sur proposition du gouvernement ou des assemblées, il peut soumettre certains projets de loi au référendum. Après consultation du gouvernement et des présidents de l'Assemblée et du Sénat, il peut dissoudre l'Assemblée nationale. Il peut saisir le Conseil constitutionnel afin que ce dernier se prononce sur la conformité de la loi à la Constitution avant sa promulgation (voir plus bas).

La Constitution définit les pouvoirs exercés personnellement par le Président et ceux qu'il partage avec le Premier ministre, ce qui a permis le fonctionnement des institutions en période de « cohabitation » entre un Président et un Premier ministre appartenant à des majorités politiques différentes.

Le Premier ministre et le gouvernement

Le gouvernement détermine et conduit la politique de la Nation. Il dispose, à cet effet, de l'administration et de la force armée. Il est responsable devant le Parlement (art. 20). Nommé par le président de la République, le Premier ministre dirige l'action du gouvernement. Il est responsable de la défense nationale. Il assure l'exécution des lois (art. 21). Dans les limites qui lui sont conférées par la Constitution, il exerce le pouvoir réglementaire (art. 21). Ce point est fondamental : en effet, alors que la loi est votée par le Parlement, le règlement (décrets et arrêtés ministériels) est une émanation du gouvernement, c'est-à-dire du Premier ministre et des ministres. À cet égard, la Constitution de 1958 innove en opérant une nette distinction entre le domaine de la loi, désormais défini de manière limitative à l'article 34, et celui du règlement qui s'étend à toutes les matières autres que celles qui sont du domaine de la loi (art. 37). Le pouvoir réglementaire peut exceptionnellement être élargi, si le Parlement autorise le gouvernement à prendre par ordonnance, pendant un délai limité, des mesures qui sont normalement du domaine de la loi (art. 38).

Indépendamment du pouvoir réglementaire, le gouvernement détient, comme dans tous les régimes parlementaires, l'initiative des lois au même titre que les membres du Parlement. Mais il jouit d'une incontestable prééminence car c'est lui qui fixe l'ordre du jour des assemblées (art. 48) et peut recourir au vote bloqué. Enfin et surtout, le Premier ministre peut décider d'engager la responsabilité du gouvernement devant l'Assemblée nationale soit sur son programme, soit sur une déclaration de politique générale, soit sur le vote d'un texte (art. 49, alinéa 3). Ce texte est considéré comme adopté, sauf si une motion de censure, déposée à l'Assemblée nationale, recueille la majorité des voix des députés. En ce cas, le Premier ministre doit remettre au président de la République la démission de son gouvernement. Cette disposition, unique en Europe occidentale, permet d'éviter toute politique d'obstruction parlementaire systématique à l'action du gouvernement.

En tant que chef du gouvernement, le Premier ministre a une situation prééminente face aux autres ministres et secrétaires d'État et dispose en outre de moyens administratifs particuliers, tel le Secrétariat général du gouvernement. Le nombre des ministres et secrétaires d'État varie en fonction des priorités et des équilibres politiques recherchés. Les membres du gouvernement participent à la conduite de la politique de la nation lors des réunions des instances gouvernementales ainsi que par le contreseing qu'ils apposent aux actes du gouvernement relatifs à leur domaine de compétence. Ils doivent, par ailleurs, défendre la politique menée par leur ministère devant le Parlement. Enfin, leur incombe la bonne application des mesures gouvernementales par les services administratifs qu'ils dirigent. La fonction de membre du gouvernement est incompatible avec celle de parlementaire de même qu'avec un emploi public ou une activité professionnelle privée. En revanche, les membres du gouvernement peuvent détenir des mandats électifs locaux. La composition de l'équipe qui entoure chaque ministre – le cabinet ministériel – constitue une spécificité française. La sélection des membres du cabinet dépend du ministre. La plupart d'entre eux sont issus de la haute administration. Ils exercent leurs fonctions en s'appuyant sur l'administration centrale et sur les services déconcentrés de l'État dans les départements, les régions et parfois à l'étranger.

Premier conseil des ministres du gouvernement de Lionel Jospin, juin 1997, sous la présidence de M. Jacques Chirac. Le conseil des ministres réunit les membres du gouvernement chaque mercredi au Palais de l'Élysée

Les membres du gouvernement sont individuellement responsables devant le Premier ministre et le président de la République. Leur démission peut être spontanée (pour convenance personnelle), automatique (démission collective du gouvernement) ou provoquée (divergence avec le Premier ministre ou le président de la République). Par ailleurs, la loi constitutionnelle du 27 juillet 1993 (titre X de la Constitution) rend les membres du gouvernement « pénalement responsables des actes accomplis dans l'exercice de leurs fonctions et qualifiés crimes et délits au moment où ils ont été commis. Ils sont jugés par la Cour de justice de la République. »

Le pouvoir législatif : les compétences du Parlement

L'Assemblée nationale (appelée Chambre des députés sous les précédentes Républiques), qui siège au Palais Bourbon, et le Sénat, qui se réunit au Palais du Luxembourg, constituent le Parlement. La Constitution de 1958 confère au Parlement un rôle éminent en qualité d'organe d'élaboration des lois et dans sa fonction de contrôle du gouvernement. L'article 34 de la Constitution définit le domaine de compétence du Parlement : vote annuel de la loi de finances (budget) ainsi que des lois de programme qui déterminent les objectifs et les cadres de l'action économique sociale et de défense de l'État. Avant d'adopter la loi, le Parlement peut consulter le Conseil économique et social ; celui-ci, composé de personnalités représentatives de l'ensemble des catégories socioprofessionnelles, se voit confier régulièrement des études sur les grands problèmes de l'économie et de la société qui touchent la vie de la nation.

L'initiative d'une loi peut émaner du gouvernement (projet de loi) ; le texte est alors délibéré en Conseil des ministres après avis du Conseil d'État (voir plus bas) avant d'être déposé sur le bureau de l'une des deux assemblées. Elle peut aussi provenir du Parlement (proposition de loi). Projets et propositions de loi sont débattus pendant les sessions parlementaires et font la « navette » entre les deux assemblées, afin d'être votés dans les mêmes termes par chacune d'elles. Si l'accord ne se fait pas sur un texte identique, il existe des mécanismes de conciliation. En cas d'échec, l'Assemblée nationale a le dernier mot (art. 45). Dans la pratique, on constate qu'au cours des dernières législatures les lois votées étaient rarement d'origine parlementaire (moins de une sur cinq), ce qui nourrit un débat permanent sur le rôle effectif du Parlement.

L'Assemblée nationale

L'Assemblée nationale comprend 577 députés élus au suffrage universel direct, au scrutin uninominal majoritaire à deux tours, dans le cadre d'une circonscription de taille variable (un député pour environ 100 000 habitants). La durée d'une législature est de cinq ans ; toutefois, elle peut être abrégée si le président de la République décide de dissoudre l'Assemblée, comme ce fut le cas le 21 avril 1997, pour la cinquième fois depuis le début de la Vᵉ République. La révision constitutionnelle d'août 1995 a instauré une session unique, qui s'ouvre le premier jour ouvrable d'octobre et s'achève le dernier jour ouvrable de juin.

Peuvent s'y ajouter des sessions extraordinaires, ouvertes et closes par décret du président de la République. La plupart des séances sont publiques. La presse rend compte des débats, dont le contenu intégral est publié au *Journal officiel*. La séance hebdomadaire du mercredi, retransmise à la télévision, est réservée aux questions d'actualité des parlementaires aux membres du gouvernement.

Lionel Jospin, Premier ministre, à la tribune de l'Assemblée nationale, juin 1997

Les députés sont, pour la plupart, inscrits à l'un des groupes politiques de l'Assemblée, mais ce n'est pas obligatoire. Chaque député appartient à l'une des six commissions permanentes de l'Assemblée et participe à ses travaux : Affaires culturelles, familiales et sociales, Affaires étrangères, Défense nationale et forces armées, Finances, économie générale et plan, Lois, Production et échanges.

Contrairement au Sénat, l'Assemblée nationale dispose du pouvoir de sanctionner le gouvernement par le vote d'une motion de censure. Par ailleurs, les projets de lois de finances lui sont soumis en priorité (art. 39).

Le Sénat

Le Sénat comprend 321 sénateurs élus pour neuf ans au suffrage universel indirect par un collège électoral composé, dans chaque département, des députés, conseillers régionaux, conseillers généraux et représentants des conseils municipaux. Le Sénat est renouvelé par tiers tous les trois ans et comporte une forte proportion d'élus locaux.

À l'instar du député, le sénateur est avant tout un législateur. Son pouvoir, dans ce domaine, s'exprime essentiellement par le droit d'amendement. L'examen des projets et propositions de lois s'effectue au Sénat comme à l'Assemblée nationale, c'est-à-dire, dans un premier temps, par l'intermédiaire de six commissions permanentes (Affaires culturelles, Affaires économiques, Affaires étrangères, Défense et forces armées, Affaires sociales, Finances et Lois), puis en séance publique. À l'exception du vote d'une motion de censure, les sénateurs ont des pouvoirs identiques à ceux de leurs collègues députés en

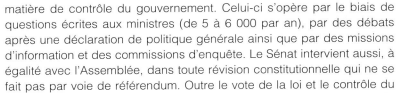

matière de contrôle du gouvernement. Celui-ci s'opère par le biais de questions écrites aux ministres (de 5 à 6 000 par an), par des débats après une déclaration de politique générale ainsi que par des missions d'information et des commissions d'enquête. Le Sénat intervient aussi, à égalité avec l'Assemblée, dans toute révision constitutionnelle qui ne se fait pas par voie de référendum. Outre le vote de la loi et le contrôle du gouvernement, la Constitution de 1958 a chargé le Sénat d'assurer la représentation des collectivités territoriales de la République, c'est-à-dire des communes, des départements, des régions ainsi que des territoires d'outre-mer. Les Français établis hors de France sont également représentés au Sénat.

Le Sénat, installé au Palais du Luxembourg, à Paris

Le mode de scrutin, la durée du mandat des séna-teurs et le fait que le Sénat ne peut être dissous ont pour conséquence une grande stabilité politique de la Haute Assemblée. Cela explique que la Constitu-tion confie au président du Sénat l'exercice provi-soire des fonctions de président de la République en cas de vacance ou d'empêchement du Président élu. Une telle situation s'est produite à deux repri-ses : en 1969, après la démission du général de Gaulle et en 1974, à la mort du Président Pompidou. Le Sénat apparaît ainsi comme l'institution qui assure la continuité du fonctionnement des pouvoirs publics et donc de l'État.

Le Conseil constitutionnel, gardien de la Constitution

Organe juridictionnel, le Conseil constitutionnel com-prend neuf membres, dont le mandat est de neuf ans, non renouvelable et irrévocable. Il se renouvelle par tiers tous les trois ans. Trois de ses membres sont désignés par le président de la République, les six autres l'étant respectivement et à parts égales par les présidents de l'Assemblée nationale et du Sénat. Les anciens présidents de la Répu-blique en sont membres de droit, toutefois aucun d'entre eux n'y a siégé. Le président du Conseil constitutionnel est nommé par le prési-dent de la République et a voix prépondérante en cas de partage.

Les attributions du Conseil constitutionnel sont stricte-ment définies par la Constitution (articles 58 à 61) et ses décisions ne sont susceptibles d'aucun recours (art. 62). Ses deux principaux pôles de compétence concernent le contentieux électoral et le contrôle de constitutionnalité des lois. Il lui incombe, par ailleurs, de constater l'éventuel empêchement du président de la République. Enfin, il doit être consulté avant que le président de la République ne soit investi des pouvoirs exceptionnels (art. 16).

S'agissant du contrôle des élections et des référendums, le Conseil constitutionnel est compétent pour l'élection présidentielle, les élections législatives et sénatoriales, les référendums, ainsi que pour le contrôle des inéligibilités et incompatibilités. Concernant le référendum, le Conseil détient une double fonction : consultative, au préalable, et juridictionnelle, a posteriori, puisqu'il est chargé d'examiner les réclamations relatives au déroulement du scrutin. Quant au contrôle de constitutionnalité, il convient de distinguer le contrôle obligatoire (conformité des règlements des assemblées et des lois organiques) de celui exercé à titre facultatif (constitutionnalité des lois ordinaires et des traités ou engagements internationaux). En ce dernier domaine, le Conseil constitutionnel peut être saisi par le président de la République, le

Premier ministre, le président de l'Assemblée nationale, le président du Sénat et, depuis 1974, par soixante députés ou soixante sénateurs. Cette dernière disposition permet aux partis d'opposition de présenter un recours contre une loi adoptée par la majorité parlementaire.

Le Conseil constitutionnel, ainsi que le Conseil d'État, siègent au Palais-Royal à Paris

En ce qui concerne la mission de contrôle de constitutionnalité, le Conseil constitutionnel a pris une décision importante en 1971. Depuis cette date, l'examen du Conseil porte sur la conformité des lois non seulement à la Constitution de 1958, mais également aux textes auxquels elle se réfère, le préambule de la Constitution de 1946 et la Déclaration des Droits de l'homme et du citoyen de 1789, ainsi qu'aux principes fondamentaux reconnus par les lois de la République. Par cette décision, le Conseil constitutionnel est devenu le protecteur des droits et libertés fondamentales des citoyens. En témoigne une jurisprudence désormais abondante, précise et rigoureuse.

L'autorité judiciaire

L'organisation judiciaire en France est caractérisée par la distinction fondamentale entre les juridictions de l'ordre administratif et les juridictions de l'ordre judiciaire.

La juridiction administrative

Contrairement à la tradition anglo-saxonne, le droit qui s'applique aux citoyens et aux entreprises privées n'est pas celui qui prévaut pour les administrations publiques et les collectivités territoriales lorsqu'elles agissent en qualité de personnes morales de droit public. Elles relèvent alors du droit administratif, doté de ses propres règles et de ses propres tribunaux. Statut des personnels, urbanisme, contrats publics, l'ensemble du contentieux du secteur public dépend des tribunaux administratifs. La juridiction suprême de l'ordre administratif est le Conseil d'État dont les membres (environ deux cents) bénéficient d'un statut qui garantit leur indépendance. Le Conseil d'État exerce des attributions juridictionnelles et consultatives.

Sur le plan juridictionnel, le Conseil d'État – juge en droit et en fait – statue, d'une part, directement sur la légalité des actes administratifs les plus importants et, d'autre part, en sa qualité de juge d'appel, sur des affaires jugées par les tribunaux administratifs et les cours administratives d'appel. À ce titre, il lui incombe de juger en dernier recours les litiges dans lesquels l'État et les collectivités publiques sont mis en cause. Il peut également être saisi de recours en annulation des actes réglementaires signés par le président de la République ou le Premier ministre. Cette éventualité permet aux administrés de se prémunir contre tout arbitraire de l'État.

Ses attributions consultatives en font le conseiller juridique du gouvernement. Il examine les projets de loi avant délibération en Conseil des ministres (art. 39) ainsi que certains projets de décrets. Le gouvernement peut solliciter son avis sur diverses questions d'ordre juridique.

L'administration est par ailleurs contrôlée, du point de vue budgétaire, par la Cour des comptes (qui comprend deux cent cinquante magistrats), relayée par les Cours régionales des comptes. Également réputée pour son indépendance, la Cour examine et juge les comptes de tous les comptables publics ; elle surveille la gestion des autorités administratives et des responsables du secteur public, qui inclut les grandes entreprises publiques. Son activité est rendue publique dans un rapport annuel.

Assemblée plénière de la Cour de Cassation. Au sommet de la hiérarchie judiciaire, la Cour de Cassation exerce un contrôle sur l'application des règles de droit et peut casser les jugements prononcés par les tribunaux

L'ordre judiciaire

À l'instar de tous les régimes démocratiques, l'ordre judiciaire français comporte une haute instance, la Cour de cassation. Celle-ci examine, en droit, les recours formés contre les arrêts des vingt-sept cours d'appel. Ces dernières se prononcent, en droit et en fait, par la voie de l'appel, sur les jugements des juridictions du premier degré, qui se divisent elles-mêmes en deux ensembles distincts : les juridictions civiles et les juridictions pénales.

Les affaires civiles et les infractions pénales relèvent respectivement des tribunaux de grande instance, des tribunaux d'instance (pour certains types de contentieux), des tribunaux correctionnels (délits) et des tribunaux de police (contraventions). Tous sont composés de magistrats professionnels. Les affaires commerciales relèvent des tribunaux de commerce, formés de juges élus par un collège de délégués consulaires comprenant des commerçants. Les conflits du travail sont jugés par les conseils des prud'hommes, dont les juges siègent selon un principe paritaire (représentants des employeurs et des salariés). Quant aux affaires criminelles, elles relèvent des cours d'assises qui ont la particularité d'être composées d'un président et de deux assesseurs – magistrats professionnels – et de neuf jurés, simples citoyens tirés au sort sur les listes électorales. Autre singularité, il n'y a pas d'instance d'appel pour les cours d'assises ; jusqu'à présent, seul le recours sur des questions de droit devant la Cour de cassation est possible.

Droit français et droit européen

La France étant à la fois membre de l'Union européenne et du Conseil de l'Europe, le droit français et son application ont été sensiblement modifiés au cours des vingt dernières années. En effet, la Constitution de 1958, dans son article 55, reconnaît au droit international une « autorité supérieure » sur le droit interne.

Le droit communautaire repose sur les traités (CEE, CECA, Euratom, UE) ainsi que sur le « droit dérivé » établi par les institutions européennes, sous la forme de règlements, directives et décisions. La légalité de l'ensemble de ces normes est garantie par la Cour de justice de l'Union européenne, établie à Luxembourg. Celle-ci a fondé sa jurisprudence sur deux grands principes : l'effet direct et la primauté du droit communautaire. Le principe de l'effet direct (arrêt de 1963) permet à toute personne d'invoquer devant le juge national une grande partie du droit communautaire. Quant au principe de primauté (arrêt de 1964), il pose la prééminence de la règle communautaire sur la règle nationale. Ainsi, en France, la Cour de cassation – depuis 1975 – et le Conseil d'État – depuis 1989 – appliquent le principe de primauté pour opposer la norme communautaire à toute loi nationale postérieure qui ne serait pas compatible avec elle.

Par ailleurs, la France a ratifié en 1974 la Convention européenne des droits de l'homme, aux termes de laquelle le respect des droits de l'homme est assuré par la Cour européenne des droits de l'homme, établie à Strasbourg. La Convention européenne des droits de l'homme garantit à toute personne résidant dans un État membre du Conseil de l'Europe un ensemble très complet et très élaboré de droits. Applicable par le juge en vertu du principe de primauté, la Convention connaît une notoriété croissante depuis 1981, date à laquelle la France a ratifié l'article 25 relatif au droit de recours individuel. Désormais, toute personne physique ou morale peut saisir la Commission sous réserve de l'épuisement des voies de recours

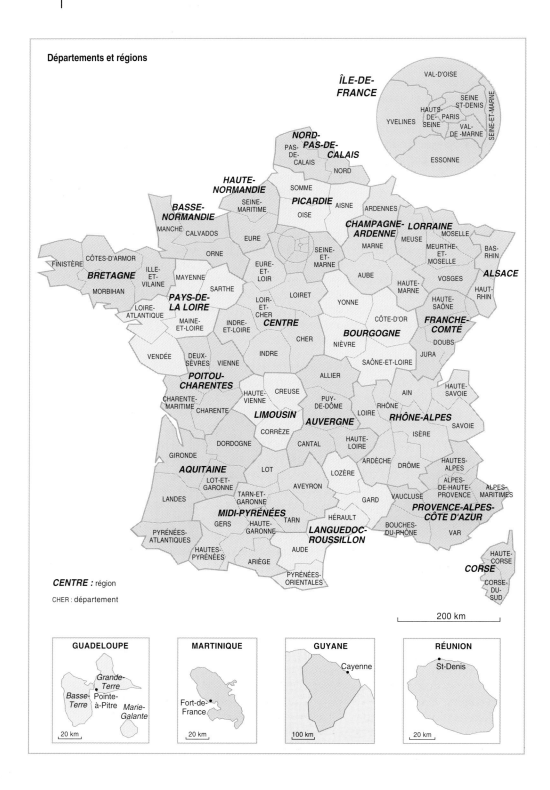

Départements et régions

ÎLE-DE-FRANCE

VAL-D'OISE

SEINE-ST-DENIS

HAUTS-DE-SEINE PARIS

YVELINES VAL-DE-MARNE

SEINE-ET-MARNE

ESSONNE

NORD-PAS-DE-CALAIS

PAS-DE-CALAIS

NORD

HAUTE-NORMANDIE

SOMME

PICARDIE AISNE

ARDENNES

BASSE-NORMANDIE

SEINE-MARITIME

OISE

CHAMPAGNE-ARDENNE

LORRAINE

MANCHE CALVADOS

EURE

MARNE

MEUSE

MOSELLE

MEURTHE-ET-MOSELLE

BAS-RHIN

FINISTÈRE

CÔTES-D'ARMOR

ORNE

SEINE-ET-MARNE

ALSACE

BRETAGNE

ILLE-ET-VILAINE

MAYENNE

EURE-ET-LOIR

AUBE

HAUTE-MARNE

VOSGES

HAUT-RHIN

MORBIHAN

SARTHE

LOIRET

YONNE

HAUTE-SAÔNE

FRANCHE-COMTÉ

PAYS-DE-LA LOIRE

LOIRE-ATLANTIQUE

MAINE-ET-LOIRE

LOIR-ET-CHER

CENTRE

CÔTE-D'OR

BOURGOGNE

DOUBS

INDRE-ET-LOIRE

CHER

NIÈVRE

JURA

VENDÉE

DEUX-SÈVRES

VIENNE

INDRE

SAÔNE-ET-LOIRE

POITOU-CHARENTES

ALLIER

AIN

HAUTE-SAVOIE

CHARENTE-MARITIME

CHARENTE

HAUTE-VIENNE

CREUSE

PUY-DE-DÔME

RHÔNE

LIMOUSIN

AUVERGNE

LOIRE

RHÔNE-ALPES

SAVOIE

CORRÈZE

ISÈRE

DORDOGNE

CANTAL

HAUTE-LOIRE

GIRONDE

ARDÈCHE

DRÔME

HAUTES-ALPES

AQUITAINE

LOT

LOZÈRE

ALPES-DE-HAUTE-PROVENCE

ALPES-MARITIMES

LOT-ET-GARONNE

AVEYRON

VAUCLUSE

LANDES

TARN-ET-GARONNE

GARD

PROVENCE-ALPES-CÔTE D'AZUR

MIDI-PYRÉNÉES

TARN

HÉRAULT

BOUCHES-DU-RHÔNE

VAR

GERS

HAUTE-GARONNE

LANGUEDOC-ROUSSILLON

PYRÉNÉES-ATLANTIQUES

AUDE

HAUTE-CORSE

HAUTES-PYRÉNÉES

ARIÈGE

CORSE

PYRÉNÉES-ORIENTALES

CORSE-DU-SUD

CENTRE : région

CHER : département

200 km

GUADELOUPE

Grande-Terre

Basse-Terre Pointe-à-Pitre

Marie-Galante

20 km

MARTINIQUE

Fort-de-France

20 km

GUYANE

Cayenne

100 km

RÉUNION

St-Denis

20 km

internes. L'ensemble des liens juridiques entre la France et les organes du Conseil de l'Europe confirme toute l'importance attachée par la France aux principes fondateurs de cette organisation et à la constante amélioration de la mise en application de ses procédures.

L'administration territoriale

Héritière d'une longue tradition centralisatrice, l'administration territoriale a connu des évolutions importantes au cours des vingt dernières années. Son organisation peut paraître complexe au premier abord ; en effet, la France est l'un des rares États de l'Union européenne à conjuguer quatre niveaux d'administration territoriale : État, région, département, commune.

La loi de décentralisation du 2 mars 1982 et les textes qui l'ont complétée marquent la volonté politique de modifier les rapports entre l'État et les collectivités territoriales (régions, départements, communes). Ces dernières détiennent désormais une autonomie de décision beaucoup plus large, les nouveaux textes ayant opéré un partage des compétences et des responsabilités administratives et budgétaires entre le pouvoir central et les pouvoirs locaux.

L'administration locale : une organisation à trois niveaux

L'organisation territoriale de la France comprend trois niveaux d'administration, la commune, le département et la région, qui sont à la fois des circonscriptions administratives de l'État et des collectivités territoriales décentralisées. Sur le plan juridique, une collectivité territoriale décentralisée est une personne morale de droit public (avec une dénomination, un territoire, un budget, du personnel, etc.), disposant de compétences propres et d'une certaine autonomie par rapport au pouvoir central.

À ces collectivités s'ajoutent les territoires d'outre-mer ainsi que les collectivités territoriales à statut particulier (Paris, Marseille et Lyon, la Corse, Mayotte et Saint-Pierre-et-Miquelon).

La commune

Instituée dès 1789, la commune est la structure de base de l'organisation administrative française. On en compte près de 37 000, chiffre très supérieur à celui des autres pays de l'Union européenne mais qui s'explique par le fait que le terme de commune, en France, s'applique à toutes les municipalités, quelle que soit leur population (80 % d'entre elles ont moins de 1 000 habitants). Cette situation a conduit les pouvoirs publics à inciter au regroupement communal, sous forme notamment de communautés urbaines et syndicats intercommunaux. De plus, la loi du 6 février 1992 a proposé de nouvelles formes de coopération susceptibles de rationaliser la gestion des municipalités, en fonction de leur communauté d'intérêts. Dans les faits, ces rapprochements se limitent souvent à la mise en commun de quelques services et les fusions sont extrêmement rares, la commune restant un cadre identitaire fort pour ses habitants et ses élus.

Comme le département et la région, la commune dispose d'un organe délibérant, le conseil municipal, et d'une autorité exécutive, le maire, élu par le conseil municipal. Le nombre de conseillers municipaux est proportionnel à la population. Élus pour six ans au suffrage universel direct, les conseillers municipaux adoptent les grandes orientations de la politique communale, votent le budget, gèrent les biens de la commune, en particulier les bâtiments et équipements scolaires du premier cycle de l'enseignement, et définissent le fonctionnement de l'administration communale.

La mairie de Conches et celle de Savigny-le-Temple (Seine-et-Marne)

Les attributions du maire sont de deux ordres, car il est à la fois l'autorité élue de la commune et le représentant de l'État sur le territoire communal. En sa qualité d'autorité exécutive de la commune, il met en œuvre les délibérations du conseil municipal, représente la commune sur le plan juridique, propose et exécute le budget, assure la conservation et l'administration du patrimoine communal et délivre les permis de construire. Le maire détient également des pouvoirs propres. À ce titre, il est responsable de la sécurité et de la salubrité publiques et dispose de l'administration communale, dont il est le chef hiérarchique. En tant que représentant de l'État, le maire est officier d'état civil (célébration des mariages, etc.) et officier de police judiciaire sous l'autorité du procureur de la République. Enfin, il assure certaines fonctions administratives : publicité des lois et règlements, établissement des listes électorales. Les actes du maire sont des actes administratifs unilatéraux, généralement des arrêtés, soumis au contrôle de légalité lorsqu'il agit en tant qu'exécutif communal, et au pouvoir hiérarchique du préfet (voir plus bas) quand il agit en qualité de représentant de l'État.

Les compétences propres à la commune concernent donc les actions de proximité ; elles se sont étendues dans le domaine économique et social, où elles furent longtemps limitées à l'octroi d'aides aux entreprises créant des emplois et de secours divers aux familles dans le besoin. La commune est ainsi devenue un acteur important de la politique de lutte contre le chômage et l'exclusion et un agent actif de la restructuration économique et du développement de nouvelles activités.

Le département

La France compte 100 départements, dont 96 en métropole et 4 outre-mer (Martinique, Guadeloupe, Réunion et Guyane). Institué en 1789, le département a vu son statut évoluer de celui de collectivité territoriale semi-décentralisée à celui de collectivité territoriale à part entière (depuis 1982). Son rôle a été prééminent sur le plan de l'organisation administrative et géographique du territoire. Les compétences propres au département concernent essentiellement l'action sanitaire et sociale, l'équipement rural, la voirie départementale et les dépenses d'investissement et de fonctionnement des collèges.

Pendant près de deux siècles (1800-1982), le préfet fut le détenteur du pouvoir exécutif dans le département. La loi de mars 1982 a modifié ses compétences. Nommé par le gouvernement, le préfet reste le dépositaire unique de l'autorité de l'État dans le département. À ce titre, il représente le Premier ministre ainsi que chacun des membres du gouvernement ; il a autorité sur les services extérieurs de l'État dans le département ; enfin, il assure le contrôle administratif des collectivités territoriales du département.

L'hôtel du département
à Avignon (Vaucluse)

Mais depuis l'adoption de la loi du 2 mars 1982, l'autorité exécutive du département est le président du conseil général. Le conseil général est l'organe délibérant du département. Il est composé de conseillers généraux élus pour six ans au scrutin uninominal majoritaire à deux tours, dans le cadre d'un canton (la France compte 3 500 circonscriptions administratives de ce type). Élu par les conseillers généraux, le président du conseil général prépare et exécute les délibérations du conseil, y compris sur le plan budgétaire ; il représente le département en justice ; il dirige l'administration départementale ; enfin, en sa qualité de responsable de la gestion du domaine départemental, il exerce les pouvoirs de police, de la conservation du domaine et ceux de la circulation sur la voirie départementale, sous réserve des pouvoirs dévolus en la matière aux maires et au préfet.

La région

La France compte 26 régions, dont 22 en métropole et 4 outre-mer qui coïncident avec les 4 départements d'outre-mer (DOM). Créée en 1955 pour servir de cadre à l'aménagement du territoire, la région est devenue collectivité territoriale en 1982. Ses compétences propres concernent principalement la planification, l'aménagement du territoire, le développement économique, la formation professionnelle ainsi que la construction, l'équipement et les dépenses de fonctionnement des lycées.

L'organe délibérant de la région est le conseil régional. Les conseillers régionaux, élus pour six ans, sont assistés d'un comité économique et social régional. Cette assemblée, à vocation consultative, est composée de représentants des entreprises, des professions libérales, des organisations syndicales et de salariés, des associations à vocation régionale, etc. La consultation de ce comité est obligatoire pour ce qui concerne la préparation et l'exécution du plan national, l'établissement du plan régional de développement ainsi que la définition des grandes orientations du budget régional. Par ailleurs, le comité peut intervenir librement sur toute question intéressant la région ou, à l'initiative du président du conseil régional, sur tout projet à caractère économique, social ou culturel. L'autorité exécutive de la région est le président du conseil régional, élu par les conseillers régionaux. Ses attributions sont identiques à celles du président du conseil général et s'exercent dans les domaines où la région a compétence.

Permanence et évolution de l'organisation territoriale

L'article 72 de la Constitution dispose que les collectivités territoriales de la République s'administrent librement par des conseils élus. La réforme de 1982 n'a pas introduit de modifications sur ce plan. Le principe de la libre administration des collectivités ainsi que celui de l'élection des membres des organes délibérants restent des fondements de l'administration territoriale française.

S'il y a donc permanence, s'agissant des structures et des fondements, et distinction évidente, s'agissant des domaines de compétence, les lois de décentralisation ont introduit certaines évolutions, en particulier concernant le contrôle. En effet, la liberté de s'administrer, la nécessaire cohérence des actions dans un État unitaire, mais aussi le principe d'égalité entre les citoyens ainsi que la sauvegarde des intérêts généraux de la nation impliquent un contrôle *a posteriori* sur les actes des collectivités territoriales.

Sur le plan financier, la loi de mars 1982 prévoit également plusieurs novations. Tout transfert de compétence de l'État vers une collectivité territoriale doit s'accompagner d'un transfert de ressources (essentiellement fiscales). De fait, les impôts locaux ont tendance à augmenter. Par ailleurs, cette même réforme reconnaît aux comptables des communes, des départements et des régions le statut de comptables directs principaux du Trésor. Enfin, elle confie à une nouvelle juridiction, la Chambre régionale des comptes, le soin du contrôle *a posteriori* de la comptabilité des collectivités territoriales.

Le processus de décentralisation a changé en profondeur l'administration territoriale de la France. Le nouveau système apparaît incontestablement plus coûteux que l'ancien pour les deniers publics et introduit une certaine fragmentation des objectifs et des choix, les collectivités territoriales agissant en priorité pour leur intérêt propre plutôt que pour l'intérêt national. Cependant, la décentralisation contribue à une meilleure répartition des tâches et à une responsabilité accrue des collectivités territoriales dans l'ensemble des secteurs de la vie publique et donc à plus de démocratie dans l'administration et la gestion du territoire.

Le conseil régional des Pays-de-la-Loire siège à Nantes (Loire-Atlantique)

Pour en savoir plus :

Sur les institutions de la Ve République

Le Président de la Ve République, La Documentation française, collection Documents d'études, n° 1.06, 1995.

Constitution française du 4 octobre 1958, La Documentation française, collection Documents d'études, n° 1.04, 1998.

D. Maus, *Les grands textes de la pratique institutionnelle de la Ve République*, La Documentation française, collection Retour aux textes, 1998.

B. Tricot, R. Hadas-Lebel, D. Kessler, *Les institutions politiques françaises*, Presses de la FNSP-Dalloz, collection Amphithéâtre, 1995.

P. Ardant, *Les institutions de la Ve République*, Hachette, 1995.

O. Duhamel, *Le pouvoir politique en France*, Le Seuil, 1995.

J.-L. Sauron, *L'application du droit de l'Union européenne en France*, La Documentation française, collection Réflexe Europe, 1995.

Institutions et vie politique en France, La Documentation française, collection Les Notices, 1997.

Sur l'administration territoriale

J.-P. Lebreton, *L'administration territoriale : le système général*, La Documentation française, collection Documents d'études, n° 2.02, 1996.

Les collectivités locales en France, La Documentation française-CNFPT, collection Les Notices, 1996.

P. Duran, J.-C. Thoenig, « L'État et la gestion publique territoriale », *Revue française de sciences politiques*, vol. 43, n° 4, 1996.

Ministère de l'Intérieur, *Les collectivités locales en chiffres*, édition 1996, La Documentation française, 1997.

7

La vie politique

Par tradition, les Français font preuve d'un intérêt soutenu pour la chose publique. Durant la Révolution, l'essor des gazettes, des clubs et des cercles traduit l'intérêt d'une partie importante de la population pour la politique, activité jusque-là réservée au cercle restreint de l'entourage du monarque. L'instauration du suffrage universel direct masculin, en 1848, permet l'expression des opinions politiques par le vote, mais c'est essentiellement sous la IIIᵉ République (1875-1940) que les Français se sont forgés une conscience politique, à la faveur de la constitution de véritables partis politiques, de l'essor du syndicalisme et grâce au rôle accru de la presse. Cette dernière a contribué à la diffusion des idéologies et des idées nouvelles et a permis aux citoyens de participer davantage aux grands débats de l'époque, sur la séparation de l'Église et de l'État ou, par exemple, sur l'affaire Dreyfus. Les institutions, les partis et les médias ne sont cependant pas les seuls responsables de l'animation de la vie politique, à laquelle tout citoyen peut contribuer.

Fondements historiques et constitutionnels de la vie politique

La vie politique française est profondément enracinée dans le passé ; aussi les références historiques y sont-elles omniprésentes.

Les fondements historiques

L'instauration du suffrage universel, en 1848, sous la IIᵉ République, est à l'origine d'une vie politique intense et riche. Cette possibilité donnée au peuple d'exercer sa souveraineté permet à chaque Français de se sentir pleinement citoyen, membre du corps social et partie prenante des décisions politiques. D'autres mesures prises par l'Assemblée constituante élue en 1848 encouragent l'essor de l'action citoyenne. Ainsi en est-il de l'abolition de la peine de mort pour motif politique, de l'affirmation de la liberté de la presse et de la liberté de tenir des réunions publiques.

La IIIᵉ République a ensuite joué un rôle essentiel : elle a ancré progressivement l'idée républicaine dans les mentalités françaises. Sa longévité y a été pour beaucoup. Grâce à elle, la République a cessé d'apparaître, aux yeux de certains Français sensibles aux idées contre-révolutionnaires, comme un facteur de troubles et une menace pour la paix civile. Peu à peu, la République parlementaire, fondée sur la légitimité démocratique du suffrage universel, s'impose comme le régime politique qui recueille l'adhésion du plus grand nombre. La IIIe République est en effet porteuse de certaines valeurs auxquelles les Français se sont mis à croire avec ferveur. La foi en l'école, en la démocratie et en la patrie constitue dès lors le credo républicain.

Discours de Jean Jaurès au Pré-Saint-Gervais, le 25 mai 1913, lors d'une manifestation contre la loi instituant trois ans de service militaire

Toutefois, alors que jusqu'en 1905 la IIIe République est véritablement la République des citoyens, elle tend par la suite à devenir une simple République des parlementaires. L'absence de gouvernements qui soient véritablement l'expression d'une majorité cohérente et l'incessant jeu des alliances et des coalitions commencent à séparer le citoyen de l'exercice du pouvoir, alors que le rôle des partis et des formations politiques s'accroît.

Avant 1900, la France ne connaît pas réellement de partis politiques, ceux-ci se structurant au début du XXe siècle mais demeurant modestes en comparaison de ce qu'ils représentent dans les autres démocraties occidentales. Cependant, après la première guerre mondiale, leur rôle s'affirme. Outre les cercles, les sociétés de lecture ou d'instruction, les réunions publiques et les banquets républicains, le café et l'entreprise deviennent les lieux privilégiés de la vie politique. Au café, les discussions s'engagent à la faveur de la lecture des journaux où sont diffusées les idées politiques, contribuant à l'échange des points de vue et à l'animation du débat. L'entreprise, et en particulier l'usine, joue aussi un rôle de socialisation et d'éveil de la conscience citoyenne par le biais du syndicalisme qui répand dans les milieux ouvriers les idées politiques, et notamment l'idéologie marxiste.

Après la seconde guerre mondiale, la IVe République (1945-1958) se caractérise par une grande instabilité. La Libération, le droit de vote accordé aux femmes et la condamnation par le général de Gaulle du régime des partis de la IIIe République font naître de grands espoirs, reposant sur des partis rénovés, porteurs d'idéologies nouvelles, capables de moraliser la vie publique et dont la majorité des cadres sont des figures de la Résistance. Ces espoirs sont déçus. Trop nombreux, bureaucratisés ou, au contraire, totalement dépourvus de structure, divisés et déstabilisés par des luttes internes entre des personnes ou entre des courants, les partis politiques d'alors ne se montrent pas à la hauteur de la situation. L'échec de la IVe République est aussi le leur.

Les fondements institutionnels

La Constitution de la Ve République a cherché à restaurer l'autorité de l'État, affaiblie sous la IVe République, en renforçant le pouvoir exécutif par rapport au pouvoir législatif. Le président de la République, chef de l'État, est le pivot de ce nouveau régime. Il doit apparaître comme un arbitre national, situé au-dessus des luttes politiques et chargé d'assurer le fonctionnement régulier des institutions.

À partir de 1962, le président de la République est élu au suffrage universel direct, au scrutin majoritaire à deux tours. On pourrait croire que, dès lors, l'opinion publique, devenue indifférente, sinon méfiante, à l'égard de partis largement discrédités par l'exercice du pouvoir sous la IVe République, se confierait au seul charisme d'un homme. Ce serait, globalement, une erreur. En effet, la Constitution de la Ve République reconnaît pour la première fois un rôle aux partis politiques et l'inscrit même dans son article 4 : les partis et groupements concourent à l'expression du suffrage. Ils se forment et exercent leur activité librement. Ils doivent respecter les principes de la souveraineté nationale et de la démocratie. Même si, juridiquement, ils n'appartiennent qu'à la catégorie

des associations (loi de 1901), ils exercent en fait une médiation entre l'opinion publique et l'État. À l'écoute des préoccupations et des problèmes des citoyens, ils élaborent des programmes susceptibles d'y répondre et soumettent au peuple des projets distincts, dans lesquels chaque citoyen pourra se reconnaître, ou non, à l'occasion d'un scrutin.

Le référendum de 1962 : les partisans du non sont actifs mais le projet – l'élection du président de la République au suffrage universel – est approuvé à 61,7 % des voix

La Constitution de la Ve République a donc institutionnalisé le rôle des partis politiques. Ils sont représentés dans les deux Chambres du Parlement, sous la forme de groupes parlementaires autour desquels s'organisent les débats, les propositions de loi et leur vote. Ce système permet de réaliser un équilibre entre l'agitation inhérente au multipartisme et la stabilité du régime, qui rend possible l'alternance gouvernementale, voire la cohabitation. En effet, l'élection du président de la République au suffrage universel direct, parce qu'elle requiert la majorité absolue des suffrages exprimés, maintient chaque parti dans l'incapacité de faire élire son représentant avec ses seules voix. Pour être élu, il est nécessaire de rassembler au-delà de son électorat en construisant autour de soi une coalition de partis, réunis autour d'un même programme ou d'une plate-forme commune de gouvernement. Ainsi, une fois élu, le président de la République apparaît bien comme un arbitre au-dessus des partis, à commencer par ceux qui composent la coalition qui l'a fait élire. Selon la tradition gaulliste, le Président n'est en fait responsable que devant le peuple qui l'a élu.

Les événements de la vie politique : élections et référendums

Les élections constituent un événement majeur dans la vie politique du pays. À l'exception des élections sénatoriales, elles se déroulent toutes au suffrage universel direct. Elles concernent un peu plus de 40 millions de personnes (sur une population de 58 millions d'habitants). Pour être électeur, il faut être majeur, c'est-à-dire âgé d'au moins 18 ans, de nationalité française, sauf pour les élections municipales et les élections au Parlement européen, avoir fait la démarche de s'inscrire sur les listes électorales de la commune où l'on réside et jouir de tous ses droits civiques. En effet certaines condamnations pénales, pour crimes ou délits graves, peuvent entraîner la privation des droits civiques pour une durée déterminée. Les conditions requises pour être éligible sont identiques pour toutes les élections, seul l'âge minimum varie selon le mandat : 18 ans pour être conseiller municipal, 21 ans pour être conseiller régional, 23 ans pour être député ou président de la République, 35 ans pour être sénateur.

Bureau de vote à Arradon (Morbihan) lors du premier tour des élections législatives, le 25 mai 1997

Les électeurs sont appelés à se prononcer lors des diverses consultations afin d'élire leurs représentants au niveau de la commune, du département, de la région ou de la nation. Le président de la République lui-même peut, sur proposition du gouvernement ou du Parlement, soumettre directement un projet de loi ou une décision d'importance à l'approbation des citoyens : il s'agit alors d'un référendum. Au cours des dix dernières années, les Français ont été amenés deux fois à se prononcer selon cette procédure : le 6 novembre 1988 sur le statut de la Nouvelle-Calédonie et le 20 septembre 1992 sur la ratification du traité sur l'Union européenne. La révision constitutionnelle d'août 1995 a élargi le champ du référendum à des projets de loi portant sur des réformes relatives à la politique économique ou sociale de la nation et aux services publics qui y concourent.

Les élections locales

Dans leur commune, les citoyens français et les résidents ressortissants de l'Union européenne élisent au suffrage universel direct, pour un mandat de six ans, les conseillers municipaux qui, à leur tour, élisent le maire. Leur nombre est proportionnel à la population. Les élections municipales se déroulent selon un mode de scrutin variable en fonction de la population de la commune :

    – dans les communes de moins de 3 500 habitants est appliqué le scrutin plurinominal majoritaire à deux tours, avec possibilité de panachage des listes, c'est-à-dire la possibilité de modifier l'ordre des candidats ou d'en changer ;

    – dans les communes de plus de 3 500 habitants est utilisé le scrutin de liste majoritaire à deux tours sans panachage et attribution partielle de sièges à la proportionnelle.

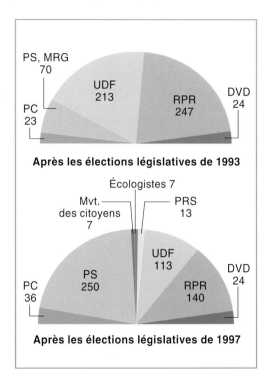

Après les élections législatives de 1993

Après les élections législatives de 1997

L'Assemblée nationale après les élections législatives de 1993 et de 1997
PC : Parti communiste
PS : Parti socialiste
MRG : Mouvement des radicaux de gauche
PRS : Parti radical-socialiste
UDF : Union pour la démocratie française
RPR : Rassemblement pour la République
DVD : Divers droite

    Au niveau du département, les Français votent lors des élections cantonales. Ces élections sont destinées à élire pour six ans les conseillers généraux, au scrutin uninominal majoritaire à deux tours,

Élections sénatoriales de septembre 1998 (situation au 6 octobre 1998)	
Groupe Rassemblement pour la République :	99 sénateurs
Groupe socialiste :	78 sénateurs
Groupe communiste, républicain et citoyen :	16 sénateurs
Groupe de l'Union centriste :	52 sénateurs
Groupe des Républicains et indépendants :	49 sénateurs
Groupe Rassemblement démocratique et social européen :	21 sénateurs

dans le cadre du canton, circonscription administrative du département. Le renouvellement du conseil général a lieu par moitié tous les trois ans.

En 1982, les lois sur la décentralisation ont fait de la région une collectivité territoriale de la République. Les membres du conseil régional sont élus pour six ans au scrutin de liste départemental, à la représentation proportionnelle avec répartition des restes à la plus forte moyenne, type de scrutin qui permet aux minorités et aux petits partis de se trouver représentés.

Les élections nationales

Les élections législatives permettent d'élire les 577 députés qui siègent à l'Assemblée nationale ; ils sont élus pour cinq ans au suffrage universel direct et au scrutin uninominal majoritaire à deux tours. Chaque député est élu dans une circonscription électorale, qui est une entité de taille variable représentant en moyenne 100 000 habitants. Le scrutin majoritaire a été instauré par le général de Gaulle afin de lutter contre l'instabilité gouvernementale qui avait sévi sous la IVᵉ République, du fait notamment du scrutin proportionnel. Celui-ci, rétabli pour les élections de 1986 par le gouvernement socialiste – qui recherchait une meilleure représentation des petites formations –, a été de nouveau remplacé par le scrutin majoritaire pour l'élection de 1988 et conservé depuis.

Les 321 membres du Sénat sont élus, lors des élections sénatoriales, pour neuf ans, au suffrage universel indirect par un collège électoral de grands électeurs composé, dans chaque département, des députés, des conseillers généraux, des conseillers régionaux et de représentants des conseils municipaux. Les effectifs du Sénat sont renouvelés par tiers tous les trois ans.

L'élection présidentielle constitue bien entendu un événement majeur de la vie politique française, par lequel le peuple passe une sorte de contrat moral avec un dirigeant. Le Président est élu au suffrage universel direct, pour un mandat de sept ans renouvelable, au scrutin uninominal majoritaire à deux tours. Pour pouvoir se présenter, les candidats doivent recevoir le parrainage d'au moins cinq cents élus nationaux ou locaux.

Enfin, les élections européennes, au suffrage universel direct et au scrutin proportionnel de liste nationale, permettent d'élire les 87 députés français au Parlement européen pour un mandat de cinq ans. En vertu du traité sur l'Union européenne, les ressortissants de l'Union résidant en France peuvent voter pour l'une des listes de candidats qui se présentent en France.

Chaque consultation électorale ou référendaire est précédée d'une période de campagne électorale au cours de laquelle l'animation de la vie politique s'intensifie. C'est le moment privilégié, pour chaque candidat, d'aller à la rencontre des électeurs et de leur exposer son programme et ses projets. Les candidats disposent pour cela de plusieurs moyens. Ils peuvent rencontrer les électeurs directement sur leurs lieux de vie, les marchés, les centres commerciaux, la rue... Ils peuvent également se servir de la presse écrite ou audiovisuelle comme d'une tribune qui leur est largement ouverte en période de campagne électorale. Toutefois, par souci d'égalité de traitement entre les candidats, le Conseil supérieur de l'audiovisuel, instance de régulation des médias audiovisuels, veille à ce que tous les candidats ou toutes les formations politiques disposent d'un temps de parole équivalent sur chaque station de radio ou chaîne de télévision, où la publicité politique est interdite. En dernier lieu, chaque électeur reçoit, dans les semaines précédant la consultation, une enveloppe électorale où sont rassemblés toutes les professions de foi et les programmes des candidats. Par ailleurs, afin de ne pas influencer l'électorat, la loi a interdit la publication, une semaine avant chaque scrutin, des sondages d'opinion, qui jouent un rôle croissant dans la vie politique française.

En application des lois du 22 décembre 1990 et du 19 janvier 1995 sur le financement des partis et des campagnes électorales, les partis politiques et les comités de soutien des divers candidats sont tenus de publier leurs comptes de campagne – qui doivent être équilibrés – et d'y faire figurer notamment tout frais occasionné par des opérations de communication politique ; ils sont contraints, dans la période d'un an précédant la date de l'élection, de ne pas dépasser un certain budget (90 millions de francs pour le premier tour de l'élection présidentielle, 120 millions de francs pour le second tour, soit respectivement 16 et 21 millions de dollars). L'affichage sur des panneaux publicitaires commerciaux est prohibé quatre mois avant l'ouverture de la campagne officielle. Le financement des partis

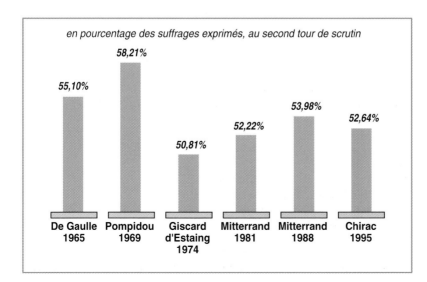

en pourcentage des suffrages exprimés, au second tour de scrutin

58,21%

55,10%

53,98%

52,64%

52,22%

50,81%

| De Gaulle 1965 | Pompidou 1969 | Giscard d'Estaing 1974 | Mitterrand 1981 | Mitterrand 1988 | Chirac 1995 |

L'élection des présidents de la Vᵉ République : depuis l'élection de V. Giscard d'Estaing, le rapport droite-gauche frise toujours l'équilibre

Le vieillissement du corps électoral

En 1995, année d'élections présidentielles et municipales, l'Institut national d'études démographiques (INED) a publié des travaux montrant que l'âge moyen de l'électeur s'était élevé en France : les personnes de plus de 65 ans représentent 19,6 % de la population en âge de voter, soit près d'un électeur sur cinq, alors que, par rapport à la population totale, cette catégorie ne constitue que 15 %. Depuis l'élection présidentielle de 1988, cette proportion a augmenté de 1,5 %. Parallèlement, la tranche des 18-24 ans ne représente plus que 13,1 % du corps électoral, contre 14,4 % en 1988. Selon une étude de 1991 relative aux conséquences de l'âge sur le choix électoral, le fait que les personnes âgées soient plus conservatrices s'expliquerait par leur appartenance « à un groupe où sont sur-représentés les individus ayant de fortes chances de préférer la droite à la gauche, notamment les femmes, les travailleurs indépendants, les catholiques pratiquants réguliers et les possesseurs d'un patrimoine ». L'INED relève ainsi un paradoxe : dans cette situation, ce sont des électeurs plus âgés qui doivent débattre des solutions aux difficultés des jeunes générations.

politiques a également fait l'objet de mesures contraignantes, tout d'abord avec le plafonnement drastique des ressources et l'obligation de déclarer les fonds provenant des entreprises, groupes industriels et donateurs particuliers, puis avec l'interdiction totale du financement des partis par les entreprises. Le remboursement d'une partie des dépenses de campagne par l'État lui-même est fonction des résultats obtenus (1 million de francs, soit 0,18 million de dollars, pour tout candidat aux élections présidentielles, auquel s'ajoutent 8 % du plafond des dépenses pour ces candidats et 36 % du plafond pour ceux ayant obtenu plus de 5 % des suffrages au premier tour). Ces dispositions ont pour but de moraliser la vie politique en limitant les dépenses et les gaspillages et en assurant une certaine équité entre les candidats.

Le paysage politique actuel

Les formations politiques jouent le rôle essentiel de médiateurs entre les citoyens et la politique. Elles enregistrent en France des transformations assez fréquentes qui rendent les positions et les alliances plus complexes qu'aux États-Unis, au Royaume-Uni ou en Allemagne, où la structure des partis apparaît plus stable. Les partis politiques français connaissent ainsi, depuis plus d'une décennie, une baisse

Le 5 mars 1998 au Zénith (Paris), les principaux représentants de la gauche plurielle lors de la campagne des élections régionales : au premier rang R. Hue, D. Voynet, L. Jospin, M.-G. Buffet et D. Strauss-Kahn

significative de leurs adhérents, comme d'ailleurs les centrales syndicales. Cette désaffection traduit une certaine méfiance de l'opinion face
à des organisations dont le financement a parfois donné lieu à des
dérives condamnées par les tribunaux. Pour réconcilier les citoyens et
la vie politique, les gouvernements qui se sont succédé depuis une
dizaine d'années se sont efforcés de clarifier le financement des partis
et de renouveler leurs dirigeants, en rajeunissant les cadres et en accordant une place plus large aux femmes.

La victoire de la gauche aux élections législatives de
1997 a conduit à une nouvelle cohabitation droite-gauche. C'est la troisième de la Vᵉ République, après celles de 1986-1988 et 1992-1995.
Cette fois, le Président appartient à la droite et le gouvernement à la
gauche, contrairement aux cohabitations antérieures. Cette situation, si
elle n'affecte guère la politique internationale du pays, le président de la
République et le Premier ministre parlant d'une seule voix lors des
grandes conférences, ne réduit pas l'opposition traditionnelle entre la
gauche et la droite sur le plan intérieur.

La défaite de la droite aux élections législatives, puis
son recul lors des élections régionales de 1998, ont contribué à son
morcellement, d'autant que la division est confortée par les ambitions
personnelles de nombreux chefs de partis. Les deux composantes
essentielles de la droite, le
Rassemblement pour la République (RPR) et l'Union pour la
Démocratie française (UDF),
sont soumises à des forces
centrifuges. Certes, l'Alliance
réunit depuis mai 1998 les
composantes de « l'opposition
républicaine », c'est-à-dire le
RPR, l'UDF et Démocratie libérale, mais si elle regroupe les
états-majors, elle ne trouve
guère d'écho sur le terrain et
n'a pas effacé les divisions
internes de la droite.

Les responsables de
l'Alliance pour la France
lors d'un rassemblement
organisé le 27 juin 1998
à Port-Marly (Yvelines) :
N. Sarkozy, A. Madelin,
Ph. Séguin et F. Bayrou

Regroupés depuis 1978 au sein de l'UDF, à l'initiative de
l'ancien président de la République, Valéry Giscard d'Estaing, les libéraux et les centristes se sont séparés en 1998. Une partie des libéraux
se retrouve aujourd'hui dans la formation Démocratie libérale, qui succède au Parti républicain et qui est dirigée par Alain Madelin. D'autres
libéraux sont demeurés au sein de l'UDF, dans le Pôle républicain, indépendant et libéral. Les centristes, qui constituent désormais la majorité
de l'UDF, se sont regroupés autour de Force démocrate, dirigée par
François Bayrou. Ce parti réunit depuis 1995 l'ancien Centre des Démo-
crates-sociaux (CDS) et le Parti social-démocrate (PSD). D'autres formations, enfin, ont été constituées par d'anciens membres de l'UDF,
comme le Mouvement des Réformateurs de Jean-Pierre Soisson,

La Droite de Charles Millon, ou le Mouvement pour la France de Philippe de Villiers.

Le RPR lui-même, s'il conserve une unité apparente, en dépit des séquelles de la concurrence entre Jacques Chirac et Édouard Balladur lors des élections présidentielles de 1995, rassemble des sensibilités différentes, comme le montre le mouvement créé par Charles Pasqua, Demain la France.

La division de la droite républicaine tient aujourd'hui pour une large part à des attitudes divergentes face au Front national. Quelques-uns de ses représentants se sont rapprochés de la formation d'extrême droite avec laquelle ils dirigent certaines assemblées régionales ; d'autres, au contraire, s'opposent à toute concession au Front national. Ce dernier, qui profite de la crise sociale et de la désaffection d'une partie de l'électorat pour les partis républicains, s'implante dans plusieurs régions. Il se fait le défenseur d'un nationalisme opposé à la construction européenne et qui s'accompagne de la dénonciation des principaux partis.

La gauche elle-même est divisée. Certes, le Parti socialiste reste, de loin, la composante la plus forte de l'actuelle majorité de gauche, dite gauche plurielle. Ses conflits internes, qui avaient trouvé un large écho durant les années quatre-vingt, à la faveur des luttes entre les tendances, se sont estompés depuis la victoire aux dernières législatives bien que quelques critiques apparaissent parfois à l'égard du gouvernement. À la gauche du Parti socialiste, Jean-Pierre Chevènement dirige le Mouvement des Citoyens (MDC).

Le Parti communiste, après avoir perdu une forte partie de ses militants et de son électorat depuis une vingtaine d'années, en partie au profit du Parti socialiste, a réussi ces dernières années à stabiliser son audience entre 9 et 10 % de l'électorat. Désormais plus pragmatique, le Parti communiste cherche à renouveler son image mais la direction se heurte aux « rénovateurs », qu'ils soient encore membres du Parti ou non.

Élections présidentielles de 1995	
Premier tour : (principaux candidats)	
Lionel Jospin (PS)	23,2 %
Jacques Chirac (RPR)	20,4 %
Édouard Balladur (RPR)	18,5 %
Jean-Marie Le Pen (FN)	15,2 %
Robert Hue (PCF)	8,7 %
Second tour :	
Jacques Chirac	52,7 %
élu président de la République	
Lionel Jospin	47,3 %

Le Parti Radical socialiste (PRS), surtout implanté dans le sud-ouest du pays, peine à se faire entendre de son allié socialiste.

Les écologistes, quant à eux, apparus en 1974 dans le paysage politique national, sont divisés en fractions rivales, dont les « Verts », qui participent au gouvernement. Une de ces fractions, Génération Écologie, dirigée par Brice Lalonde, s'est rapprochée du RPR et de l'UDF.

Les élections législatives de 1997 ont enfin souligné la montée de l'extrême gauche dont Lutte ouvrière, avec Arlette Laguiller, apparaît comme la principale formation, devant la Ligue communiste révolutionnaire. Contestant une partie des mesures adoptées par le gouvernement, l'extrême gauche prend appui sur les mouvements de chômeurs et les défenseurs des étrangers sans papiers.

Les principales formations politiques

Parti socialiste (PS)

Le Parti socialiste a pris la relève de la SFIO (Section française de l'Internationale ouvrière), née au début du siècle sous l'impulsion de Jules Guesde et de Jean Jaurès et dirigée par Léon Blum. Fondé en 1971 par François Mitterrand au congrès d'Épinay, le parti socialiste, rénové, est devenu en dix ans un des premiers partis de France et a permis à son Premier secrétaire d'accéder à la présidence de la République en 1981. Son Premier secrétaire actuel, François Hollande, a remplacé à ce poste Lionel Jospin, nommé Premier ministre à la suite de la victoire de la gauche aux élections législatives de 1997.

Parti communiste français (PCF)

Au congrès de la SFIO (Section française de l'Internationale ouvrière) à Tours, en 1920, le courant majoritaire, admettant les « 21 conditions » composant la Charte communiste, crée la SFIC (Section française de l'Internationale communiste) qui deviendra le PCF (Parti communiste français). L'alliance passée avec le Parti socialiste lui a permis, au lendemain de l'élection de François Mitterrand à la présidence de la République, de participer au gouvernement de 1981 à 1984. Le Parti communiste compte deux ministres et un secrétaire d'État dans le gouvernement de Lionel Jospin formé en 1997.

Rassemblement pour la République (RPR)

Fondé en 1976 par Jacques Chirac, le Rassemblement pour la République (RPR) a succédé à l'Union des Démocrates pour la République (UDR) ; le RPR revendique sa filiation gaulliste qui remonte au Rassemblement du Peuple Français (RPF), mouvement fondé par le général de Gaulle en 1947.

◼ Union pour la démocratie française (UDF)

Fondée le 1er février 1978 à l'initiative de Valéry Giscard d'Estaing, l'Union pour la Démocratie française était une confédération de partis et non un parti unifié, jusqu'à novembre 1998 où son conseil national a décidé de transformer l'UDF en un parti unifié. Plusieurs composantes sont réunies en son sein : Force démocrate, le Parti populaire pour la démocratie française, le Parti radical, le Pôle républicain, indépendant et libéral, formations auxquelles s'ajoutent des adhérents directs.

◼ Front national (FN)

Fondé en 1972 par Jean-Marie Le Pen, le Front national se réclame de la droite nationaliste et populiste. Resté marginal dans ses résultats électoraux entre 1972 et 1982, il a développé, depuis 1983, son implantation électorale.

Pour en savoir plus :

J.-J. Becker, *Histoire politique de la France depuis 1945*, A. Colin, collection Cursus, 1996.

P. Bréchon, *La France aux urnes, cinquante ans d'histoire électorale*, La Documentation française, collection Les Études, 1998.

CEVIPOF, *L'électeur a ses raisons*, Presses de sciences po, 1997.

D. Chagnollaud (sous la dir. de), *La vie politique en France*, Le Seuil, collection Points Essais, 1993.

Institutions et vie politique, La Documentation française, collection Les Notices, 1997.

J. Massot, *Alternances et cohabitation sous la Ve République*, La Documentation française, collection Les Études, 1997.

Y. Mény, *Le système politique français*, Montchrestien, collection Clefs politiques, 1996, traduit en anglais et en espagnol dans la collection Getting to know French administration, La Documentation française - IIAP, 1998.

J.-F. Sirinelli (sous la dir. de), *Dictionnaire historique de la vie politique française au XXe siècle*, PUF, 1995.

C. Ysmal, *Les partis politiques sous la Ve République*, Montchrestien, Domat politique, 1989.

LA FRANCE
DANS
LE MONDE

8

La politique étrangère

Vieille nation européenne, inspiratrice des idéaux inscrits dans la Déclaration universelle des droits de l'homme, membre permanent du Conseil de sécurité, la France a toujours revendiqué et exercé une influence sur les affaires du monde.

Au lendemain de la seconde guerre mondiale, la volonté de mettre un terme aux rivalités qui déchirèrent longtemps le vieux continent l'a conduite à bâtir, avec ses voisins, la Communauté européenne qui est ensuite devenue l'Union européenne (UE). Elle a continué de développer des relations privilégiées en Afrique, au Moyen-Orient et en Asie et a milité en faveur du développement des pays du Sud, et en particulier des Pays les Moins Avancés. Avec le continent américain, elle entretient des rapports étroits et anciens forgés par l'histoire. De la Révolution de 1789, la France a conservé les grands principes républicains de liberté, d'égalité et de fraternité destinés à l'ensemble de l'humanité. L'activité qu'elle déploie sur la scène internationale en faveur de la démocratie et de la paix en est la preuve.

Principes

Les objectifs qui inspirent la politique étrangère française sont constants. L'influence qu'elle exerce a naturellement évolué depuis la fin de la seconde guerre mondiale, mais elle n'a pas cessé de se fonder sur le respect de certains principes.

La France attache un prix particulier à son indépendance, principe qui a guidé la politique étrangère engagée sous l'impulsion du général de Gaulle dans les années soixante. Celui-ci a fondé son action sur la mise en œuvre d'une capacité de défense autonome et crédible, reposant sur la dissuasion nucléaire. Dans le même esprit, certaines initiatives diplomatiques spectaculaires ont été prises, notamment au Proche-Orient ou en Asie, démontrant que la France demeurait pleinement maîtresse de ses analyses et de ses choix de politique étrangère. Cette volonté n'a pas faibli au cours des décennies suivantes.

Cependant, le souci d'indépendance n'exclut pas la recherche de solidarités. Tout au long de la guerre froide, la France a affirmé et démontré son appartenance au monde libre. Elle exerce des responsabilités qui résultent de son statut international, soit comme membre permanent du Conseil de sécurité des Nations unies, soit comme membre d'alliances qu'elle a contractées. Elle est enfin guidée par l'ambition de voir triompher, partout dans le monde, les valeurs dont elle a été l'inspiratrice et que les institutions internationales ont consacrées en des textes solennels.

Au lendemain de la guerre froide, ces principes et ces ambitions ont conservé toute leur actualité. Ils dessinent les axes principaux de la politique de la France sur la scène internationale : poursuivre la construction de l'Europe de manière à garantir la stabilité et la prospérité du continent ; agir au sein de la communauté internationale afin de favoriser les progrès de la paix, de la démocratie et du développement.

La France et la construction européenne

Depuis 1945, la construction de l'Europe s'est constamment trouvée au cœur de la politique étrangère française. Trois considérations ont fait de ce grand dessein une priorité : la volonté de mettre un terme aux conflits qui, par deux fois en trente ans, avaient déchiré le continent européen et affaibli la France ; la nécessité, dans le contexte de la guerre froide, d'asseoir la stabilité et de garantir la sécurité des États démocratiques situés à l'ouest du rideau de fer ; le souci, enfin, de construire un espace économique homogène, adapté aux conditions modernes de production, garantissant la prospérité des peuples européens.

Deux Français initiateurs du projet de construction européenne, Robert Schuman et Jean Monnet, étaient convaincus de la nécessité de réunir au sein d'une même organisation les nations du continent. Ils ont fait le pari d'organiser entre ces États une solidarité économique en vue de hâter un rapprochement politique. Dans cette perspective s'est constituée, le 18 avril 1951, la Communauté européenne du charbon et de l'acier (CECA), dont les institutions serviront de modèle au développement de la construction européenne. Le 25 mars 1957, les six États membres de la CECA, Allemagne, Belgique, France, Italie, Luxembourg et Pays-Bas, signent le traité de Rome instituant la Communauté économique européenne (CEE). Ces pays s'engagent à lier leur destin économique, en abolissant entre eux toute barrière douanière et en organisant une politique agricole commune (PAC).

Lors de son accession à la présidence de la République, en 1958, le général de Gaulle affirme sa volonté de poursuivre dans cette voie. Durant les trois décennies suivant la conclusion du traité de Rome, la France participe ainsi activement aux progrès réguliers de la construction de l'Europe. À l'union douanière succède, le 1er janvier 1973, sous Georges Pompidou, un premier élargissement de la Communauté à trois nouveaux membres : le Royaume-Uni, le Danemark et l'Irlande. Les années soixante-dix sont marquées par d'importantes réformes politiques, la création du Conseil européen (réunissant les chefs d'État ou de gouvernement) et l'élection des membres du Parlement européen au suffrage universel, ainsi que par l'élaboration du Système monétaire européen (SME), à l'initiative du président Valéry Giscard d'Estaing et du chancelier allemand Helmut Schmidt. Bientôt, la volonté d'aider les régimes démocratiques du sud de l'Europe appelle un nouvel élargissement : la Grèce intègre la Communauté en 1981, l'Espagne et le Portugal en 1986. Enfin, sous l'impulsion de François Mitterrand, d'Helmut Kohl et de Jacques Delors, président de la Commission, l'Acte unique est adopté en février 1986. Son objectif est de créer un véritable grand marché européen, garantissant la libre circulation des personnes, des marchandises et des capitaux, ainsi que la libre prestation des services, sur le territoire de la Communauté. Pour l'essentiel, c'est chose faite depuis 1993.

Aujourd'hui, l'Union européenne

Avec ses partenaires, la France s'est attelée à la réalisation d'un nouveau dessein : la mise en œuvre du traité sur l'Union européenne, signé le 7 février 1992 dans la ville néerlandaise de Maastricht. Ce document élargit les compétences de la Communauté dans plusieurs domaines importants : l'environnement, la protection des consommateurs, l'enseignement et la formation professionnelle, la politique sociale. Il modifie des mécanismes institutionnels pour accroître le rôle du Parlement européen et faire prévaloir le principe de subsidiarité réservant à l'Union européenne les questions qui ne peuvent pas être réglées à l'échelon national. Il prévoit aussi, pour les citoyens de l'Union, le droit de voter aux élections municipales et européennes, là où ils résident, quel que soit leur État d'origine.

Le traité innove en ajoutant à la construction européenne deux nouveaux piliers : la Politique étrangère et de sécurité commune (PESC) visant la mise en place d'une défense commune ; la coopération dans les domaines de la justice et des affaires intérieures.

L'intégration accrue des États européens rencontre parfois des résistances nationales. La France, pour sa part, a choisi : après d'importants débats, la ratification du traité de Maastricht a finalement été approuvée par référendum le 20 septembre 1992. L'engagement européen de la France en est renforcé.

En cette fin des années quatre-vingt-dix, le grand projet d'approfondissement de l'Union européenne est la monnaie unique, l'euro. Celui-ci voit jour le 1er janvier 1999. Onze (France, Allemagne, Italie, Bénélux, Irlande, Espagne, Portugal, Autriche et Finlande) des quinze États membres de l'Union européenne sont engagés dans cette entreprise audacieuse.

Pour la France, l'euro représente une étape majeure de la construction européenne. L'euro consacre l'attachement de la France à une politique économique et financière coordonnée avec ses partenaires européens. Avec la création de la Banque centrale européenne, chargée de la gestion de l'euro, l'Union européenne dispose d'une autorité monétaire indépendante, s'imposant également à tous les États participants. L'euro consolide l'Union comme acteur international de poids, notamment face au dollar, et contribue à la promotion d'une Europe politique, allant au-delà de l'intégration économique. Enfin, la monnaie unique favorise les efforts en faveur de la croissance et de l'emploi.

Vers une Europe élargie

Le principe de l'élargissement de l'Union européenne est acquis. Il concerne d'abord certains pays de l'Association européenne de libre échange (AELE) : l'Autriche, la Finlande et la Suède ont ainsi rejoint l'Union européenne le 1er janvier 1995.

Les nouvelles démocraties d'Europe centrale et orientale (Bulgarie, Hongrie, Pologne, République tchèque, Roumanie, Slovaquie) et les États baltes (Estonie, Lettonie, Lituanie) ont également vocation à rejoindre l'Union européenne. À l'est et au sud du continent, d'autres États sont intéressés par cette perspective. La France avait maintenu avec eux des liens d'amitié et de solidarité. Elle entend aujourd'hui favo-

Le ministre
des Affaires étrangères
Hubert Védrine signe,
le 2 octobre 1997,
le Traité d'Amsterdam

riser leur intégration au sein d'un espace européen élargi : l'Union européenne a adopté des mesures destinées à aider ces pays à mener à bien les réformes nécessaires à la consolidation de l'État de droit et au passage à l'économie de marché.

D'importants programmes d'aide et de coopération technique ont été mis en place afin de contribuer à la rénovation des principales infrastructures, à la formation des hommes et à la mise en place de nouvelles institutions. Globalement, la part de l'Union européenne dans le programme d'assistance à l'Europe centrale et orientale et aux États baltes, au sein du groupe des vingt-quatre pays industrialisés, s'élève ainsi à plus de 60 % du total des fonds dégagés à cet effet.

Par ailleurs, afin de faciliter le développement du commerce et les flux d'investissement direct, des accords européens ont été conclus entre ces pays et l'Union européenne. Ces accords prévoient l'institution d'un dialogue politique, l'octroi de facilités commerciales conduisant à la réalisation progressive d'une zone de libre-échange pour les produits industriels et la mise en place d'une vaste coopération. Si bien que l'Union européenne est aujourd'hui le premier client et le premier fournisseur des pays d'Europe centrale et orientale ainsi que la principale source des capitaux investis.

En juin 1993, lors du Conseil européen de Copenhague, les douze chefs d'État et de gouvernement de l'UE ont confirmé la vocation des pays d'Europe centrale et orientale ainsi que des États baltes à rejoindre l'Union européenne. Dans cette perspective, ils ont décidé de les associer dès à présent à la Politique étrangère et de sécurité commune (PESC).

Depuis 1990, la France a multiplié les initiatives pour créer des institutions permettant de garantir la sécurité et la stabilité du continent européen.

Adepte de la diplomatie préventive, elle s'est trouvée à l'origine de la création, au sein de la CSCE (Conférence sur la sécurité et la coopération en Europe), d'une Cour de conciliation et d'arbitrage. Elle a appuyé les efforts du Secrétaire général de l'ONU, Boutros Boutros-Ghali, en vue de créer un tribunal pénal international, mis en place à La Haye en novembre 1993 pour juger les responsables de crimes de guerre commis dans l'ancienne Yougoslavie. La même année, sur la proposition du Premier ministre Édouard Balladur, elle a soumis à ses partenaires de l'Union européenne un projet de Pacte sur la stabilité en Europe, pour prévenir les conflits potentiels légués par l'histoire européenne. Cette initiative a permis aux pays d'Europe centrale et orientale ainsi qu'aux États baltes de négocier des accords de bon voisinage, consolidant les frontières et respectant les minorités nationales. Ce projet, adopté par l'Union européenne à la conférence inaugurale de Paris en mai 1994, a été signé dans la capitale française en mars 1995. L'Union européenne a mis ses institutions économiques et politiques au service de ce dessein, dont le suivi a été confié à l'OSCE (Organisation pour la sécurité et la coopération en Europe). La France a par ailleurs proposé l'adoption d'une charte de sécurité rassemblant l'ensemble des membres de l'OSCE.

La signature de l'Accord de partenariat et de coopération avec la Russie, à l'occasion du Sommet européen de Corfou (juin 1994), est un autre exemple des efforts déployés par les Européens pour renforcer la stabilité et la prospérité de l'ensemble du continent.

L'OTAN et la Russie ont renforcé leur coopération en signant le 27 juin 1997 à Paris un Acte fondateur. Le Sommet atlantique de Madrid du 8 juillet 1997 a posé le principe de l'adhésion de la Pologne, de la République tchèque et de la Hongrie tout en ouvrant une perspective à la Roumanie et à la Slovénie.

En décembre 1997, le Conseil européen de Luxembourg lance l'élargissement à l'Est. Le 30 mars 1998, des négociations d'adhésion s'ouvrent avec Chypre, la Hongrie, la Pologne, l'Estonie, la République tchèque et la Slovénie. Au même moment, un processus de pré-paration à l'adhésion est enclenché avec la Roumanie, la Slovaquie, la Lettonie, la Lituanie et la Bulgarie. L'ensemble des pays candidats et ayant vocation à adhérer, y compris la Turquie, sont, par ailleurs, invités à participer à une Conférence européenne.

Naturellement, les institutions européennes, conçues pour une coopération d'États en nombre restreint, devront être adaptées afin de tenir compte de ces nouvelles adhésions éventuelles. La France prépare ce rendez-vous en réfléchissant, avec ses partenaires, aux formules répondant à quatre objectifs fondamentaux : préserver l'effica-cité de l'Union européenne ; accroître la représentativité de ses institu-tions ; préciser la notion de subsidiarité ; rapprocher l'Europe de ses citoyens.

Comme le prévoyait le Traité de Maastricht, une Confé-rence intergouvernementale (CIG) s'est tenue de mars 1996 à juin 1997. Son objet était précisément de procéder à l'adaptation des institutions de l'Union européenne. Elle a accouché du Traité d'Amsterdam, signé le 2 octobre 1997. Ce traité répond partiellement aux attentes de la France. Certes, il permet, selon une procédure bien lourde, aux États qui souhaitent aller plus vite et plus loin de le faire (mécanisme des coopérations renforcées). Mais aucune réforme véritable des institutions n'est intervenue, « grands » et « petits » États restant en désaccord sur la réduction du nombre des commissaires, ainsi que sur la « repondéra-tion » des votes des États au sein du Conseil des ministres en cas de décision à la majorité qualifiée.

Plusieurs pays, dont la France, souhaitent que cette réforme institutionnelle intervienne avant que les futurs élargissements ne soient effectifs.

Assurer la stabilité du continent européen

La fin de la guerre froide a créé une nouvelle situation conduisant les nations européennes à se fixer de nouveaux objectifs en matière de sécurité. En effet, des revendications anciennes, des pas-sions ethniques ou nationalistes, des désordres politiques menacent la stabilité du continent européen. La guerre qui a fait rage sur le territoire de l'ancienne Yougoslavie démontre que les risques de nouveaux conflits sont sérieux et appellent une réaction collective.

Plusieurs institutions sont concernées par cette pers-pective.

La plus ancienne, le Conseil de l'Europe, a été créée en 1949 à l'initiative du ministre français Georges Bidault. Ayant son siège à Strasbourg, il rassemble les nations attachées à la démocratie et au plura-lisme politique. Les nouvelles démocraties d'Europe centrale et orientale, ainsi que les États baltes, ont progressivement pris part à ses travaux.

L'Organisation pour la sécurité et la coopération en Europe – OSCE – (appelée Conférence pour la sécurité et la coopération en Europe – CSCE – jusqu'en décembre 1994) regroupe 52 États, dont les États-Unis et le Canada, et l'ensemble des anciennes Républiques soviétiques. Le rôle de cette enceinte, créée en 1975 dans le cadre de la détente Est-Ouest par l'Acte final d'Helsinki, s'est considérablement élargi avec la fin de la guerre froide.

Le Sommet de Paris de novembre 1990 a abouti à la signature de la Charte pour une nouvelle Europe. Il a entériné un accord de désarmement conventionnel de très grande ampleur, le Traité sur les forces armées conventionnelles en Europe, signé par 22 États membres de l'Alliance atlantique et de l'ex-pacte de Varsovie, et prévu la création d'un nouveau Forum de sécurité ainsi que d'un Centre de prévention des conflits.

Enfin, les organisations militaires, l'Organisation du traité de l'Atlantique Nord (OTAN) et l'Union de l'Europe occidentale (UEO), sont amenées à évoluer à leur tour : à l'UEO incombent des ambitions nouvelles dans le cadre du traité de Maastricht ; le Conseil de coopération de l'Atlantique Nord (COCONA) a été créé afin d'établir un dialogue entre les pays d'Europe centrale et orientale, les États baltes et les États membres de l'OTAN, qui a débouché sur le Partenariat pour la Paix lors du sommet du 11 janvier 1994.

L'Acte fondateur,
signé le 27 juin 1997
à Paris, renforce
la coopération entre
l'OTAN et la Russie

Le couple franco-allemand

À chaque nouvelle étape de la construction européenne, la France et l'Allemagne ont joué les premiers rôles. Sans la réconciliation entre Français et Allemands, cet édifice européen ne pouvait être bâti, ainsi que l'avaient déjà compris le général de Gaulle et le chancelier Adenauer. Dès 1958, l'ancien chef de la France Libre reçoit le chancelier ouest-allemand, fondateur de la République fédérale, avant de se rendre à son tour en Allemagne. De leurs efforts conjoints naît le rapprochement franco-allemand : le 23 janvier 1963, le traité de l'Élysée est signé. L'agenda des rencontres prévoit deux sommets franco-allemands par an, une rencontre trimestrielle des ministres des Affaires étrangères et des réunions régulières des responsables de la défense, de l'éducation et de la jeunesse. L'Office franco-allemand pour la jeunesse (OFAJ) voit le jour quelques mois plus tard. Il permet à des dizaines de milliers de jeunes des deux pays de se rencontrer, d'étudier ou de travailler ensemble.

Au-delà des liens étroits noués entre les dirigeants successifs des deux pays, trente ans de relations privilégiées ont permis davantage. Aujourd'hui, l'habitude des sommets franco-allemands, des réunions d'harmonisation, de préparation en commun des dossiers européens a multiplié les relations à tous les échelons des deux administrations et permis de porter les relations bilatérales à un degré de convergence unique au monde.

Les commissions bilatérales touchent pratiquement tous les secteurs de l'activité publique. Ainsi, le Comité monétaire associe le président de la Bundesbank, le gouverneur de la Banque de France et les deux ministres des Finances. La Commission de défense a pris corps avec la création de la brigade franco-allemande en 1987, embryon d'une force européenne, le Corps européen, créé en 1993 et renforcé par la Belgique, le Luxembourg et l'Espagne. Enfin, la chaîne de télévision culturelle franco-allemande Arte, installée à Strasbourg, diffuse depuis 1992 des programmes conçus en commun à l'intention des téléspectateurs français et allemands, mais également belges, suisses et autrichiens. Arte est ouverte aux autres États européens intéressés.

Rencontre entre le président de la République, Jacques Chirac, et Gerhard Schröder, Chancelier de la République fédérale d'Allemagne, le 1er octobre 1998 à Paris

Un exemple de coopération franco-allemande : la chaîne de télévision Arte, issue du Traité signé entre les deux pays le 2 octobre 1990, a une vocation européenne

La participation de la France à l'action de l'ONU

Dès la création de l'Organisation des Nations unies (ONU), le 26 juin 1945, la France appartient à son instance suprême : le Conseil de sécurité. Elle y détient un siège permanent au même titre que les États-Unis, la Grande-Bretagne, la Russie et la Chine. Elle s'est, depuis lors, prononcée en faveur de l'élargissement du Conseil de sécurité, notamment à l'Allemagne et au Japon, et a précisé que les représentants du monde en développement ne devaient en aucune façon se trouver marginalisés dans le cadre de la future réforme proposée. Le français est l'une des six

CONFÉRENCE DE PAIX SUR L'EX-YOUGOSLAVIE
PARIS

langues officielles de l'ONU et l'une des deux langues de travail. Paris accueille le siège de l'Organisation des Nations unies pour la science, la culture et l'éducation, l'UNESCO.

La France est le quatrième contributeur au budget de l'organisation. Sa quote-part au budget de l'ONU s'élève, en 1998, à 6,49 % ; sa part dans la richesse mondiale est d'environ 3,5 % en1996. Ainsi la France a versé, en 1997, 930 millions de francs (155 millions de dollars) de contributions obligatoires aux institutions du système des Nations unies.

Le 14 décembre 1995 sont signés à Paris les accords de Dayton qui concluent la Conférence de paix sur l'ex-Yougoslavie ; sur la photographie Bill Clinton, président des États-Unis, Jacques Chirac, président de la République et Helmut Kohl, Chancelier de la République fédérale d'Allemagne

Les contributions françaises au budget des principales organisations du système de l'ONU en 1998

Bénéficiaires	Contributions en monnaie d'appel (en millions)	Contributions en millions de francs
ONU	68,37 US$	410,2
Organisation mondiale de la santé (OMS)	27 US$	162
UNESCO	8,8 US$ et79,9 MF	132,9
Organisation internationale du travail (OIT)	21,4 MF suisses	88,8
Organisation pour l'alimentation et l'agriculture (OAA)	21,9 US$	131,3

À cela s'ajoutent 416 millions de francs (69,3 millions de dollars) au titre des opérations de maintien de la paix. Dans ce domaine, la part de la France en 1997 était de 7,96 % (472 millions de francs, soit 80,6 millions de dollars). Il s'agit d'un poste en diminution, du fait de la liquidation de certaines de ces opérations (en particulier en ex-Yougoslavie). Au 31 mai 1998, la France était au neuvième rang des contributeurs de troupes et de matériel et au premier rang parmi les membres permanents du Conseil de sécurité.

Cette place éminente impose à la France d'importantes responsabilités. Elle les assume en participant activement au renouveau des Nations unies, chargées de nouvelles tâches depuis la fin de la guerre froide : mettre fin aux conflits régionaux hérités de cette période et faire prévaloir le respect du droit sur la scène internationale. La France est particulièrement attachée à la place des Nations unies qui est la seule organisation universelle et qui, à ce titre, a le monopole pour autoriser le recours à la force, en dehors du cas de légitime défense.

Le ministre délégué aux Affaires européennes, Pierre Moscovici, lors d'une conférence de presse commune avec son homologue estonien, Toomas-Hendrik Ilves, Tallinn, décembre 1997

La première grande crise internationale des années 1990, l'invasion du Koweït par l'Iraq, en est un exemple. Le Conseil de sécurité, que ne paralysait plus la rivalité entre les États-Unis et l'Union soviétique, a adopté sans difficulté les résolutions condamnant l'invasion de l'Émirat par les troupes de Saddam Hussein et exigeant leur retrait, puis la résolution qui autorisait l'intervention de la coalition internationale. Un contingent français de 12 000 hommes a participé aux opérations qui ont abouti à la libération du Koweït.

Sept années après la fin de la guerre du Golfe, la France œuvre activement en faveur de l'application entière par l'Iraq de ses obligations en matière de désarmement, qui ouvrira la voie à la levée des sanctions économiques. Dans la dernière crise iraquienne, la France s'est attachée avec succès à rechercher une solution politique aux différends qui opposaient l'Iraq au Conseil de sécurité.

Au Moyen-Orient, en Afrique et en Asie, les conflits régionaux affectent des pays avec lesquels la France a noué de longue date des relations d'amitié. Elle prend donc une part active aux efforts de la communauté internationale afin de trouver une solution équitable.

Au Proche-Orient, en particulier, la France a toujours cherché à apaiser les crises déchirant la région. En 1967, au lendemain de la guerre des Six jours, elle a soutenu la résolution 242 du Conseil de sécurité exigeant le retrait immédiat des territoires occupés par Israël, position réaffirmée depuis avec constance : la France reconnaît à la fois le droit d'Israël d'exister au sein de frontières sûres et reconnues et le droit des Palestiniens de disposer d'un État ; elle s'est efforcée de favoriser le dialogue direct entre l'État hébreu et l'Organisation de libération de la Palestine (OLP), qui dispose depuis 1975 d'un bureau à Paris. Elle a approuvé la conclusion de l'accord d'Oslo, signé à Washington le 19 septembre 1993, et décidé, avec ses partenaires de l'Union européenne, d'apporter immédiatement son soutien au processus de paix en dégageant un fonds de 500 millions d'ECU (560 millions de dollars) destiné à la reconstruction des territoires occupés. Au-delà de l'accord israélo-palestinien, la diplomatie française encourage activement la recherche d'un règlement de paix global au Proche-Orient. Au Liban, la France, lors du conflit d'avril 1996, a œuvré pour qu'intervienne un accord de cessez-le-feu supervisé par un comité de surveillance que la France co-préside avec les États-Unis.

L'Afrique, continent sur lequel se déroule la plupart des crises, constitue une priorité. La France entretient des relations privilégiées avec de nombreux États africains : un sommet annuel des chefs d'État de France et d'Afrique est la traduction concrète de ce dialogue fondamental. La France ne ménage pas ses efforts diplomatiques pour résoudre les conflits et les crises politiques qui affectent ces pays, que ce soit au sein de l'ONU ou en liaison avec certains États de la région. Elle a ainsi soutenu les efforts de la communauté internationale destinés à amener la République sud-africaine à abolir le régime de l'apartheid et à élaborer une constitution démocratique. Elle a participé à l'opération des Nations unies cherchant à rétablir la paix civile en Somalie et à assurer la sécurité de l'approvisionnement alimentaire. Pendant l'été 1994, elle s'est portée au secours des populations rwandaises menacées : elle a dépêché des forces chargées de créer une zone humanitaire sûre. L'opération Turquoise, autorisée par la résolution 929 du Conseil de sécurité, a ainsi permis de mettre des milliers de Rwandais à l'abri des combats et déclenché une mobilisation internationale.

En République centrafricaine, la France a apporté un soutien logistique et financier à la Force interafricaine de la MISAB, en 1997, dont le Conseil de sécurité a reconnu le bien-fondé par sa résolution 1125. La France a ensuite soutenu la création d'une opération de maintien de la paix (la MINURCA), pour succéder à la MISAB en 1998. La France a consenti un important effort financier et humain (200 casques bleus français y participent) pour lancer cette opération.

En matière de prévention des conflits et de déploiement rapide, la France est, avec les États-Unis et le Royaume-Uni, à l'origine d'une initiative pour le renforcement des capacités des armées africaines à participer aux opérations de maintien de la paix sous l'égide des Nations unies. Elle apporte à ce sujet la plus grosse contribution bilatérale.

La France n'a pas davantage oublié les liens qui l'attachent aux pays de la péninsule indochinoise. Elle a favorisé en 1991 la signature des accords de Paris, destinés à mettre en œuvre la réconciliation nationale au Cambodge. Architecte avec l'Indonésie de cette réconciliation, elle a joué un rôle prépondérant sur le terrain durant toute la phase de transition. Les 1 500 casques bleus français ont ainsi constitué le contingent principal mis à la disposition de l'Autorité provisoire des Nations unies au Cambodge (APRONUC), chargée de désarmer les parties en conflit, de veiller au respect du cessez-le-feu et de préparer la restauration de la démocratie. La visite du président Mitterrand à Phnom Penh, en février 1993, symbolise la part prise par la France au processus qui a finalement conduit à la tenue d'élections libres en mai 1993, puis au retour du Prince Sihanouk sur le trône du Cambodge.

La France a également pris part aux actions militaires conduites en ex-Yougoslavie par l'Alliance atlantique avec un mandat de l'ONU et y a déployé une Force de réaction rapide pour protéger les casques bleus. Avec les États-Unis, la Russie, le Royaume-Uni et l'Allemagne, elle fait partie du « Groupe de contact » qui s'est employé, au nom de la communauté internationale, à amener les belligérants à accepter un plan de paix global. Ces efforts ont conduit à la signature à Paris, le 14 décembre 1995, de l'Accord de paix négocié à Dayton (États-Unis) : leur mise en œuvre est assurée par une force militaire de l'OTAN (SFOR) et une force de police des Nations unies (GIP) à laquelle appartiennent plus de 120 gendarmes français. Longtemps premier État contributeur de troupes et de matériel en raison de sa participation à la FORPRONU (ex-Yougoslavie), la France occupe actuellement le neuvième rang des États participant aux opérations de maintien de la paix engagées sous l'égide des Nations unies. Ses « casques bleus » sont présents au Liban, au Sahara occidental, en Haïti,

Lors de sa visite officielle en Chine, le Premier ministre Lionel Jospin, est accueilli par son homologue chinois, Zhu Rongji, devant le Palais du peuple, place Tienanmen à Pékin, septembre 1998

en Géorgie, en Angola, à la frontière irano-irakienne, à Jérusalem, en ex-Yougoslavie et en République centrafricaine. Plus généralement, la France encourage toutes les réformes visant à améliorer le fonctionnement des Nations unies dans le domaine du maintien de la paix. Elle est à l'origine du système des « forces en attente » qui a contribué à accélérer sensiblement la rapidité de déploiement de casques bleus.

La France n'a pas ménagé ses efforts au sein des Nations unies, et du Conseil de sécurité en particulier, pour faire respecter la justice internationale : elle a été, avec d'autres États, à l'origine des résolutions du Conseil de sécurité créant les Tribunaux pénaux internationaux pour l'ex-Yougoslavie (en 1993) et pour le Rwanda (en 1995). Elle accorde depuis son plein soutien à ces deux juridictions internationales qui ont vocation à juger des personnes responsables des violations graves du droit humanitaire international. Elle a participé activement aux négociations qui ont présidé en 1998 à la naissance de la cour criminelle internationale.

Les droits de l'homme

Si les droits de l'homme sont aujourd'hui universellement reconnus et défendus, ils revêtent une importance historique particulière pour la France. La tradition française d'attachement aux droits de l'homme prend sa source au XVIIIᵉ siècle, dans les Lumières, et la France fut une des premières nations à élaborer une déclaration les proclamant, la Déclaration des droits de l'homme et du citoyen du 26 août 1789. En 1948, c'est à Paris, au Palais de Chaillot où siégeait l'Assemblée générale des Nations unies, qu'a été adopté la Déclaration universelle des droits de l'homme. Un grand juriste français, René Cassin, qui a exercé par la suite les fonctions de président de la Cour européenne des droits de l'homme et à qui a été décerné le prix Nobel de la Paix, fut un des principaux artisans de son élaboration.

Fidèle à sa tradition, la France mène à l'époque contemporaine une

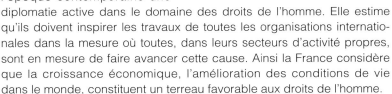

diplomatie active dans le domaine des droits de l'homme. Elle estime qu'ils doivent inspirer les travaux de toutes les organisations internationales dans la mesure où toutes, dans leurs secteurs d'activité propres, sont en mesure de faire avancer cette cause. Ainsi la France considère que la croissance économique, l'amélioration des conditions de vie dans le monde, constituent un terreau favorable aux droits de l'homme.

Affiche de la
commémoration
du 50ᵉ anniversaire de la
Déclaration universelle
des droits de l'homme

La France est aujourd'hui partie à presque tous les accords internationaux de promotion des droits de l'homme et plusieurs experts indépendants français siègent dans les « comités conventionnels » qui sont chargés de veiller à leur respect par les États. Elle est, par ailleurs, un membre permanent de la Commission des droits de l'homme des Nations unies. Elle met en application, dans cette enceinte privilégiée, son approche constructive de la question des droits de l'homme. Sans qu'il s'agisse de transiger avec les principes fondamentaux de respect des droits de l'homme qui peuvent conduire la communauté internationale à condamner vigoureusement des pratiques les enfreignant, voire à formuler des injonctions, la diplomatie française met en effet l'accent sur la nécessité de développer la coopération entre les États plutôt que de s'inscrire dans une perspective de confrontation. Elle favorise par exemple le dialogue entre la Chine et la communauté internationale, ce qui a été vraisemblablement un des éléments pris en compte par les autorités chinoises dans leur décision de devenir partie au Pacte international relatif aux droits économiques, sociaux et culturels, et peut-être dans un second temps au Pacte international sur les droits civils et politiques.

Dans les développements récents de la vie internationale, la France a soutenu la création des deux tribunaux pénaux internationaux chargés de juger les auteurs de crimes contre l'humanité ou d'actes de génocide commis sur les territoires de l'ex-Yougoslavie et du Rwanda. La France avait préalablement joué un rôle de premier plan dans les efforts de la communauté internationale pour assurer le respect des droits de l'homme dans ces territoires. Elle a aussi appuyé le principe de l'institution d'une cour pénale internationale permanente qui sera compétente pour sanctionner les violations graves des droits de l'homme.

Au plan européen, la France accueille sur son sol, à Strasbourg, le Conseil de l'Europe. Celui-ci fut installé dès sa fondation, en 1949, dans cette ville d'Alsace qui symbolisait la réconciliation franco-allemande. Le Conseil de l'Europe est chargé de réaliser une union toujours plus étroite entre les États européens, basée sur leur respect commun de la démocratie pluraliste, des droits de l'homme et de l'État de droit. Capitale européenne des droits de l'homme, Strasbourg accueille aussi la Cour européenne des droits de l'homme qui veille au respect de la Convention européenne de sauvegarde des droits de l'homme et des libertés fondamentales de 1950. La France a ratifié la Convention et a adhéré au mécanisme qui permet aux personnes physiques ou morales s'estimant victimes d'une violation de leurs droits d'introduire un recours individuel. En application du protocole n° 11 à la Convention, le système juridictionnel de la Cour a été renforcé à partir du 1er novembre 1998, les particuliers se voyant reconnaître un droit d'interjeter appel des décisions de première instance.

La France joue aussi un rôle important dans la protection des droits de l'homme dans le cadre de l'Organisation pour la sécurité et la coopération en Europe (OSCE). C'est à Paris, en 1990, qu'a été adoptée la Charte pour une nouvelle Europe, par laquelle les États européens rassemblés ont affirmé leur attachement aux principes de la démocratie, des droits de l'homme et de l'État de droit, en soulignant qu'ils sont la base de la prospérité économique et sociale et qu'ils sont indispensables à la promotion de la paix. Le pacte de stabilité en Europe, adopté à Paris en 1995, est également issu d'une initiative française. Un de ses aspects principaux concerne le respect des droits des personnes appartenant à des minorités.

Dans ses relations bilatérales, la France mène de très nombreuses actions de coopération dans le monde pour assurer la promotion et la protection des droits de l'homme, dans des domaines aussi variés, par exemple, que les droits de l'enfant, les droits des femmes ou la lutte contre l'esclavage. La France conduit aussi dans des pays des cinq continents des actions de formation aux droits de l'homme et aux règles internationales de leur respect.

Au plan national, la Déclaration des droits de l'homme et du citoyen fait partie, de même que le Préambule de la Constitution de 1946 la complétant, des textes constitutionnels actuellement en vigueur sous l'empire de la Constitution du 4 octobre 1958. Les accords internationaux de promotion des droits de l'homme ont par ailleurs une valeur supérieure à celle des lois et sont, pour beaucoup d'entre eux, directement invoquables par les particuliers devant les juridictions. L'ampleur de la législation nationale consacrée aux droits de l'homme atteste également de l'importance fondamentale que la France attache à leur respect.

Le gouvernement français a institué, dès 1947, une Commission nationale consultative des droits de l'homme dont le fondateur fut René Cassin. Sa compétence s'étend à la totalité des questions intéressant les droits de l'homme. La CNCDH remet notamment chaque année au gouvernement un rapport sur la lutte contre le racisme et la xénophobie. Chaque année également, la Commission décerne le « Prix des droits de l'homme de la République française » qui distingue des actions de promotion des droits de l'homme. Et c'est devant la CNCDH que le Premier ministre a annoncé en avril 1998, année du cinquantième anniversaire de la Déclaration universelle, sa décision de faire de la défense des droits de l'homme une « Grande cause nationale 1998 ».

La CNCDH s'efforce de promouvoir la création d'institutions semblables à l'étranger. Aujourd'hui, une quarantaine d'institutions nationales existent et, en 1991, des « Principes de Paris » sur leurs statuts et leurs compétences ont été définis dans la capitale française. L'Assemblée générale des Nations unies a adopté le texte des « Principes de Paris » en 1993.

La France est, au total, un acteur très actif de la scène internationale en matière de droits de l'homme. Si elle a joué historiquement un rôle de première importance dans leur reconnaissance, elle est aussi résolument tournée vers l'avenir et la définition des nouveaux droits de l'homme que l'évolution du monde contemporain appelle. À la fin des années soixante-dix, la France fut ainsi un des premiers États à garantir les droits de l'individu face à l'informatique. Plus récemment, le gouvernement français s'est fait l'avocat de la reconnaissance d'un droit humanitaire s'imposant à l'action des États, d'un « devoir d'assistance humanitaire » de la communauté internationale qui a depuis trouvé quelques applications. Et, après l'adoption de la Convention européenne sur les droits de l'homme et la biomédecine en 1997, c'est aussi sur une initiative dont le gouvernement français est un des auteurs qu'a été conclu à Paris, en 1998, son protocole interdisant le clonage des êtres humains.

L'aide au développement

Attachée au respect de la démocratie et des droits de l'homme, la France a toujours été convaincue que cet objectif est indissociable du combat pour le développement. L'ancienneté des relations nouées avec de nombreux pays du Sud et le sentiment de solidarité particulier qui les lie l'ont amenée à définir une politique de coopération ambitieuse.

Les présidents de la République ont tous souligné, depuis 1958, l'engagement de la France dans ce domaine.

L'action menée par la France en faveur du développement répond à cette conviction largement partagée : en volume, la France est en 1997 le deuxième donateur mondial, avec un montant d'aide publique au développement de 37 milliards de francs (6,35 milliards de dollars), derrière le Japon mais devant les États-Unis et l'Allemagne ; ce montant représente maintenant 0,45 % de son PNB (moyenne des pays riches : 0,22 %), ce qui la place au premier rang des sept pays les plus industrialisés (G7) et au sixième rang des États membres du Comité d'aide au développement de l'OCDE.

La France a plaidé avec constance, au sein des instances internationales, la cause des pays en développement afin de faciliter la gestion de leur dette. Elle a même annulé en 1992 les créances qu'elle détenait à l'égard des pays les moins avancés. Elle a pris de nombreuses initiatives favorables à la stabilisation du cours des produits de base dont dépendent les recettes d'exportation des pays du Sud. Concernant l'Afrique francophone, la France a pris en 1994 des mesures d'aide particulières pour limiter les effets sur les populations de la dévaluation du franc CFA (monnaie soutenue par la Banque de France), ce qui a permis aux pays intéressés de renouer avec les institutions financières internationales. Un an plus tard, les économies de ces pays pouvaient redémarrer et leurs projets de développement pouvaient reprendre.

La répartition géographique de l'aide bilatérale fait apparaître une forte concentration sur l'Afrique subsaharienne, qui a été bénéficiaire en 1996 de 42,2 % des versements nets, soit 12,4 milliards de francs (2,06 milliards de dollars). Les liens historiques privilégiés unissant la France et ce continent expliquent ce pourcentage élevé, qui n'empêche pas cependant une diversification croissante de la distribution géographique de l'aide.

À cette politique de coopération nationale viennent s'ajouter les mesures

Montant de l'aide publique au développement en provenance des pays du Comité d'aide au développement (CAD), en 1997. La France est le deuxième donateur mondial après le Japon

	en millions de dollars	en % du PNB
Allemagne	5 913	0,28
Australie	1 076	0,28
Autriche	531	0,26
Belgique	764	0,31
Canada	2 146	0,36
Danemark	1 635	0,97
Espagne	1 227	0,23
États-Unis	6 168	0,08
Finlande	379	0,33
France	**6 348**	**0,45**
Irlande	187	0,31
Italie	1 231	0,11
Japon	9 358	0,22
Luxembourg	87	0,50
Norvège	1 306	0,86
Nouvelle-Zélande	145	0,25
Pays-Bas	2 946	0,81
Portugal	251	0,25
Royaume-Uni	3 371	0,26
Suède	1 672	0,76
Suisse	839	0,32
Total pays du CAD	**47 580**	**0,22**
dont pays membres de l'Union européenne	26 542	0,33

Source : OCDE.

adoptées dans le cadre communautaire. Dès 1963, la convention de Yaoundé associait aux États de la Communauté européenne dix-huit États africains et malgache, bénéficiant de conditions commerciales préférentielles. Renouvelé à cinq reprises, cet accord - qui a pris le nom de Convention de Lomé - définit une politique de coopération plus ambitieuse, concernant soixante-dix États d'Afrique, des Caraïbes et du Pacifique (ACP).

L'expérience acquise a permis d'améliorer l'efficacité de cette aide. Comme ses partenaires de l'Union européenne, la France contribue à promouvoir les efforts d'intégration régionale et les ajustements macro-économiques réalisés sous l'égide des instances internationales. Enfin, en 1990, lors du sommet franco-africain de La Baule, la France a annoncé son intention de lier le niveau de sa coopération bilatérale aux progrès réalisés par chaque pays en matière de démocratie et de respect des droits de l'homme.

L'action humanitaire

L'action humanitaire française répond au principe d'exigence morale de secourir les populations civiles en situation de détresse physique ou mentale où qu'elles se trouvent. Pour ce faire, l'action humanitaire française appuie techniquement et financièrement en partenariat les opérations d'organisations non gouvernementales (ONG) et d'organismes institutionnels français (Sécurité civile, Samu mondial, service de santé des armées), outre les contributions aux programmes des organisations humanitaires internationales.

La France joue un rôle important au sein de l'Office humanitaire européen (ECHO), pour lequel elle contribue à hauteur de 18 % de son budget. Les principaux terrains d'action de l'aide humanitaire européenne sont la région des Grands lacs en Afrique, l'Europe centrale et les pays du Caucase.

La lutte contre les mines anti-personnel et le déminage humanitaire font partie des priorités de l'action de la France. Son engagement dans le domaine du déminage et de l'assistance aux victimes des mines remonte à plus de vingt ans. Depuis 1994, plus de 50 millions de francs (8,3 millions de dollars), dont 28 millions (4,6 millions de dollars) pour la seule année 1997, ont été consacrés à des opérations de déminage humanitaire, dans le cadre de programmes bilatéraux ou par le biais des Nations unies. À cette somme vient s'ajouter la quote-part ver-

Les accords d'Ottawa interdisant les mines anti-personnel ont été signés le 3 décembre 1997 par le ministre délégué chargé de la Coopération et de la Francophonie, Charles Josselin

sée par la France aux programmes mis en œuvre dans le cadre de l'Union européenne. Pour la seule période 1996-1997, ces programmes ont représenté, pour l'Union européenne, un engagement financier de plus de 50 millions d'écus (environ 320 millions de francs, soit 53 millions de dollars). La part financée par la France s'élève à 68 millions de francs (11 millions de dollars). En outre, les forces armées françaises, qui disposent d'une grande expérience en la matière, ont effectué depuis 1978 une vingtaine d'opérations extérieures de déminage et surtout de formation au déminage, notamment au Liban, au Tchad et au Cambodge. La France a ratifié la Convention d'Ottawa d'interdiction totale des mines anti-personnel le 1er juillet 1998. Elle a fait une déclaration annonçant son intention de procéder à la destruction de ses stocks avant la date fixée par la Convention.

La Francophonie : échanges et solidarité

Aujourd'hui 105 millions de personnes utilisent le français comme première langue, 55 millions s'en servent de manière occasionnelle. En nombre de locuteurs, le français est la neuvième langue dans le monde. Il est présent dans les systèmes éducatifs de toutes les régions du monde. Avec l'appui de la France, mais aussi d'autres États francophones, la communauté francophone est devenue une véritable enceinte de coopération, tant linguistique et culturelle qu'économique et politique. Plusieurs institutions rassemblent ainsi la famille francophone. L'Agence de la Francophonie (ACCT), qui a son siège à Paris, met en œuvre des programmes couvrant des domaines aussi divers que l'éducation et la formation, l'environnement et le développement durable, la culture et la communication, la coopération juridique et judiciaire. Les efforts déployés par l'Association des universités partiellement ou entièrement de langue française (AUPELF) ont abouti, en 1987, à la création de l'Université des réseaux d'expression française (UREF). Ces deux enceintes ont été fusionnées pour constituer l'Agence de la Francophonie. Par ailleurs, la chaîne de télévision francophone TV5, née en Europe en 1984, s'est progressivement élargie à l'Amérique (TV5 Québec-Canada, 1988), à l'Afrique et à l'Amérique latine (1992).

Sept sommets de la Francophonie se sont tenus à Versailles (1986), Québec (1987), Dakar (1989), Paris (1991), Port-Louis (1993), Cotonou (1995) et Hanoï (1997). Réunissant 52 États, la rencontre de Hanoï a créé un poste de secrétaire général à la Francophonie, qui a été attribué à l'Égyptien Boutros Boutros-Ghali, ancien secrétaire général des Nations unies.

Parallèlement, une politique active de promotion des échanges culturels, scientifiques et techniques est conduite à travers le monde. En 1999, cette action s'organise autour de deux grands axes. D'une part, les projets de coopération couvrent les secteurs les plus variés (agriculture, santé, environnement, administration publique, urbanisme, énergie...) ; de nombreux projets touchent quelque 120 pays développés, émergents et en transition. D'autre part, le réseau lie

300 lycées et écoles accueillant 150 000 élèves (dont 60 000 sont Français). La présence culturelle française s'appuie également sur environ 130 établissements culturels, installés dans 56 pays et offrant des cours de français à 140 000 adolescents et adultes.

L'Alliance française, quant à elle, dispose d'un réseau de 1 060 centres répartis dans 140 pays, qui enseignent le français à 318 000 étudiants.

Au total, ces quelque 1 500 institutions, auxquelles il convient d'ajouter 25 instituts de recherches en sciences sociales ou humaines installés dans 20 pays et 203 missions de fouilles archéologiques, concourent à la présence française à l'étranger. Par ailleurs, en 1998, on comptait près de 150 000 étudiants étrangers en France, dont 18 000 bénéficiaient de bourses du gouvernement français. L'évocation de ce dispositif, largement aidé par l'État, illustre l'importance que la France attache, dans le cadre de sa politique étrangère, à la promotion réciproque des cultures.

La médiathèque du centre culturel français à Oslo, en Norvège, représente une des nombreuses formes de la présence culturelle française dans le monde

Pour en savoir plus :

L'Union politique de l'Europe. Jalons et textes, documents rassemblés par P. Gerbet, F. de La Serre et G. Nafilyan, préf. de J. Delors, La Documentation française, collection Retour aux textes, 1998.

Y. Doutriaux, C. Lequesne, *Les institutions de l'Union européenne*, nouvelle édition mise à jour, La Documentation française, collection Réflexe Europe, 1998.

Une politique pour le français, Ministère des Affaires étrangères, Direction générale des relations culturelles, scientifiques et techniques.

La Direction générale des relations culturelles, scientifiques et techniques, Ministère des Affaires étrangères, 1998.

J. Dalloz, *La France et le monde depuis 1945*, Armand Colin, collection Cursus, 1993.

J. Doise et M. Vaisse, *Diplomatie et outil militaire ; politique étrangère de la France 1871-1991*, Le Seuil, collection Points, 1992.

A. Grosser, *Affaires extérieures : la politique étrangère de la France 1944-1989*, Flammarion Champs, 1989.

P.-M. de La Gorce et A.-D. Schor, *La politique étrangère de la Ve République*, PUF, collection Que sais-je ?, 1992.

Ph. Moreau Defarges, *La France dans le monde du XXe siècle*, Hachette, collection Les fondamentaux, 1994.

Politique étrangère de la France, recueil bimestriel des déclarations officielles de politique étrangère réalisé par la Direction de la communication et de l'information du ministère des Affaires étrangères, édité et diffusé par La Documentation française.

Site internet du ministère des Affaires étrangères :
http ://www.france.diplomatie.gouv.fr

9

La politique de défense

Son histoire, sa situation géographique, son potentiel économique et ses responsabilités internationales commandent à la France d'apporter une attention particulière à sa politique de défense. Tout en restant attachée au principe d'indépendance nationale et soucieuse de la protection de ses intérêts dans le monde ainsi que du respect des valeurs démocratiques, la France adapte constamment sa politique de défense et de désarmement à un contexte international évolutif. La publication par le gouvernement en 1994 d'un Livre blanc sur la défense, la réforme des forces armées décidée en 1996 et l'adoption d'une loi de programmation militaire pour 1997-2002 ont permis d'actualiser les objectifs et les moyens de cette politique, pour tenir compte des bouleversements intervenus depuis quelques années dans les relations internationales et, en conséquence, sur le plan stratégique.

Le concept français

Le concept français de défense, défini dans l'ordonnance du 7 janvier 1959, est global. Il assigne à la politique de défense de la France trois objectifs.

– Défendre les intérêts vitaux du pays, dont la définition relève du président de la République et qui comprennent notamment la population, le territoire et le libre exercice de la souveraineté. À cet égard, la Constitution de 1958 confère au président de la République le rôle de garant de l'intégrité du territoire (article 5), ainsi que celui de chef des armées (art. 15). Parallèlement, la France doit également assurer la protection de ses intérêts stratégiques au niveau international, tout en contribuant à la prévention des conflits, au maintien ou au rétablissement de la paix, au respect du droit international et des valeurs démocratiques dans le monde. Dans ces domaines, son statut de membre permanent du Conseil de sécurité des Nations unies lui confère à la fois des prérogatives et des responsabilités.

– Œuvrer au développement de la construction européenne et à la stabilité du continent. La France a fait ce choix dès la fin de la seconde guerre mondiale en participant activement à l'Union de l'Europe occidentale (UEO), à l'Organisation du traité de l'Atlantique Nord (OTAN) et à la Conférence sur la sécurité et la coopération en Europe (CSCE), devenue Organisation pour la coopération et la sécurité en Europe (OSCE) en décembre 1994.

– Mettre en œuvre un concept de défense globale qui ne se compose pas uniquement d'un aspect militaire. En effet, la sécurité et la stabilité d'un État dépendent non seulement de ses forces armées et de sa police, mais également de son organisation sociale, de son système éducatif et de son mode de fonctionnement en matière de solidarité. Le concept de défense est, de fait, indissociable de celui de nation. Ainsi, la sécurité civile assure la protection de la population, le maintien de l'ordre public et donc la continuité de l'État. Elle englobe la prévention et la protection face aux risques naturels et technologiques majeurs, la sécurité des installations et des réseaux sensibles. Enfin, elle assure la bonne répartition des ressources en temps de crise.

Défilé du 14 juillet 1998 sur les Champs-Élysées, Paris

Un nouvel environnement stratégique

Après la chute du mur de Berlin, la dissolution du pacte de Varsovie et de l'Union soviétique, et l'amorce d'un réel désarmement conventionnel et nucléaire de la principale puissance militaire du continent européen, la France ne connaît plus aujourd'hui de menace militaire directe à ses frontières. De plus, le traité sur les Forces nucléaires intermédiaires (FNI) conclu en 1987 entre les États-Unis et l'URSS a abouti à l'élimination de tous les missiles nucléaires à moyenne portée déployés à terre par ces deux puissances en Europe.

Les traités START (*Strategic Arms Reduction Talks*) de 1991 et 1993 conduiront d'ici fin 2007 à un abaissement respectif des arsenaux stratégiques américains et russes à 3 000 et 3 500 ogives (contre plus de 12 000 et 11 000 en 1990). Le traité sur les Forces armées conventionnelles en Europe (FCE), signé à Paris le 19 novembre 1990, dans le cadre de la CSCE, par 22 États membres de l'Alliance atlantique et de l'ex-pacte de Varsovie, a imposé aux parties des plafonds pour les armements lourds terrestres et aériens (les ELT : Éléments Limités par Traités). Il a imposé aux forces de l'ex-Pacte de Varsovie la destruction de près de 34 000 pièces d'armement lourd.

En 1997, la stabilité stratégique a été renforcée par la signature à Paris de l'Acte fondateur entre l'OTAN et la Russie, puis par la décision prise au sommet de Madrid de faire adhérer la Hongrie, la République tchèque et la Pologne.

À côté de ces facteurs positifs qui ont mis fin à l'affrontement Est-Ouest, la disparition du bloc de l'Est a coïncidé avec l'apparition de nouvelles tensions provenant des conflits frontaliers ou liés à des minorités ethniques. De telles tensions font peser des menaces réelles sur la stabilité du continent qui, pour la première fois depuis 1945, a vu renaître sur son sol des conflits armés. Cette instabilité est aggravée par les difficultés de certains pays d'Europe centrale, orientale et balkanique ou de l'ex-URSS à s'intégrer dans la communauté internationale au moyen de réformes structurelles politiques, économiques et sociales. Ces pays conservent d'importantes capacités d'armement conventionnel. Par ailleurs, la prolifération des armes non conventionnelles, nucléaires, biologiques et chimiques, et de leurs vecteurs, missiles balistiques et de croisière, reste une source d'inquiétude pour la communauté internationale. En outre, le terrorisme continue de menacer non seulement les populations civiles, mais aussi les réseaux de communication et les installations industrielles. Enfin, le trafic organisé de stupéfiants représente une menace non seulement pour la santé publique mais pour la sécurité internationale en apportant, notamment, son soutien financier aux guérillas. Il s'agit là de nouveaux risques de déstabilisation des États et même d'enjeux de conflits.

Une stratégie adaptée au nouveau contexte international

Face à cette double évolution du contexte international, la France a adapté sa stratégie.

Sur le plan politique et diplomatique, la France a cherché à favoriser la stabilité et la paix sur le continent européen, notamment grâce à un Pacte de stabilité entre les États de l'Union européenne et les pays d'Europe centrale, orientale et balte, ainsi qu'au moyen d'accords d'association entre ces pays et l'UEO. « Le Partenariat pour la paix » a été développé au sein de l'Alliance atlantique depuis 1994 avec les anciens pays du bloc de l'Est.

Sur le plan militaire, la France a réaffirmé que sa sécurité reposait sur la dissuasion, ce qui impliquait le maintien de ses forces à un niveau suffisant de crédibilité. Les moyens conventionnels jouent aujourd'hui un rôle stra-

Des ressortissants de toutes nationalités, encadrés par des militaires français, convergent vers l'aéroport de Brazzaville d'où les avions militaires français les évacueront vers Libreville, au Gabon, juin 1997

tégique propre et ne sont plus considérés uniquement comme un apport à la force de dissuasion nucléaire.

Selon le Livre blanc sur la défense, la France doit désormais être en mesure de faire face à des crises d'une ampleur limitée, de gérer et prévenir des crises longues, d'intensité variable et dont les théâtres d'opération peuvent être éloignés du territoire national. Certains de ces conflits ne mettent pas en cause directement les intérêts vitaux de la France, mais contreviennent à certains principes tels que le respect du droit international ou de la souveraineté des États, principes que son statut de membre permanent du Conseil de sécurité lui confère la responsabilité de défendre. La participation de la France à la prévention des conflits et à des opérations de maintien de la paix s'exerce donc, en coopération avec des partenaires ou des alliés, dans un cadre multilatéral. Face à ce nouvel environnement, la France s'est fixé pour objectif de mieux maîtriser l'intelligence des situations (par une amélioration du renseignement) et d'appréhender la complexité de conflits comportant des dimensions à la fois politiques et militaires et se déroulant sur des théâtres régionaux. Ceci implique une plus grande mobilité stratégique de ses forces. Il faut toutefois tenir compte du fondement de la stratégie française qui est toujours la dissuasion nucléaire. Cette doctrine repose sur la perception par tout adversaire potentiel des risques inacceptables pour lui, c'est-à-dire hors de proportion avec l'enjeu du conflit, qu'entraînerait une agression. La France continue de rejeter toute confusion entre dissuasion et emploi des forces nucléaires.

Les moyens conventionnels sont, quant à eux, définis en fonction de leur aptitude propre à contribuer à la prévention, à la limitation ou au règlement par la force des crises ou conflits régionaux. Pour mener à bien cette mission, la France met l'accent sur les moyens de renseignement qui permettent, par les informations qu'ils fournissent (notamment à partir de l'observation spatiale), d'intervenir à tous les stades de la crise, y compris celui de la prévention. La France dispose également de forces prépositionnées hors du territoire national qui peuvent être activées en cas de besoin.

La non-prolifération et le désarmement, facteurs de sécurité

Dans la mise en œuvre de sa politique de défense, la France agit également en faveur d'un désarmement contrôlé et pour la lutte contre la prolifération des armes de destruction massive en vue de renforcer la sécurité internationale.

Concernant les armes nucléaires, la France a longtemps appelé de ses vœux la réduction du surarmement des deux principales puissances, alors que ses propres forces reposaient sur le concept de suffisance.

Prenant en compte l'évolution du contexte stratégique, elle a procédé sans attendre à des réductions unilatérales de ses forces. Dès 1992, l'évolution du contexte stratégique l'a amenée à retirer du service les missiles Pluton et à les démanteler. Le 22 février 1996, après avoir annoncé la fermeture du centre d'expérimentations nucléaires du Pacifique, le président de la République a fait part de sa décision de retirer définitivement du service et de faire procéder au démantèlement des missiles Hadès et des missiles stratégiques sol-sol basés au plateau d'Albion. La décision a également été prise de fermer définitivement et de démanteler les usines produisant des matières fissiles pour les armes nucléaires, plutonium à Marcoule et uranium hautement enrichi à Pierrelatte.

S'agissant des essais nucléaires, la France a suspendu unilatéralement, le 2 avril 1992, ses essais souterrains en Polynésie française. Puis en 1993, elle s'est jointe au consensus de la communauté internationale en faveur de la négociation – dans le cadre de la conférence du désarmement de Genève – d'un traité d'interdiction totale des essais nucléaires à condition qu'il soit universel et internationalement vérifiable.

La France a été la première puissance nucléaire à se prononcer, en 1995, en faveur de « l'option zéro », c'est-à-dire d'une interdiction complète des essais nucléaires quelle que soit leur puissance. Ouvert à la signature le 24 septembre 1996, le traité d'interdiction des essais nucléaires a été signé le jour même par la France.

Le ministre des Affaires étrangères, Hervé de Charette, signe au siège de l'ONU, à New York, le 24 septembre 1996, le traité d'interdiction des essais nucléaires (TICE)

La France, qui n'avait pas adhéré au traité de non-prolifération des armes nucléaires (TNP) au moment de son entrée en vigueur en 1970, en a toujours respecté les principes. Dès 1991, elle avait pris la décision de ne plus exporter de technologies et de matières nucléaires à des fins pacifiques qu'aux États ayant au préalable accepté de placer toutes leurs installations nucléaires sous le contrôle de l'Agence internationale de l'énergie atomique (AIEA). Le nouveau contexte stratégique provoqué par la désintégration de l'Union soviétique et la montée des risques liés à la prolifération nucléaire l'a décidée à annoncer en 1991 son adhésion au TNP. Elle l'a ratifié formellement en 1992, rejoignant ainsi les autres puissances nucléaires reconnues et entraînant un nombre important de pays à suivre son exemple.

La France soutient également le renforcement de la sécurité régionale par la création de zones exemptes d'armes nucléaires. Déjà adhérente aux protocoles du traité de Tlatelolco créant une telle zone en Amérique latine, elle a ratifié en 1996 les protocoles des traités instituant de telles zones en Océanie (traité de Rarotonga) et en Afrique (traité de Pélindaba).

Dans le domaine des armes chimiques, la France est déjà dépositaire du protocole de Genève de 1925 qui interdit l'emploi à la guerre mais non la fabrication. Elle a mobilisé la communauté internationale, en particulier après la guerre Iraq-Iran pour relancer, en janvier 1989, la négociation, par la Conférence du désarmement de Genève, d'un traité interdisant non seulement l'emploi mais aussi la mise au point, la fabrication et le stockage des armes chimiques.

Ce traité a été signé à Paris en janvier 1993 par plus de 130 États et comptait, fin 1997, 165 signataires. Il est entré en vigueur le 29 avril 1997, après la 65e ratification. Aujourd'hui plus de 100 États, dont les cinq membres permanents du Conseil de Sécurité, l'ont ratifié. Comme la France l'a souhaité, son application est soumise à une stricte vérification, mise en œuvre par des inspecteurs internationaux.

En ex-Yougoslavie, trois militaires français de la Brigade multinationale, automne 1995

Par ailleurs, la France a adhéré en 1984 à la Convention de 1972 sur l'interdiction des armes biologiques. Elle a cherché dès 1991 à doter cet instrument international, qui en était dépourvu, de moyens de vérification. Des travaux d'experts ont été lancés, à son initiative, en 1993, et ils doivent être suivis par l'élaboration d'un protocole adjoint à la convention.

Enfin, en ce qui concerne les armements conventionnels, la France participe à l'adaptation du traité FCE au nouveau contexte géostratégique tout en veillant à maintenir son caractère d'instrument essentiel de sécurité.

Avec ses partenaires, elle procède à une mise à jour des mesures de confiance et de sécurité (Document de Vienne, 1994) pour tenir compte de l'évolution du contexte géostratégique : disparition de la confrontation bloc à bloc, mais aussi émergence de tensions régionales. Elle vise à promouvoir la transparence dans les activités militaires : c'est ce que devrait permettre, sous forme d'inspections aériennes, l'entrée en vigueur du traité « Ciel Ouvert » (1992), dès sa ratification.

Dans le cadre des Nations unies, elle est à l'origine de la création d'un registre sur les exportations et les importations d'armements, qui devrait jouer un rôle dissuasif à l'égard des transferts susceptibles de renforcer ou d'introduire des déséquilibres régionaux.

Enfin, la France a été l'un des tout premiers États à prendre des initiatives en vue de lutter contre les mines anti-personnel qui causent des ravages parmi les populations de nombreuses régions. À titre national, elle a prononcé des moratoires sur l'exportation, la production et l'emploi de ces armes. Sur la scène internationale, la France a été à l'initiative de la révision de la Convention de 1980 sur certaines armes classiques, qui a abouti au renforcement du Protocole II relatif à l'emploi et au transfert des mines anti-personnel. Par ailleurs, elle a contribué activement au processus ayant conduit à la signature, le 3 décembre 1997, de la Convention d'Ottawa portant interdiction totale des mines anti-personnel. Elle continuera à agir dans toutes les enceintes internationales pour que la lutte contre les mines anti-personnel fasse partie des priorités majeures de la communauté internationale.

Les moyens de défense de la France

Dans un tel contexte, la politique de défense de la France doit disposer des moyens adéquats.

L'organisation de la défense nationale

Le président de la République est le chef des armées (article 15 de la Constitution) et dispose, à ce titre, du pouvoir d'engager, en cas de besoin, les forces nucléaires. Le Premier ministre est, pour sa part, responsable de la défense nationale (art. 21), le ministre de la Défense étant chargé de l'organisation et de la mobilisation des forces.

Le 22 février 1996, le président de la République Jacques Chirac annonçait la professionnalisation des forces armées et l'abandon d'une armée mixte à partir du 31 décembre 2002. La loi du 28 octobre 1997 portant réforme du service national suspend l'appel sous les drapeaux pour les jeunes nés après le 31 décembre 1978, tout en conservant la possibilité de le rétablir à tout moment. Elle organise également la phase de transition vers l'armée professionnelle.

Entre 1996 et 2002, l'armée est engagée dans une profonde réforme qui doit la mener d'une armée de conscription, forte de 548 000 hommes, à une armée entièrement professionnelle de 440 000 hommes répondant aux nouveaux besoins de défense. C'est la phase de transition.

Durant cette phase, les jeunes hommes nés avant le 1er janvier 1979 effectuent leur service national dans les conditions actuelles.

Hélitreuillage
de forces spéciales
par un hélicoptère Puma

Le nouveau service national s'applique aux jeunes hommes nés après le 31 décembre 1978 et aux jeunes femmes nées après le 31 décembre 1982.

Il comprend :

– le recensement obligatoire dont l'âge sera progressivement abaissé à 16 ans ;

– l'enseignement obligatoire des principes et de l'organisation de la défense, à partir de la rentrée 1998, dans le cadre des programmes des établissements du second degré des premiers et seconds cycles ;

– la participation obligatoire à un « appel de préparation à la défense » d'une journée entre le recensement et l'âge de 18 ans ;

– la possibilité d'effectuer, après « l'appel de préparation à la défense », une préparation militaire, un volontariat d'un an renouvelé chaque année dans la limite de cinq ans, ou d'accéder aux réserves, dans les armées ou la gendarmerie nationale.

La loi de programmation militaire 1997-2002

Le nouveau modèle d'armée, arrêté par le président de la République le 22 février 1996, représente un changement d'une ampleur inégalée depuis les débuts de la Ve République. La loi de programmation militaire 1997-2002 est une loi de transition, marquant la première étape du cheminement vers ce modèle d'armée. Elle prend en compte une véritable rupture et se caractérise par un fort investissement dans la réforme structurelle de l'appareil de défense français. Son enjeu majeur est l'accomplissement de la professionnalisation.

Pour la première fois, une loi concerne la totalité des dépenses de défense (investissement et fonctionnement) et concerne aussi bien les autorisations de programme que les crédits de paiement. La valeur de référence de chaque annuité de programmmation est, hors pensions, de 185 milliards de francs (valeur 1995, soit 30,8 milliards de dollars), dont 99 milliards (16,5 milliards de dollars) consacrés aux dépenses courantes et 86 milliards de francs (14,3 milliards de dollars) consacrés aux dépenses en investissements, en diminution de 18 % par rapport à la loi précédente. Cette somme représentait, en 1997, 2,3 % du PIB français.

**Le porte-avions
Lafayette**

La participation du ministère de la Défense à l'effort gouvernemental décidé en 1997, pour tenir compte à la fois des dépenses de solidarité sociale et de la réduction des déficits publics conforme aux exigences de la monnaie unique européenne, a entraîné un fléchissement des dépenses en investissements pour les deux premières annuités de la programmation, ramenées à 84,9 milliards de francs (14,15 milliards de dollars) en 1997 et 81 milliards de francs (13,5 milliards de dollars) pour 1998. La volonté de rétablir la cohérence de la programmation a amené, fin 1997, à un exercice interministériel de « revue des programmes » consistant à stabiliser les dépenses à 85 milliards de francs (en francs constants 1998), soit 14 milliards de dollars, pour chacune des quatre annuités restant à courir de la loi de programmation, de 1999 à 2002, et à décider un certain nombre d'adaptations et d'ajustements de programmes, les programmes majeurs étant intégralement préservés.

Char Leclerc
en exercice

La loi de programmation militaire 1997-2002 comporte trois priorités, confirmées par l'exercice de la revue de programmes.

1. Le passage d'une armée de conscription à une armée professionnelle, qui doit être réalisé d'ici 2002. Les effectifs militaires passeront ainsi de 499 300 en 1996 à 356 000 en 2002, alors que ceux des personnels civils augmenteront, passant de 73 750 à 81 820 pendant la même période. Le service militaire obligatoire aura disparu en 2002 ; il sera remplacé par un volontariat qui devrait attirer dans les armées environ 27 000 jeunes gens par an.

La professionnalisation des armées implique une réforme profonde des réserves. Concentrée, compétente et disponible, la nouvelle réserve est une partie intégrante de l'armée professionnelle. Le volume prévu est de 100 000 hommes (dont 50 000 pour la gendarmerie). 30 % environ de ces personnels peuvent être rappelés dans des délais très brefs, venant compléter rapidement, en cas de besoin, les unités d'active dans lesquelles ils sont directement intégrés. En 1998, une loi spécifique a fixé les conditions d'emploi et le statut du réserviste, notamment vis-à-vis des structures civiles d'emploi.

2. La poursuite de la modernisation des équipements

Conformément aux décisions annoncées par le président de la République, la dissuasion s'appuie depuis 1996 sur une nouvelle posture, plus réduite mais suffisante face au nouveau contexte géostratégique, des forces nucléaires françaises et sur l'acquisition d'une capacité de simulation.

La programmation prévoit la modernisation des deux composantes qui subsistent : océanique et aéroportée. Les sous-marins nucléaires lanceurs d'engin (SNLE) de nouvelle génération, du type Triomphant, entreront progressivement en service et le développement du missile ASMP amélioré sera entamé.

L'effort de modernisation des forces classiques sera poursuivi afin d'améliorer les capacités de prévention et de projection.

C'est ainsi que les moyens d'observation et de communication spatiaux tels qu'Hélios 2 et Trimilsatcom continueront d'être développés, en coopération avec d'autres pays européens, et que l'interopérabilité des systèmes de commandement sera améliorée.

Cette loi, dont les ambitions par rapport à la précédente ont été diminuées, tant en termes d'échéances de livraisons que de quantités de matériels à acquérir, verra les mises en service des premiers Rafale, du porte-avions Charles de Gaulle, d'un TCD et de 33 chars Leclerc par an, ainsi que le développement des frégates Horizon, des hélicoptères Tigre et NH 90.

3. La restructuration de l'industrie d'armement

L'adaptation au nouvel environnement du secteur de l'armement, composante essentielle de la politique de défense de la France, est indispensable. Elle s'articule autour de quatre grands axes :

– la réduction des coûts :

un objectif de réduction des coûts de 30 % est assigné à la Délégation générale pour l'armement sur la période de programmation. Pour y parvenir, l'appel aux technologies duales sera étendu et un rapprochement avec les secteurs concurrentiels sera recherché ;

– la construction de pôles industriels :

depuis juin 1997, le gouvernement français a donné un signal fort à ses partenaires européens en créant un pôle électronique de défense autour de Thomson, avec Alcatel, Aérospatiale et Dassault Électronique, et en accélérant la constitution d'un pôle aéronautique par le transfert à Aérospatiale des actions de Dassault détenues par l'État. Dans le secteur électro-mécanique, conformément aux objectifs de la programmation, Giat Industries continue à se recentrer en se réorganisant autour de ses métiers principaux et la Direction des constructions navales (DCN) est mise au défi d'améliorer sa productivité par l'ouverture à la diversification et une mise en concurrence accrue avec les chantiers privés ;

– une industrie européenne disposant d'une base de défense compétitive, performante et adaptée. La constitution d'une telle base, la réduction des surcapacités existantes, la création d'une réelle complémentarité entre les pays partenaires doivent s'appuyer sur des projets concrets en coopération. La France a décidé fin 1997, en accord avec l'Allemagne, l'Espagne, l'Italie et le Royaume-Uni, de

En 1998, les effectifs totaux des forces armées françaises s'élèvent à :

235 834 personnes dans l'Armée de terre

83 446 dans l'Armée de l'air

65 195 dans la Marine

95 242 dans la Gendarmerie

27 111 dans les autres services (Service de santé, service des essences, administration centrale...)

La mission nucléaire

La dissuasion repose, depuis les décisions de février 1996, sur deux composantes, l'une balistique emportée par les sous-marins nucléaires lanceurs d'engins (SNLE), l'autre aérobie emportée par les aéronefs (Mirage 2000 N de l'Armée de l'air et Super Étendard embarqués de la Marine), tous deux équipés du missile air-sol de moyenne portée ASMP et ravitaillés par les avions KC 135 FR de l'Armée de l'air.

Les forces de combat comprennent :

– le Corps blindé mécanisé (CMB), corps de manœuvre d'équipement lourd, qui compte quelque 900 chars de combat et 350 hélicoptères ;

– la Force d'action rapide (FAR) et ses 44 000 hommes et femmes répartis en 4 divisions.

À compter du 1er juillet 1998, l'Armée de terre opère un regroupement de toutes ses forces sous l'autorité d'un seul commandement, le CFAT (commandement de la force d'action terrestre) auquel sera associé le CFLT (commandement de la force logistique terrestre) ;

– les forces aériennes de combat, réparties sur une quarantaine de bases, qui comprennent, pour l'essentiel, 380 avions de combat (Mirage 2000, Mirage F1, Jaguar), une centaine d'avions de transport tactique et logistique, 14 avions ravitailleurs ainsi que des systèmes de détection et de communication (dont 4 Awacs) ;

– la force d'action navale (FAN), composante maritime des forces projetables, qui regroupe 20 grands bâtiments de combat de haute mer, dont un porte-avions et des bâtiments amphibies armés par 5 600 hommes ;

– le Groupe d'action sous-marine (GASM), la Force de guerre des mines et des forces de soutien, qui complètent en cas de besoin les forces maritimes projetables et rassemblent, au 1er janvier 1998, 89 bâtiments.

L'ensemble de ces forces rassemble 123 aéronefs.

- Les forces de Gendarmerie, enfin, dont la contribution aux missions de sécurité est essentielle et qui comptent environ 180 véhicules blindés et une cinquantaine d'aéronefs.

Il convient d'y ajouter les forces françaises établies outre-mer, composées d'éléments terrestres, navals et aériens, prépositionnées en de multiples points du globe. Ces quelque 20 000 hommes et leur équipement sont présents de façon permanente dans les départements et territoires d'outre-mer.

On compte également près de 8 000 hommes stationnés dans plusieurs États africains liés par des accords de défense. Ce dispositif va être ramené à un peu plus de 5 000 hommes d'ici 2001, dans le cadre d'un redéploiement des forces visant à leur donner une plus grande mobilité ; simultanément, la France participe au « renforcement des capacités africaines de maintien de la paix » (RECAMP).

Enfin, la France fournit en permanence des contingents importants de « caques bleus » dans le cadre d'opérations de maintien de la paix ou d'interventions à caractère humanitaire, placées sous l'égide des Nations unies. Au total, il y avait 13 500 hommes engagés sur les théâtres extérieurs en 1995, dont 8 600 en ex-Yougoslavie ; il n'y en avait plus que 9 000 en 1997, essentiellement en raison d'un redimensionnement du dispositif en ex-Yougoslavie, ramené à 3 800 hommes dans le cadre de la SFOR.

donner une impulsion forte au regroupement des industries aéronautiques et spatiales européennes ;

– la recherche de nouveaux marchés, indispensable pour que les entreprises de défense françaises acquièrent une plus grande indépendance vis-à-vis du budget des armées.

Pour en savoir plus :

APHG et SIRPA, *Éléments de géostratégie et défense de la France*, La Documentation française, 1995.

G. Ayade et A. Demant, *Armements et désarmement depuis 1945*, Complexe, 1991.

M. Long (sous la dir. de), *Livre blanc sur la défense*, La Documentation française, collection des Rapports officiels, 1994.

Mémento défense-armement : L'Europe et la sécurité internationale, Groupe de recherche et d'information sur la paix (GRIP), 1997.

H. Prévost, *La France, économie et sécurité*, Hachette, collection Pluriel, 1994.

J.-P. Hébert, *Production d'armement. Mutation du système français*, La Documentation française, collection Les Études de la DF, 1995.

Textes législatifs et réglementaires, Secrétariat général de la Défense nationale, Organisation générale de la Défense nationale, *Journal officiel*.

« La France et sa défense », *Cahiers français*, n° 283, La Documentation française, octobre-décembre 1997.

« Les jeunes et la défense. Opinion publique et service militaire », *Les Champs de mars*, Cahiers du centre d'études en sciences sociales de la défense, n° 2, 1997.

P. Buffolot, « La réforme du service national », *Problèmes politiques et sociaux*, n° 769, La Documentation française.

L'année stratégique, sous la dir. de P. Boniface, 1997.

P. Buffolot, *La défense en Europe. Les adaptations de l'après-guerre froide*, La Documentation française, collection Les Études de la DF, 1997.

Revues

Armées d'aujourd'hui, revue mensuelle des Armées (DICOD).

Défense nationale (mensuel).

10

Les échanges extérieurs

Parce qu'elle a su s'ouvrir largement au monde depuis 1945, abandonnant sa vieille tradition protectionniste, la France est restée un acteur de premier plan de l'économie mondiale. Elle participe aujourd'hui pleinement au mouvement de mondialisation et son économie s'internationalise fortement, ce qui se traduit par une croissance importante de ses échanges. La France produit plus de 5 % du PIB mondial, au 4e rang derrière les États-Unis, le Japon et l'Allemagne et réalise environ 6 % des échanges commerciaux de la planète, se classant au 2e rang mondial derrière les États-Unis pour les exportations de produits agricoles et de services et au 4e rang mondial pour les exportations de produits industriels. La France est aussi un des tout premiers investisseurs mondiaux et le 3e pays d'accueil au monde pour les capitaux étrangers.

Des échanges excédentaires

Après avoir été déficitaire pendant quinze ans, la balance commerciale de la France est redevenue positive en 1992, l'excédent des exportations sur les importations atteignant 31 milliards de francs (5 milliards de dollars) cette année-là. Le solde commercial s'est considérablement renforcé depuis, atteignant 122 milliards de francs (20,3 milliards de dollars) en 1996 et 173 milliards de francs (28,8 milliards de dollars) en 1997.

Cette performance apparaît solide et durable. En 1992 et 1993, le redressement pouvait sembler fragile, car lié à une baisse sen-

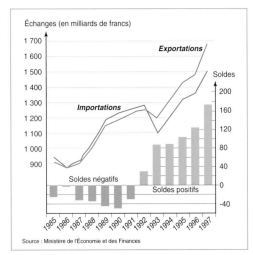

Échanges (en milliards de francs)

Exportations

Importations

Soldes

Soldes négatifs

Soldes positifs

1985 1986 1987 1988 1989 1990 1991 1992 1993 1994 1995 1996 1997

Source : Ministère de l'Économie et des Finances

Depuis 1992, le solde du commerce extérieur de la France est en progression constante et a atteint 173 milliards de francs en 1997

sible des importations qui traduisait le ralentissement de l'activité économique. Mais les excédents enregistrés depuis ont été réalisés en dépit d'une croissance soutenue des achats à l'étranger : la valeur des importations est passée d'environ 1 100 milliards de francs (183,3 milliards de dollars) en 1993 à près de 1 500 milliards de francs (250 milliards de dollars) en 1997. C'est donc bien une hausse structurelle des exportations qui place désormais la France dans une situation créditrice en ce qui concerne ses échanges extérieurs de marchandises.

La vente à l'étranger de biens d'équipement professionnel est le secteur qui a le plus contribué à l'amélioration du solde de la balance commerciale, principalement dans les branches « construction aéronautique », « machines de bureau et matériel électronique professionnel » et « équipements industriels ». Les échanges agro-alimentaires, traditionnellement positifs, les industries d'armement, les industries du luxe, ainsi que l'automobile et les transports terrestres, participent aussi largement à l'excédent de nos échanges extérieurs. S'ajoute à cela, depuis ces dernières années, un confortable surplus dans les produits de la pharmacie et de la parachimie. Les principaux déficits sont liés aux achats de produits énergétiques (le solde déficitaire est de l'ordre de 80 milliards de francs, soit 13,3 milliards de dollars), de matières premières minérales, de produits alimentaires tropicaux et de produits des industries traditionnelles (textile-habillement, cuirs et peaux, chaussure...).

Dans le port de commerce de Lorient (Morbihan), un navire charge 6 000 tonnes de poulets pour l'Iran

Si l'on ajoute aux échanges de biens les échanges immatériels concernant les services, en particulier le tourisme, et les échanges financiers, on constate que la balance des paiements de la France est largement excédentaire. Les transactions courantes ont ainsi généré un solde positif de plus de 230 milliards de francs (38,3 milliards de dollars) en 1997, l'excédent dégagé par les services et les revenus des placements financiers s'ajoutant au solde commercial.

L'Europe, partenaire privilégié

La France réalise 78 % de ses échanges avec les pays riches de l'OCDE et 62 % avec ses partenaires de l'Union européenne (50 % avec la zone euro). La part de l'Europe dans le commerce extérieur de la France n'a cessé de se renforcer au cours de ces dernières décennies et a gagné près de vingt points depuis les années soixante. Il y a donc eu une réelle dynamique de marché liée à la construction européenne et la

France en a profité, puisque le solde de ses échanges avec les pays de l'Union est fortement excédentaire (de l'ordre de 88 milliards de francs en 1997, soit 14,6 milliards de dollars). Les cinq principaux clients de la France sont ses proches voisins européens : Allemagne, Royaume-Uni, Italie, Belgique-Luxembourg et Espagne ; on retrouve ces mêmes pays dans les premiers fournisseurs, à l'exception de l'Espagne devancée par les États-Unis. Le partenaire privilégié, qui occupe de longue date le premier rang dans les échanges avec la France, est l'Allemagne (16,3 % du commerce extérieur total de la France), devant l'Italie (9,6 %) et le Royaume-Uni (9,2 %). En 1996 et 1997, les échanges de la France avec l'Allemagne sont

Le pont Vasco de Gama, construit sur le Tage au nord de Lisbonne par une société française et long de 17 kilomètres, représente une prouesse technologique ; il a été inauguré en mars 1998

devenus excédentaires, alors qu'ils étaient chroniquement en déficit. Parmi les partenaires hors Union européenne, trois occupent une place de choix : les États-Unis et le Japon, avec lesquels les échanges sont déficitaires et la Suisse, avec laquelle ils sont largement excédentaires.

Les échanges avec les pays hors OCDE ne représentent que 20 % du commerce extérieur de la France, dont plus de 4 % avec les pays de l'Est et la Russie. La part des pays en développement d'Asie, d'Afrique et d'Amérique latine est de 14 %, plus faible donc que les échanges avec la seule Allemagne. De ces pays, la France reçoit essentiellement des produits énergétiques, miniers et des matières premières d'origine agricole, ainsi que des biens de consommation à faibles coûts de production. Elle leur vend surtout du matériel d'équipement, des biens de consommation durables et des produits agro-alimentaires. Le bilan des échanges est assez contrasté. La balance commerciale est déficitaire avec la Chine, la Russie (sauf en 1995 et 1997) et les pays d'Asie du Sud-Est ; elle est excédentaire en revanche avec l'Afrique, l'Amérique latine, le Proche et le Moyen-Orient, à l'exception de quelques États de ces régions avec lesquels la France enregistre un déficit chronique notable, en raison des importations de pétrole (Arabie Saoudite, Nigeria). Avec les pays de l'Est européen, les échanges sont en progression rapide et le solde commercial est devenu excédentaire pour la France en 1996 et 1997.

L'internationalisation de l'économie française

Les exportations de la France représentent 21 % de son PIB, ce qui traduit une internationalisation importante des échanges, plus faible certes que celle de l'Allemagne (24 %), mais plus forte que celle du

Japon (10 %) et des États-Unis (9 %). Les flux croisés d'investissements sont un autre signe de cette ouverture économique. Le stock d'investissements directs détenus par la France à l'étranger était de l'ordre de 1 000 milliards de francs en 1996 (166,6 milliards de dollars), les investissements directs étrangers en France s'élevant à la même date à près de 750 milliards de francs (125 milliards de dollars).

Entre 1990 et 1996, la France a été au troisième rang des grands investisseurs mondiaux derrière les États-Unis et le Royaume-Uni. Il existe ainsi, de par le monde, 16 000 entreprises contrôlées par des capitaux français et qui emploient 2,6 millions de salariés. En tête des implantations françaises à l'étranger, on trouve les États-Unis (1 850 entreprises et 370 000 salariés) puis, à quasi-égalité, l'Allemagne (1 100 entreprises et 224 000 salariés), le Royaume-Uni (1 200 entreprises et 221 000 salariés) et l'Espagne (1 000 entreprises et 218 000 salariés). Au total, l'Union européenne est la première zone d'accueil, regroupant 45 % des salariés employés par des entreprises françaises à l'étranger. Dans les pays en développement, le Brésil est largement en tête pour les implantations françaises à l'étranger (au 7e rang, derrière l'Italie), mais la présence française en Amérique latine stagne, de même qu'en Afrique, où l'installation de filiales françaises est ancienne mais n'a guère progressé. La poussée française est forte en revanche dans les pays d'Asie en développement rapide, où l'effectif salarié employé s'est accru de plus de 60 % entre 1990 et 1995, et dans les pays d'Europe de l'Est et de l'ex-URSS, où il a augmenté de 57 % dans le même temps.

De même, plus de 10 000 entreprises implantées en France, situées pour moitié dans la région Ile-de-France, sont financées par des investisseurs étrangers. Les investissements récents se dirigent principalement vers des secteurs « porteurs » comme les télécommunications, l'électronique, la chimie-pharmacie dans le domaine industriel et le crédit, l'hôtellerie-restauration, les loisirs dans le domaine des commerces et services. Les principaux pays investisseurs sur le territoire national sont les États-Unis, devant le Royaume-Uni, les Pays-Bas, l'Allemagne et la Belgique. Les créations d'emplois, du fait de l'implantation d'entreprises étrangères, jouent un rôle important dans un contexte de chômage élevé : elles sont de l'ordre de 20 000 par an actuellement, contre 10 000 en moyenne dans les années quatre-vingt.

Pour en savoir plus :

H. Tyrman, F. Le Gallo, C. Loisy, *Un demi-siècle d'échanges extérieurs*, INSEE Première, n° 495, novembre 1996.

A. Bavelier, J.-C. Donnelier, *Les relations économiques internationales*, PUF, collection Que sais-je ?, 1997.

DREE (Direction des relations économiques extérieures), *Les échanges commerciaux de la France*, publication annuelle du ministère de l'Économie, des Finances et de l'Industrie.

Notes bleues de Bercy, revue bimensuelle qui publie de nombreux articles et mises au point sur les échanges extérieurs (ministère de l'Économie, des Finances et de l'Industrie).

LA SOCIÉTÉ

11

Les modes de vie

Depuis les années cinquante, la croissance économique d'abord, les progrès techniques et sociaux ensuite, ont changé la France en profondeur et fait entrer la société dans l'ère de la consommation et des loisirs. En dépit des difficultés que connaît le pays depuis la crise, la population française affiche, en effet, l'un des meilleurs niveaux de vie de la planète et apparaît aux meilleurs rangs des classements des Nations unies. Ainsi l'indice de développement humain (IDH) calculé selon des critères économiques, sociaux et culturels, met la France au deuxième rang mondial derrière le Canada en 1997. Le développement économique et social a cependant entraîné une certaine uniformisation des modes de vie et des habitudes de consommation, notamment entre les villes et les campagnes. Malgré tout, les identités régionales demeurent et contribuent largement à faire de la France une mosaïque géographique et culturelle qui reflète la diversité européenne et vaut à l'Hexagone d'être la destination touristique la plus appréciée du monde.

Plus qu'un sport, le roller est devenu un moyen de transport privilégié pour certains citadins ; ici à Paris sur les berges de la Seine

Une société plus riche
et moins inégalitaire

Entre 1955 et 1995, le pouvoir d'achat moyen des Français a quadruplé. Malgré la crise, sa progression, quoique plus ralentie, s'est poursuivie puisque le revenu des ménages a augmenté de 50 % de 1975 à 1995, soit une hausse moyenne de 2 % par an. Les Français se sont davantage enrichis au cours de ces quarante années que depuis le début de la Révolution industrielle, qui a amorcé le décollage économique du pays. Dans le même temps, la protection sociale s'est étendue à la totalité de la population et tout individu ne disposant pas de ressources est aujourd'hui assuré d'un « minimum social », revenu de base qui peut prendre la forme du RMI (revenu minimum d'insertion), de l'allocation spécifique de solidarité versée aux chômeurs en fin de droits ou de la prestation spécifique dépendance des personnes âgées. Au total, sur la longue durée, les inégalités sociales se sont réduites de même que l'éventail des revenus et des patrimoines, même si les deux décennies de crise ont eu tendance à creuser à nouveau le fossé entre la frange la plus pauvre et la frange la plus riche de la société : les 10 % des Français les plus pauvres se partagent 2,3 % des revenus alors que les 10 % les plus riches disposent de 27 % du revenu national. Cependant, malgré ces écarts, la société française reste l'une des moins inégalitaires.

En moyenne le revenu des ménages, salariés et non salariés, est compris entre 15 000 francs (2 500 dollars) et 16 000 francs (2 660 dollars) par mois avant impôt, sachant que la taille moyenne d'un ménage est de 2,5 personnes. Sur l'ensemble, les salaires représentent la moitié du revenu et les prestations sociales le tiers ; le reste provient d'activités non salariées et des revenus des placements et du patrimoine. L'éventail des salaires s'est resserré au cours de ces trente dernières années et la rémunération moyenne, en 1996, est comprise dans une fourchette allant de 1 à 3 : 20 760 francs (3 460 dollars) pour les cadres, catégorie la mieux payée, à 7 020 francs (1 170 dollars) pour les ouvriers non qualifiés, catégorie la moins bien payée. En moyenne, les salariés ont perçu 10 685 francs net par mois (1 780 dollars) en 1997 (13 550 francs brut), pour un temps plein, primes éventuelles non comprises. En 1950, la France a été le premier pays en Europe à instituer un salaire minimum applicable à tous les emplois. En 1998, le SMIC (salaire minimum interprofessionnel de croissance) brut est de 6 797 francs

Le niveau de vie dans l'Union européenne en 1995 : le PIB par habitant

Allemagne	131
Autriche	124,2
Belgique	117,8
Danemark	129,6
Espagne	63,3
Finlande	108,5
France	117,3
Grèce	48,5
Irlande	79,7
Italie	82,6
Luxembourg	187,7
Pays-Bas	113,5
Portugal	45
Royaume-Uni	83,3
Suède	115,5

Source : Eurostat (base 100 : moyenne de l'Union européenne).

par mois (1 132 dollars) et concerne 1,5 million de travailleurs, soit 11,2 % des salariés. Il s'agit surtout de jeunes, de femmes et d'hommes sans qualification, employés dans des petites et moyennes entreprises. En 1997, le pouvoir d'achat des salaires nets a progressé de 2,5 %, connaissant sa plus forte hausse depuis 7 ans. Toutefois, 4,5 millions de personnes, soit un actif sur 6, ne perçoivent pas de salaire et vivent des prestations sociales : 1,8 million de chômeurs indemnisés et 2,7 millions de personnes percevant les minima sociaux.

Le niveau de vie des Français varie non seulement selon leur revenu mais aussi en fonction de l'importance de leur patrimoine, constitué pour plus de la moitié de sa valeur moyenne par des biens immobiliers et fonciers (immeubles, bâtiments, terrains) et pour le reste par des valeurs financières, parmi lesquelles les produits d'assurance et les titres boursiers (actions et obligations) occupent une place croissante : leur part relative a été multipliée par cinq en vingt ans. Le patrimoine moyen brut des ménages dépasse 1 million de francs mais présente un éventail allant de 1 à 8 selon les groupes socioprofessionnels : il varie d'un peu moins de 500 000 francs pour les familles d'ouvriers et d'employés à près de 4 millions de francs pour les professions libérales.

Logement : une majorité de propriétaires

Les Français consacrent en moyenne 22 % de leur revenu au logement et aux charges qui lui sont liées (chauffage, éclairage, etc.). Cette part a doublé depuis 1960 parce qu'un nombre croissant de ménages a accédé à la propriété en s'endettant sur une période de quinze à vingt ans et aussi car les logements, qui offrent plus d'espace et de confort qu'auparavant, sont plus coûteux. Aujourd'hui, près de 6 ménages sur 10 sont propriétaires de leur logement, alors qu'ils n'étaient que 4 sur 10 en 1960.

L'accession à la propriété a comblé une aspiration forte d'une majorité de Français. Elle a été permise par la hausse du niveau de vie et encouragée par des politiques spécifiques d'aide à l'achat des résidences principales. Les politiques mises en place au début des années soixante ont surtout favorisé l'achat d'appartements dans des immeubles collectifs. En 1977, la création des prêts aidés d'accession à la propriété, dits prêts PAP, a relancé l'achat de logements qui s'essoufflait et s'est surtout traduite par l'acquisition de maisons individuelles, en particulier de pavillons dans les lotissements qui ont poussé à la péri-

Le temps passé devant la télévision a augmenté de plus de 30 % depuis 1982 et représente en moyenne 2 h 45 mn par jour, soit près de 20 % de la vie éveillée

phérie des villes. Les maisons individuelles constituent actuellement 56 % du parc total de logements. Dès la fin des années quatre-vingt, le mouvement d'accession à la propriété s'est ralenti, en raison sans doute de la faible croissance du pouvoir d'achat à cette période, mais aussi en raison du coût élevé de l'immobilier et des crédits. Ces facteurs se sont actuellement améliorés et les achats de logements sont nettement plus nombreux depuis 1994, le mouvement ayant été encouragé par la réforme de l'accession à la propriété, en octobre 1995, qui a créé le prêt à taux zéro pour certaines catégories de personnes.

Les conditions de logement

Les conditions de logement se sont sensiblement améliorées en qualité et en quantité. La taille moyenne des habitations approche aujourd'hui 90 m² pour un ménage français standard de 2,5 personnes, alors que dans les années soixante, les ménages moyens comptaient trois personnes pour une surface moyenne des logements de l'ordre de 60 m². On estime que la surface habitable par Français a doublé depuis la guerre. Le nombre de logements disposant du « tout confort » a aussi augmenté ; ainsi en 1955, 87 % des logements ne possédaient pas de sanitaires de base (WC intérieur et salle de bains) ; cette proportion est tombée à moins de 4 % aujourd'hui. Par le jeu des opérations de rénovation et de réhabilitation, qui ont touché des quartiers entiers dans les villes et qui ont également bénéficié à l'habitat rural, le parc ancien de logements a atteint un niveau de qualité équivalent à celui du parc de logements neufs ou récents.

Aujourd'hui, l'amélioration des conditions de logement se poursuit sous diverses formes. Les opérations de réhabilitation des cités d'habitat collectif construites dans les années soixante et au début des années soixante-dix (environ 200 ZUP – zones urbaines prioritaires –, soit 800 000 logements) sont conduites activement dans le cadre des politiques de la ville. La loi de 1998 permettant l'annulation des dettes sous conditions réglera, à terme, le sort des ménages qui ont accédé à la propriété dans des situations difficiles et ne peuvent honorer leurs échéances. Il est enfin nécessaire de loger les familles les plus démunies et dans l'incapacité de payer momentanément un loyer. Le plan d'urgence décidé à cet égard en 1995 a permis de constituer un stock de 20 000 logements destinés à une occupation temporaire.

De nouveaux modèles de consommation

La progression générale du niveau de vie a entraîné une hausse continue de la consommation, en moyenne de 3 % par an depuis 1970, mais avec un ralentissement dans les années récentes (+1,5 % en 1995 et +1,9 % en 1996) et de fortes variations selon les années. Cette évolution s'est accompagnée de modifications importantes dans la structure des dépenses effectuées par les ménages. La part occupée par l'alimentation et l'habillement a fortement reculé, passant de 44 % des dépenses en 1960 à 23 % en 1997. De même, les achats de biens d'équipement du logement ont diminué, passant de 11 % en 1960 à 7 % aujourd'hui. Les postes qui ont nettement augmenté sont ceux qui concernent le financement et l'entretien du logement (22 % en 1997 contre 10,4 % en 1960), la santé (10,3 % en 1997 contre 5 % en 1960), les transports et communications (16,7 % en 1997 contre 11,6 % en 1960) et les loisirs et la culture (7,4 % en 1997 contre 6 % en 1960). Globalement, la France présente une structure de consommation de pays riche, dans laquelle la part des dépenses nécessaires diminue au profit de celle des dépenses de confort.

En % des dépenses	1960	1980	1997
Produits alimentaires, boissons, tabacs	33,3	21,4	17,8
Habillement et chaussures	11,0	7,3	5,2
Logement, chauffage, éclairage	10,4	17,5	22,2
Meubles et articles ménagers	11,0	9,6	7,3
Services médicaux, santé	5,0	7,7	10,3
Transports et communications	11,6	16,6	16,7
Loisirs, spectacles, enseignement, culture	6,0	7,3	7,4
Autres biens et services	11,7	12,6	13,0

Évolution de la structure de la consommation des ménages : la part de l'alimentation et de l'habillement est passée de 44 % en 1960 à moins de 25 % aujourd'hui

L'ère du multimédia

Même si les Français consacrent une part plus faible de leur revenu à la satisfaction des besoins élémentaires, les dépenses effectives réalisées en ce domaine restent considérables : plus de 1 000 milliards de francs ont été affectés en 1997 à l'alimentation et à l'habillement, c'est-à-dire deux fois plus en francs constants que les sommes qui étaient réservées à ces postes en 1960. Par ailleurs, l'équipement des ménages est devenu très complet et les dépenses sont majoritairement destinées au renouvellement plutôt qu'à l'acquisition des produits. Près de 8 ménages sur 10 ont une automobile, 3 sur 10 en ont au

En 1998, 23 % des ménages ont un micro-ordinateur. Pour les autres, il existe des lieux accessibles au public comme les « cyber cafés » (ici à Paris, rue de Médicis), où les internautes peuvent se familiariser avec Internet

moins deux et il semble de plus en plus que ceux qui ne sont pas équipés appartiennent aux catégories qui ne peuvent l'être (personnes âgées en particulier) ; plus de 95 % des ménages disposent d'un réfrigérateur, d'un téléviseur et d'un lave-linge. C'est vers des équipements comme le magnétoscope, le caméscope, l'ordinateur personnel et les produits multimédias que les Français orientent de préférence leurs achats depuis les années quatre-vingt. La progression est rapide en ce domaine puisque 23 % des ménages disposent d'un micro-ordinateur en 1998, soit deux fois plus qu'en 1992.

La santé : une priorité

La part croissante des dépenses de santé dans le budget des Français relève de plusieurs phénomènes. D'une part la population vieillit, ce qui exige des soins accrus et qui ne feront qu'augmenter. D'autre part, si la sécurité sociale couvre encore les trois quarts des dépenses de santé, les cotisations des ménages n'ont cessé d'augmenter et leur contribution directe s'est accrue. Enfin, on assiste à une médicalisation de plus en plus systématique des difficultés de la vie ainsi qu'à une volonté de plus en plus marquée d'éliminer ce qui était auparavant considéré comme une fatalité : douleurs, disgrâces physiques, effets du vieillissement.

Consommation de masse, consommation sélective

Ces indicateurs montrent une mutation profonde des modes de vie et une société de plus en plus ancrée dans la consommation et les loisirs. On assiste à une standardisation relative des pratiques des consommateurs, qui se traduit par la montée du « prêt-à-consommer », qu'il s'agisse de produits surgelés, de restauration rapide, de produits jetables, de cures d'amaigrissement ou de voyages, séjours ou loisirs organisés. Dans le même temps, des habitudes bien enracinées reculent : la consommation de vin et de pain s'est effondrée et celle de tabac est en recul constant, les campagnes conduites au nom de la santé publique ayant sans doute joué en ce domaine autant que le changement des mœurs. Cependant, comme pour compenser ces évolutions, les produits de qualité, voire de luxe, sont très appréciés : les achats de champagne, de grands vins, d'articles de luxe et l'engouement pour la grande cuisine ne sont plus le fait des seuls consommateurs aisés mais touchent désormais les classes moyennes.

Le Mondial de l'automobile de septembre 1998, à Paris, a reçu plus de 1,2 million de visiteurs, un record d'affluence

Famille : de nouvelles valeurs

La famille et les pratiques matrimoniales ont évolué de manière complexe en même temps que la société se diversifiait et que la hausse du niveau de vie changeait en profondeur les conditions d'existence de la population. L'exode rural et l'urbanisation, qui ont atteint leur aboutissement dans les années soixante-dix, sont les facteurs fondamentaux d'effacement des structures et des liens familiaux traditionnels, phénomène accentué par l'extension aux populations des campagnes d'un mode de vie citadin et par le travail des femmes.

L'éclatement du groupe familial traditionnel s'est traduit par une baisse marquée de la cohabitation entre personnes âgées et générations plus jeunes – plus fréquente autrefois – et par une hausse du nombre des divorces. Parallèlement s'opère une certaine dilution des hiérarchies à l'intérieur de la famille, où l'autorité reposait autrefois sur l'âge et le rang de naissance. Ces mutations s'accompagnent d'un recul du mariage et d'une montée du divorce. On se marie de moins en moins et de plus en plus tardivement (l'âge moyen au premier mariage est passé à 27 ans chez les femmes et 29 ans chez les hommes) et le nombre de célibataires s'accroît : ils représentaient 7 % de la génération née en 1940, on estime qu'ils pourraient représenter plus de 30 % de la génération née en 1970. On compte aujourd'hui quasiment un divorce pour deux mariages (environ 285 000 mariages par an et plus de 130 000 divorces) ; il y a trente ans, le rapport était de 1 à 10, avec environ 40 000 divorces pour 400 000 mariages.

Les Français se marient moins (environ 285 000 mariages par an) et les célibataires pourraient représenter plus de 30 % de la génération née en 1970. Ici, mariage à la mairie de L'Isle-d'Abeau (Isère)

Évolution des mœurs, adaptation du droit

En fait, on assiste à une évolution des modèles plus qu'à leur disparition. La cellule familiale et le couple restent des références fortes dans notre société mais se sont adaptés à des conceptions et à des pratiques moins rigides, et les liens juridiques et sociaux qui fondaient ces institutions se sont assouplis. Il y avait environ 400 000 couples non mariés dans les années soixante, il y en a deux millions actuellement et près de 4 naissances sur 10 ont lieu hors mariage. On parle aujourd'hui de familles monoparentales pour désigner les ménages composés d'un seul adulte élevant ses enfants et de famille recomposée pour désigner les ménages où les enfants vivent avec un parent biologique et un beau-parent. Plus de deux millions d'enfants vivent dans une famille monoparentale ou recomposée. La loi s'adapte d'ailleurs à ces nouvelles exigences et un assouplissement de la législation concernant l'organisation de la cellule familiale, le mariage et le divorce est en cours en 1998.

Solidarité familiale

La famille reste pourtant un refuge privilégié face aux difficultés du temps. Les enfants la quittent de plus en plus tardivement en raison du prolongement des études et des difficultés d'insertion dans la vie professionnelle : les départs ont lieu autour de 25 ans en moyenne alors qu'ils intervenaient majoritairement vers 20-21 ans dans les années soixante. Il apparaît aussi que le renforcement des solidarités et des réseaux d'entraide à l'intérieur des familles permet d'amortir les effets du chômage et des difficultés économiques. Les aides financières entre parents et enfants sont estimées à 135 milliards de francs (22,5 milliards de dollars) par an en moyenne, les flux allant très majoritairement des générations les plus âgées vers les plus jeunes et se prolongeant souvent, même quand les bénéficiaires ont un âge avancé. On sait, par ailleurs, que bon nombre de personnes sans domicile fixe (SDF) sont en rupture de toute attache familiale, ce qui montre bien que l'absence de famille favorise les mécanismes d'exclusion.

Les Français au travail

Grâce aux progrès technologiques et à une meilleure organisation de la production, on travaille beaucoup moins aujourd'hui que par le passé, mais beaucoup plus efficacement. La réduction du temps de travail est surtout perçue à travers la diminution de la durée hebdomadaire du travail, fixée à 48 heures en 1919, à 40 heures en 1936, à 39 heures en 1982 et à 35 heures en 1998 (décision applicable en l'an 2000). Mais le phénomène est aussi imputable à d'autres éléments que l'on perçoit mieux si l'on observe l'ensemble de la vie active : la carrière professionnelle commence beaucoup plus tard et se termine beaucoup plus tôt, on ne travaille plus sept jours sur sept, ni douze mois sur douze (la durée légale des congés payés est de 5 semaines). En tenant compte de tous ces éléments, on peut conclure que, depuis 1870, la durée effective du travail par actif a été divisée par deux... Pourtant, dans le

Campagne d'affichage pour les « 35 heures » du ministère de l'Emploi et de la Solidarité, septembre 1998

Du temps pour soi.
Une chance pour l'emploi.

35^h

" JE VIENS DE TROUVER DU TRAVAIL GRÂCE AUX 35 HEURES. ICI ÇA MARCHE, ET CHEZ VOUS ? "

Informations : 0803 35 2000 (1,09 F/mn) ; www.35h.travail.gouv.fr

même temps, le produit intérieur brut (PIB) de la France a été multiplié par 14 et la productivité horaire du travail par 20. Il reste cependant des inégalités inhérentes aux diverses professions et, si le salarié travaille en moyenne 1 630 heures par an en 1996, l'agriculteur, le chauffeur routier ou le petit commerçant travaillent davantage.

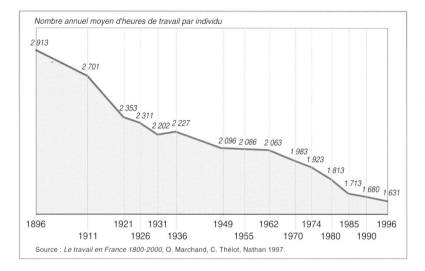

Nombre annuel moyen d'heures de travail par individu

2 913
2 701
2 353
2 311
2 202 2 227
2 096 2 086 2 063
1 983
1 923
1 813
1 713
1 680 1 631

1896 1921 1931 1949 1962 1974 1985 1996
1911 1926 1936 1955 1970 1980 1990

Source : *Le travail en France 1800-2000*, O. Marchand, C. Thélot, Nathan 1997.

Le temps de travail a diminué de 45 % en cent ans, mais il est inégalement partagé selon les salariés : 13 % d'entre eux travaillent moins de 30 heures par semaine et 6 % plus de 50 heures

Vers la semaine travaillée de 35 heures

La crise économique, les nouveaux modes d'organisation de la production, le recours accru à des machines ou à des systèmes remplaçant l'individu pour exécuter des tâches de plus en plus complexes ont changé le monde du travail. L'apparition du chômage chronique, à la fin des années soixante-dix, dans une conjoncture démographique qui voyait des générations nombreuses affluer sur le marché de l'emploi, a également contribué à modifier le rapport au travail. Un certain nombre d'ajustements s'opèrent face à ces exigences nouvelles. Le travail à temps partiel se développe rapidement : il concernait 6 % des salariés au début des années soixante-dix contre 17 % actuellement. De même, le télétravail permet le développement des tâches à domicile. L'aide aux personnes âgées, les besoins sociaux nouveaux, l'attention croissante portée à l'environnement, sont aussi l'occasion de créer de nombreux emplois de proximité et donc de répondre en partie aux demandes de travail. Face à l'importance du chômage, la réduction du temps de travail décidée en 1998 apparaît comme une des solutions possibles. Cependant cette mesure est controversée car elle est susceptible d'accroître les difficultés de certaines entreprises et de les rendre moins concurrentielles face à la plupart des pays où la législation sociale est moins évoluée. La négociation des modalités de passage aux 35 heures hebdomadaires dans les entreprises devrait pourtant aboutir à des consensus acceptables dans la plupart des cas.

En effet, les conditions et l'organisation du travail sont négociées entre employeurs et salariés d'une même branche professionnelle et fixées par des conventions collectives bénéficiant de la garantie de l'État. Par ailleurs, depuis 1982, une série de lois et d'ordonnances a renforcé les institutions représentatives des salariés, le rôle des organisations syndicales et instauré un droit à la négociation. Toujours très importante dans des pays comme l'Allemagne et les États scandinaves, l'audience des syndicats est en recul chez les salariés français, en dépit d'une tradition pourtant ancienne. Le taux de syndicalisation est de l'ordre de 10 % actuellement (pour 81 % en Suède) et la plupart des grandes organisations syndicales (CGT, CFDT, FO pour les plus importantes) ont perdu entre le quart et plus de la moitié de leurs effectifs en vingt ans. Les relations de travail sont aujourd'hui vécues sur un mode moins revendicatif que par le passé.

L'apprentissage du temps libre

Le temps libre est incontestablement une conquête de ce siècle. Outre la baisse continue de la durée quotidienne du travail salarié, les travailleurs bénéficient en général de deux jours de repos

hebdomadaire (le repos dominical n'ayant été imposé qu'en 1906) et de cinq semaines de congés payés (deux semaines accordées en 1936, trois en 1956, quatre en 1963 et cinq en 1981). Les sociologues ont ainsi calculé que sur une année de vie, un salarié passe en moyenne 20 % de son temps à travailler et dans les transports, 33 % à dormir et emploie le reste, soit 47%, à d'autres occupations, certaines passives comme la télé-

Il y a en France 12,5 millions de jardins potagers ou d'agrément ; ici, les Hortillonnages à Amiens (Somme)

vision, d'autres actives comme le bricolage, le jardinage ou la pratique d'un sport, mais toutes considérées par les usagers comme des activités de détente.

Télévision : la première des distractions

La télévision apparaît comme le premier des loisirs. Les Français lui consacrent en moyenne près de 1 000 heures par an, soit 17 % de leur vie éveillée, ce qui représente 2 h 45 par jour, durée qui a augmenté de 30 % depuis 1982. Instrument d'ouverture pour certains (la télévision est souvent devenue une compagne irremplaçable des personnes qui vivent seules, en particulier des personnes âgées), fléau culturel pour d'autres, le petit écran s'est imposé dans la vie quotidienne des Français, d'autant que la multiplication des chaînes et la transmission par câble ou satellite autorisent aujourd'hui un choix étendu de programmes. Cette tendance illustre un réel attrait pour les loisirs domestiques qui permettent de se détendre à domicile. C'est ainsi que se multiplient les consoles vidéo et leur panoplie de plus en plus sophistiquée de jeux et de loisirs culturels comme les cédéroms et bien sûr la connexion au réseau Internet, appelée à se populariser davantage dans l'avenir, avec entre autres la possibilité d'utiliser le Minitel comme moyen de connexion au réseau. L'accès à ces nouvelles technologies s'est accompagné d'une certaine désaffection à l'égard des spectacles traditionnels : le cirque n'est plus guère qu'un vestige et le théâtre ne survit souvent que grâce à des subventions. Le nombre de spectateurs de cinéma a été presque divisé par trois en quarante ans : 412 millions en 1957, 148 millions en 1997. Le cinéma français garde cependant certains atouts, grâce à une politique active de soutien, et a mieux résisté que celui des autres pays européens à la concurrence américaine. La France produit environ 130 films par an et les films français représentent 36 % de part de marché dans l'hexagone (contre 54 % pour les films américains).

La détente, entre jardinage et bricolage

Si certains loisirs traditionnels sont en recul, comme la chasse qui comptait 2,3 millions de pratiquants en 1976 contre 1,5 million en 1996, d'autres résistent bien à l'usure du temps. Deux activités gardent ainsi toute la faveur des Français : le bricolage, qui représente un marché annuel d'environ 90 milliards de francs et le jardinage, passe-temps favori d'un ménage sur deux (il y a 12,5 millions de jardins potagers ou d'agrément en France), qui lui consacrent un budget annuel de 35 milliards de francs. La lecture reste aussi une occupation répandue : un quart seulement des Français déclare n'avoir lu aucun livre dans l'année (contre 35 % en 1986) et 35 % déclarent en avoir lu plus de cinq. Les enquêtes montrent cependant que la lecture est en recul chez les catégories les plus jeunes, sous l'effet conjugué de la télévision et des jeux vidéos.

Une nation sportive

Comme pour compenser le poids croissant de ces loisirs sédentaires, les activités sportives sont en plein essor. Les deux tiers des hommes et la moitié des femmes déclarent pratiquer un sport et le nombre de licenciés dans les fédérations sportives a triplé depuis 1970, représentant désormais près d'un Français sur quatre. Ce dynamisme sportif se reflète dans les performances sportives internationales. En effet, en se classant au cinquième rang mondial aux Jeux Olympiques d'Atlanta de 1996 avec 37 médailles, derrière les États-Unis, la Russie, l'Allemagne et la Chine, les Français ont démontré leur progression constante dans la compétition sportive de haut niveau.

Les sports les plus populaires comme le football, le rugby, le cyclisme ou le tennis sont l'objet de grandes compétitions nationales et internationales, qui attirent de nombreux spectateurs et recueillent une audience record à la télévision ou à la radio. Le Tour de France cycliste fait ainsi figure de véritable fête nationale, sa popularité dépasse désormais les contours de l'Hexagone et revêt une dimension européenne.

La France est aussi organisatrice de rencontres internationales prestigieuses, comme les Jeux Olympiques d'hiver de Grenoble en 1968, d'Albertville en 1992 et la Coupe du monde de football, en 1998, au cours de laquelle elle devient championne du monde de football.

Sur un score de 3-0 face au Brésil, la France remporte pour la première fois de son histoire la finale de la Coupe du monde. La victoire des « Bleus » (surnom donné à l'équipe nationale) est célébrée partout en France dans une immense liesse populaire.

Les Français ont, outre ces sports populaires, la possibilité de pratiquer toutes les disciplines sportives ; ils bénéficient, en raison des atouts géographiques et physiques de la France, de larges capacités pour la pratique d'activités nautiques, des sports de neige et de glace. Dans certaines spécialités, les sportifs français se rangent parmi les meilleurs du monde: voile, judo, escrime, course automobile.

Le match de finale du Mondial 98, France-Brésil, 12 juillet 1998 ; la France remporte pour la première fois la Coupe du monde de football

Les vacances au plus près de la nature

En hiver et en été, la pratique des sports est souvent liée aux vacances : en se livrant aux joies du ski, du nautisme, du golf, du vélo ou de la marche, le vacancier allie détente et activité physique. 62 % des Français partent en vacances, contre un peu plus de 40 % au début des années soixante. Les vacances d'été voient le départ d'environ 36 millions de personnes, contre 20 millions environ pour les vacances d'hiver. Les vacances se diversifient ; les longs séjours consacrés uniquement au repos sont remplacés par des formules plus courtes, impliquant les participants dans des activités sportives, artisanales ou culturelles. Partout en France se sont multipliés les festivals, les activités de découverte en milieu rural, ainsi que les visites d'entreprises et de sites industriels qui suscitent un intérêt croissant. Les séjours à l'étranger attirent 11 millions de touristes français ; l'Espagne, le Portugal, l'Italie, les Iles Britanniques, le Maroc, l'Allemagne, l'Autriche et la Tunisie sont les destinations les plus prisées.

Agriculteurs, artisans et petits commerçants sont encore sensiblement moins nombreux à partir en vacances que les salariés, qui ont profité le plus des départs en vacances au cours de ces deux dernières décennies. Le troisième âge, qui a profité de la revalorisation des retraites, de l'action des communes et des comités d'entreprises et des organismes spécialisés dans l'organisation de séjours, fournit aussi des contingents de plus en plus nombreux de touristes. Enfin, l'instauration du chèque-vacances, financé en partie par l'employeur, contribue également au développement du tourisme.

Balade dans les Alpes
en Haute-Savoie,
lors de l'été 1997
qui fêtait les cinquante
ans des sentiers de
grande randonnée

Pour en savoir plus :

L'état de la France 98-99, La Découverte, 1998.

« Les chiffres de l'économie et de la société », *Alternatives économiques*, Hors série n° 34, 4e trimestre 1998.

« Qui sont les Français ? », *Sciences humaines*, n° 10, septembre-octobre 1995.

O. Marchand, C. Thélot, *Le travail en France*, Nathan, 1997.

L. Dirn, *La société française en tendance 1975-1995 : deux décennies de changement*, PUF, 1997.

G. Mermet, *Francoscopie 1998*, Larousse, 1998.

France, portrait social 1997, INSEE, 1998.

12

La protection sociale

La France dispose d'un système de protection sociale qui figure parmi les plus performants du monde. Longtemps réservé à une partie des salariés, il a été progressivement étendu, depuis la seconde guerre mondiale, à l'ensemble de la population ; il répond à des besoins sociaux fondamentaux comme la santé, les retraites, la politique familiale, l'indemnisation du chômage et un revenu minimum pour les personnes qui ne bénéficient d'aucun autre droit.

Les dépenses annuelles de protection sociale approchent les 2 800 milliards de francs (466 milliards de dollars), soit plus de 35 % du PIB, ce qui est l'un des niveaux les plus élevés de l'Union européenne, avec le Danemark, la Finlande, l'Autriche et les Pays-Bas.

Les dépenses de sécurité sociale bénéficient de ressources et font l'objet d'une gestion distincte du budget de l'État, tandis que les dépenses d'action sociale destinées aux plus démunis sont inscrites au budget de l'État et des collectivités locales.

Assurée sans grande difficulté durant les trois décennies de forte croissance qui ont suivi la seconde guerre mondiale, la sécurité sociale est l'objet d'une grande attention des pouvoirs publics qui adaptent en permanence les moyens disponibles aux besoins de la population et assurent la pérennité du système grâce à des réformes régulières depuis la création de l'institution en 1945.

Répartition des dépenses de protection sociale en 1997	
Maladie, invalidité, accidents du travail	34 %
Vieillesse, survie	43,7 %
Famille, maternité	9,5 %
Chômage, promotion de l'emploi	8,1 %
Logement	4,7 %

Les années de crise économique – qui ont limité les ressources et fragilisé certaines catégories de la population –, l'évolution de la demande et le remarquable essor de l'offre de santé ont pesé lourdement sur l'équilibre des comptes. Aujourd'hui, la sécurité sociale retrouve une situation économique plus acceptable avec un déficit de 13,3 milliards de francs (2,2 milliards de dollars) en 1998 et un équilibre prévu pour 1999.

La santé

L'offre de santé compte deux secteurs : les hôpitaux (environ 51 % des dépenses de santé de la sécurité sociale) et la médecine libérale dite de « ville ».

Le secteur de la santé emploie près de 2 millions de personnes dont environ 600 000 dans les hôpitaux. Il a été l'un des plus gros créateurs d'activité au cours des dernières décennies. Son dynamisme conduit à une amélioration constante des équipements de recherche, de diagnostic et de soins, notamment dans les secteurs des médicaments et de l'imagerie médicale (échographie, scanner, imagerie à résonance magnétique nucléaire). Parallèlement aux progrès techniques, l'organisation du système public de soins a été rénovée. Les équipements de santé sont programmés et régionalisés, dans le cadre d'une carte sanitaire qui permet de les répartir plus harmonieusement en fonction des besoins de la population. Ces progrès se sont effectués dans le respect du système de santé traditionnel qui laisse une large place à la médecine libérale et au libre choix du malade.

La politique de la santé vise à assurer un égal accès aux soins à tous les habitants du pays. Si des disparités persistent, qu'elles résultent du niveau de vie, de l'éducation ou du lieu de résidence, elles sont moins importantes que pour bien d'autres postes de la consommation.

Les pouvoirs publics s'efforcent aussi de développer la médecine préventive par la mise en place d'un suivi pré et post-natal systématique, par la multiplication des consultations sur les lieux de travail et par l'organisation de grandes campagnes d'information concernant les principales pathologies. C'est notamment le cas pour la lutte contre le tabagisme et l'alcoolisme, ainsi que la détection précoce des cancers et la prévention du sida.

Ces efforts de la collectivité se soldent par des résultats remarquables : la mortalité infantile de la France est l'une des plus faibles du monde et la longévité l'une des plus élevées, l'espérance

Les dépenses de santé ont doublé depuis 1980, mais la France est l'un des pays du monde où l'espérance de vie est la plus élevée

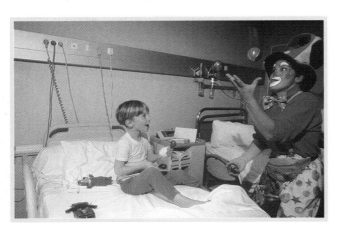

de vie moyenne des individus augmentant d'environ 100 jours chaque année.

La quasi-totalité de la population est aujourd'hui couverte en ce qui concerne les dépenses liées au risque de maladie. Cette couverture du risque est totale pour les maladies graves, longues et coûteuses et les interventions chirurgicales. Elle est partielle pour les petits risques et les dépenses dites de confort. Pour ces dépenses, les usagers de la sécurité sociale ont la possibilité de contracter une assurance complémentaire privée ou d'adhérer à une mutuelle.

Toutefois, afin de rendre véritablement effectif l'accès aux soins pour tous, une réforme d'ampleur de la protection sociale a été décidée pour 1998, à travers la création d'une couverture maladie universelle et la garantie d'une protection complémentaire, ainsi que l'instauration d'une dispense d'avance de frais pour les plus démunis.

Aujourd'hui, les dépenses consacrées à la santé représentent au total près de 800 milliards de francs (133 milliards de dollars) : ce chiffre comprend les dépenses de l'État, des particuliers, de la sécurité sociale, des mutuelles et autres assurances complémentaires facultatives. Chaque Français dépense en moyenne et par an 12 400 francs (2 066 dollars) pour se soigner. Près de 10 % du PIB sont ainsi consacrés à la santé et alimentent un secteur économique important.

Pour tenir compte de l'évolution de besoins toujours plus grands en matière de santé, l'État a mis en œuvre une politique de responsabilisation des acteurs du système de santé. Le Parlement se prononce chaque année sur le niveau des dépenses. Ses décisions permettent aux pouvoirs publics de conclure des conventions avec les caisses de sécurité sociale et en particulier avec la Caisse nationale d'assurance maladie. La Caisse, à son tour, signe des conventions avec les médecins et les professionnels de santé.

Les patients sont eux-mêmes sensibilisés à la modération des dépenses par des campagnes de communication. Ils seront prochainement dotés d'une carte à puce, la carte «Sésame Vitale», outil de technologie très avancée qui permettra aux praticiens de connaître le dossier médical du patient et les traitements suivis.

Service de puériculture
dans une clinique de Nice

Depuis 1998, le financement de la santé est assuré non plus par un prélèvement sur la seule masse salariale dans les entreprises mais par un impôt sur l'ensemble des revenus du capital grâce à la contribution sociale généralisée (CSG).

Les personnes âgées et handicapées

Classées dans la rubrique «vieillesse-survie» des comptes sociaux, les prestations destinées à assurer des ressources aux personnes âgées et dépendantes constituent le premier poste de la protection sociale et représentent près de 13 % du PIB, soit environ 1 000 milliards de francs (166,6 milliards de dollars). Cette somme recouvre à la fois les retraites de base versées par la sécurité sociale pour 380 milliards de francs (63,3 milliards de dollars), les retraites complémentaires obligatoires qui s'élèvent à environ 250 milliards de francs (41,6 milliards de dollars). Environ 10 millions de retraités bénéficient de ces prestations.

Une résidence pour
personnes âgées
à Saint-Herblain
(Loire-Atlantique)

Les retraites sont financées par des cotisations des employeurs et des salariés prélevées sur les salaires.

Le système des retraites en France est un système contributif par répartition alliant la solidarité, qui est institutionnalisée avec par exemple le fonds de solidarité vieillesse, et la valorisation de l'épargne-retraite.

L'arrivée progressive à l'âge de la retraite des générations nombreuses, nées après 1946, va en effet peser sur le système financier des retraites. Des mesures ont été prises pour garantir un certain équilibre. La réforme de 1993 portait ainsi progressivement à 40 ans la durée de cotisation ouvrant droit à une retraite au taux plein (à raison d'un trimestre supplémentaire chaque année à partir de 1994, la réforme étant totalement effective à partir de 2003) et établissait la base de calcul des prestations sur les 25 meilleures années de salaire, au lieu des 10 meilleures auparavant.

Bien que reposant sur le principe de la contribution, la protection vieillesse s'étend également aux personnes qui n'ont pas de droit à pension ou qui en ont peu, faute d'avoir cotisé ou exercé une activité professionnelle pendant une durée suffisante : c'est le cas de nombreuses femmes âgées. Un minimum vieillesse, créé en 1956, vient en aide aux personnes âgées de plus de 65 ans dont les ressources sont trop faibles. Il a été fortement revalorisé au cours de ces dernières années et s'élève à environ 3 470 francs (578 dollars) pour une personne seule et 6 226 francs (1 037 dollars) pour un couple.

La loi du 30 juin 1975 a créé une obligation nationale d'éducation et d'insertion professionnelle et sociale des personnes atteintes d'un handicap, et institué des allocations (allocation adulte handicapé) et des structures destinées à les aider à s'insérer dans le monde du travail, ordinaire ou protégé. On compte en France 2,5 millions de personnes handicapées, dont plus d'un million et demi sont en âge de travailler. Parmi elles, seules 170 000 exercent une profession en milieu ordinaire et 80 000 en établissements de travail protégé.

Formulaire de Sécurité sociale rempli par un médecin : il y indique le prix de la consultation que le patient pourra se faire rembourser par sa Caisse de sécurité sociale et, éventuellement, par sa mutuelle

La politique de la famille

La France consacre une part importante de son PIB (près de 4 %) à la politique familiale, soit plus que les autres pays européens. C'est au début du siècle que furent versées les premières allocations aux familles nombreuses nécessiteuses et à certains fonctionnaires. Il a fallu cependant attendre 1932 pour que les allocations familiales soient étendues aux salariés et 1939 pour que les actifs non salariés en bénéficient aussi. Dans le même temps, les entreprises ont été obligées de s'affilier à une caisse de compensation en matière d'allocations familiales. Le Code de la famille a, par ailleurs, institué en 1939 une prime à la première naissance, une allocation pour la mère au foyer et accordé certains avantages fiscaux aux familles nombreuses. Ces mesures visaient avant tout à encourager une reprise de la natalité dans une France malthusienne.

Depuis les années soixante-dix, la politique familiale revêt un rôle distributif plus que nataliste, privilégiant les familles à revenu modeste et les parents isolés. La politique de la famille est ainsi devenue une politique sociale plus que démographique. Le financement de ces prestations familiales est largement pris en charge par les entreprises dont la contribution est calculée depuis 1990 sur la totalité des salaires versés. C'est la Caisse nationale d'allocations familiales qui redistribue ces cotisations, ainsi que la participation de l'État. Elle procède au versement des différentes allocations familiales et des prestations spécifiques comme les aides au logement et le revenu minimum d'insertion (RMI).

L'aide aux familles revêt essentiellement la forme d'allocations versées aux parents ; les plus importantes, les allocations familiales, représentent 28 % des prestations et concernent plus de 4 millions de familles. De nombreuses aides s'y ajoutent : allocation pour jeune enfant, allocation parentale d'éducation, complément familial, allocation de soutien familial, allocation de parents isolés, aide à l'emploi d'une assistance maternelle, allocation de rentrée scolaire, allocation logement dont le montant est lié au nombre d'enfants. Au total, plus de 270 milliards de francs (45 milliards de dollars) sont ainsi versés à plus de 10 millions de familles. Si on ajoute les avantages indirects – réduction d'impôts, tarifs réduits, allégements sur les intérêts des prêts immobiliers, prise en charge partielle ou totale par la collectivité de certains besoins (crèches, loisirs, vacances) – c'est un total de plus de 300 milliards de francs (50 milliards de dollars) qui est consacré aux familles.

Répartition de l'ensemble des prestations versées par la branche famille en 1995

Les prestations famille en 1995 : au total, plus de 270 milliards de francs versés à plus de 10 millions de familles, soit un ménage sur deux

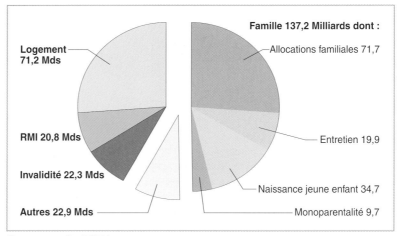

Source : enquête INSEE.

La lutte contre la nouvelle pauvreté

Dans un contexte de chômage élevé, la difficulté de nombreux jeunes à s'insérer dans le marché du travail, la séparation des couples ou leur surendettement ont contribué à l'essor d'une nouvelle pauvreté. L'État et les départements, qui ont hérité de compétences sociales avec la décentralisation, dépensent de plus en plus d'argent pour lutter contre cette montée de la précarité : quelque 170 milliards de francs (28 milliards de dollars) sont versés aux ménages les plus démunis, ce qui représente environ 6 millions de personnes. Le revenu minimum d'insertion (RMI) est le principal instrument de ces aides. Créé en décembre 1988, il est actuellement versé à 1,5 million de ménages, ce qui représente environ 2 millions de personnes si l'on tient compte des conjoints et des enfants. En 1998, le montant du RMI est fixé à 2 627 francs (437 dollars) pour une personne seule et à un peu plus de 5 300 francs (883 dollars) pour un couple avec deux enfants. Cette allocation, dont peut bénéficier toute personne de plus de 25 ans ayant, par mois, moins de 2 000 francs (333 dollars) de ressources, est destinée à favoriser l'insertion ou la réinsertion professionnelle, ce qui lui confère un caractère social novateur. Elle est financée pour l'essentiel par l'État et distribuée par les caisses d'allocations familiales. Par ailleurs, des prestations spécifiques sont distribuées à près de 500 000 chômeurs en fin de droit ; ceux-ci perçoivent une allocation de solidarité financée par l'État et dont le montant minimal équivaut au RMI. La solidarité nationale doit aussi prendre en compte les 2,8 millions de salariés qui travaillent à temps partiel, en intérim ou sous contrat à durée déterminée et gagnent moins que le SMIC (salaire minimum) ; diverses prestations compensatoires peuvent leur être attribuées.

La lutte contre la pauvreté et l'exclusion est devenue un enjeu national et mobilise de nombreux acteurs aux côtés des institutions spécialisées et de l'État, qui a engagé un grand programme visant à garantir à chacun l'accès aux droits fondamentaux (emploi, logement, santé, éducation, culture...) et à prévenir les nouvelles situations d'exclusion. Les collectivités territoriales s'impliquent de plus en plus dans cette bataille mais il faut souligner le rôle particulièrement efficace d'associations comme ATD-Quart monde ou les Restos du cœur, dont l'action sur le terrain est souvent décisive pour faire reculer la pauvreté.

Des volontaires du Samu social de Paris viennent en aide aux personnes sans abri

La lutte contre le chômage

Comme bon nombre de pays industrialisés, la France doit faire face depuis vingt ans à une progression continue du chômage, qui touche 2,9 millions de personnes en 1998, soit 11,8 % de la population. Depuis 1997, la tendance est cependant orientée à la baisse. Jusqu'en 1974, le taux de chômage était inférieur à 3 % et le million de chômeurs n'a été dépassé qu'en 1977. Le chômage affecte plus particulièrement les femmes - dont le taux de chômage est de 14,2 % contre 10,8 % pour les hommes - et les jeunes - le taux de chômage est de 27 % pour les moins de 25 ans. Les personnes non qualifiées et sans diplômes sont les plus touchées, avec un taux de chômage de 17 %, alors qu'il n'est que de 7 % pour les diplômés de l'enseignement supérieur.

La lutte pour l'emploi, entreprise dès le début de la décennie 1970, a pris pour axe, successivement puis simultanément, le traitement économique et le traitement social du chômage. Le premier vise à encourager les entreprises à maintenir leurs effectifs, ou mieux, à embaucher. Dans ce but, l'État s'efforce de créer un environnement favorable. Il prend à sa charge tout ou partie des cotisations sociales pesant sur les entreprises qui s'engagent à créer des emplois, diminue la taxe professionnelle et l'impôt sur les bénéfices réinvestis. Plus récemment, il a décidé de budgétiser progressivement les allocations familiales qui étaient jusqu'alors à la charge des entreprises. Ces aides multiples prennent en retour pour les entreprises la forme de contrats d'embauche, à durée déterminée généralement. Au total, 1,5 million de personnes ont été embauchées selon ces diverses formules, dont les plus usitées sont le contrat initiative-emploi, qui concerne plus de 400 000 personnes, ainsi que le contrat emploi-solidarité et le contrat d'apprentissage, qui en touchent chacun plus de 300 000. Depuis 1997, le gouvernement s'est attaqué au problème des jeunes en créant de nouvelles activités de services utiles à la collectivité ; 350 000 jeunes bénéficieront de ce programme d'ici l'an 2000.

Le traitement social, lui, consiste à jouer sur les conditions et la durée du travail : abaissement de l'âge de la retraite, généralisation du système de préretraite à partir de 55 ans dans les branches en crise. Cette politique s'accompagne de mesures pour favoriser le travail à mi-temps ou à temps partiel et pour aider à la formation et à la requalification des chômeurs, notamment par le biais de stages rémunérés. Enfin, parce que la croissance ne suffit pas à résoudre le chômage, le gouvernement a lancé une réduction négociée de la durée du temps de travail.

Ces mesures ont certes permis de freiner la progression du chômage et de limiter l'exclusion, mais plus de 3 millions d'actifs restent sans travail et la solidarité nationale s'exerce à leur égard. Les indemnités de chômage sont versées aux personnes ayant perdu leur emploi par l'Unedic (Union pour l'emploi dans l'industrie et le commerce), qui gère l'assurance chômage et dont le budget (116 milliards de francs en 1997, soit 20 milliards de dollars), provient pour 36 % des cotisations salariales et pour 64 % des cotisations patronales. Ces indemnités représentent en moyenne 4 700 francs (783 dollars) par chômeur et par mois en 1998, soit près de 100 milliards de francs ;

Les jeunes, particulièrement les non diplômés, et les femmes sont les plus touchés par le chômage : un jeune de moins de 25 ans sur quatre (hors étudiants) est sans emploi

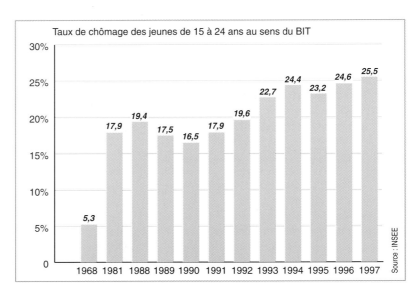

Taux de chômage des jeunes de 15 à 24 ans au sens du BIT

Source : INSEE

elles sont dégressives et la durée maximale d'indemnisation est de 60 mois, dans le meilleur des cas. Les 500 000 chômeurs en fin de droit perçoivent l'Allocation de solidarité spécifique, financée par l'État mais distribuée aussi par l'Unedic. Les autres chômeurs n'ont pas droit à une indemnisation directe, car ils n'ont jamais travaillé ni cotisé et sont donc pris en charge par d'autres instruments de la protection sociale, en particulier le RMI.

Au total, si l'on ajoute à l'indemnisation des chômeurs, qui s'élève à 150 milliards de francs (25 milliards de dollars) par an environ, le coût des politiques pour l'emploi, on arrive à une dépense totale de l'ordre de 320 milliards de francs (53,3 milliards de dollars) consacrée chaque année par la collectivité à la lutte contre le chômage. Les efforts consentis peuvent apparaître cependant comme peu efficaces et certains pays, comme les États-Unis et le Royaume-Uni, semblent avoir obtenu de meilleurs résultats à moindre coût. On se trouve là face à un choix politique, car les pays développés où le chômage a reculé ont réussi cette performance grâce à un recul de la protection sociale et à une multiplication de l'emploi précaire faiblement rémunéré. De telles recettes n'ont pas été retenues par les pouvoirs publics en France.

Il reste néanmoins que, dans le domaine de l'indemnisation du chômage comme dans celui de la politique de la santé, de la famille ou de l'aide aux personnes âgées, le système de protection sociale doit être repensé pour limiter la hausse vertigineuse des coûts enregistrée ces dernières années et pour être plus efficace. Les réformes en cours concernant les retraites et l'assurance maladie vont dans ce sens, de même que la budgétisation de plus en plus poussée du système par le biais de l'augmentation de la CSG ; celle-ci se substitue progressivement à des cotisations diverses, lesquelles s'étaient ajoutées les unes aux autres au fil du temps. Ces évolutions ne constituent pas un recul de la protection sociale, comme on le dit parfois, mais une adaptation du système à de nouvelles exigences : elles n'ont pas empêché une extension de la protection sociale à des domaines de plus en plus variés et à des catégories de plus en plus larges de la population.

Répartition des dépenses pour l'emploi en 1996

Dépenses passives	**48 %**
dont	
Indemnisation du chômage	38,4 %
Incitation au retrait d'activité	9,6 %
Dépenses actives	**52 %**
dont	
Formation professionnelle	28,1 %
Promotion de l'emploi	15,1 %
Autres	8,8 %

Source : INSEE. *Tableaux de l'économie française*, 1998-1999.

Pour en savoir plus :

Bilan économique et social de la France, Ministère de l'Emploi et de la Solidarité, Ministère de l'Économie, des Finances et de l'Industrie, La Documentation française, 1997.

L'année sociale, Éditions de l'Atelier-Alternatives économiques, collection Points d'appui, 1998.

La protection sociale en France, sous la dir. de M. de Montalembert, La Documentation française, collection Les Notices, 1997.

J.-P. Cendron, *Le monde de la protection sociale*, Nathan, 1997.

J.-B. de Foucauld, J.-F. Chadelat et C. Zaïdman, Commissariat général du Plan, *Le financement de la protection sociale*, La Documentation française, collection des Rapports officiels, 1995.

T. Lecomte, A. Mizrahi, *Précarité sociale, cumul des risques sociaux et médicaux*, CREDES, 1996.

Ministère du Travail et des Affaires sociales, *40 ans de politique de l'emploi*, La Documentation française, 1996.

Les dépenses courantes de santé en 1996

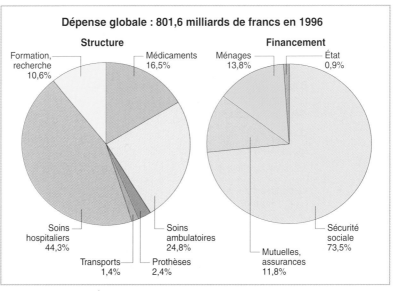

Dépense globale : 801,6 milliards de francs en 1996

Structure

Formation, recherche 10,6%

Médicaments 16,5%

Soins hospitaliers 44,3%

Soins ambulatoires 24,8%

Transports 1,4%

Prothèses 2,4%

Financement

Ménages 13,8%

État 0,9%

Sécurité sociale 73,5%

Mutuelles, assurances 11,8%

Source : Secrétariat d'État à la Santé.

13

L'éducation et la formation

En deux siècles, depuis les décrets de 1792 et 1793 qui assignaient à l'État un rôle primordial en matière d'éducation, la France s'est dotée de l'un des systèmes d'enseignement et de formation les plus avancés au monde. Ses missions sont cependant de plus en plus complexes, compte tenu de la rapidité des changements sociaux, économiques et technologiques et des attentes croissantes des familles et de la société.

En 1997-1998, les élèves et étudiants sont plus de 15 millions, soit le quart de la population, et le budget de l'Éducation nationale, de l'enseignement supérieur et de la recherche est le premier de la nation. Il s'élève à 334,4 milliards de francs (55,7 milliards de dollars) en 1998, en hausse de plus de 3 % par rapport à celui de 1997, et représente 21 % des dépenses de l'État. Le système éducatif est aussi le plus important employeur du pays, avec un personnel d'encadrement de 1,2 million de personnes, soit plus de la moitié des agents de la fonction publique d'État. Si l'on ajoute aux dépenses de l'État celles des collectivités territoriales, des ménages et des entreprises, on constate que le poste « éducation-formation » représente 7,4 % du PIB national, soit 580 milliards de francs (96,6 milliards de dollars) en 1998.

	1975	1997
Dépense totale (milliards de francs)	330	592
Dépense moyenne par élève (en francs)	21 400	35 700
Part dans le PIB	6,5 %	7,3 %

Évolution des dépenses intérieures d'éducation (au prix 1997). En vingt ans, la dépense moyenne par élève a augmenté de 65 % : l'éducation s'est affirmée comme un choix prioritaire pour l'État

Les débats relatifs à l'enseignement

Afin de s'adapter aux profondes mutations socio-économiques et culturelles de ces trente dernières années, le système éducatif français est en constante évolution, comme dans la plupart des pays industriels. Les changements ont affecté tous les niveaux de l'édifice, de l'échelon scolaire à l'échelon universitaire. Ces transformations se sont accompagnées de nombreux débats sur les missions fondamentales de l'éducation, en particulier sur l'équilibre nécessaire entre un enseignement visant à préparer les jeunes à la vie active et un enseignement dont la finalité serait de donner à tous des éléments de culture générale permettant à chacun la liberté de ses choix et le plein exercice de la citoyenneté. Se sont ainsi affrontées diverses conceptions sur la laïcité, la formation des maîtres, le rapport enseignant-enseigné, le développement de pédagogies nouvelles, etc.

Les choix opérés ont permis à l'institution de continuer à fonctionner mais quelques principes fondamentaux ressortent, en particulier la volonté d'élargir au plus grand nombre l'accès au lycée, puis au baccalauréat et aux formations universitaires, le tout en cherchant à préserver au mieux l'éventail disciplinaire et les contenus, équation bien difficile à résoudre. S'est affirmée aussi la tendance à accorder une autonomie plus large aux établissements, une véritable politique de décentralisation étant néanmoins limitée par des principes républicains encore en vigueur mais qui font l'objet d'attaques en règle, comme par exemple le caractère national des diplômes et du recrutement des professeurs dans le cycle secondaire de l'enseignement.

Permanence et mutations du système

Le système éducatif relève principalement de l'État et donc du ministère de l'Éducation nationale. Parfois un ministère ou un secrétariat d'État responsable d'un secteur spécifique (enseignement

scolaire, enseignement supérieur, formation professionnelle) lui est adjoint. D'autres ministères peuvent également être compétents, tel celui de l'Agriculture pour les lycées d'enseignement agricole.

L'école a toujours eu une dimension symbolique en France. C'est à elle que l'on confie au départ la mission de constituer et de maintenir l'unité nationale, en délivrant à tous le même enseignement sans

Les examens publics sont ouverts à tous les élèves. Ici, l'épreuve du baccalauréat à la maison des examens d'Arcueil (Val-de-Marne)

considération des origines sociales et géographiques, ce qui permet notamment l'intégration des enfants nés de parents étrangers. Quatre grands principes régissent le service public de l'éducation : l'égalité d'accès, la non-discrimination, la neutralité et la laïcité. L'ouverture d'une école, d'un établissement d'enseignement secondaire ou supérieur est libre, sous réserve du respect de ces principes et à condition de satisfaire à certaines règles en matière d'hygiène, de sécurité et de respect de l'ordre public. Le système éducatif public est gratuit, à l'exception des droits d'inscription à l'université, très modérés cependant en comparaison de ce qui se pratique dans la plupart des grands pays développés. La définition et la création des grades et diplômes sont réservées à l'État ; les examens publics sont ouverts à tous les élèves.

Durant de longues années, le système éducatif a été très centralisé, hiérarchisé et uniforme dans son organisation et ses fonctions. Cette situation a changé à partir des années soixante. Deux tendances sont apparues : d'une part, les programmes et les méthodes d'enseignement ont été actualisés et les décisions relatives à l'organisation interne des établissements sont discutées au sein de conseils d'établissement, favorisant ainsi la participation des élèves, des familles et des élus locaux ; d'autre part, l'État a dû prendre les dispositions nécessaires pour faire face à une augmentation importante des effectifs à tous les niveaux, liée à des raisons démographiques et, plus fondamentalement, à l'allongement de la durée des études et à la politique délibérée des pouvoirs publics d'assurer aux jeunes un accès de plus en plus étendu au lycée et à l'université, afin de disposer des compétences nécessaires au développement du pays.

L'école maternelle : une réussite méconnue

Ni garderies ni jardins d'enfants, les écoles maternelles, créées en 1887, sont des établissements d'éducation qui reçoivent les enfants de 2 à 6 ans. L'enseignement y est assuré en majorité par des institutrices.

La scolarisation en maternelle n'est pas obligatoire, mais elle fait l'objet d'une forte demande. À cet égard, le cas de la France est exceptionnel : plus de 99 % des enfants de trois ans fré-

Les apprentissages précoces sont un gage de réussite scolaire et les enfants entrent de plus en plus tôt en maternelle. Initiation au livre et à l'image dans une école maternelle à Tremblay-en-France (Seine-Saint-Denis)

quentent l'école maternelle, en majorité dans l'enseignement public. Des observations rigoureuses ont permis de démontrer la bonne influence de la préscolarisation sur la suite de la scolarité. Elle permet aux 2,1 millions d'enfants scolarisés de faire l'apprentissage de la vie en société, de former leur personnalité et de développer la pratique du langage. Elle permet aussi le dépistage des difficultés sensorielles, motrices ou intellectuelles et favorise leur traitement précoce. Pour les enfants de milieux défavorisés, elle est un instrument efficace d'insertion. Enfin, les plus grands peuvent y commencer l'apprentissage de la lecture.

La construction et l'entretien des écoles maternelles relèvent de la compétence des communes, qui fournissent également le personnel auxiliaire. Les enseignants dépendent, quant à eux, du ministère de l'Éducation nationale.

Les nouveaux défis de l'école primaire

À de rares exceptions près, l'enfant entre à l'école primaire à six ans. L'école publique est communale : depuis 1833, la commune - ou le groupement de communes - en assure la construction, l'équipement et l'entretien. Depuis les lois votées sous l'impulsion de Jules Ferry (1881-1882), l'instruction primaire est obligatoire et l'enseignement à l'école publique est laïc et gratuit.

L'État, pour sa part, gère les carrières des personnels qu'il recrute, majoritairement sur concours. Les professeurs des écoles, comme les professeurs de l'enseignement secondaire, sont formés dans les Instituts universitaires de formation des maîtres (IUFM) et les instituteurs, formés auparavant dans le cadre des Écoles normales d'instituteurs, sont progressivement intégrés au nouveau corps de professeur des écoles. Les coûts de fonctionnement et les salaires des maîtres des écoles privées sous contrat sont assurés respectivement par les communes et par l'État.

La durée normale de la scolarité est de cinq ans : les trois premières années, celles du cours préparatoire et du cours élémentaire, sont regroupées avec la dernière année de maternelle en un cycle des apprentissages fondamentaux. Le cycle d'approfondissement (cours moyen 1 et 2) couvre le reste de la scolarité et comprend l'initiation obligatoire à une langue étrangère depuis la rentrée 1998-1999.

Les jeux de la récréation dans une école primaire de Vironchaux (Somme)

L'école primaire scolarise actuellement 6,4 millions d'enfants (dont 800 000 dans l'enseignement privé), encadrés par 300 000 enseignants. Les effectifs ont diminué de près de 900 000 élèves en trente ans, avec une baisse qui s'est accélérée depuis le début des années 1990, en raison de la diminution des naissances enregistrée à partir de 1981-1982. Cette évolution a entraîné la diminution du nombre d'élèves par classe, mais elle a également pour conséquence des fermetures de classes, parfois d'écoles dans les régions les moins peuplées, ce qui risque de contribuer au dépeuplement des zones rurales, en dépit de la mise en place d'un système de transport scolaire collectif.

Dans certaines communes urbaines et périurbaines, l'école primaire est confrontée au problème de l'hétérogénéité culturelle et linguistique, du fait de l'immigration. Les enfants d'origine étrangère, qui représentent environ 10 % de l'effectif total, sont inégalement répartis géographiquement et scolarisés à 97 % dans les écoles publiques.

	1985		1997	
	(en francs)	*(en %)*	(en francs)	*(en %)*
Préélémentaire	51 600	*33,5*	76 400	*39,1*
Élémentaire	102 300	*66,5*	119 200	*60,9*
Total	153 900	*100*	195 600	*100*

Évolution du coût de la formation préélémentaire et élémentaire d'un élève (au prix de 1997) : un investissement de près de 200 000 francs est nécessaire pour qu'un élève accède en classe de 6e au collège

Collège : le maillon essentiel

Les collèges – près de 7 000 établissements – accueillent plus de trois millions d'élèves. Les études au collège durent quatre ans : classe de sixième (cycle d'adaptation), classes de cinquième et quatrième (cycle central) et classe de troisième (cycle d'orientation). Depuis 1975, tous les élèves, quel que soit leur niveau, entrent au collège. De ce fait, les effectifs ont augmenté de près d'un million par rapport à ce qu'ils étaient il y a trente ans. L'immense majorité des élèves accomplit dans sa totalité cette première étape de l'enseignement secondaire. Ceux qui atteignent l'âge de seize ans avant ce terme peuvent arrêter leurs études ; mais, au total, 94 % d'une classe d'âge atteint le niveau du Certificat d'aptitude professionnelle (CAP), du Brevet d'enseignement professionnel (BEP) ou entre en classe de seconde, c'est-à-dire au lycée.

Environ 80 % des élèves fréquentent des collèges publics. Dans le cadre de la décentralisation, leur construction, leur équipement, leur entretien et leur fonctionnement relèvent des départements. L'État, pour sa part, recrute, forme, rémunère et affecte les personnels, gère leurs carrières, assure la fourniture des manuels scolaires et des matériels (ordinateurs, audiovisuel, etc). Il accorde des crédits supplémentaires aux établissements implantés en zones dites d'éducation prioritaire (ZEP), impliquant un effort particulier en raison de l'environnement socioculturel difficile. En vingt ans, les effectifs scolarisés dans les collèges privés ont augmenté en moyenne de 2,5 %. S'agissant des collèges privés sous contrat d'association avec l'État (seuls 10 000 élèves sont scolarisés

Les collèges accueillent plus de trois millions d'élèves. Ici, le collège Victor Hugo à Noisy-le-Grand (Seine-Saint-Denis), situé devant les Arènes Picasso (architecte : M. Nunez)

dans des établissements privés hors contrat), l'État prend en charge la totalité des traitements du personnel enseignant. Les frais de fonctionnement des établissements se répartissent entre l'État et le département.

Alors que, dans l'enseignement primaire, le principe est celui d'un maître unique polyvalent par classe, les professeurs de collège enseignent généralement une seule matière. Durant les deux premières années, les élèves font l'apprentissage d'une langue vivante étrangère. À l'entrée en classe de quatrième, ils choisissent une deuxième langue. Actuellement, chaque établissement scolaire doit se doter de son propre projet pédagogique, inspiré des recommandations établies à l'échelon national, adapté aux réalités régionales, voire locales, et répondant, le cas échéant, à la spécificité des élèves.

La réforme Haby de 1977 qui a créé le «collège unique», puis la suppression en 1989 du palier d'orientation en fin de cinquième, ont bouleversé la constitution des classes dont le niveau est, de fait, hétérogène : en effet, jusqu'alors, les élèves en difficulté étaient accueillis dans des classes spéciales (classes pré-professionnelles de niveau, classes de préparation à l'apprentissage, etc.) ; certes, il existe toujours des formules de soutien, des classes passerelles et des sections d'éducation spécialisée, mais une réflexion est engagée par le ministère de l'Éducation nationale et ses partenaires afin de mieux faire face à l'impératif de remise à niveau des élèves en difficulté. En effet, 85 % des élèves entrés en 6e avec un an de retard atteignent la 3e, mais seulement 8 % d'entre eux finissent par obtenir le baccalauréat.

Le lycée : objectif 80 % de bacheliers

La majorité des élèves effectue sa scolarité dans des lycées relevant du ministère de l'Éducation nationale. Les 2 600 lycées publics accueillent en effet 78 % des élèves. On distingue deux types de lycées.

Pour les lycéens, l'objectif d'un taux de 80 % de réussite au baccalauréat est en vue. Le lycée Martin Luther King à Bussy-Saint-Georges (Seine-et-Marne)

– Les lycées d'enseignement général conduisent plus d'un million et demi d'élèves soit à un baccalauréat d'enseignement général, soit à un baccalauréat technologique, après trois ans d'études en seconde, première et terminale. Le baccalauréat d'enseignement général, souvent modifié au fil des ans, reste un examen national considéré comme le premier grade universitaire ; il a été réorganisé autour de trois séries : lettres (L), sciences (S), économie (ES). Le baccalauréat technologique comprend également plusieurs séries : sciences et technologies tertiaires (STT), sciences et technologies industrielles (STI), sciences et technologies de laboratoire (STL) et sciences médico-sociales (SMS).

– Les lycées professionnels préparent 700 000 élèves environ aux métiers de l'industrie et des services. La préparation aux CAP (en trois ans) a subi une forte érosion, tandis que les BEP, en deux ans, sont en forte augmentation. Le baccalauréat professionnel, créé fin 1985, est aujourd'hui préparé par plus de 100 000 élèves. Les formations dispensées dans les lycées professionnels et leur contenu sont déterminés, au niveau national, en relation avec les professions. Mais elles se heurtent, plus que d'autres, à la difficulté à s'adapter aux besoins quantitatifs et qualitatifs des entreprises. Dans cet objectif, le ministère de l'Éducation nationale essaie de développer des enseignements en alternance avec les entreprises et d'évaluer, à l'aide de contrôles continus, les acquisitions des élèves.

Ce sont les lycées qui ont subi la plus forte augmentation d'effectifs par le simple effet de l'arrivée de classes d'âge plus nombreuses, nées à la fin des années soixante-dix et au début des années quatre-vingt, mais surtout du fait de la volonté politique de conduire 80 % d'une classe d'âge au niveau du baccalauréat. Alors que, dans les années cinquante, moins de 10 % des jeunes atteignaient ce niveau et moins de 30 % en 1980, près de 70 % y sont parvenus en 1997, le taux de réussite à l'examen, toutes filières confondues, étant de 79 % en 1998.

Un centre
d'apprentissage prépare
les élèves au CAP
de soudure, à Clermont
(Oise)

Le réseau des établissements secondaires est fixé par région, dans le cadre d'un schéma régional des formations. Les régions assurent la construction, l'équipement et le fonctionnement des lycées. L'État pourvoit ces établissements en postes budgétaires et en personnels ainsi qu'en matériel pédagogique ; de gros investissements ont ainsi été consentis pour l'équipement informatique des établissements, l'objectif actuel étant de relier tous les lycées au réseau Internet. De leur côté, les régions ont réalisé des efforts financiers considérables, depuis une décennie, pour rénover le patrimoine immobilier des lycées et construire de nouveaux établissements.

Enseignement supérieur : préparer le troisième millénaire

Les enseignements supérieurs sont tous ceux qui se situent après la fin des études secondaires sanctionnées par l'obtention du baccalauréat. En 1998, 95 milliards de francs (15,8 milliards de dollars) ont été consacrés à l'enseignement supérieur, toutes dépenses confondues, soit 2,5 fois plus qu'il y a 25 ans. Il a en effet fallu faire face à une croissance extraordinaire du nombre d'étudiants. Ils étaient 123 000 en 1946, 850 000 en 1970, 1,2 million en 1980 et 2,1 millions en 1998. L'Université emploie près de 130 000 enseignants et chercheurs.

Une partie des enseignements, c'est-à-dire les formations en deux ans après le baccalauréat, est donnée dans les lycées et relève administrativement de l'enseignement secondaire, pour des raisons historiques et techniques. Il s'agit essentiellement des brevets de techniciens supérieurs (BTS) préparés par plus de 200 000 élèves – trois fois plus qu'il y a dix ans – auxquels il faut ajouter environ 80 000 élèves préparant en deux ans les concours d'accès aux grandes écoles. Les enseignements supérieurs sont en effet partagés entre grandes écoles, auxquelles les étudiants n'accèdent qu'après avoir réussi à un concours très sélectif, et universités dont l'accès est autorisé à tout détenteur du baccalauréat.

L'Institut de mécanique de l'INSA à Saint-Étienne-du-Rouvray (Seine-Maritime) ; de nombreux établissements d'enseignement supérieur ont été ouverts depuis 1990 pour faire face à une demande sans cesse croissante

Les grandes écoles sont apparues dès le XVIIIe siècle, dans les périodes de crise de l'Université et à l'initiative des pouvoirs publics afin de pourvoir en cadres, par concours, les administrations ; elles ont également été créées à l'initiative des professionnels pour que les entreprises disposent des compétences nécessaires à leur développement. Actuellement rattachées à différents ministères, ces écoles comptent plus de 200 000 élèves et couvrent tous les domaines du savoir et de la connaissance, des sciences fondamentales aux arts, en passant par les sciences humaines et de l'ingénieur, ainsi que les disciplines littéraires, juridiques et administratives. Certaines de ces écoles, parmi les plus prestigieuses, étaient initialement destinées à former les personnels les plus qualifiés des grands corps de l'État : Écoles normales supérieures pour l'enseignement, Polytechnique et Saint-Cyr pour l'armée, École des Chartes pour les archives et les conservateurs du patrimoine national, École nationale d'administration (ENA), créée en 1945, pour former les personnels civils de la haute fonction publique. Tout en conservant ces objectifs, la plupart de ces établissements ont élargi leurs formations et les étudiants qui en sortent ne se destinent plus nécessairement au service de l'État. Parallèlement, les écoles de commerce et de gestion, telles que HEC, l'ESSEC ou l'École supérieure de commerce, ainsi que les écoles d'ingénieurs (ENSI), ont attiré un nombre sans cesse croissant de candidats, les besoins des entreprises en personnels hautement qualifiés de ce type étant de plus en plus forts.

La grande majorité des étudiants, 1,5 million environ, dont environ 10 % d'étrangers originaires principalement d'Afrique, fréquente les universités, ouvertes aux titulaires du baccalauréat ou d'un diplôme équivalent. L'entrée aux IUT, Instituts universitaires de technologie, qui préparent en deux ans au diplôme universitaire de technologie et comptent près de 110 000 étudiants, se fait en revanche par une sélection sur dossier. Les étudiants se répartissent entre les lettres et sciences humaines (35 %), le droit et les sciences économiques (24 %), les sciences (20 %), la médecine, la pharmacie et l'odontologie (14 %) ; les autres sont les étudiants des IUT et d'éducation physique et sportive. Les études sont organisées en trois cycles ; le premier, de deux ans, est sanctionné en général par un diplôme d'études universitaires générales (DEUG) ; le second, de deux ans, par la licence, puis la maîtrise ; le troisième, accessible sur sélection, conduit soit à des diplômes d'études supérieures spécialisées (DESS), soit à des diplômes d'études approfondies (DEA) qui permettent de poursuivre jusqu'au doctorat. Environ 60 % des étudiants accèdent au deuxième cycle, après un succès au DEUG obtenu dans des délais variables : 28 % en deux ans, 32 % en trois ans ou plus.

L'organisation des universités est restée remarquablement stable depuis 1896, date de leur refondation par la Troisième République, jusqu'à la loi Edgar Faure de 1968 – qui répondait aux nécessités de réforme exprimées par la revendication étudiante – et la loi Savary de 1984 – qui a institué l'autonomie administrative, pédagogique et financière des universités. Deux nouvelles instances ont remplacé les facultés : d'une part, les Unités de formation et de recherche (UFR), avec à leur tête des directeurs disposant de pouvoirs pour assurer une coordination pédagogique ; d'autre part, l'université, qui

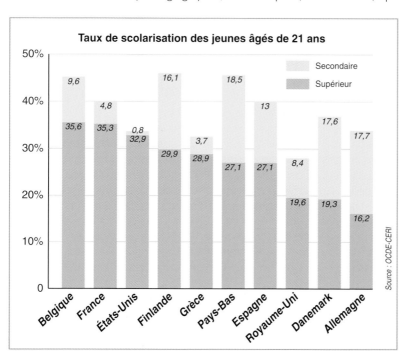

Environ 40 % des jeunes de 21 ans sont scolarisés en France, dont 35 % à l'université

regroupe les UFR, les services communs (bibliothèque, service d'information et d'orientation, service de formation continue) ainsi que les instituts et écoles qui lui sont éventuellement rattachés. Le président de chaque université, élu pour cinq ans, dispose de services administratifs et financiers ; il gère un budget comprenant les crédits attribués par l'État et des ressources propres (donations, soutien d'entreprises, subventions des collectivités territoriales, droits d'inscription). Les universités sont autonomes, bien que la grande majorité de leurs ressources proviennent de l'État, que leur personnel soit d'État et que le secrétaire général soit nommé par le ministère. À l'administration de l'université participent des conseils élus par l'ensemble des personnels et les étudiants, l'un de ces conseils appelant des personnalités extérieures à siéger en son sein. Les réformes qui se sont succédé dans les années quatre-vingt et quatre-vingt-dix ont cherché à adapter l'université aux besoins plus diversifiés de l'économie et de la société, ainsi qu'au nombre plus élevé d'étudiants et à leur plus grande hétérogénéité. La dernière, datant d'avril 1997, a instauré l'organisation de l'année universitaire en semestres permettant des réorientations plus rapides qu'auparavant ; elle a aussi généralisé les unités d'enseignement capitalisables, introduit une unité d'expérience professionnelle et créé un tutorat. Il est actuellement question d'aller plus loin, en jouant la carte de la décentralisation et de la professionnalisation des études.

Les universités et les établissements de statut universitaire sont de très inégale importance et souffrent de disparités dans leur répartition à travers le territoire national. La ville de Paris, à elle seule, compte près du sixième des étudiants du pays. Si l'on ajoute les universités des académies voisines de Versailles et de Créteil, la région parisienne en rassemble le quart. Les petites universités sont généralement caractérisées par leur polyvalence et l'importance du nombre de leurs étudiants de premier cycle. Les grandes métropoles de province, quant à elles, comptent plusieurs universités, souvent plus spécialisées, avec des effectifs importants en deuxième et troisième cycles. C'est le cas de Lille, Toulouse, Lyon, Aix-en-Provence, Bordeaux, Grenoble, Montpellier, Nancy.

L'augmentation constante du nombre des étudiants et les participations financières demandées aux collectivités territoriales, en partie pour faire face à cet afflux, ont entraîné la création d'antennes universitaires dans de très nombreuses villes moyennes. Le plan «Université 2000», lancé au printemps 1990, a prévu 32 milliards de francs (5,3 milliards de dollars) pour faire face à ces nouveaux besoins, investissement supporté pour moitié par l'État et pour moitié par les collectivités territoriales ; depuis, un plan «U 3000» a été annoncé par le Premier ministre Lionel Jospin en novembre 1997, pour répondre aux nouvelles demandes du prochain millénaire. Les délocalisations sont un levier important du développement régional et de l'essaimage de nouvelles activités dans les provinces. Elles favorisent aussi la démocratisation de l'enseignement supérieur, d'autant qu'un système d'aides, sous forme de bourses pour les plus défavorisés et, de façon plus générale, sous forme de restaurants et de logements universitaires, complète le dispositif d'accueil et de soutien aux étudiants.

Le souci de permettre aux universités françaises d'être de plus en plus présentes dans l'ordre international, notamment européen, conduit à accroître leur autonomie de gestion. Le même souci a suscité une politique ministérielle d'encouragement à la création d'un petit nombre de pôles européens. Dans une même ville diverses universités se rapprochent, se lient entre elles et à des équipes de recherche importantes. Ces universités qui développent une politique volontariste d'échanges internationaux ont alors une dimension suffisante pour constituer des centres dynamiques et renommés, capables de travailler et participer à des programmes européens d'échanges entre universités et de partenariat avec les entreprises. Tel est le cas, par exemple, des universités de Grenoble, Toulouse, Lille et Rennes-Nantes.

Adapter la formation professionnelle

L'expression formation professionnelle recouvre un ensemble de dispositifs destinés aux personnes engagées dans la vie active et comprenant des préparations à des diplômes professionnels, mais surtout des stages d'insertion, de conversion, de perfectionnement et d'adaptation. La formation professionnelle dépend conjointement des ministères de l'Éducation nationale, de l'Enseignement supérieur, mais aussi du ministère de l'Emploi et de la Solidarité. Les lois de décentralisation du début des années quatre-vingt ont donné compétence aux régions en ce domaine. L'État s'est réservé, par exception, les actions en faveur des publics prioritaires : jeunes sans qualification, demandeurs d'emploi, travailleurs migrants, femmes souhaitant une réinsertion dans la vie professionnelle.

Le financement des actions de formation est assuré soit par des fonds publics, principalement d'État, soit par des fonds privés. Ceux-ci proviennent du versement obligatoire, pour tout employeur ayant un minimum de dix salariés, de 1,1 % de la masse salariale brute. Ces sommes peuvent être utilisées pour financer directement des actions de formation du personnel de l'entreprise, ou sont versées au Fonds d'assurance formation, à des organismes de formation agréés ou au Trésor public. Le coût annuel total de la formation, toutes sources de financement confondues, approche 140 milliards de francs (23,3 milliards de dollars) et les actions de formation profitent chaque année à un actif sur trois.

Les actions pour les salariés du secteur privé, pour les personnels des administrations (dans l'un et l'autre cas, elles se déroulent souvent dans le cadre d'un congé formation) et en faveur des publics prioritaires sont réalisées soit par des organismes privés, soit par des formateurs publics. Près de 4 000 organismes privés couvrent plus de 87 % du marché de la formation. Les établissements publics interviennent dans les conditions du marché. Les intervenants principaux sont divers et les fonctions nettement réparties entre eux. L'Association pour la formation professionnelle des adultes (AFPA), qui dispose de plus de 100 centres, prépare à plus de 300 métiers et s'adresse en priorité à des demandeurs d'emploi et à des salariés sous contrat de travail ou en congé individuel de formation. Les Groupements d'établissements de l'Éducation nationale (GRETA) offrent des stages négociés avec les entreprises, des stages pour publics prioritaires (notamment le cinquième des jeunes en première insertion), des stages d'initiation, de perfectionnement, de promotion. Les organismes privés à but non lucratif, quant à eux, accueillent le tiers des jeunes en première insertion et près d'un tiers des chômeurs. Les centres des administrations publiques et les organismes privés à but lucratif accueillent la moitié des actifs salariés en formation.

Entre 1983 et 1996, les dépenses pour la formation professionnelle continue ont augmenté de 75 %

Dépenses pour la formation professionnelle continue
(en Milliards de francs au prix de 1996)

Source : MEN - DEP

Pour en savoir plus :

Direction de l'évaluation et de la prospective, *L'état de l'école* (rapport périodique), Ministère de l'Éducation nationale.

« Le système éducatif », *Cahiers français*, n° 285, La Documentation française, mars 1998.

M. Allaire, M.-T. Frank, *Politiques de l'éducation en France : de la maternelle au baccalauréat*, La Documentation française, collection Retour aux textes, 1995.

B. Bouyx, *L'enseignement technologique et professionnel*, La Documentation française - CNDP, collection Systèmes éducatifs, 1997.

R. Fauroux, G. Chacornac, *Pour l'école*, Commission de réflexion sur l'école, Calmann-Lévy-La Documentation française, 1996.

J. Fialaire, *L'école en Europe*, La Documentation française-IIAP, collection Vivre en Europe, 1996.

R. Hérin, R. Rouault, V. Veschambre, *Atlas de la France scolaire : de la maternelle au lycée*, La Documentation française, collection Dynamiques du territoire, 1994.

R. Périé, J. Simon, *Organisation et gestion de l'Éducation nationale*, Berger-Levrault, 1998.

C. Rault, *La formation professionnelle initiale*, in *Notes et Études documentaires*, n° 4987, La Documentation française, 1994.

L'ÉCONOMIE

14

La politique économique

La France est la quatrième puissance économique du monde et le quatrième exportateur. En 1997, le produit intérieur brut (PIB) du pays a atteint 8 183 milliards de francs (1 363 milliards de dollars), ce qui permet aux Français de figurer parmi les habitants disposant de l'un des niveaux de vie les plus élevés de la planète. Cette situation traduit la forte croissance économique qui a marqué le pays depuis la seconde guerre mondiale. Profitant de la construction européenne dans laquelle elle joue un rôle essentiel, ainsi que du dynamisme de son commerce extérieur, la France a en effet connu au cours du dernier demi-siècle un bouleversement considérable de son économie. Son agriculture a enregistré une modernisation spectaculaire lui permettant souvent de rivaliser avec celle des États-Unis sur bien des marchés extérieurs ; son industrie s'est restructurée et orientée vers les hautes technologies ; enfin, le secteur tertiaire, appuyé sur des infrastructures de transport performantes, est devenu, notamment grâce aux banques, à la distribution et au tourisme, l'un des fers de lance de l'économie nationale (sur les secteurs économiques, voir chapitre suivant).

Des impératifs changeants

La crise des années trente et la seconde guerre mondiale ont laissé l'économie française exsangue. En 1945, les infrastructures sont détruites, l'appareil de production est obsolète, les finances ruinées et le commerce extérieur anéanti. Cependant, tout comme les autres pays industriels, la France connaît de 1945 à 1974 une période de croissance de longue durée – les « Trente Glorieuses » – qui lui permet de remettre sur pied son économie et de sortir de son isolement commercial.

De 1945 à 1958, le pays se lance dans la reconstruction et en particulier la modernisation de son appareil industriel. L'État joue alors un rôle essentiel par le biais de la planification et de l'extension du secteur public. Il prend le contrôle des grandes banques, des charbonnages, de la distribution du gaz et de l'électricité et d'une partie de l'industrie, en nationalisant des entreprises comme Renault. Il bénéficie par ailleurs de l'aide américaine, octroyée dans le cadre du plan Marshall.

Les pouvoirs publics donnent dans un premier temps la priorité aux transports, à la production énergétique et à l'industrie lourde. Dès 1948, le niveau de production d'avant-guerre est atteint et le besoin de main-d'œuvre est tel que le plein emploi est assuré. Le pays entre dans la société de consommation et la forte croissance démographique soutient la demande intérieure. Sur le plan commercial, la France demeure cependant assez isolée dans le cadre de son ancien empire colonial. En 1958, les exportations ne représentent que 9 % du PIB et les anciennes colonies assurent encore le quart des importations et près du tiers des exportations françaises.

De 1958 à 1973, la croissance s'accélère, avec un taux annuel moyen de 5,5 %, contre 4,8 % en République fédérale d'Allemagne et 3,9 % aux États-Unis. Seul le Japon fait mieux. Le PIB en francs constants double durant cette période et la production industrielle augmente au rythme annuel de 5,7 % l'an. Les entreprises privées prennent le relais de l'État dans l'investissement et connaissent une première vague de concentration. Elles profitent du faible coût de l'énergie et des matières premières et les dévaluations de la monnaie nationale permettent de maintenir leur compétitivité sur les marchés extérieurs, en dépit d'une inflation française supérieure à celle de nombreux concurrents. Dans le même temps, le pays connaît une large ouverture commerciale à la suite de la décolonisation et surtout de l'adhésion à la Communauté européenne du charbon et de l'acier (CECA) en 1951, puis à la Communauté économique européenne (CEE) en 1957. En 1973, les pays de la zone franc, c'est-à-dire les anciennes colonies, ne représentent plus que 3,5 % des importations et 5,1 % des exportations nationales. Les pays industrialisés, en revanche, assurent plus de 76 % du commerce extérieur de la France, 64 % des flux s'effectuant désormais dans le cadre de la CEE. L'agriculture et l'industrie poursuivent leur modernisation. L'État développe les infrastructures de transport, notamment autoroutières, et soutient de grands programmes industriels

Évolution du produit intérieur brut, 1972-1997

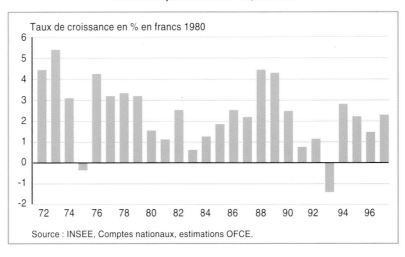

Taux de croissance en % en francs 1980

Source : INSEE, Comptes nationaux, estimations OFCE.

dans la construction aéronautique et la filière nucléaire. Par ailleurs, le déséquilibre économique entre Paris et la province s'atténue grâce à la décentralisation industrielle et à la mise en place d'une politique d'aménagement du territoire.

Les Trente Glorieuses prennent fin avec l'instabilité monétaire qui se développe, après 1971, à la suite de la suppression de la convertibilité du dollar en or et surtout du premier choc pétrolier de 1973. Une nouvelle hausse brutale du pétrole survient en 1979 et elle est amplifiée par le renchérissement du dollar. La facture énergétique de la France passe de 14 milliards de francs (2,3 milliards de dollars) en 1972 à 187 milliards (31 milliards de dollars) en 1984. Il faut attendre 1985 pour voir baisser le prix du baril et le cours du billet vert, ce qui allège la contrainte extérieure. Durant ces années, le taux de croissance diminue et, de plus, il connaît de fortes fluctuations d'une année à l'autre. Pour améliorer leur compétitivité, les entreprises augmentent leur productivité et réduisent leurs effectifs. Jusqu'à la fin des années quatre-vingt, le pays doit aussi faire face à une forte inflation, qui pèse sur les prix au moment où il se trouve confronté à une double concurrence : celle des États-Unis et du Japon pour les technologies de pointe et celle des pays en développement pour les biens de consommation courants. Certains secteurs industriels tels que le textile, les chaussures, les jouets, la sidérurgie et les appareils électroniques ont souffert de cette concurrence. Le choc est d'autant plus rude que ces industries sont souvent les activités dominantes, voire uniques, de certaines régions ou de quelques villes. Il en résulte un véritable drame social, comme le montrent les taux de chômage élevés qui s'imposent alors dans les vallées textiles des Vosges ou dans les anciens bassins sidérurgiques de Valenciennes et de Longwy.

Une économie assainie

Ces dernières années, la France a enregistré une sensible amélioration de la plupart de ses indicateurs économiques, ce qui lui a permis de répondre aux critères définis par le traité de Maastricht pour participer à l'Union monétaire, dès 1999, aux côtés de dix autres partenaires.

En premier lieu, la croissance s'est accélérée. Après une période de progression moyenne, entre 1990 et 1996, elle a atteint 2,3 % en 1997 et approche les 3 % en 1998. Cette reprise traduit la bonne tenue des marchés étrangers, en particulier ceux des pays industriels avec lesquels la France effectue plus de 80 % de ses échanges. Elle souligne aussi la progression du marché intérieur depuis 1997, tant en raison de la demande accrue des ménages que de la hausse des investissements des entreprises désirant rattraper le retard enregistré pendant plusieurs années. Les carnets de commande s'accroissent et les stocks se reconstituent.

L'inflation, qui a été longtemps supérieure à celle de nos principaux partenaires commerciaux, est désormais jugulée. Alors que la hausse des prix atteignait 14 % l'an au début des années quatre-vingt, ce chiffre a été ramené à moins de 3 % dès 1991 et les derniers résultats confirment la tendance : 1,5 % en 1996, 1,3 % en 1997 et environ 1 % en 1998. C'est le résultat d'un long consensus et d'une politique continue de stabilité des prix, menée depuis plus d'une décennie par les gouvernements successifs, quelle que soit la majorité au pouvoir.

Les remarquables résultats du commerce extérieur constituent un autre indicateur favorable de l'économie nationale. Alors qu'il était structurellement déficitaire jusqu'au début de la décennie 90, celui-ci voit ses excédents gonfler de manière spectaculaire : 31 milliards de francs (5,1 milliards de dollars) en 1992, 122 milliards de francs (20 milliards de dollars) en 1996 et 175 milliards (29 milliards de dollars) en 1997. Le solde est aussi redevenu positif pour les biens manufacturés depuis 1992 et la France enregistre des excédents avec la plupart de ses partenaires de l'Union européenne, pays avec lesquels elle assure plus de 60 % de ses échanges extérieurs.

Le chômage, en revanche, demeure un grave problème économique et social, comme d'ailleurs dans la plupart des pays européens. Le nombre de personnes sans-emploi enregistre une montée inquiétante depuis plus de 20 ans : 430 000 en 1974, 1 400 000 en 1980, 2 483 000 en 1990 et près de 3 000 000 en 1998. La majeure partie des pertes d'emplois a été enregistrée dans le bâtiment et les industries manufacturières. Le secteur tertiaire a, quant à lui, gagné des effectifs en dépit de l'amélioration considérable de la productivité. La lutte contre le chômage est devenu l'objectif prioritaire de tous les gouvernements, quelle que soit leur couleur politique. Depuis plusieurs mois, on constate une légère baisse du taux de chômage, à la faveur du retour de la croissance et des politiques de l'emploi, notamment

L'inflation jugulée :
taux de croissance annuel
des prix à la
consommation,
de 1962 à 1997

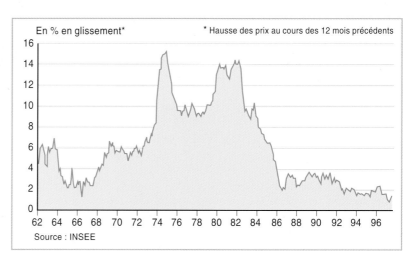

En % en glissement*   * Hausse des prix au cours des 12 mois précédents

Source : INSEE

l'allègement des charges sociales pour les bas salaires. Il n'en demeure pas moins que la France obtient dans ce domaine des résultats inférieurs à ceux de ses principaux partenaires.

Les déficits publics constituent un autre problème d'envergure. Le déficit budgétaire reste élevé, comme dans les pays voisins. La situation, après une grave détérioration au début de la décennie 90, s'améliore cependant depuis 1994. Le besoin de financement des administrations, qui atteignait alors 5,8 % du PIB, n'en représente plus que 4,2 % en 1996, 3,1 % en 1997 et 3 % en 1998. Cette amélioration s'explique par le redressement des comptes de l'État, des administrations publiques locales et de la sécurité sociale. Alors qu'en 1995 le déficit budgétaire atteignait 323 milliards (53,8 milliards de dollars), la France a bouclé son budget 1997 sur un déficit ramené à 268 milliards de francs (44,6 milliards de dollars). Le gouvernement français, comme ceux des autres pays européens, a engagé un programme de réduction des déficits publics, dit programme de convergence, en procédant à une gestion plus rigoureuse tout en développant des actions sélectives dans les secteurs sensibles au cycle économique pour réduire le chômage et la dette. En effet, le poids des dépenses publiques entraîne des prélèvements obligatoires élevés, qu'il s'agisse des impôts ou des cotisations sociales, et surtout accroît la dette publique. Cette dernière atteint 58 % du PIB. Ce taux est certes inférieur à ceux de la plupart des pays européens, mais le remboursement des intérêts de cette dette représente aujourd'hui plus de 14 % des dépenses budgétaires de l'État.

Un environnement européen favorable

La construction européenne a profondément influencé l'économie française. Elle a d'abord imposé aux entreprises un effort accru de compétitivité non seulement pour résister à de nouveaux concurrents, mais aussi pour saisir les occasions que leur offrait un vaste marché. L'application du principe de la libre circulation des personnes, des marchandises, des services et des capitaux, développée en 1993 dans le cadre du marché unique, a ouvert aux entreprises françaises un espace peuplé de 376 millions de consommateurs et profité à tous les secteurs de l'économie nationale.

La Politique agricole commune, ou PAC, a constitué pour la France un facteur essentiel de modernisation. Fondée sur la libre circulation

La construction du tunnel de Puymorens, entre la France et l'Espagne (ici, l'entrée côté Pyrénées-Orientales), a été financée en partie par l'Union européenne

des produits, la solidarité financière et la préférence communautaire, elle a contribué à l'amélioration du revenu des agriculteurs, à l'accroissement des investissements et donc à l'augmentation rapide de la production. Le Fonds européen d'orientation et de garantie agricole (FEOGA), qui gère la PAC, octroie des aides importantes à l'aménagement de l'espace rural, à la modernisation des exploitations et à la bonification des terres. Il accorde aussi un soutien régulier à l'agriculture des montagnes et des autres régions défavorisées. La France, premier pays agricole européen, bénéficie chaque année de plus de 55 milliards de francs (9 milliards de dollars) d'aides diverses du FEOGA.

Dans le domaine industriel, la libre circulation des marchandises et des capitaux a tout particulièrement stimulé les entreprises. Il en a résulté des taux d'investissement plus élevés, une forte concentration financière et la multiplication des filiales à l'étranger. Près de 40 % des filiales des entreprises françaises se situent dans les pays de l'Union européenne, l'Allemagne, le Royaume-Uni et l'Espagne figurant en tête des pays d'accueil. L'Union européenne a par ailleurs adopté un certain nombre de mesures favorables aux entreprises françaises. Elle a d'abord facilité la restructuration des vieilles industries par des aides diverses et une limitation des importations. Ainsi, elle a obtenu, dans le cadre des Accords multifibres, ou AMF, que les pays du tiers monde, gros exportateurs de textiles, limitent leurs exportations vers les pays européens. Elle s'efforce aussi de promouvoir les industries de pointe en encourageant la coopération entre les laboratoires, les universités et les entreprises des pays membres et elle a multiplié les programmes de recherche pour permettre aux pays européens de réduire leur retard sur les États-Unis et le Japon. Elle encourage par ailleurs l'internationalisation des PME au sein du marché européen, en mettant à leur service des structures d'information et de coopération.

Le secteur tertiaire a aussi profité de la dynamique européenne. La Communauté, par des aides et des prêts, a contribué à la modernisation du réseau de transport, participant au financement de grands ouvrages comme le tunnel de Puymorens, entre la France et l'Espagne. L'instauration de la libre concurrence et l'harmonisation des moyens techniques et juridiques ont aussi contribué à la modernisation des différents modes de transport. Par la libre circulation, la Communauté a facilité le développement du tourisme au sein de l'hexagone, la clientèle européenne assurant plus des quatre cinquièmes des flux. Elle a aussi dynamisé les secteurs de la banque et de l'assurance, en conduisant les sociétés françaises à se moderniser, à se regrouper pour faire face à la concurrence étrangère et à se lancer à l'assaut des marchés voisins.

La coopération européenne a également contribué à stabiliser les monnaies et à limiter les fluctuations de change préjudiciables à une saine concurrence, indispensable au bon fonctionnement du Marché commun. La mise en place du Système monétaire européen (SME), en 1979, a permis dans un premier temps de fixer des marges de fluctuations étroites entre les monnaies et de déterminer une coopération entre les banques centrales des pays y participant. Le traité sur l'Union européenne, entré en vigueur le 1er janvier 1993, a engagé la France et ses partenaires dans le processus visant à constituer une Union économique et monétaire (UEM). Il a, de ce fait, permis une certaine convergence économique entre les pays membres et notamment la réduction des déficits budgétaires. La mise en place de l'euro, depuis le 1er janvier 1999, permet d'éliminer les risques de change et les frais de conversion monétaire, pour le plus grand bénéfice des particuliers et des entreprises. L'Union économique et monétaire constitue aujourd'hui, pour la France et ses partenaires, un élément fondamental pour conforter la construction européenne.

Des entreprises dynamiques

L'État joue en France un rôle économique important. Il est d'abord le premier employeur, le premier producteur et le premier client du pays. Il est aussi le premier transporteur, le premier propriétaire foncier et immobilier.

L'État, qui définit les grandes orientations de la politique économique, s'est longtemps appuyé sur la planification, mise en place en 1947. Bien qu'incitative et non impérative, celle-ci a permis d'orienter les investissements vers les secteurs prioritaires, puis de favoriser la construction des grandes infrastructures et l'aménagement du territoire. L'État est longtemps intervenu dans la production en contrôlant de nombreuses entreprises mais les alternances politiques qui ont marqué le pays depuis une vingtaine d'années ont entraîné des changements considérables. Le poids de l'État s'est d'abord renforcé en 1982 par une vague de nationalisations visant à moderniser l'appareil productif et à restructurer les entreprises. Le quart de l'industrie et 90 % des dépôts bancaires passent alors sous son contrôle. L'arrivée d'une nouvelle majorité au pouvoir, en 1986-1988, conduit le gouvernement à privatiser une douzaine de sociétés. Après une nouvelle alternance, le retour aux affaires de cette même majorité, en mars 1993, s'accompagne d'un nouveau programme de privatisations portant sur vingt-et-une grandes entreprises industrielles, banques et compagnies d'assurances. Le programme est poursuivi en 1995 avec la privatisation de plusieurs entreprises industrielles comme Péchiney, Usinor-Sacilor et Elf-Aquitaine et de plusieurs banques et compagnies d'assurances comme la BNP et l'UAP. Depuis la nouvelle alternance de 1997, l'État a réduit sa participation dans plusieurs entreprises et s'apprête à le faire dans d'autres, comme le montre la privatisation prochaine du Crédit lyonnais.

Les entreprises ont, quant à elles, connu une forte concentration financière. Celle-ci a conduit à la naissance de grands groupes. La tendance est cependant moins forte que chez bien des concurrents. La France ne compte en effet que neuf entreprises parmi les cent premières mondiales, loin derrière les États-Unis (31) et le Japon (21) mais aussi l'Allemagne (12). La première entreprise française, Elf-Aquitaine, ne se classe qu'au 28ᵉ rang mondial. Les grandes entreprises françaises demeurent caractérisées par un jeu complexe de participations croisées mêlant les grandes banques du pays. Elles font généralement moins appel que la plupart de leurs concurrentes étrangères au marché boursier pour accroître leur capital, bien que les deux dernières décennies aient été marquées par un engouement important du grand public pour les placements boursiers, notamment à la suite des nombreuses privatisations.

Alors que les grandes entreprises réduisent leurs effectifs, les PME, plus souples et mieux adaptées aux changements rapides de stratégie, constituent les nouveaux fers de lance de l'économie nationale. Près de la moitié des salariés de l'industrie sont désormais employés dans des entreprises de moins de 500 salariés et celles-ci réalisent 42 % des ventes. Certaines de ces entreprises, spécialisées dans des secteurs très performants, occupent une position de choix sur le marché mondial. C'est, entre autres, le cas de Zodiac pour les bateaux pneumatiques et les toboggans de secours des avions, de Bénéteau et de Jeanneau pour la navigation de plaisance ou de Salomon et de Rossignol pour le matériel de ski. Les PME sont particulièrement actives dans les secteurs de l'agro-alimentaire, du bâtiment et de la confection. Elles souffrent cependant d'une insuffisante présence sur

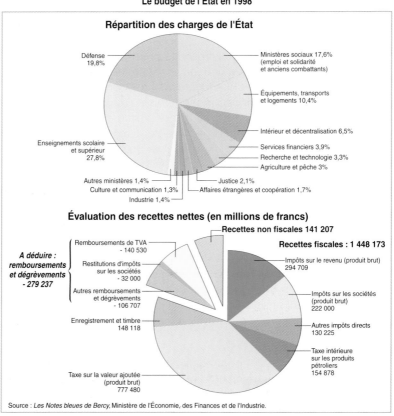

Le budget de l'État en 1998

Répartition des charges de l'État

- Défense 19,8%
- Ministères sociaux 17,6% (emploi et solidarité et anciens combattants)
- Équipements, transports et logements 10,4%
- Intérieur et décentralisation 6,5%
- Enseignements scolaire et supérieur 27,8%
- Services financiers 3,9%
- Recherche et technologie 3,3%
- Agriculture et pêche 3%
- Autres ministères 1,4%
- Culture et communication 1,3%
- Industrie 1,4%
- Justice 2,1%
- Affaires étrangères et coopération 1,7%

Évaluation des recettes nettes (en millions de francs)

Recettes non fiscales 141 207

Recettes fiscales : 1 448 173

A déduire : remboursements et dégrèvements - 279 237

- Remboursements de TVA - 140 530
- Restitutions d'impôts sur les sociétés - 32 000
- Autres remboursements et dégrèvements - 106 707
- Enregistrement et timbre 148 118
- Taxe sur la valeur ajoutée (produit brut) 777 480
- Impôts sur le revenu (produit brut) 294 709
- Impôts sur les sociétés (produit brut) 222 000
- Autres impôts directs 130 225
- Taxe intérieure sur les produits pétroliers 154 878

Source : *Les Notes bleues de Bercy,* Ministère de l'Économie, des Finances et de l'Industrie.

les marchés extérieurs, c'est pourquoi l'État encourage le développement des initiatives publiques ou privées susceptibles de faciliter la pénétration des marchés étrangers.

La modernisation des entreprises a permis d'améliorer leur compétitivité. Par ailleurs, la main-d'œuvre française qualifiée présente des coûts salariaux inférieurs de 25 % à ceux de l'Allemagne, notre premier partenaire commercial, ce qui contribue à l'implantation de nombreuses firmes étrangères sur le sol national, notamment en Lorraine et en Alsace. Si l'écart des salaires est défavorable avec l'Italie, l'Espagne et le Royaume-Uni, ce handicap est compensé, en totalité ou en partie, par une productivité plus élevée. La situation est plus délicate par rapport aux pays en voie de développement, qui offrent des coûts de production parfois trente à cinquante fois inférieurs à ceux des entreprises françaises, ce qui peut accentuer les délocalisations industrielles, notamment vers les pays du Sud-Est asiatique. Pour freiner ces départs, les pouvoirs publics s'efforcent de réduire le coût du travail par un allégement des charges pesant sur les entreprises et par la promotion de nouvelles technologies susceptibles de réduire les coûts de production.

Après la période d'intense modernisation de la fin des années soixante-dix et durant les années 1987-1988, l'effort d'investissement s'est quelque peu ralenti au début des années quatre-vingt-dix. Il connaît depuis 1997 un nouvel élan. Les entreprises profitent de la reprise économique, d'autant plus facilement qu'elles disposent aujourd'hui d'une marge de manœuvre financière plus importante. Renforcer les capacités d'innovation, investir dans les nouvelles technologies et se redéployer vers les marchés porteurs sont désormais les mots clés de la réussite économique pour les entreprises françaises.

Pour en savoir plus :

Annuaire statistique de la France, édition 1997, INSEE, 1997.

Les tableaux de l'économie française 1998-1999, INSEE, 1998.

L'économie française. Rapport sur les comptes de la Nation 1998-1999, Le Livre de poche, 1998.

Le budget de l'État 1998, Les Éditions de Bercy, Ministère de l'Économie et des Finances, 1998.

Études économiques de l'OCDE, France, OCDE, 1997.

J.-F. Eck, *La France dans la nouvelle économie mondiale*, PUF, 1994.

S. Marti, V. Ragot, *L'euro en poche*, La Documentation française, 1998.

J.-P. Vesperini, *L'économie française sous la Ve République*, Économica, 1993.

Revues

Cahiers français, La Documentation française ; *Capital* (mensuel) ; *L'Expansion* (bi-mensuel) ; *Le Nouvel Économiste* (hebdomadaire) ; *Le Revenu français* (hebdomadaire) ; *Valeurs actuelles* (hebdomadaire) ; *La Vie française* (hebdomadaire) ; *Problèmes économiques*, La Documentation française (hebdomadaire).

15

Les grands secteurs économiques

L'agriculture

La France est la première puissance agricole de l'Union européenne, devant l'Allemagne. Elle assure 22 % de la production totale des quinze pays membres. Elle est aussi le second exportateur mondial de produits agroalimentaires, derrière les États-Unis, et l'excédent de la balance commerciale a dépassé les 50 milliards de francs (8,3 milliards de dollars) en 1997. Bien qu'elle n'emploie plus que 6 % des actifs et n'assure que 2 % du produit intérieur brut national, l'agriculture constitue l'une des activités les plus dynamiques du pays. Elle a connu depuis trois décennies une modernisation remarquable qui a permis des progrès spectaculaires de la productivité et des rendements. Ce bouleversement a non seulement affecté les paysages ruraux et les structures de production, mais aussi les hommes et les mentalités. Ainsi, aux paysans de jadis ont succédé des chefs d'exploitation, véritables techniciens et gestionnaires de l'agriculture.

Une agriculture de plus en plus performante

L'espace agricole s'étend sur 33,4 millions d'hectares, soit 55 % du territoire français. Les terres arables en occupent 61 %. Elles devancent largement les superficies toujours en herbe (35 %) et les cultures permanentes, notamment les vignes et les vergers (4 %).

La modernisation de l'agriculture s'est accompagnée d'une concentration continuelle des exploitations dont le nombre est passé de 1 588 000 à 735 000 entre 1960 et 1997. Il en est résulté un doublement de leur superficie moyenne, qui atteint désormais 39 hectares. Le regroupement des terres s'est surtout effectué au profit des grandes unités de plus de 100 hectares. Si elles ne représentent que 10 % du nombre total des exploitations, elles couvrent désormais 40 % de la superficie agricole. Elles sont surtout nombreuses dans le Bassin parisien, notamment sur les riches terroirs de la Beauce, de la Brie et de la Picardie, alors que les petites exploitations occupent encore une large place dans le Sud-Ouest et dans les régions littorales méditerranéennes. L'État, soucieux de promouvoir des structures compétitives, facilite le remodelage des exploitations par l'intermédiaire des Sociétés d'aménagement foncier et d'établissement rural (SAFER). Ces organismes, qui bénéficient d'un droit de préemption, achètent des terres, les aménagent parfois et les revendent à des agriculteurs désireux d'étendre leur domaine ou à de nouveaux exploitants. Dans le même temps, l'État incite les agriculteurs âgés à prendre leur retraite et il aide les jeunes exploitants à s'installer. Il encourage aussi l'association entre exploitants, notamment par le biais des groupements agricoles d'exploitation en commun (GAEC). Le faire-valoir direct, qui est longtemps demeuré le mode d'exploitation le plus répandu, est désormais devancé par le fermage qui concerne 63 % de la superficie agricole. Quant au métayage, il a quasiment disparu des campagnes françaises.

Les grandes exploitations céréalières : la plaine de la Beauce, en Eure-et-Loir

La concentration des terres s'est accompagnée d'un remodelage des paysages agraires. Le remembrement a touché plus de 40 % de la superficie agricole, facilitant la constitution de vastes parcelles géométriques favorables à la mécanisation. Il s'est surtout développé dans la France du Nord et de l'Est. Dans les régions de l'Ouest, il s'est accompagné, comme en Bretagne, de la destruction de la plupart des haies qui formaient autrefois le bocage. Dans le sud du pays, en revanche, la présence de nombreuses cultures spécialisées et le maintien d'un faire-valoir direct important contribuent à limiter les restructurations. Par ailleurs, l'irrigation et le drainage se développent rapidement, en particulier dans le Sud-Ouest et dans le Bassin parisien.

Plus étendues, les exploitations sont aussi mieux équipées. La France compte aujourd'hui 1 310 000 tracteurs et de nombreux agriculteurs en possèdent plusieurs. Les autres machines se sont également multipliées, de la moissonneuse-batteuse à la machine à vendanger, en passant par les arracheuses de pommes de terre et de betteraves. De nouveaux matériels apparaissent sans cesse, comme les machines à tailler la vigne. Cette mécanisation explique le repli rapide de la main-d'œuvre agricole, passée de 2 700 000 à 1 080 000 actifs depuis 1970.

Les progrès de l'agriculture traduisent aussi le recours croissant à la chimie. La consommation d'engrais a été multipliée par six depuis 1950 et l'usage massif des produits phytosanitaires a permis d'éliminer la plupart des maladies et des plantes parasites qui affectaient les récoltes. Les rendements français figurent aujourd'hui parmi les plus élevés du monde, d'autant que les recherches génétiques ont permis de mettre au point des variétés de plantes de plus en plus performantes. Les résultats sont aussi remarquables dans le domaine de l'élevage. Les vaccinations, le contrôle laitier et la sélection des races grâce à l'insémination artificielle contribuent à l'augmentation des rendements en lait comme en viande et à une meilleure qualité des produits.

Les productions végétales

Les productions végétales assurent un peu plus de la moitié des recettes agricoles. Les céréales viennent toujours en bonne place tant pour la production que pour les exportations. Avec 36 millions de tonnes de blé, la France se classe au 4e rang mondial et au 1er rang dans l'Union européenne. Cette céréale privilégie les terres riches du Bassin parisien, du Berry et du Toulousain. Avec 17 millions de tonnes en 1997, le maïs devance désormais l'orge dont la production stagne depuis une décennie (10 millions de tonnes). Longtemps limité au sud-ouest du pays, le maïs, grâce à l'irrigation par aspersion et à la mise aux points d'hybrides, s'est étendu au Bassin parisien. Les autres céréales, que ce soit l'avoine ou le seigle, déclinent rapidement.

Les oléagineux et les protéagineux, en revanche, soutenus par une forte demande industrielle, se sont étendus depuis une quinzaine d'années. Le colza, surtout présent au nord de la Loire, et le tournesol, cultivé dans le Sud-Ouest et le Bassin parisien, assurent l'essentiel des livraisons. Plus récemment, le soja s'est développé dans le Midi et la vallée du Rhône.

Souvent associée aux céréales, la betterave à sucre fait de la France le premier producteur du monde, avec 34,2 millions de tonnes en 1997, devant l'Allemagne. S'ajoute à cette production celle de sucre de canne provenant de la Martinique, de la Guadeloupe et de la Réunion. Quant à la pomme de terre, autre plante industrielle, sa culture décline malgré la diversification des utilisations par les industries agroalimentaires.

Les cultures spécialisées ont une extension moindre mais elles procurent des revenus à l'hectare souvent élevés. C'est d'abord le cas de la vigne. En 1997, la production totale de vin s'élevait à 56 millions d'hectolitres, dépassant ainsi celle de l'Italie (54 millions). La France vient également en tête pour les vins de qualité. Ces derniers sont produits par des régions bien délimitées dont la production bénéficie d'une Appellation d'origine contrôlée (AOC). Il s'agit notamment de la Champagne, du Bordelais, de la Bourgogne, du Val de Loire et de la vallée du Rhône. D'autres vignobles, comme ceux d'Armagnac et de la région de Cognac, servent à la fabrication d'eaux-de-vie renommées. Quant au Languedoc, qui livre surtout des vins de table, il a entamé une grande restructuration et s'oriente vers une amélioration de la qualité de ses productions par un changement de cépages et la réduction des rendements.

En ce qui concerne les fruits et légumes, la France occupe le troisième rang européen, derrière l'Italie et l'Espagne. La production est surtout assurée par les régions méditerranéennes, comme le Roussillon et le Comtat Venaissin, les vallées de la Garonne et de la Loire et les ceintures maraîchères qui se sont constituées autour des grandes agglomérations. Quant aux cultures florales, elles privilégient les littoraux et les basses vallées de Provence.

Les productions animales

La France figure aussi au premier rang de l'Union européenne pour la production de viande. Elle possède le premier cheptel bovin, avec 20,6 millions de têtes. Le troupeau est largement concentré dans les régions océaniques de l'Ouest, où l'humidité favorise la pousse

de l'herbe, comme la Normandie, la Bretagne, les Pays de la Loire et Poitou-Charentes. Il est aussi présent dans les moyennes montagnes humides comme le Jura et les Préalpes du Nord. Toutes ces régions privilégient la production laitière. Cette dernière, toujours régulée dans le cadre des quotas européens visant à lutter contre la surproduction, permet à la France de figurer dans les premiers rangs mondiaux pour le fromage et le

La France est le premier producteur de viande bovine de l'Union européenne : ici le GAEC des Essarts à Plan (Isère)

beurre. Ces régions assurent aussi une large part de la production de viande bovine, mais l'engraissement des bêtes est concentré dans les pays d'embouche disposant de grasses prairies, comme le Charolais et la bordure limousine du Massif Central.

Le cheptel porcin figure au second rang européen, derrière celui de l'Allemagne. Il regroupe plus de 15 millions d'animaux, soit une progression de près de 50 % depuis 1970. Comme dans les autres pays européens, la viande de porc, plus économique, voit sa consommation croître rapidement (34,2 kilos par habitant). Elle devance même celle de viande bovine (26 kilos par habitant). L'élevage porcin familial a cédé la place à des élevages industriels, largement concentrés dans le Nord et en Bretagne. L'aviculture a connu une évolution comparable et les grandes batteries d'élevage hors sol se sont multipliées dans l'Ouest et le Sud-Ouest. Cependant, pour répondre aux exigences des consommateurs, des élevages fermiers se spécialisent dans des productions de qualité, garanties par des labels, notamment pour la production de foie gras en Alsace et dans le Sud-Ouest, ou de poulets, comme en Bresse.

L'élevage ovin connaît une certaine reprise depuis deux décennies. Il profite de la demande accrue en viande et en fromages, comme celui de roquefort. Avec 10 millions de têtes, le cheptel demeure cependant modeste. Il se concentre dans les régions méridionales comme les Causses, les Alpes du Sud, le Pays basque et la Corse. À l'Ouest, les agneaux élevés sur les prés salés de Bretagne et de Normandie bénéficient d'une bonne renommée.

L'industrie agro-alimentaire

L'industrie agro-alimentaire est le premier client de l'agriculture. Point fort de l'économie française, elle pèse à elle seule un chiffre d'affaires de plus de 750 milliards de francs (125 milliards de dollars). Près de la moitié de son chiffre d'affaires provient de la transformation des produits d'origine animale (industrie des viandes et produits laitiers) ; les secteurs des boissons et alcools, fruits et légumes et produits pour animaux enregistrent de bonnes performances. Avec près de 400 000 salariés, le secteur agro-alimentaire est le troisième employeur de l'industrie française. 4 200 entreprises contribuent à son dynamisme, parmi lesquelles on compte de nombreuses PME et coopératives agricoles.

Les grandes entreprises agro-alimentaires comprennent notamment Générale des Grandes sources, Miko et Fromageries Bel.

L'industrie agro-alimentaire est, en outre, un marché très ouvert à l'exportation, ce qui lui a permis de dégager en 1997 un excédent commercial record de 50 milliards de francs (8,3 milliards de dollars). Les ventes de vin et de spiritueux viennent en tête des produits les plus exportés, enregistrant un excédent commercial de 31 milliards de francs en 1997 (5,1 milliards de dollars) ; suivent les céréales (25 milliards de francs, soit 4 milliards de dollars) et les produits laitiers avec un solde excédentaire de 13 milliards de francs (2 milliards de dollars).

Vers de nouvelles exigences

La réussite de l'agriculture française résulte pour une part de la Politique agricole commune (PAC) européenne, qui assure un large soutien à la production et contribue à la modernisation des campagnes par le financement de divers aménagements comme le drainage ou la construction de chemins ruraux. La progression rapide des rendements a conduit, comme dans la plupart des autres pays européens, à l'existence de larges excédents en dépit des mesures de régularisation adoptées depuis une vingtaine d'années. C'est pourquoi, depuis sa dernière réforme de 1992, la Politique agricole commune s'est orientée vers une baisse des prix garantis pour les rapprocher des cours mondiaux, ceci afin de faciliter les exportations. Elle multiplie par ailleurs les aides en faveur des petits exploitants et encourage le développement d'une agriculture extensive, plus respectueuse de l'environnement. Enfin, pour freiner la désertification de certaines régions rurales, elle prône l'essor de la pluriactivité des exploitants en accordant notamment des aides au reboisement et à la promotion de l'agritourisme. L'agriculteur français de l'an 2000 reste certes avant tout un producteur, mais il est appelé à jouer un rôle sans cesse croissant dans l'équilibre écologique du monde rural.

L'énergie

Bien qu'elle ne dispose que de faibles ressources, la France parvient néanmoins à assurer 51 % de ses besoins énergétiques, contre 24 % en 1973. Ce résultat traduit une indépendance comparable à celle de l'Allemagne et très supérieure à celle de l'Italie et du Japon. L'amélioration de la situation énergétique tient surtout à l'essor de la production d'électricité d'origine nucléaire, qui place aujourd'hui la France au second rang mondial pour ce type d'énergie, derrière les États-Unis. Elle résulte aussi d'une progression ralentie de la consommation. Après avoir doublé tous les dix ans durant les années de forte croissance, celle-ci a vu son essor freiné par les mesures d'économie adoptées depuis 1973 et par le repli des industries grosses consommatrices comme la sidérurgie. La consommation énergétique nationale s'élève à 237 millions de tep (tonnes équivalent-pétrole) en 1997, contre 183 millions en 1973. Si la dépendance reste lourde (50 %), la facture énergétique a cependant diminué. Elle s'élève en 1997 à 85 milliards de francs (14,1 milliards de dollars) contre 187 milliards en 1984, année record.

La consommation
d'énergie primaire
en 1979 et en 1998

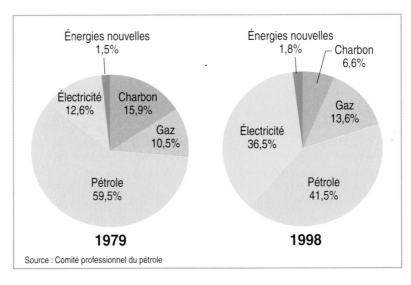

Énergies nouvelles
1,5%

Électricité
12,6%

Charbon
15,9%

Gaz
10,5%

Pétrole
59,5%

1979

Énergies nouvelles
1,8%

Charbon
6,6%

Gaz
13,6%

Électricité
36,5%

Pétrole
41,5%

1998

Source : Comité professionnel du pétrole

La primauté des hydrocarbures

La France est encore très dépendante des hydrocarbures. La production de pétrole, assurée par les gisements des Landes et de Brie, atteint seulement 2,1 millions de tonnes, quand les importations s'élèvent à 83 millions de tonnes de pétrole brut, auxquelles s'ajoutent 25 millions de tonnes de produits raffinés. Les pays du Moyen-Orient assurent encore 38,7 % des importations de pétrole brut, l'Arabie Saoudite 22 %. Cependant, la politique de diversification des fournisseurs permet à la Mer du Nord de figurer en seconde position avec 35 % des approvisionnements.

La production de gaz naturel est concentrée dans le Sud-Ouest. Le gisement de Lacq, après avoir couvert plus de 50 % de la consommation nationale, s'épuise et ne livre plus que 3 milliards de m³. Pour remédier à ce déclin de la production, la France a développé ses achats à l'étranger en multipliant les contrats à long terme pour garantir son approvisionnement. Les importations proviennent de la CEI (33 %), de l'Algérie (22 %), la Norvège (30 %) et les Pays-Bas (15 %).

Le second équipement nucléaire du monde

La production électrique française a été pratiquement multipliée par 10 en 43 ans : elle atteint 490 TWh (térawatts/heure) en 1998 contre 50 en 1955. Elle couvre ainsi plus de 40 % des besoins énergétiques totaux du pays. Électricité de France (EDF) est devenue l'une des premières compagnies mondiales d'électricité. Elle exporte plus de 72 milliards de kWh (kilowatt/heure) chaque année. Ce résultat est le fruit de la politique d'équipement développée depuis 1974. L'électricité nucléaire représente aujourd'hui 75 % de la production électrique totale. EDF dispose de 57 réacteurs totalisant une puissance installée de 60 000 MW (mégawatts). Les centrales sont situées sur la Loire et le Rhône. Le surgénérateur Superphénix de Creys-Malville, fonctionnant au plutonium, est désormais arrêté.

Les centrales thermiques classiques n'assurent plus que 11 % de la production électrique.

La production d'électricité d'origine nucléaire couvre 40 % des besoins énergétiques français : la centrale nucléaire de Dampierre-en-Burly (Loiret)

Quant aux centrales hydrauliques, implantées dans les Alpes, les Pyrénées et le Massif central, elles fournissent 13 % de la production électrique nationale contre 55,7 % en 1960.

L'inexorable déclin du charbon

Le charbon ne représente plus que 6,6 % de la consommation énergétique nationale, contre 22,7 % en 1970. Après avoir culminé à 60 millions de tonnes en 1958, la production n'a cessé de décliner pour atteindre 7 millions en 1997, auxquels s'ajoutent 900 000 tonnes de lignite. Les mines du Nord-Pas-de-Calais sont fermées depuis 1990 et toutes les autres, en Lorraine comme à la périphérie du Massif central, le seront d'ici 2005. Les gisements français souffrant de leur faible productivité, c'est le charbon importé qui assure aujourd'hui l'essentiel de la consommation nécessaire aux centrales électriques ou aux hauts fourneaux. Les États-Unis, l'Australie et l'Afrique du Sud sont les principaux fournisseurs.

Le rôle encore marginal des énergies nouvelles

Les énergies nouvelles n'assurent que 3,6 % de la consommation énergétique, en dépit des travaux de recherche poursuivis en ce domaine. La géothermie permet cependant de chauffer plus de 200 000 logements en région parisienne et dans le Sud-Ouest. L'énergie solaire est également utilisée pour le chauffage des maisons dans les régions méridionales. Quant aux éoliennes et à la biomasse, leur rôle reste également modeste. On assiste cependant depuis quelques années à l'apparition de nouveaux carburants, comme l'éthanol ou le diester, extrait du colza et employé par les autobus de plusieurs grandes villes.

L'industrie

L'industrie française est la seconde d'Europe et la quatrième du monde, derrière celles des États-Unis, du Japon et de l'Allemagne. Le secteur secondaire, y compris le bâtiment et les travaux publics, assure 29 % des emplois, 40 % des investissements et près de 80 % des exportations françaises. Toutefois, bien que l'industrie ait vu sa production quadrupler depuis 1950, elle a perdu près de 1,5 million d'emplois au cours des vingt dernières années. Ce repli témoigne de l'amélioration constante de la productivité, mais aussi de la restructuration du tissu industriel consécutive aux chocs pétroliers et à la mondialisation de l'économie. L'industrie française a connu à cet égard une concentration accélérée de ses entreprises et un essor rapide de ses investissements directs à l'étranger. Les entreprises françaises contrôlent aujourd'hui 15 788 filiales hors de l'hexagone et elles emploient 2 548 000 personnes. Ces investissements permettent aux entreprises nationales d'atteindre une taille critique et d'accéder à de nouveaux marchés. Il en est de même avec la prise de contrôle d'entreprises étrangères. Ainsi, Michelin a acquis Uniroyal et Alcatel-Alsthom le groupe américain ITT. En revanche, les 2 860 entreprises contrôlées par des capitaux étrangers majoritairement originaires des États-Unis, d'Allemagne, de Suisse et du Royaume-Uni, assurent 28 % de la production, 24 % de l'emploi et 30 % du secteur secondaire national. La France se place au troisième rang mondial, derrière les États-Unis et le Royaume-Uni, pour l'accueil des investissements étrangers. Ces derniers sont surtout présents dans l'informatique, la pharmacie, la machine-outil et les instruments de précision.

L'ensemble de l'industrie manufacturière dégage un confortable excédent commercial depuis quelques années. Ce résultat traduit le savoir-faire français dans différents secteurs des industries traditionnelles comme la construction automobile, le matériel ferroviaire, la haute couture et les industries agro-alimentaires, mais aussi le succès des technologies de pointe telles la filière électronucléaire, les télécommunications et la construction aéronautique et spatiale.

Les industries traditionnelles

Longtemps considérées comme le symbole de la puissance économique, les industries de base voient, comme dans les autres pays développés, leur rôle diminuer progressivement. La stagnation de la demande et la concurrence croissante des pays étrangers ont entraîné des réductions sensibles des capacités de production et bouleversé la géographie des implantations.

La sidérurgie, avec une production annuelle de 17 millions de tonnes d'acier, se classe au douzième rang mondial et elle est devancée au sein de l'Union européenne par l'Allemagne, l'Italie et le Royaume-Uni. La production a diminué de plus d'un tiers depuis 1974 et la main-d'œuvre de 70 %. Ce repli traduit les effets conjugués de la crise, de la concurrence d'autres produits tels l'aluminium et les matières plastiques, et de l'apparition de nouveaux grands concurrents, comme les pays de l'Est, le Brésil et la Corée du Sud. Les mesures de réduction des capacités et de restructuration adoptées dans le cadre de l'Union européenne ont permis aux entreprises de moderniser leur équipement, de concentrer leur production sur les sites les plus rentables et de retrouver une santé financière. La production, marquée par l'essor de l'acier à l'oxygène, est dominée par le groupe Usinor-Sacilor, qui se classe au quatrième rang mondial. La production d'acier est désormais assurée pour plus de 45 % par la région du Nord-Pas-de-Calais, et notamment par le grand pôle sidérurgique sur l'eau de Dunkerque, qui

Démoulage de plaques en fonderie dans l'usine d'aluminium du groupe Péchiney, à Dunkerque (Nord)

a supplanté les anciens foyers de l'intérieur. De même, en Lorraine, la production se concentre sur la vallée de la Moselle, comme à Gandrange, au sud de Thionville. À ces régions s'ajoutent des centres dispersés, tels Fos-sur-mer, près de Marseille, ou Ugine dans les Alpes.

La métallurgie de l'aluminium, implantée à l'origine dans les Alpes et les Pyrénées à proximité des centrales hydroélectriques, s'est déplacée vers des sites portuaires plus aptes à réceptionner la bauxite importée. Pechiney, qui possède aussi plusieurs usines dans le monde, notamment en Australie, aux États-Unis et en Grèce, domine la production et figure au troisième rang mondial de la branche. Privatisée fin 1995, l'entreprise dispose à Dunkerque, près de la centrale nucléaire de Gravelines, d'une usine ultramoderne. Elle valorise sa production par la fabrication de produits finis et elle a ainsi pris le contrôle, en 1988, du grand groupe américain d'emballage, *American Can*.

Parmi les industries de première génération, celles du **textile et de l'habillement** emploient encore 254 000 personnes et totalisent plus de 170 milliards de francs (28 milliards de dollars) de chiffre d'affaires. Bien qu'elles exportent le tiers de leur production, ces industries enregistrent un déficit commercial de 26 milliards de francs (4,3 milliards de dollars) en 1997 et, surtout, elles ont perdu plus de 250 000 emplois depuis 1974. Elles souffrent de la faible progression de la demande intérieure et surtout d'une concurrence internationale de plus en plus pressante. Celle-ci émane de l'Italie et de l'Allemagne, et surtout de l'Europe de l'Est, du Bassin méditerranéen et du Sud-Est asiatique. Ces dernières régions, qui offrent des coûts de production très inférieurs aux tarifs français, attirent de plus en plus les industriels de l'hexagone qui y multiplient les délocalisations.

En amont, **l'industrie textile** proprement dite, notamment vouée à la filature, au tissage, à l'impression et à la fabrication de tapis et de moquettes, reste une branche capitalistique. Elle est dominée par de grandes entreprises comme Chargeurs-Textiles, premier groupe mondial pour le commerce de la laine, et DMC, société mulhousienne spécialisée dans le coton. Ces entreprises travaillent des matières premières importées, comme le coton et la laine, mais surtout des fibres chimiques, en particulier des fibres synthétiques. S'ajoutent à ces grands groupes des PME familiales. Pour faire face à la concurrence, les entreprises textiles ont engagé un processus de concentration financière et technique et massivement investi dans la modernisation de l'équipement pour accroître leur productivité. Les industries textiles restent souvent localisées sur leur implantation initiale. Ainsi, Roubaix-Tourcoing et Armentières privilégient toujours la filature et le tissage de la laine et du coton, Mulhouse reste spécialisée dans le coton et l'impression sur étoffes, la région lyonnaise règne sur la soie et les fibres synthétiques et Troyes sur la bonneterie.

En aval, l'habillement demeure, en revanche, une industrie de main-d'œuvre, morcelée entre de nombreuses PME plus ou moins spécialisées. L'habillement est concentré dans les grandes agglomérations des régions Nord-Pas-de-Calais, Rhône-Alpes et Ile-de-France. Pour améliorer leur compétitivité, les entreprises ont de plus en plus recours à des techniques de pointe comme le tracé des pièces de tissu par ordinateur et la découpe des tissus par laser ou jet d'eau à haute pression, mais elles multiplient aussi les délocalisations. Elles s'appuient enfin sur les accords conclus entre les pays développés et les principaux exportateurs du tiers monde dans le cadre des Accords multifibres

Haute couture :
essayage d'un modèle
chez Christian Dior

(AMF). Ces accords, qui doivent être progressivement démantelés dans le cadre de l'Organisation mondiale du commerce (OMC), permettent de limiter momentanément les importations de produits à bas prix. D'autres entreprises s'appuient sur des circuits courts, adaptés aux changements rapides de la mode. C'est le cas dans le quartier du Sentier à Paris.

Comme le textile, **les industries du cuir** doivent affronter la concurrence des pays à bas salaires, notamment pour les produits de bas de gamme. La production française de chaussures a chuté d'un tiers depuis 1970 et la ganterie a perdu neuf dixièmes de ses effectifs en 25 ans. Des centres spécialisés comme Romans et Fougères ont été durement affectés par ce repli.

Le pont de Normandie, construit par les groupes français Bouygues et Campenon-Bernard et par une société danoise, permet de franchir l'estuaire de la Seine ; sa travée centrale s'étire sur 856 mètres et culmine à 52 mètres au-dessus de la Seine

Le bâtiment et les travaux publics emploient directement 1,4 million de personnes et fournissent presque autant d'emplois induits. Excellent baromètre de la conjoncture économique, ce secteur a connu ces dernières années de nombreuses pertes d'emplois, mais il enregistre cependant une légère reprise. Il représente un chiffre d'affaires de près de 800 milliards de francs (133,3 milliards de dollars). **Les travaux publics** constituent le domaine privilégié des grandes entreprises qui ont connu un ample mouvement de concentration depuis deux décennies. Les plus importantes sont Bouygues, la SGE (Société

Générale d'Entreprise), Dumez-GTM, Eiffage, Spie-Batignolles et Sogea. Ces sociétés s'appuient sur des techniques de plus en plus sophistiquées, du béton armé précontraint aux ponts à haubans en passant par les plates-formes off-shore. Elles opèrent dans le cadre national pour la construction des autoroutes, du Stade de France, du pont de Normandie ou du tunnel de Puymorens. Elles sont également très actives hors de France où elles se heurtent cependant à la concurrence de groupes étrangers, notamment ceux des nouveaux pays industrialisés. La Lyonnaise des Eaux et la Générale des Eaux, aujourd'hui dénommée Vivendi, ont conclu de nombreux contrats à l'étranger pour la mise en place des systèmes de distribution et de traitement des eaux dans de grandes métropoles comme Buenos Aires et Pékin.

Le bâtiment, au contraire, présente une structure très morcelée, avec 30 000 petites et moyennes entreprises. Pour améliorer leur productivité, ces sociétés industrialisent les procédés de construction, notamment pour les charpentes et les menuiseries. L'activité de ce secteur est étroitement liée aux mesures publiques adoptées en faveur de la construction de logements, sous formes d'aides diverses et de prêts bonifiés, au total quelque 120 milliards de francs (20 milliards de dollars) par an. Or, les mises en chantier ont connu un net déclin depuis une vingtaine d'années, passant de 556 000 en 1973 à près de 300 000 en 1997. Il est vrai que la pression démographique est aujourd'hui moins forte.

Les biens d'équipement

La chaîne de fabrication
automatisée de la Renault
Scénic : soudage
de la caisse

Les industries de biens d'équipement, y compris la construction automobile, tiennent une place essentielle dans le tissu industriel français. Elles représentent un chiffre d'affaires de plus de 1 200 milliards de francs (200 milliards de dollars) et emploient 1,5 million de salariés. Si plusieurs branches, comme la construction navale, la machine-outil, la motocyclette et la bicyclette ont connu un net repli devant la concurrence étrangère, d'autres manifestent un réel dynamisme.

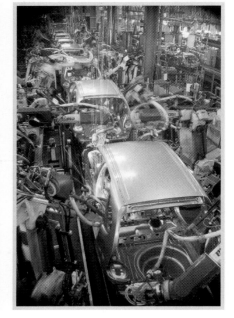

C'est notamment le cas de la **construction automobile** qui a enregistré en 1997 un excédent commercial de près de 31 milliards de francs (5 milliards de dollars). La France est le troisième exportateur mondial de voitures particulières, avec une production de 3,4 millions de voitures, et fabrique plus de 500 000 véhicules utilitaires. Elle se classe ainsi au quatrième rang mondial des constructeurs. La branche automobile emploie directement plus de 350 000 personnes auxquelles s'ajoutent plus de 2,6 millions d'emplois induits, ce qui lui confère une place de choix dans l'économie nationale. Renault et le groupe privé PSA, qui contrôle les marques Peugeot et Citroën, assurent la quasi-totalité de la production. Les équipementiers ont connu une importante concentration d'où émergent quelques groupes importants tels Michelin, leader mondial des pneumatiques après le rachat d'Uniroyal, Valéo, spécialisé dans les équipements électriques, ou encore Epéda-Bertrand Faure, qui fabrique les sièges.

Les constructeurs français exportent plus de 60 % de leur production, mais ils ont dû céder 40 % du marché intérieur à leurs concurrents, en particulier à l'Allemagne et à l'Italie. De plus, dans le cadre d'un accord conclu entre l'Union européenne et le Japon, l'importation des voitures nipponnes se libère à compter de 1999. Afin de renforcer leur compétitivité, les constructeurs français ont investi massivement dans la robotisation, ce qui a conduit à une réduction importante des effectifs. Ils ont par ailleurs multiplié les accords de coopération technique, adopté la stratégie des flux tendus et développé leur présence sur les marchés extérieurs, notamment en Espagne, au Portugal et au Brésil.

La construction navale a notablement réduit ses activités, victime de la surcapacité de la flotte mondiale et de la concurrence des chantiers asiatiques. Alors qu'elle figurait encore aux premiers rangs dans les années soixante-dix, elle joue aujourd'hui un rôle marginal. Quelques sites de production tels les Chantiers de l'Atlantique de Saint-Nazaire et les Ateliers et Chantiers du Havre se sont spécialisés dans la construction de grands paquebots de croisière et de méthaniers. Par ailleurs, la France est l'un des premiers constructeurs du monde de bateaux de plaisance avec les chantiers vendéens Bénéteau et Jeanneau.

La France est l'un des premiers constructeurs mondiaux de bateaux de plaisance : chantier naval à Lorient (Morbihan)

La chimie place la France au quatrième rang mondial. Son chiffre d'affaires annuel dépasse les 430 milliards de francs (71 milliards de dollars) et elle emploie 250 000 personnes. La chimie de base repose sur la transformation de matières premières nationales, comme la potasse d'Alsace, le soufre de Lacq et le sel de Lorraine et de Camargue, ou sur le traitement de produits importés, ce qui explique la concentration d'une partie des activités dans les ports. La pétrochimie, dominée par la Compagnie française des pétroles (CFP-Total) et Elf-Aquitaine, s'est substituée à l'ancienne carbochimie. Orkem, l'ancienne filiale des Charbonnages de France, Atochem, du groupe Elf, Rhône-Poulenc et Air liquide, leader mondial des gaz industriels implanté dans plus de 50 pays, dominent la branche. Vouée en grande partie à la fabrication d'engrais, de matières plastiques et de fibres synthétiques, la chimie de base connaît cependant une croissance faible.

En revanche, **la parachimie et la pharmacie** sont très dynamiques et dégagent de larges excédents commerciaux (plus de 50 milliards de francs, soit 8,3 milliards de dollars). Mobilisant de lourds investissements et une recherche coûteuse, elles sont dominées par de grands groupes. Dans la parachimie, c'est le cas des géants étrangers tel Procter et Gamble, Unilever et Colgate-Palmolive pour les lessives et les détergents, alors que la firme nationale L'Oréal vient en tête pour les produits de beauté, pour lesquels on peut aussi citer les grands parfumeurs tels Saint-Laurent et Chanel. Dans la pharmacie, les laboratoires connaissent une forte concentration au profit des grands groupes comme Rhône-Poulenc, qui a pris le contrôle de l'entreprise américaine Rorer et figure au septième rang mondial en ce domaine. Synthélabo, qui appartient au groupe L'Oréal, a absorbé les laboratoires Delagrange et Delalande. Sanofi, filiale d'Elf-Aquitaine, est un autre grand de la branche.

Les industries de pointe

Tributaires de progrès techniques très rapides, mais aussi de la recherche et d'un personnel hautement qualifié, les industries de pointe assurent 20 % des emplois industriels et des exportations. La France constitue l'un des pays les plus performants dans la construction aéronautique et spatiale ainsi que dans les industries de l'armement. Pour faire face à une concurrence internationale accrue et réduire les coûts de recherche et de production, les entreprises françaises se sont rapprochées de leurs homologues. Ainsi, le programme Airbus est issu d'une coopération entre la France, l'Allemagne, le Royaume-Uni et l'Espagne. Par ailleurs, l'Aérospatiale est associée à l'Italien Alenia et à British Aerospace dans l'ATR, avion de transport régional.

Principalement implantée dans la région parisienne, qui rassemble près de 40 % des emplois, et dans le Sud-Ouest, notamment à Toulouse et à Bordeaux, **l'industrie aérospatiale** emploie près de 100 000 personnes et exporte près de la moitié de sa production. Elle comprend de nombreuses entreprises à capitaux d'État comme l'Aérospatiale et la Snecma. Alors qu'Airbus et ATR fournissent des avions civils, Dassault-Industrie est spécialisée dans la fourniture d'appareils militaires, tels les Mirage et le Rafale, et d'avions d'affaires comme le Falcon. La Snecma, associée à l'Américain General Electric, livre des réacteurs et des moteurs.

L'industrie spatiale s'est également développée dans le cadre d'une coopération internationale regroupant une quinzaine d'États dont certains, comme la Norvège et la Suisse,

Lancement réussi de la fusée Ariane 5 depuis le centre de Kourou, en Guyane, octobre 1997

n'appartiennent pas à l'Union européenne. C'est notamment le fait du programme Arianespace qui dispose d'un plan de charge très dense pour les prochaines années, avec Ariane 5, qui permet de placer en orbite une charge de 6 tonnes, contre 4 tonnes pour Ariane 4. Le succès d'Ariane tient à la fiabilité des lanceurs qui permet d'attirer de nombreux clients étrangers en dépit de la concurrence des États-Unis, de la Russie et, plus récemment, de la Chine. Les fusées sont tirées depuis le centre de Kourou, en Guyane. La France est également présente dans le domaine des satellites de télécommunications et d'observation, tels SPOT ou Hélios. Ces satellites sont construits par Matra Espace, Alcatel Espace et Aérospatiale Espace.

Les industries électriques et électroniques sont caractérisées par une grande diversité des productions. Elles sont aussi dominées par de grandes entreprises et dépendent largement des commandes publiques. Alcatel-Alsthom, qui a réalisé de nombreuses acquisitions depuis dix ans, demeure la première entreprise mondiale dans les télécommunications. Alsthom, associée à la société britannique GEC, est, outre le matériel ferroviaire (TGV), spécialisée dans les équipements pour centrales électriques. Elle occupe ainsi le premier rang mondial pour les générateurs de turbines à cycle combiné. Thomson couvre une large gamme de productions, de l'électronique appliquée à la défense, avec Thomson-CSF, aux biens d'équipement ménager et au matériel grand public avec Thomson Multimédia. Schneider tient une place dominante dans le secteur de l'électromécanique et Legrand est le leader mondial de l'appareillage électrique.

Si la France est bien placée dans les télécommunications et la télématique, notamment avec France Télécom, les résultats sont moins probants dans l'informatique. Certes, l'industrie du logiciel et surtout du service, avec Cap Gemini-Sogeti, est performante, mais la France dépend largement de l'étranger pour la fabrication des micro-processeurs, souffrant de la concurrence des États-Unis et du Japon dont les entreprises bénéficient d'un marché intérieur plus étendu. SGS-Thomson se classe certes au troisième rang européen des fabricants de puces électroniques, mais avec moins de 3 % de la production mondiale. Si la filière dégage des excédents commerciaux pour le matériel électrique et les télécommunications, ceux-ci ne compensent pas les déficits enregistrés dans l'informatique ou dans l'électronique grand public.

Les industries d'armement connaissent depuis quelques années un net repli, à la suite de la fin de la guerre froide et des réductions du budget de la défense. Elles placent la France au cinquième rang mondial des exportateurs et l'excédent commercial dépasse en moyenne les 30 milliards de francs (5 milliards de dollars). Il s'agit d'une industrie stratégique, de haute technologie et dépendant largement de l'État qui décide des programmes d'équipement par le biais de la Délégation générale à l'armement et contrôle les exportations. Les grandes entreprises dominent la production. C'est le cas de GIAT-Industries pour les armements terrestres, de Dassault et de l'Aérospatiale pour les avions, de l'Aérospatiale, de Thomson-CSF et de Matra pour les missiles. Pour lutter contre la surcapacité de production et les coûts élevés de certains projets, les entreprises françaises se regroupent – exemple de la fusion intervenue en 1998 entre Aérospatiale et Matra Hautes Technologies – et multiplient les accords avec leurs homologues européennes, comme Eurocopter pour la production d'un hélicoptère de combat. La majeure partie de l'industrie d'armement est concentrée en Ile-de-France, en Bretagne, dans le Sud-Ouest et la région Provence-Alpes-Côte d'Azur.

Les bio-industries constituent un enjeu de taille. Que ce soit dans le domaine des fermentations, des arômes, du génie génétique utilisé notamment en agriculture pour la mise au point de nouvelles semences, la France est bien placée. Les activités sont très variées et touchent bien des branches économiques : l'innovation pharmaceutique

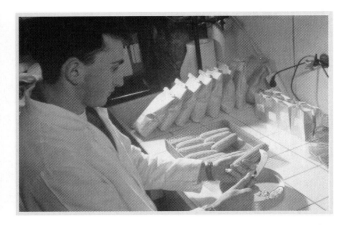

avec les antibiotiques, le secteur agro-alimentaire avec le génie enzématique utilisé pour l'industrie laitière, l'horticulture avec la culture « in vitro » déjà largement utilisée par le rosiériste Delbard, l'énergie et les industries de l'environnement avec la production de diester ou d'éthanol. Ainsi, les entreprises industrielles opérant sur le « marché vert » ou éco-industries enregistrent un chiffre d'affaires de 30 milliards de francs (5 milliards de dol-

À l'INRA (Gif-sur-Yvette, Essonne), sélection de semences pour croisement génétique et amélioration des espèces de maïs

lars). Le traitement de l'eau constitue le premier domaine d'intervention, suivent le traitement de l'air et les déchets. De nombreux organismes spécialisés sont impliqués dans la recherche, tels l'Inserm, l'INRA et l'Institut Pasteur qui bénéficient d'aides de l'État, mais aussi des groupes industriels : des entreprises de l'agro-alimentaire comme BSN, chimiques comme Rhône-Poulenc et Lafarge-Coppée, pétrolières comme Elf-Sanofi ou encore pharmaceutiques comme Roussel-UCLAF.

Une nouvelle carte industrielle

L'industrie demeure très inégalement répartie sur le territoire. Il existe toujours une nette opposition entre une France située au Nord-Est d'une ligne Le Havre-Marseille et une France du Sud-Ouest où l'industrialisation, plus récente, demeure encore discrète. Cette opposition, très marquée dans les années cinquante, s'estompe cependant assez rapidement. En effet, la politique de décentralisation industrielle conduite dans les décennies soixante et soixante-dix a contribué à la diffusion de l'industrie dans les régions de l'Ouest, à l'image de la construction automobile à Caen, Rennes et Le Mans et des industries électriques et électroniques en Bretagne du nord. La périphérie du Bassin parisien, notamment les régions Centre et Bourgogne, ont également été de grandes bénéficiaires de ces mesures. Au total, plus d'un million d'emplois ont été créés en province et le tiers des emplois industriels se situe désormais au sud-ouest d'une ligne Le Havre-Marseille, alors que la région parisienne n'en concentre plus que 20 % (contre 25 % en 1950). Sans aller jusqu'à l'image d'une « France inverse », on peut noter une meilleure répartition de la fonction industrielle au sein de l'hexagone, d'autant que les évolutions disparates des branches favorisent les reclassements régionaux.

Les vieilles régions industrielles, appuyées sur des industries de première ou seconde génération, comme le Nord et la Lorraine, sont en crise. L'emploi dans le secteur secondaire diminue rapidement et les friches industrielles se multiplient. Ces anciens foyers d'accueil sont désormais devenus des terres d'émigration. Les autres régions industrielles, comme la région parisienne et Rhône-Alpes, ont été moins touchées par la crise. Elles le doivent à un tissu industriel plus diversifié, à la présence d'industries de pointe et d'un réseau de PME performantes. Il en est de même de l'Alsace qui bénéficie du marché allemand proche. Le dynamisme industriel est aujourd'hui le fait des régions méridionales. De nouveaux pôles industriels se sont développés à Sophia-Antipolis, première technopôle française, à Montpellier et à Toulouse. Ces villes, qui n'ont pas à supporter le poids de la reconversion, profitent en outre d'une forte attractivité liée à un environnement privilégié, notamment sur le plan climatique.

Les services

Le secteur tertiaire fournit désormais 70 % du PIB et 65 % des emplois. Qu'il s'agisse des services non marchands assurés par l'administration, la santé ou les agents des collectivités locales, ou encore des services marchands, comme l'hôtellerie, la restauration, le commerce ou les banques, le secteur reste le grand pourvoyeur d'emplois au moment où s'intensifie la lutte contre le chômage. Cependant, depuis quelques années, les gains de productivité considérables, enregistrés notamment grâce à l'informatisation, contribuent à diminuer les offres.

Les banques et les assurances

Le système bancaire occupe une place importante dans l'économie française. Les activités bancaires contribuent pour près de 4 % au PIB, soit une part comparable à celles des secteurs des transports, de l'énergie ou encore de l'agriculture, de la sylviculture et de la pêche. Les principaux groupes bancaires comptent parmi les plus grandes entreprises françaises par les effectifs qu'ils emploient (400 000 salariés) ou par leur capitalisation boursière. Le développement du système bancaire s'apprécie également par le nombre total des établissements de crédit (1 400) et par celui des guichets bancaires de plein exercice installés en France, soit 25 500 environ, non compris les 17 000 bureaux du réseau de La Poste.

Le secteur bancaire a connu de grands bouleversements depuis le début des années soixante. L'opposition classique entre banques de dépôts et banques d'affaires s'est estompée à la suite des investissements des premières dans le monde industriel et de la possibilité pour les secondes de mettre en place un réseau d'agences. Les grandes banques comme le Crédit Lyonnais, la BNP et la Société Générale disposent d'un vaste réseau qui couvre tout le pays et s'étend même hors de France ; plus de 1 000 établissements français sont présents dans 139 pays étrangers. Les anciennes banques d'affaires – Paribas et Suez – privilégient toujours les investissements industriels et contrôlent bon nombre d'entreprises françaises ou étrangères, dans le cadre de participations croisées dessinant un écheveau complexe. À ces établissements s'ajoutent ceux qui s'appuient sur des réseaux régionaux comme les Banques Populaires et des établissements à vocation régionale. Il faut y ajouter le réseau des Caisses d'épargne et des institutions spécialisées tels le Crédit National et le Crédit Foncier de France. Les banques ont enregistré une internationalisation croissante de leurs activités à la faveur de la mondialisation des échanges, de la volonté de la France de renforcer le poids financier de Paris et de la libre circulation des capitaux au sein de la Communauté européenne, effective depuis le

Le service de banque à distance de la Banque nationale de Paris (BNP)

1er juillet 1990. Pour améliorer leur compétitivité, elles ont recouru massivement à l'informatisation de leurs services et favorisé l'utilisation des cartes de paiement au détriment des chèques, plus coûteux à gérer. Elles ont également augmenté leurs fonds propres pour conforter leur sécurité. Certaines se sont rapprochées des compagnies d'assurances, comme le soulignent les participations croisées de la BNP et de l'UAP et la prise de contrôle du CIC par le GAN. Elles ont également multiplié les participations dans le monde industriel. Enfin, plusieurs banques ont créé des filiales spécialisées dans l'assurance-vie pour diversifier leurs activités et élargir leur clientèle. La rénovation des structures s'est accélérée à partir de 1985. En effet, la modernisation du système bancaire réalisée par la loi du 24 janvier 1984, jointe au mouvement général de libéralisation et de déréglementation des activités bancaires et financières, a été à l'origine d'un renforcement de la concurrence. L'effort d'adaptation qui en est résulté est appelé à se poursuivre avec l'achèvement de l'intégration européenne, le passage à la monnaie unique (euro) et la mondialisation de l'économie.

Dans le cadre de l'Union économique et monétaire, la France dispose désormais d'une banque centrale indépendante. Depuis sa création en 1800, à l'initiative de Napoléon Bonaparte, la Banque de France avait connu quatre réformes importantes de ses structures de décision. La loi du 24 juillet 1936 modifia son organisation pour renforcer l'autorité des pouvoirs publics sur l'Institut d'émission. Cette réforme fut le prélude à la nationalisation de la banque centrale, qui intervint après la Libération, en décembre 1945. Enfin, en 1973, un cadre modernisé fut donné à l'Institut pour lui permettre de s'adapter aux évolutions des techniques financières et du crédit. En 1993, la Banque de France est devenue indépendante. Jusqu'alors, elle avait le rôle de banque de l'État. Désormais, son statut d'indépendance lui interdit formellement d'autoriser des découverts ou d'accorder tout autre type de crédit au Trésor public ou à tout autre organisme ou entreprise publics ; elle continue à tenir le compte courant du Trésor public, à participer à la gestion de la dette publique, à tenir les comptes courants de bons du Trésor. Elle établit également la balance des paiements pour le compte de l'État.

La place financière de Paris est un marché unifié des capitaux, allant du jour le jour au plus long terme et accessible à tous les émetteurs. Le marché des actions et le marché obligataire figurent parmi les premiers marchés du monde. La place de Paris est dotée d'un marché actif de produits dérivés, tant sur le gré à gré que sur les marchés organisés : le MATIF (Marché à terme international de France) et le MONEP (Marché des options négociables à Paris). Elle ne connaît aucun obstacle technique, fiscal ou réglementaire aux mouvements internationaux de titres et de capitaux et s'est considérablement modernisée ces dernières années. Elle offre à l'ensemble des investisseurs internationaux une gamme diversifiée de marchés et de produits, dans un contexte de parfaite sécurité et de transparence. La place de Paris se situe au cinquième rang mondial, derrière celles de New York, de Tokyo, de Londres et de Francfort, pour la capitalisation boursière (4 098 milliards de francs en 1998, soit 673 milliards de dollars). La cote de la Bourse de Paris reflète la structure de l'économie française dans sa diversité sectorielle et géographique. Les quarante principales capitalisations boursières composent l'indice CAC 40, la Bourse de Paris ayant aussi développé de nouveaux indices plus larges, incluant des valeurs moyennes. Depuis 1983, les PME à fort potentiel de croissance ont accès au second marché. En 1996 a été créé le Nouveau marché, destiné lui aussi à assurer un meilleur développement aux PME. Le marché obligataire est le premier compartiment du marché financier français et il se classe au troisième rang mondial.

L'assurance française se situe au quatrième rang mondial avec un chiffre d'affaires dépassant les 1 050 milliards de francs (175 milliards de dollars). Le secteur de l'assurance compte près de 600 entreprises françaises et emploie 146 000 personnes. La branche est dominée par de grandes compagnies comme le GAN, l'UAP, les AGF et Axa. S'y ajoutent de nombreuses mutuelles telles que la GMF (Garantie mutuelle des fonctionnaires) ou la MAIF (Mutuelle assurances des instituteurs de France). Outre Paris, qui concentre la majeure partie de l'activité, Niort et Le Mans, où siègent d'importantes mutuelles, sont des centres spécialisés. Les compagnies d'assurances, propriétaires de nombreux biens immobiliers, diversifient leurs activités pour améliorer leur rentabilité. Elles prennent des participations industrielles, multiplient les investissements à l'étranger pour renforcer leur poids et diversifient également leurs produits, notamment par le biais des fonds de retraite par capitalisation. La libéralisation des services dans le cadre européen a également entraîné de grands bouleversements stratégiques et structurels. Par ailleurs, les concentrations s'accélèrent, qu'elles se fassent dans le cadre national, comme la prise de contrôle de Victoire par l'UAP et la banque Suez, ou dans le cadre européen, avec la prise de parts d'UAP dans la compagnie britannique Sun Life et l'entreprise espagnole Gesa.

Grandes surfaces et petits commerces

La distribution, qui emploie plus de 2,5 millions de personnes, a connu depuis trente ans un grand bouleversement de ses circuits et de ses méthodes de vente, avec l'essor du commerce intégré. Ce dernier, apparu au XIXe siècle avec les Grands magasins tels le

Bon Marché et la Samaritaine, situés au cœur de Paris, a connu un nouvel essor au lendemain de la seconde guerre mondiale, avec l'apparition des Prisunic et autres Monoprix, puis une véritable explosion à partir des années soixante avec l'émergence des magasins à grande surface développant le libre-service. Avec 1 120 hypermarchés (soit un pour 52 000 habitants) et 7 600 supermarchés, la France est l'un des pays du monde où le grand commerce est le plus développé. Il assure aujourd'hui plus de 60 % des produits alimentaires et 30 % des produits non alimentaires. Des groupes spécialisés tels Carrefour, Auchan et Promodès dominent le secteur, aux côtés des centres Leclerc. Ces groupes s'appuient sur de puissantes centrales d'achat imposant leurs prix aux industriels et ils se livrent une âpre concurrence, multipliant les campagnes publici-

Un centre commercial Leclerc à Ibos (Hautes-Pyrénées) : outre un hypermarché, il accueille un centre culturel avec cinéma, théâtre et lieu d'exposition

taires. Ils s'implantent à l'étranger, comme Carrefour et Auchan en Espagne, en Asie et en Amérique latine et Promodès en Allemagne. Les magasins à grande surface, après avoir privilégié le domaine alimentaire, ont rapidement diversifié leur offre vers d'autres secteurs (billeterie de spectacle, agences de voyages...). Des commerces spécialisés sont apparus dans la hi-fi et l'électro-ménager avec Darty ou le bricolage avec Castorama ou Leroy Merlin. Exigeant de vastes espaces, les hypermarchés sont implantés à la périphérie des grandes agglomérations ou dans les centres commerciaux. Ces centres regroupent des commerces spécialisés et de nombreux services : cinémas, pharmacie, Poste...

Les petits commerces connaissent en revanche une baisse rapide de leur activité et l'adoption d'une législation protectrice, limitant l'ouverture des magasins à grande surface, n'a pas suffi à freiner leur déclin. Très touchés en milieu rural, ils résistent mieux dans les villes, surtout lorsqu'ils sont spécialisés ou lorsqu'ils jouent le rôle de commerces de dépannage.

D'autres formes de distribution se sont développées, comme la vente par correspondance. Quelques groupes dominent ce secteur très concentré : La Redoute, la CAMIF et les Trois Suisses. Ces sociétés recourent de plus en plus au téléphone, au Minitel, et à Internet et s'appuient sur un traitement rapide des commandes. Ici aussi l'internationalisation se développe, comme le montrent les entreprises allemandes Neckermann et Quelle qui réussissent une belle percée sur le marché français, alors que La Redoute développe ses activités en Italie. Plus récemment, se sont multipliés les magasins d'usines et les centres de maxidiscompte qui misent sur des marges extrêmement réduites pour drainer la clientèle.

Le tourisme

Avec plus de 60 milliards de francs d'excédent en 1997 (10 milliards de dollars) et la venue de 67 millions de touristes étrangers, la France est le premier pays visité au monde. Les Européens, avec 87 % des arrivées, et en particulier les Allemands et les Britanniques, sont les étrangers les plus nombreux à fréquenter l'hexagone. S'y ajoutent plus de 35 millions de nationaux. Berceau d'un tourisme aristocratique et bourgeois au XIXe siècle, la France connaît depuis trois décennies l'avènement d'un tourisme de masse.

Paris accueille plus de 10 millions de touristes étrangers chaque année ; file d'attente pour entrer au musée du Louvre

Pour mobiliser de tels flux, la France dispose de solides atouts qui tiennent surtout à la diversité de ses reliefs et de ses paysages et à son remarquable patrimoine culturel, comme en témoignent ses 12 000 monuments classés et 1 200 musées. Bien située et remarquablement desservie par les réseaux de communication, elle possède aussi une grande capacité d'hébergement, avec plus de 17 millions de lits. L'hôtellerie recense près de 45 000 établissements totalisant plus d'un million de chambres. Le pays dispose aussi de 8 200 campings, de 830 villages de vacances, de plus de 42 000 gîtes ruraux et de 2 820 000 résidences secondaires. L'hôtellerie française connaît un dynamisme remarquable, illustré par la puissance des chaînes intégrées comme le groupe Accor qui rassemble 1 010 hôtels sur le sol national, auxquels s'ajoutent plus de 1 300 établissements à l'étranger. Le tourisme est désormais devenu un puissant moteur économique. Il fournit plus de 1,5 million d'emplois directs ou induits et la consommation touristique totale dépasse 750 milliards de francs (125 milliards de dollars). Le tourisme a aussi dynamisé certaines régions littorales comme le Languedoc et les Landes, freiné le dépeuplement des régions de montagne, stimulé le bâtiment et les travaux publics ainsi que les industries spécialisées comme la plaisance et l'habillement et les activités culturelles.

Le littoral draine près de la moitié de la clientèle. Aux stations balnéaires anciennes comme Deauville, Arcachon et Biarritz s'ajoutent des aménagements plus récents, en particulier sur le littoral languedocien et en Aquitaine. La région Provence-Alpes-Côte d'Azur figure toujours en tête pour la fréquentation et le Languedoc-Roussillon et la Corse complètent la domination des littoraux méditerranéens. Sur la façade atlantique, la Bretagne devance l'Aquitaine et la Vendée, plus tard venues au tourisme de masse. Le tourisme montagnard, né à Chamonix, a connu un rapide essor après la guerre, profitant de la diversification des activités et de l'organisation des Jeux Olympiques à Grenoble en 1968 et à Albertville en 1992. La France possède 18 % des remontées mécaniques du monde. Les Alpes du Nord concentrent l'essentiel de la clientèle. Plus élevées, mieux enneigées et remarquablement équipées, elles regroupent les grandes stations comme Chamonix, Courchevel, Les Arcs et Tignes. Les Alpes du Sud, avec des stations comme Serre-Chevalier, Vars et Isola 2 000, confortent la suprématie du massif alpin. Moins élevées et plus éloignées des grands centres émetteurs, les autres montagnes sont moins fréquentées. Les Pyrénées comptent surtout sur leurs stations thermales, comme Cauterets et Luchon, et leurs stations de ski telles La Mongie et Superbagnères. Le Massif central s'appuie avant tout sur ses volcans et ses nombreuses stations thermales. Quant au Jura et aux Vosges, ils profitent de la proximité des clientèles suisse et allemande. Le tourisme vert a connu un grand essor dans les années soixante et soixante-dix, profitant de la montée des mouvements écologistes et de prix compétitifs. Il permet aux agriculteurs de diversifier leurs ressources par l'aménagement de gîtes ruraux, de chambres d'hôtes et de campings à la ferme. Particulièrement actif dans la région Rhône-Alpes et dans le Massif central, il contribue à redonner une animation saisonnière à de nombreux villages dépeuplés.

Le tourisme de circuit privilégie surtout la région parisienne et le Val de Loire. La capitale, qui reçoit plus de 10 millions d'étrangers chaque année, compte sur un patrimoine architectural exceptionnel, sur sa fonction intellectuelle et artistique et sur un tourisme d'affaires actif, qui dégage un chiffre d'affaires de plus de 20 milliards de francs (3,3 milliards de dollars) par an. Paris est d'ailleurs le premier centre européen de congrès. Quant au Val de Loire, il doit son succès à la présence de ses nombreux châteaux dont ceux de Chambord, de Chenonceaux et d'Azay-le-Rideau sont les plus beaux fleurons.

Les transports

Les transports jouent un rôle essentiel dans le développement économique et la maîtrise du territoire. La France bénéficie en ce domaine de l'un des réseaux les plus denses et les plus performants du monde, avec 146 km de routes et 6,2 km de voies ferrées pour 100 km². Les réseaux intérieurs et internationaux sont centrés sur Paris, renforçant ainsi le poids de la capitale dans l'organisation du territoire. Longtemps construits dans une perspective d'intégration nationale, les réseaux sont désormais conçus en fonction de l'espace européen. D'ailleurs, la mise en place du grand marché européen s'accompagne d'une harmonisation progressive des techniques et des législations et d'une libéralisation des transports dans le cadre communautaire.

Un réseau routier performant

Avec plus de 965 000 km de routes, la France figure au premier rang européen. Le réseau autoroutier a fait l'objet de nombreuses réalisations depuis 1965, ce qui lui a permis d'atteindre plus de 9 000 km. Les liaisons internationales se sont multipliées avec les autoroutes Paris-Lille-Bruxelles, Macon-Genève et Perpignan-Barcelone, et les tunnels routiers du Mont-Blanc (1965), du Fréjus (1980) et du Puymorens (1994). Ralenti durant les années quatre-vingt, le programme autoroutier bénéficie de nouvelles impulsions dans le cadre d'un schéma directeur lancé en 1990, qui portera le réseau à plus de 12 000 km avant 2010.

Forte de la souplesse de sa desserte, de l'essor du parc automobile, qui comprend 25 millions de voitures de tourisme et 3,4 millions de véhicules utilitaires, et de la modernisation des techniques, la route assure aujourd'hui plus de 60 % du trafic intérieur de marchandises, contre 40 % en 1970. Elle assure aussi près de 90 % du trafic de voyageurs, essentiellement dans le cadre d'un transport individuel, bien que les transports en commun connaissent une forte progression, notamment dans le cadre du tourisme.

Le transport routier est assuré par plus de 39 000 entreprises, employant 350 000 salariés. Le secteur est très morcelé. Des groupes spécialisés comme Calberson, filiale de la SNCF, côtoient de très nombreux artisans qui travaillent souvent en sous-traitance, dans le cadre de contrats de tractionnaires. Cette dispersion des entreprises risque de handicaper le transport routier national à l'heure de l'ouverture de l'espace européen. C'est d'ailleurs pourquoi le gouvernement a demandé un délai aux autorités communautaires avant d'ouvrir l'hexagone au cabotage routier.

Rail : l'arme du TGV

Le rail, pourtant longtemps favorisé par les pouvoirs publics, n'assure plus que 20 % du trafic de marchandises, avec 50,5 milliards de tonnes-km. À la concurrence de la route s'ajoute le déclin du transport des pondéreux, notamment du charbon, du minerai de fer et des hydrocarbures. Le trafic est concentré dans le quart nord-est du pays et sur l'axe Paris-Lyon-Méditerranée. Le trafic des voyageurs résiste mieux, grâce à la densité des flux dans la banlieue parisienne et à la mise en service des lignes de TGV

Sud-Est et Atlantique. La rapidité, la ponctualité et la sécurité constituent ici des atouts précieux pour le rail qui permet, en outre, un accès direct au centre des villes. Malgré ces atouts, le rail n'assure cependant que 9 % du trafic intérieur de voyageurs. Le réseau ferroviaire s'étire sur 34 450 km, contre 52 000 km au début des années trente. Si le réseau électrifié se limite à 14 200 km, il assure 80 % du trafic total.

À la gare du Nord (Paris), l'Eurostar, qui assure la liaison Paris-Londres en trois heures et Thalys, qui joint Bruxelles en une heure 25 minutes

La SNCF, entreprise publique, souffre d'un lourd endettement et d'un grave déficit financier, en dépit de l'aide de l'État destinée à compenser les obligations du service public. Elle doit investir plus de 22 milliards de francs (3,6 milliards de dollars) par an afin de poursuivre sa modernisation. Un établissement public industriel et commercial, Réseau ferré de France (RFF), a été créé pour gérer les infrastructures du transport ferroviaire. Outre la création du réseau à grande vitesse, la modernisation se traduit par la mise en fonction de nouveaux matériels, la diversification des services (trains auto-couchettes, compartiments familiaux, formule train + hôtel) et une politique commerciale active. Dans le même temps, la course à la productivité a conduit à une réduction rapide de l'effectif du personnel, passé de 500 000 en 1939 à 180 000 en 1998. L'avenir du rail est désormais lié à l'extension du réseau TGV et à l'essor du ferroutage. Ce mode de transport, déjà utilisé sur les longues distances, est appelé à se développer, notamment entre Lille et Marseille, via Lyon, pour remédier à la saturation du réseau autoroutier, mais aussi sur des axes internationaux vers le Royaume-Uni et l'Italie, comme le souligne le récent projet d'un tunnel ferroviaire entre Lyon et Turin.

Eurostar : Londres à trois heures de Paris

Paris-Londres directement, de la gare du Nord au Terminal international de Water-loo, en trois heures, c'est ce qu'ont vécu le 14 novembre 1994 les 794 passagers du premier train Eurostar à effectuer la liaison commerciale entre les deux capitales. Aujourd'hui, il y a environ un départ toutes les heures. Le voyage Paris-Londres aller-retour revient à 690 francs (115 dollars) environ. Pour 2 750 francs (458 dollars), le voyage en première classe comprend un petit-déjeuner ou un dîner directement servi au fauteuil du passager.

Le voyage en Eurostar ressemble à un trajet aérien : terminaux futuristes, enre-gistrement 20 minutes avant le départ, cartes d'embarquement et transport séparé des bagages sont là aussi de mise. Même les temps de trajet sont compa-rables : de centre-ville à centre-ville, trois heures sont nécessaires pour rallier Paris à Londres, que l'on prenne l'Eurostar ou l'avion. Seul le paysage est diffé-rent : à bord de l'Eurostar, le voyageur traverse d'abord la Picardie à 300 km/h puis, après les 54 km du tunnel sous la Manche, la belle région du Kent à 160 km/h.

Thalys : Paris-Bruxelles en une heure vingt-cinq

Depuis le 14 décembre 1997, la durée du trajet entre Paris et Bruxelles est réduite de 45 minutes. C'est la première fois qu'un TGV relie deux capitales européennes à 300 km/h de bout en bout. De 7 h à 22 h, la fréquence est d'un départ toutes les heures ou toutes les demi-heures en période de pointe. Le prix du billet aller-retour varie entre 316 francs (52 dollars) et 996 francs (166 dollars). Thalys dessert aussi de nombreuses villes en Belgique, en Allemagne et aux Pays-Bas jusqu'à Cologne ou Amsterdam.

Un trafic fluvial modeste

La batellerie, concurrencée par le rail et le transport par tube, assure, avec 5,7 milliards de tonnes-kilomètres, moins de 2,5 % du trafic intérieur de marchandises. La profession souffre de l'effondre-ment du transport de pondéreux, qui a entraîné une baisse des taux de fret et conduit l'État et la Communauté européenne à financer la des-truction d'une partie des bateaux pour limiter la surcapacité de la flotte. L'armement français doit faire face à la concurrence de ses homologues allemands et néerlandais, plus concentrés. La batellerie souffre aussi des déficiences d'un réseau long de 8 500 km mais marqué par la vétusté de bien des canaux. Quelques grands cours d'eau ont certes été aménagés, comme le Rhin, le Rhône en aval de Lyon, la Seine en aval de Montereau, la Moselle, ainsi que quelques canaux à grand gabarit comme la liaison Dunkerque-Valenciennes, mais ils demeurent isolés et reliés par des canaux anciens de faible gabarit. 1 860 km de canaux seulement sont au gabarit européen de 1 500 tonnes. Le trafic se concentre dans la moitié nord du pays, les premiers ports fluviaux étant Paris, Strasbourg, Thionville et Rouen.

L'ouverture maritime

La flotte marchande naviguant sous pavillon français, qui dispose d'un tonnage de 6,6 millions de tjb (tonnes de jauge brute), ne rassemble qu'une partie des navires appartenant à des armateurs nationaux, soit 210 navires commerciaux. En effet, comme leurs confrères des autres pays industriels, les armateurs ont placé une partie de leurs navires sous pavillon de complaisance pour réduire leurs charges salariales et fiscales. D'autres navires voguent sous le pavillon des Kerguelen, créé en 1986 et permettant de constituer des équipages composés pour les trois quarts de marins étrangers, alors que le pavillon national impose des équipages totalement français, plus coûteux. La Compagnie Générale Maritime, privatisée en 1996, domine l'armement national et assure aussi le trafic entre le continent et la Corse par le biais d'une filiale, la Société Nationale Corse Méditerranée. Parmi les autres armateurs, les plus importants sont la compagnie SCAC/Delmas-Vieljeux/SDV, le groupe Dreyfus, spécialisé dans le transport de céréales, et la Compagnie française de Navigation, filiale de la CFP, qui achemine des hydrocarbures.

Quatrième exportateur dans le monde, la France se situe seulement au 27e rang pour sa flotte marchande. Le trafic de marchandises se répartit pour l'essentiel entre six ports sur les 70 que compte le pays. Marseille-Fos (90,7 millions de tonnes) devance Le Havre (56 millions de tonnes), Dunkerque, Calais, Nantes-Saint-Nazaire, Rouen et Bordeaux. La course à la productivité a entraîné une réduction rapide de l'effectif des dockers et l'apparition de nouvelles techniques de manutention portuaire, privilégiant notamment les conteneurs et les remorques. Le transport de passagers augmente rapidement, profitant de l'essor du tourisme. Il est particulièrement actif pour les relations trans-Manche, en dépit de l'ouverture du tunnel. Calais (1,8 million de passagers) précède Cherbourg (1,5 million), Boulogne et Dunkerque, alors qu'entre le continent et la Corse, Bastia devance Marseille et Nice.

Un carrefour aérien

Son étendue et sa situation géographique valent à la France de constituer une véritable plaque tournante du transport aérien en Europe. Profitant d'une démocratisation rapide liée aux vols charters, à l'avènement des gros porteurs et à l'essor de la concurrence, il connaît une forte croissance. Air France, compagnie nationale, a pris le contrôle de la compagnie Air Inter. Le groupe développe par ailleurs la coopération commerciale avec des compagnies étrangères. Il a transporté, en 1997, 33 millions de passagers à l'international, à travers ses 164 escales réparties dans 92 pays. S'agissant du trafic intérieur, il a transporté 15 millions de passagers malgré la concurrence que lui font des compagnies comme AOM et Air Liberté.

Aéroport de Paris se situe au second rang européen derrière Londres et au septième rang mondial. Il a enregistré 60,4 millions de passagers en 1997 et 644 500 mouvements d'avions commerciaux. Il devance les aéroports de Nice-Côte d'Azur, Marseille-Provence, Lyon, Toulouse et Bordeaux.

Les télécommunications

En 1997, La Poste a acheminé plus de 24 milliards d'objets, qu'il s'agisse de lettres, de colis, de journaux ou de périodiques. L'une des spécificités de la poste française est sa fiabilité et sa rapidité d'acheminement. En créant une dizaine de filiales, le groupe La Poste a développé trois activités majeures : les services financiers et les services courrier et colis en distribution accélérée. Employant près de 310 000 personnes, ses services ont été dissociés de ceux du téléphone en 1990 : deux sociétés de droit public ont été créées, France Télécom prenant en charge les télécommunications. Grâce à un important effort d'investissement de l'État dans les années soixante-dix et quatre-vingt, on compte aujourd'hui plus de 33 millions de lignes téléphoniques sur le territoire. Les tarifs connaissent une baisse continue, en particulier pour les communications à longue distance, avec l'essor de la concurrence entre France Télécom et des opérateurs privés comme Cégétel ou Bouygues. La croissance fulgurante de la téléphonie mobile (plus de 8 millions d'abonnés au réseau depuis sa mise en place en 1996) est également l'objet d'une âpre concurrence.

Le téléphone mobile connaît une croissance fulgurante depuis 1996 ; France Télécom, Cégétel et Bouygues, les trois principaux opérateurs, se livrent une âpre concurrence

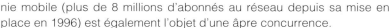

Du Minitel à l'Internet : une rapide conversion

Le développement de la télématique française, avec ses 7,4 millions de terminaux informatiques Minitel, ses 30 000 services accessibles et ses 85 millions d'heures de connexions annuelles, a ralenti la croissance d'Internet. La France cherche aujourd'hui à combler son retard en matière d'utilisation d'Internet grâce à une politique volontariste de l'État, qui a confié à France Télécom le pilotage de plusieurs projets dans le domaine des nouvelles technologies de l'information et de la communication.

Les débuts sont prometteurs et la croissance rapide. Ainsi, le nombre d'internautes avoisine les trois millions fin 1998 grâce notamment aux fournisseurs d'accès comme Wanadoo, le service d'accès de France Télécom, Club-Internet, AOL, Micronet, etc. Le nombre de sites français a essaimé en un temps record : on en dénombre quelque 44 000 ; administrations, journaux, télévisions, radios, entreprises et associations sont accessibles via le Web.

Pour en savoir plus :

Les chiffres-clés de l'industrie française 1997-1998, Ministère de l'Industrie, Direction générale des stratégies industrielles, Service des statistiques industrielles, SESSI, 1998.

G. Colletis, J.-L. Levet, *Quelles politiques pour l'industrie française ?* Commissariat général du Plan, La Documentation française, 1997.

B. Coriat, D. Taddéï, *Made in France*, LGF, 1993.

La France, industries et services depuis 1945, Sirey, 1994.

P. Le Roy, *Les agricultures françaises face aux marchés mondiaux*, A. Colin, 1993.

L'agriculture, la forêt et les industries agroalimentaires, Graph Agri France 1998, Ministère de l'Agriculture et de la Pêche, 1998.

L'agriculture et l'agroalimentaire dans les régions, Graph Agri 1998, Ministère de l'Agriculture et de la Pêche, 1998.

D. Zerah, *Le système financier français : dix ans de mutation*, La Documentation française, collection Les Études, 1993.

« Le commerce international », *Cahiers français*, n° 253, La Documentation française.

D. Plihon, *Les banques. Nouveaux enjeux, nouvelles stratégies,* La Documentation française, collection Les Études, 1998.

16

L'aménagement du territoire et l'action régionale

Marquée par des siècles de tradition centralisatrice, tant sur le plan politique que sur le plan économique, la France offre au lendemain de la seconde guerre mondiale de fortes disparités régionales, qui se traduisent d'abord par le poids excessif de la capitale – Paris rassemble alors plus de 15 % de la population –, ensuite par le contraste existant entre une France riche, industrielle et urbaine dans sa moitié nord-est et une France demeurée rurale et plus pauvre dans la moitié sud-ouest, enfin par une opposition générale entre les villes et les campagnes, ces dernières enregistrant un niveau de développement sensiblement inférieur. Pour remédier à ces inégalités, les pouvoirs publics ont conduit depuis le milieu des années soixante une active politique d'aménagement du territoire visant à instaurer une meilleure répartition des hommes et des activités.

Des objectifs renouvelés

Après la seconde guerre mondiale, la prise de conscience des déséquilibres régionaux aboutit en 1949 à la création, par l'État, d'une Direction de l'aménagement du territoire. Dès lors, va s'affiner la perception de déséquilibres rendus de plus en plus complexes à la suite des mutations économiques. En 1955, l'État définit des régions de programme et met en place des structures et des moyens de financement spécialisés. Ainsi, la DATAR, Délégation à l'aménagement du territoire et à l'action régionale, instituée en 1963, devient l'instrument privilégié d'intervention. Elle pilote l'aménagement en s'appuyant sur divers organismes locaux, compétents notamment en matière d'équipement touristique, d'industrialisation ou d'aménagement des aires métropolitaines et est depuis 1997 mise à la disposition du ministre de tutelle. S'ajoutent à la DATAR le Comité interministériel à l'aménagement du territoire (CIAT), qui détermine les objectifs et prend les décisions, et le Fonds d'intervention pour l'aménagement du territoire (FIAT) qui assure le financement des opérations aux côtés des autres partenaires comme les collectivités locales et les entreprises publiques ou privées. Dans un premier temps, l'État détermine les objectifs de l'aménagement dans le cadre de la planification et il assure la maîtrise des opérations.

La DATAR conduit plusieurs types d'interventions. Elle coordonne des réalisations de grande ampleur pour favoriser le développement économique de certaines régions. C'est ainsi que vont être conduits, dans les années soixante et au début des années soixante-dix, l'équipement touristique des littoraux languedocien et aquitain et la construction de grandes stations de sports d'hiver dans les Alpes. Elle participe aussi à la construction des deux grandes zones industrialo-portuaires de Dunkerque et de Fos, destinées à promouvoir les industries lourdes littorales en favorisant l'approvisionnement par des matières premières et des produits énergétiques importés.

Pour réduire la suprématie parisienne, la DATAR encourage aussi, à compter de 1964, l'essor de huit métropoles d'équilibre en favorisant le développement de l'industrie et des services de haut niveau : universités, centres hospitaliers universitaires... Pour rééquilibrer la structure des agglomérations, elle contribue par ailleurs à la création de villes nouvelles autour de Paris, comme Marne-la-Vallée et Saint-Quentin-en-Yvelines, de Lille, avec Villeneuve-d'Ascq, et de Lyon, avec L'Isle-d'Abeau. À toutes ces interventions directes s'ajoutent des mesures destinées à restructurer l'espace national. C'est ainsi qu'est encouragée la décentralisation industrielle et tertiaire par l'octroi de primes aux entreprises s'implantant dans certaines régions. Les régions périphériques du Bassin parisien, comme le Centre et la Picardie, et la Bretagne verront ainsi s'accroître rapidement leurs emplois industriels. À l'inverse, les installations dans d'autres régions, notamment l'Ile-de-France, sont soumises à l'agrément des pouvoirs publics et aux versements de taxes.

L'État montre aussi l'exemple en délocalisant certains de ses services, comme la fabrication des billets de banque qui est implantée près de Clermont-Ferrand ou la météorologie nationale qui s'installe à Toulouse. Au total, toutes ces actions ont contribué à la création de plus de 600 000 emplois industriels dans les régions périphériques de la Région parisienne et à une densification importante des équipements au sein de métropoles régionales beaucoup mieux desservies. Par ailleurs, les dynamiques régionales ont été bouleversées : les régions de l'Ouest et du Sud, jusqu'alors peu industrialisées, enregistrent un développement plus rapide que les vieilles régions industrielles du Nord et de l'Est. Seule ombre au tableau : les campagnes continuent à perdre des habitants.

Le ralentissement de la croissance à compter de 1974 et la crise qui affecte bon nombre de branches industrielles anciennes, tels le textile et la sidérurgie, conduisent l'État à réviser les objectifs de l'aménagement du territoire, d'autant que ses moyens financiers diminuent. Les grandes opérations d'aménagement sont délaissées et les actions visent avant tout à faciliter la reconversion des vieux foyers industriels par la réhabilitation des paysages, par la requalification de la main-d'œuvre et par l'implantation de nouvelles activités. Ainsi, l'État encourage l'arrivée des constructeurs automobiles français ou étrangers dans le Nord et en Lorraine. Par ailleurs, pour limiter l'effet de métropolisation qui affecte bon nombre de régions au profit de la capitale régionale, il privilégie les interventions en faveur des villes moyennes, puis des « pays ». Il doit aussi faire face à deux problèmes qui s'accentuent : la désertification du monde rural et les difficultés de certains quartiers urbains.

Au cours des dernières décennies, plus de 40 % des communes rurales ont perdu des habitants. C'est notamment le fait des campagnes situées dans la « diagonale du vide » qui traverse la France des Pyrénées centrales aux Ardennes, ainsi que dans les Alpes du Sud, en Corse et en Bretagne intérieure. Pour lutter contre l'hémorragie démographique, l'État, assisté par les subventions de la Communauté européenne, multiplie les aides à l'agriculture et encourage l'implantation de nouvelles activités, en particulier la sylviculture et le tourisme. Certaines de ces régions font l'objet de la création de parcs naturels destinés à la préservation des équilibres et susceptibles d'attirer des touristes.

L'impact de la régionalisation

Les lois de décentralisation, votées en 1982 et 1983, ont conduit l'État à se désengager progressivement de l'aménagement du territoire en transférant aux collectivités locales une large part de ses moyens d'action. Les régions, devenues des collectivités territoriales à part entière, disposent de nombreuses compétences, notamment en matière d'aménagement du territoire. Elles élaborent des programmes d'aménagement concerté du territoire, ou PACT, en liaison avec l'État et dans le cadre du plan national. Ces contrats de plan regroupent les

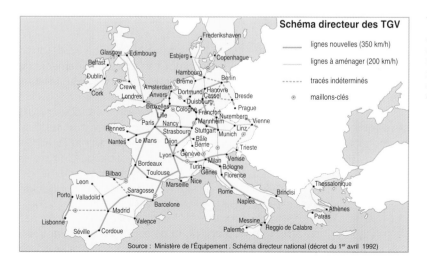

Schéma directeur des TGV

—— lignes nouvelles (350 km/h)

—— lignes à aménager (200 km/h)

----- tracés indéterminés

⊛ maillons-clés

Source : Ministère de l'Équipement . Schéma directeur national (décret du 1er avril 1992)

Pionnière en matière de liaisons ferroviaires à grande vitesse, la France est bien placée pour tirer les bénéfices de son insertion dans le réseau européen

fonds octroyés par les divers opérateurs : l'État, la région, le Fonds national pour l'aménagement du territoire (FNADT) et les aides éventuellement octroyées par la Communauté européenne. Pour la période 1994-1998, les contrats de plan représentent un crédit de plus de 250 milliards de francs (42 milliards de dollars), réparti comme suit : 85 milliards de francs (14 milliards de dollars) de la part de l'État, 85 milliards de francs émanant des régions, près de 40 milliards de francs (6,6 milliards de dollars) financés par les autres collectivités locales et 55 milliards de francs (9 milliards de dollars) attribués par la Communauté européenne. Le domaine routier en absorbe près du tiers, le développement économique 18 %, la politique de la ville 10 % ; la mise en œuvre du schéma Université 2000, l'environnement et la culture, sont également de gros postes d'investissement.

Les autres collectivités territoriales, dont les pouvoirs ont été accrus dans le cadre de la régionalisation, voient également leurs compétences élargies. C'est le cas des 36 500 communes du pays qui bénéficient d'une grande autonomie en matière d'urbanisme. Ainsi, elles adoptent un Plan d'occupation des sols (POS) déterminant les fonctions des différentes parties du territoire communal (agriculture, habitat, espaces verts...) et le maire attribue désormais les permis de construire. Les départements, quant à eux, assurent une partie des aménagements agraires, comme le remembrement, et gèrent le réseau des routes départementales.

Par ailleurs, l'Union européenne a accru le poids de ses interventions. Les différents fonds structurels communautaires représentent pour la période 1994-1999 un apport important pour la France. Ces aides privilégient les régions en retard de développement, comme la Corse et les départements d'outre-mer, les régions touchées par le déclin industriel, comme le Nord-Pas-de-Calais et la Lorraine, et les régions rurales fragiles. Elles visent aussi à faciliter la lutte contre le chômage et la réinsertion des travailleurs licenciés. Le Fonds européen de développement régional (FEDER) est l'instrument privilégié de ces interventions, aux côtés du Fonds social européen et du FEOGA-Orientation.

De nouvelles perspectives : un rééquilibrage en faveur de l'emploi et de l'environnement

De nouvelles orientations de l'aménagement du territoire ont été définies. La loi d'orientation du 4 février 1995, révisée par le projet de loi adopté en Conseil des ministres en 1998 et présenté au Parlement en 1999, met l'accent sur le développement durable du territoire et engage une démarche nouvelle de planification avec la volonté de rééquilibrer le rôle de l'État et des collectivités locales. Un budget de 1,8 milliard de francs (0,3 milliard de dollars) lui est consacré.

Les actions prioritaires de la politique d'aménagement à l'horizon 2020 porteront sur la réduction des inégalités entre territoires ruraux et territoires urbains. Il s'agit d'abord de poursuivre la lutte contre la désertification de plus de 400 cantons dans les campagnes mais aussi de soutenir les zones rurales encore peuplées mais fragiles afin d'éviter que la trame du monde rural ne s'étiole. Pour cela, il a été décidé de freiner les fermetures de services publics et d'encourager une diversification des emplois. Par ailleurs, un fonds de gestion des milieux naturels des espaces ruraux sera créé.

Il est également prévu de réhabiliter des zones urbaines en difficulté (périphéries urbaines, zones en reconversion industrielle, outre-mer...), condition indispensable à une meilleure harmonie sociale. Amorcée dans les années soixante-dix, la politique de la ville s'est développée dans les années quatre-vingt et surtout après 1990. Elle vise avant tout à l'amélioration du cadre de vie par la réhabilitation de l'habitat, la création d'espaces verts et d'équipements collectifs. Elle multiplie également les actions favorisant les initiatives locales en matière d'emploi.

Le développement durable est intégré à la politique d'aménagement du territoire (voir chapitre sur la protection de l'environnement) qui vise à rééquilibrer le développement des villes et des campagnes en renforçant les communautés territoriales façonnées par la géographie, l'histoire ou l'économie. Le cadre géographique de la politique territoriale a été modifié et comporte désormais trois niveaux : les régions, les agglomérations et les « pays ». Ces groupements de communes présentant une cohérence géographique, culturelle, économique ou sociale peuvent s'associer sur la base d'un projet de développement commun : on en compte aujourd'hui 70. Les agglomérations sont aussi incitées à organiser leur coopération et leur solidarité dans le cadre de « l'intercommunalité ».

Face à la désertification des campagnes, la politique d'aménagement du territoire vise à soutenir les zones rurales encore peuplées

Enfin, en cette fin du XXᵉ siècle, la recomposition de l'espace français s'effectue dans le cadre européen et non plus dans les seules limites du pays. Aujourd'hui, les régions françaises sont beaucoup moins en compétition entre elles qu'avec leurs homologues européennes, comme la Flandre, le Bade-Wurtemberg, la Bavière ou la Lombardie, avec lesquelles, d'ailleurs, elles développent des accords de coopération. Paris n'est plus en concurrence avec Lyon, Lille ou Marseille, mais doit plutôt s'affirmer face à Londres, Bruxelles, Francfort et demain Berlin. C'est d'ailleurs pourquoi la capitale s'efforce d'accroître son influence et d'attirer les grands décideurs étrangers et les sièges sociaux de multinationales en leur offrant des facilités d'ordre fiscal, en développant le parc de bureaux et d'hôtels et en multipliant les équipements pour congrès et séminaires. En contrepoids de l'expansion parisienne, il est envisagé de réactiver l'espace national autour d'une douzaine de métropoles urbaines régionales à vocation européenne et internationale, comme Lyon, Marseille, Lille, Strasbourg, Bordeaux, Rennes, Nancy, Metz, Nantes, Toulouse, Grenoble et Clermont-Ferrand, en s'appuyant sur leurs infrastructures tertiaires, leurs réseaux de communications et leurs équipements généraux.

Les nouvelles perspectives se traduisent aussi par l'identification de nouveaux domaines nécessaires au développement comme l'éducation, la recherche ou encore les technologies de l'information qui répondent aux besoins de mobilité des personnes.

Le nouveau terminal
de l'aéroport
de Roissy-Charles
de Gaulle

Pour en savoir plus :

F. Auriac et V. Rey (coord. par), *Atlas de France*, volume 8, *L'espace rural*, Reclus-La Documentation française, 1998.

J. Bourdin, J. Boyon, A. Zeller, Commissariat général du Plan, *Économie et territoires*, La Documentation française, 1997.

J.-P. Delevoye, Commissariat général du Plan, *Cohésion sociale et territoires*, La Documentation française, 1997.

R. Brunet, « L'aménagement du territoire en France », in *La Documentation Photographique*, n° 7041, La Documentation française, 1997.

J.-P. de Gaudemar (sous la dir. de), DATAR, *Environnement et aménagement du territoire*, La Documentation française, 1996.

M. Kotas, DATAR, *Politique de pays*, La Documentation française, collection Rapport de mission, 1997.

SCIENCES, TECHNOLOGIE, CULTURE ET MÉDIAS

17

Sciences et technologie

Fidèle à une longue tradition, la science française se situe actuellement à un haut niveau de compétitivité internationale. Elle contribue dans toutes les disciplines au développement des connaissances scientifiques fondamentales et des technologies qui leur sont associées.

Recherche fondamentale : une tradition poursuivie

L'*école mathématique* française, prolongeant et élargissant considérablement l'œuvre entamée pendant l'entre-deux-guerres par le groupe « Bourbaki », demeure l'une des premières du monde. Récompensée par sept médailles Fields, dont deux décernées en 1994, elle fait autorité dans les domaines suivants : la géométrie fractale, les équations aux dérivées partielles ou la théorie du chaos (c'est-à-dire l'étude mathématique des phénomènes complexes très sensibles aux conditions initiales ou aux contraintes, par exemple les fluctuations boursières, la croissance des tumeurs cancéreuses, la météorologie ou l'acoustique des salles de concert). Des mathématiciens comme Benoît Mandelbrot, Alain Connes, Jean-Pierre Serre, René Thom, Alexander Grothendieck, Pierre-Louis Lions ou Jean-Christophe Yoccoz sont des savants reconnus internationalement.

Cette qualité de recherche mathématique confère tout naturellement à la France une place éminente dans le secteur connexe des logiciels et progiciels informatiques, en particulier les logiciels complexes pour grosses machines, conçus sur mesure pour répondre à des besoins spécifiques comme le traitement du signal, l'imagerie, le calcul scientifique intensif, etc. Dans un champ encore plus porteur et riche d'avenir, d'excellentes équipes françaises, à Paris-Sud, Marseille et Grenoble en particulier, se distinguent dans la conceptualisation de langages de plus en plus naturels que devront comprendre les super-ordinateurs du futur pour permettre une interaction directe entre l'homme et la machine.

La *physique* française actuelle, héritière des travaux de prestigieux prédécesseurs – de Henri Becquerel et Pierre et Marie Curie à Alfred Kastler et Louis Néel –, continue de s'illustrer dans des domaines très divers : optique quantique, physique atomique, magnétisme et physique du solide, hydrodynamique, matériaux pour la micro-électronique. En témoigne l'attribution du prix Nobel de physique, successivement, à Pierre-Gilles de Gennes en 1991, à Georges Charpak en 1992 et à Claude Cohen-Tannoudji en 1997. Le premier a exploré avec succès de multiples champs de la physique et de la physico-chimie moléculaire contemporaine. Particulièrement tournés vers les applications concrètes, ses travaux ont abouti dans les domaines suivants : les cristaux liquides, les matériaux supraconducteurs, les solutions de polymères ou les adhésifs. On doit au second l'invention d'un détecteur ultra-sensible aux rayonnements et aux particules qui est à la base d'un grand nombre de découvertes récentes sur la structure intime de la matière. Quant au troisième, ses travaux sur le refroidissement et la capture d'atomes permettent d'étudier leurs très faibles interactions et leurs émissions, ce qui devrait trouver des applications pour les horloges atomiques du

Georges Charpak
(à droite sur la photo),
prix Nobel de physique en
1992, félicite Claude
Cohen-Tannoudji qui a
reçu le même prix en 1997

futur. Les physiciens français contribuent également au développement de grands instruments de renommée mondiale. Au sein du Centre européen de recherche nucléaire (CERN), où le plus grand accélérateur mondial de particules, le LEP 2, a été mis en service en 1996, la France participe en première ligne à l'effort européen de recherche sur la physique des particules élémentaires. Elle dispose, près de Caen, d'un accélérateur d'ions lourds de haute qualité, le GANIL (Grand accélérateur national d'ions lourds), qui permet à la communauté scientifique internationale de poursuivre ses recherches en physique atomique et nucléaire.

La *chimie* est également une discipline où s'illustrèrent de longue date les chercheurs français comme Lavoisier, Gay-Lussac ou Frédéric et Irène Joliot-Curie. Parmi les secteurs d'excellence actuels, on trouve la chimie supramoléculaire qui élabore, quasiment à la demande, des associations moléculaires complexes aux fonctionnalités inédites tels les fameux cryptands découverts par Jean-Marie Lehn, prix Nobel de chimie en 1990, capables de capturer sélectivement des ions en solution. On trouve aussi la chimie des solides, avec la synthèse des premiers solides supraconducteurs à hautes températures due au professeur Raveau, la chimie douce, élaborant des matériaux nouveaux dans des conditions ambiantes, la chimie de synthèse des médicaments, renommée notamment en matière de thérapie cancéreuse, grâce aux travaux de l'Institut de chimie des substances naturelles, mais aussi pour la production de vaccins.

Dans le secteur des *sciences de la vie*, notamment en biologie, les équipes françaises comme celles de l'Institut Pasteur et de l'Institut national de la santé et de la recherche médicale (INSERM), avec Luc Montagnier, Pierre Chambon et d'autres, sont à l'origine de travaux très importants en génétique moléculaire, en immunologie – sur les recombinaisons génétiques *in vitro* et le sida –, en hormono-logie – sur la reproduction et le développement. Il est ainsi désormais reconnu que le virus VIH a bien été isolé pour la pre-mière fois à l'Institut Pasteur à Paris. Le groupe Pasteur-Mérieux poursuit activement ses recherches sur la mise au point d'un vaccin contre le sida, domaine où les Français restent seuls en lice avec quelques sociétés américaines de bio-technologie. Il faut aussi signa-

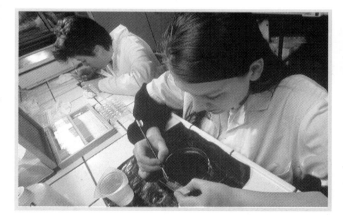

Une équipe de l'INSERM (U161) étudie des coupes de cerveaux de cobayes pour analyser les mécanismes cérébraux de la douleur

ler les travaux du professeur Étienne-Émile Baulieu, père de la pilule contraceptive RU 486, mise au point en 1982, dont l'équipe de cher-cheurs de l'INSERM a récemment mis en évidence les capacités d'une hormone féminine, la progestérone, à « réparer » des cellules nerveuses lésées, ce qui pourrait avoir d'importantes applications dans le traitement de troubles moteurs et sensitifs ou de paralysies.

Le grand chantier en cours, lui aussi dominé par la recherche américaine et française, est l'exploration du génome humain : il s'agit d'opérer le déchiffrage complet de tous les gènes de chacun des 23 chromosomes de l'homme - travail qui peut être comparé à la lecture d'un texte de 3,5 milliards de caractères écrits dans une langue inconnue -, et d'en déceler les fonctions dans l'espoir de prévenir ou de guérir un jour la plupart des maladies génétiques. Cet objectif, que per-sonne n'aurait prétendu viser il y a seulement dix ans, est le fruit d'une coopération internationale où les équipes françaises enregistrent de nombreux succès. Les découvertes se succèdent : ainsi, au Généthon d'Évry, près de Paris, l'un des laboratoires les plus modernes du monde pour l'étude du génome, Daniel Cohen a établi en septembre 1992 la première carte physique intégrale du chromosome 21 ; le mois suivant, Jean Weissenbach publiait 1 400 marqueurs couvrant la quasi-totalité du génome humain (22 chromosomes sur 23). À l'INSERM, en février 1993, l'équipe dirigée par Patrick Aubourg localisait le gène de l'adré-noleucodystrophie, maladie génétique qui détruit le cerveau. Un mois plus tard, à la suite d'expériences menées avec succès sur le rat, d'autres équipes françaises (Axel Kahn, Michel Perricaud et Marc Pes-chanski, Jacques Mallet) annonçaient une voie de traitement de la mala-die d'Alzheimer par thérapie génique et réussissaient à guérir, chez la souris, la myopathie de Duchenne par transfert génétique. Autre atout français, le Centre national de séquençage, qui se consacre à l'ADN afin d'identifier les gênes. Ainsi, en 1994, la première carte complète du génome a été produite, fruit d'une collaboration internationale à laquelle la recherche française a activement participé. Le dynamisme de la recherche génétique a par ailleurs permis la constitution de la plus importante entreprise française de biotechnologie, Genset, qui emploie 500 chercheurs et techniciens et travaille en collaboration avec les géants de l'industrie pharmaceutique.

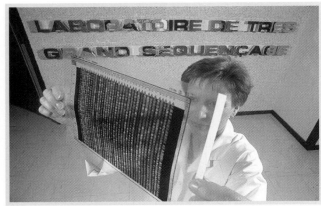

À Evry (Essonne),
un laboratoire privé de
séquençage génétique
installé dans les locaux
du Généthon

De son côté, l'Institut national de la recherche agronomique (INRA) obtient des résultats notables en matière de recher-che en biologie végétale et ani-male. Par exemple, dans les domaines viticole, horticole et céréalier, ont été mises au point la multiplication rapide, par microbouturage *in vitro*, de plants de vigne ou de fleurs ainsi que la création, par intro-duction de gènes spécifiques, de variétés résistantes à telle ou telle maladie. L'INRA est aussi le découvreur du colza hybride et a mis au point un logiciel de gestion des peuplements forestiers.

Le secteur des *sciences de la terre et de l'univers* n'est pas moins dynamique. Pour les premières, des équipes françaises ont largement contribué au développement de la sismologie et de la théorie de la tectonique des plaques. Elles participent également aux grands programmes internationaux, comme l'opération franco-américaine Famous pour l'exploration des vallées océaniques ou le programme IPOD (*International Project for Ocean Drilling*) pour l'exploration des grands fonds marins. Par ailleurs, la France occupe une place éminente dans le domaine de la recherche spatiale ; en témoignent de nom-breuses réalisations, dont plusieurs sont menées dans le cadre de coopérations européennes ou internationales : lanceur Diamant, fusée Ariane, programme SPOT (satellites pour l'observation de la Terre) pour la gestion des ressources terrestres, programme franco-américain de surveillance des océans par le satellite radar Topex-Poséidon, lancé en 1992 par la fusée Ariane, participation enfin à de nombreux projets de télécommunications, de météorologie, de recherche en astrophysique et en cosmologie.

Les *sciences humaines et sociales* sont en renouvellement constant au sein des universités et de grands établissements comme les Écoles normales supérieures, le Centre national de la recherche scientifique (CNRS), l'École pratique des hautes études, l'École des hautes études en sciences sociales, etc. La recherche historique française est reconnue comme l'une des plus illustres et des plus fécondes, en particulier avec l'« École des Annales », fondée par Lucien Febvre et Marc Bloch, mais aussi grâce à l'œuvre d'historiens de réputation internationale comme Fernand Braudel, Georges Dumézil ou Georges Duby, aujourd'hui décédés, ou encore de Jacques Le Goff, Pierre Chaunu, Jean Favier et Emmanuel Leroy-Ladurie. Parallèlement, de nombreuses missions archéologiques travaillant tant en France que sur les rives de la Méditerranée, en Asie et en Amérique latine, ont totalement renouvelé une discipline où la France s'illustrait déjà au XIXe siècle dès l'expédition en Égypte et, quelques décennies plus tard, par la fondation de l'École d'Athènes. Dans le même temps, d'autres disciplines s'affirment : la sociologie ou l'anthropologie qui doit tant à Claude Lévi-Strauss, la démographie où l'Institut national d'études démographiques (INED), encore marqué par l'impulsion donnée par Alfred Sauvy, a acquis une autorité mondiale. Quant à la recherche en sciences économiques, discipline largement dominée par les Anglo-Saxons, elle a été encouragée par la reconnaissance mondiale de Maurice Allais (lauréat du prix Nobel d'économie en 1988) et d'Edmond Malinvaud, pour leurs travaux sur le fonctionnement des économies de marché dans des situations de risques ou soumises à des effets simultanés de planification et de décentralisation. Enfin, la recherche juridique en France repose sur une tradition ancienne. Pour faire face à la complexité croissante de l'univers du droit et à l'interdépendance des spécialités, elle tend désormais à devenir de plus en plus collective. Attentive aux préoccupations du monde actuel, elle s'attache au renouvellement des thèmes fondamentaux (droit constitutionnel, libertés publiques, droit comparé, etc.) ainsi qu'à des questions plus récemment apparues (bioéthique, droit communautaire, droit de l'informatique, en particulier).

Les nouvelles technologies : la rencontre de la science et de l'industrie

Quatrième puissance industrielle, quatrième exportateur de biens et deuxième exportateur mondial de produits agricoles et alimentaires et de services, la France a su mettre au point les technologies modernes nécessaires à son essor économique et social et promouvoir l'effort de recherche et de développement indispensable à son avenir.

La compétitivité des industries de pointe françaises implique qu'elles intègrent les progrès réalisés en électronique, micro-électronique, informatique et biotechnologie, dans le domaine nucléaire ou dans celui des matériaux composites. Ces technologies trouvent des

Claudie-Andrée
Deshayes, première
femme spationaute
française

applications dans les industries innovantes ainsi que dans les industries traditionnelles qu'elles contribuent à rénover.

Les technologies stratégiques

Outre l'industrie de la défense, domaine de convergence de nombreuses technologies génériques (matériaux, mécanique de précision, électronique, informatique, etc.), les activités dans les secteurs spatial, aéronautique et énergétique contribuent à garantir l'indépendance de la France et à lui conserver une place de premier plan dans les activités de haute technologie.

Le Colibri, dernier-né
de la société franco-
allemande Eurocopter,
arrivé sur la base de
Marignane (Bouches-du-
Rhône) en janvier 1998

Dans le domaine aérospatial, la France s'est affirmée, avec l'appui de ses partenaires associés aux programmes Ariane et Airbus, comme la seule grande rivale des États-Unis. Grâce à sa conception d'ensemble, aux performances de son moteur à hydrogène liquide et à sa fiabilité, la fusée Ariane a réussi à capter la majeure partie des lancements spatiaux mondiaux. Elle permet également au programme spatial européen d'accumuler les succès technologiques dans le domaine des sciences de l'observation et de la communication. Les avancées techno-

logiques majeures mises en œuvre à l'occasion de la réalisation de l'Airbus A 340, premier au monde de sa catégorie en ce qui concerne la sobriété et la propreté de la combustion, la réduction des émissions sonores des réacteurs, l'implantation de matériaux composites dans des structures vitales au plan de la sécurité, démontrent le dynamisme et la compétence des équipes françaises engagées dans la coopération aéronautique européenne. Si l'on s'en tient aux avions commandés par les compagnies aériennes en 1997 et 1998, Airbus fait presque rang égal avec son grand rival, l'américain Boeing, premier constructeur aéronautique mondial. La France est, par ailleurs, en partenariat avec l'Allemagne, le premier constructeur mondial d'hélicoptères avec la société Eurocopter.

L'énergie est aussi un des points forts de la technologie française. La France maîtrise et exploite l'ensemble de la filière électronucléaire, du combustible au retraitement des déchets en incluant la production d'électricité. Elle dispose du plus grand centre de retraitement de déchets nucléaires de la planète, à la Hague dans le Cotentin, et son savoir-faire en la matière est reconnu puisqu'elle a pour clients des États aussi exigeants que l'Allemagne, la Suède ou le Japon. Fiabilité et sécurité caractérisent cette industrie qui démontre que l'on peut conjuguer maîtrise des dépenses énergétiques et protection de l'environnement. Dans le domaine des énergies classiques, la technologie nationale est aussi éprouvée et la France exporte ses techniques et son savoir-faire en construisant dans de nombreux pays des centrales hydroélectriques, des centrales thermiques conventionnelles, notamment celles qui sont équipées par les nouvelles turbines à gaz qui connaissent un vif succès. Il faut ajouter à cela la qualité de la recherche dans le secteur de l'exploration et des procédés pétrochimiques ainsi que la maîtrise de l'ingénierie correspondante, qui ont permis à l'industrie pétrolière française de s'implanter dans de nombreuses régions du monde.

Transports terrestres, génie civil et génie des matériaux

En ce qui concerne les technologies mises en œuvre dans le domaine des transports, la France détient plus de 12 % des brevets mondiaux et 22 % des brevets européens. Maîtrise de la propulsion thermique et électrique (synchrone ou asynchrone), fiabilité des techniques et des matériaux de freinage et de confort aéro-acoustique, performance des logiciels de sécurité, de contrôle-commande, de signalisation, légèreté des systèmes associée à la résistance accrue aux chocs, sont les points forts de la construction maritime, ferroviaire et automobile française. C'est ainsi que de nombreux marchés étrangers ont été conquis en matière de transport urbain (métros, tramways, véhicules de transport automatique de type VAL), mais aussi de transport ferroviaire classique et à grande vitesse : le TGV a été adopté en Corée du Sud et en Floride.

La France est aussi aux meilleurs rangs mondiaux pour les travaux publics et le génie civil. La Grande Arche de La Défense, à Paris, le tunnel sous la Manche, le pont de Normandie, l'ouvrage de Garabit (Cantal) sont autant de réalisations utilisant les technologies modernes dans le domaine de la construction, du génie civil et des disciplines scientifiques associées. Le plus grand pont à haubans du monde, d'une longueur de 17 kilomètres, ouvert au nord de Lisbonne sur la « Mer de Paille » en mars 1998, a été construit par les Français. S'ajoute à cela un savoir-faire internationalement reconnu en matière de réalisation d'infrastructures et d'équipements urbains, en particulier dans le secteur de l'adduction et du traitement des eaux. Les entreprises françaises occupent d'ailleurs les meilleurs rangs dans tous ces domaines : les deux premières entreprises mondiales d'approvisionnement et de traitement des eaux (CGE et Lyonnaise des eaux), ainsi que les trois premières entreprises européennes de bâtiment-travaux-publics (Bouygues, GTM, SGE), sont françaises.

Météor, le métro ultramoderne sans conducteur, inauguré en octobre 1998 sur la nouvelle ligne de métro parisienne

Électronique et industries de l'information

L'électronique occupe une place particulière dans le développement des sciences. En effet, les progrès qu'elle permet de réaliser assurent non seulement son propre développement industriel, mais servent aussi de support aux avancées dans de nombreux autres domaines : le traitement du signal et de l'image, les télécommunications, la robotique ou, plus prosaïquement, la monétique électronique, dont la carte à puce bancaire ou téléphonique, invention du Français Roland Moreno, est l'exemple le plus connu. Dans de nombreux secteurs d'activité qui touchent aussi bien au téléphone cellulaire qu'à la compression des données ou à l'imagerie virtuelle, la France a développé ses capacités, avec la force de frappe de grands groupes multinationaux (la première entreprise mondiale de télécommunications, Alcatel, est française), mais aussi de nombreuses PME innovantes qui s'imposent parfois jusqu'sur le marché américain.

La politique volontariste des pouvoirs publics en matière de télécommunications et de télématique est venue conforter la situation et l'avance prises par les entreprises françaises. Si le célèbre minitel n'a pas été exportable, il a quand même fait de la

France un précurseur en matière de télématique et pourrait connaître une seconde jeunesse, les minitels de dernière génération pouvant fonctionner comme postes d'accès à l'Internet. Alcatel a aussi développé une technologie dite ADLS, permettant l'accès à l'Internet à partir du réseau téléphonique classique. Pour sa part, le CNET, Centre national d'études des télécommunications, a mis au point une technique de transport numérique de données à très haut débit (mode de transfert asynchrone ATM), qui devrait accélérer le développement des autoroutes de l'information. Aujourd'hui, la France, qui est l'un des pays les plus « numérisés » au monde, entre dans la société de l'information.

Alimentation, santé, environnement

La renommée de la gastronomie française se trouve désormais consolidée au plus haut niveau scientifique par la maîtrise de la qualité et de la sécurité des procédés biotechnologiques et agro-alimentaires, ainsi que par la recherche permanente d'une hygiène incontestable (bactériologie prédictive) s'agissant des denrées alimentaires, des emballages et des procédés de conditionnement. Des actions de coopération scientifique et technique, très appréciées des partenaires de la France, développent aussi de grands projets pluridisciplinaires de recherche afin de protéger les cultures des pays du Sud, de mener des actions en faveur des régions sèches, de valoriser la ressource hydrique, de développer des systèmes de production agricole mieux adaptés aux zones tropicales humides. Cette démarche complète utilement l'activité immunologique et vaccinale des chercheurs français, universellement reconnue (vaccins antirabique, anti-poliomyélitique, anti-méningitique, vaccin cinq cibles, etc).

Dans le domaine de l'environnement, les techniques développées par la recherche publique et privée française concernent des domaines aussi variés que la télédétection, qui permet de prévoir et programmer les actions à entreprendre, la conservation des sols, le reboisement, la purification des eaux, le traitement des déchets et la lutte antipollution. La France détient actuellement plus de 12 % des brevets mondiaux et près de 20 % des brevets européens dans le domaine des technologies de l'environnement. Alliant ainsi tradition et originalité, la communauté scientifique française fait preuve d'une vitalité qui lui permet de nouer de fructueuses coopérations internationales tout en contribuant de manière essentielle à la compétitivité économique du pays.

Xavier Vignon
et J.-P. Renard,
chercheurs de l'INRA
et « pères » d'un veau
cloné, Marguerite,
né en mars 1998

Pour en savoir plus :

Les principaux centres de recherche français

Ministère de l'Enseignement supérieur et de la Recherche
1, rue Descartes - 75231 Paris Cedex 05
Direction de la Technologie
Télécopie : 33 1.46.34.48.58
Direction de la Recherche
Télécopie : 33 1.46.34.49.49
http://education.gouv.fr
http://www.recherche.gouv.fr
Centre national de la recherche scientifique (CNRS)
3, rue Michel-Ange - 75794 Paris Cedex 16
Télécopie : 33 1. 44.96.50.00
http://www.cnrs.fr
Centre national d'études spatiales (CNES)
2, place Maurice Quentin - 75039 Paris Cedex 01
Télécopie : 33 1.44.76.76.76
http://www.cnes.fr
Institut national de la santé et de la recherche médicale (INSERM)
101, rue de Tolbiac - 75654 Paris Cedex 13
Télécopie : 33 1.45.85.68.56
http://www.inserm.fr
Institut national de la recherche agronomique (INRA)
147, rue de l'Université - 75338 Paris Cedex 07
Télécopie : 33 1.47.05.99.66
http://www.inra.fr
Institut français de recherche pour l'exploitation de la mer (IFREMER)
155, rue Jean-Jacques Rousseau - 92138 Issy-Les-Moulineaux Cedex
Télécopie : 33 1.46.48.22.96
http://www.ifremer.fr
Commissariat à l'énergie atomique (CEA)
31-33, rue de la Fédération - 75752 Paris Cedex 15
Télécopie : 33 1.40.56.29.70
http://www.cea.fr
Institut national de recherche en informatique et automatique (INRIA)
Domaine de Voluceau. Rocquencourt. BP 105
78153 Le Chesnay
Télécopie : 33 1.39.63.59.60
http://www.inria.fr
Institut français du pétrole (IFP)
1 et 4, avenue de Bois-Préau. BP 92852. 92506 Rueil-Malmaison Cedex.
Télécopie : 33 1.47.52.70.00
http://www.ifp.fr
**Institut français de recherche scientifique pour le développement
en coopération (ORSTOM)**
213, rue La Fayette - 75480 Paris Cedex 10
Télécopie : 33 1.48.03.08.29
http://www.orstom.fr
**Centre de coopération internationale en recherche agronomique
pour le développement (CIRAD)**
42, rue Scheffer. 75116 Paris.
Télécopie : 33 1.53.70.21.33

18

La culture

L'image de la France est indissociable de sa culture : les touristes étrangers le savent, qui se rendent en grand nombre au Louvre ou au Centre Georges Pompidou et assistent aux représentations de l'Opéra-Bastille ou de la Comédie-Française. Cette effervescence artistique est parfois mise à l'actif d'une tradition française originale de politique culturelle, dans laquelle l'État intervient de façon constante, ce qui soulève des polémiques de manière récurrente.

Cette intervention s'est affirmée très tôt. Dès le XVIe siècle, l'usage du français dans la rédaction des jugements et des actes notariés fut ainsi imposé par l'ordonnance royale de Villers-Cotterêts (1539) et l'évolution de la langue surveillée par l'Académie française, créée en 1635. Au XVIIe siècle, l'État s'affirme comme le protecteur des Arts, en particulier sous le règne de Louis XIV et, à ce titre, encourage, pensionne, fait travailler les artistes et les écrivains : la construction du château de Versailles et la création de la Comédie-Française (1680) témoignent de l'ambition du monarque mécène.

En ouvrant un musée au palais du Louvre en 1793, l'État ne se fait plus seulement mécène, mais également conservateur. L'action de Mérimée, dès 1832, à la tête de la nouvelle administration des Monuments historiques, ou celle de l'architecte-restaurateur Viollet-le-Duc s'inscrivent dans cette perspective.

Il faut attendre le milieu du XXe siècle pour que soit nettement formulé, outre l'encouragement prodigué aux artistes et la conservation du patrimoine, un troisième objectif : la diffusion culturelle. L'action pionnière du ministre de l'Instruction publique et des Beaux-Arts, Jean Zay, sous le Front populaire, trouve ainsi son prolongement, à la Libération, dans une politique visant à rendre accessibles au plus grand nombre les trésors de la culture autrefois réservés à un public restreint. En témoigne le soutien apporté par l'État à l'action de

La salle des sculptures hellénistiques du Musée du Louvre

Jean Vilar, directeur du Théâtre national populaire (TNP). Sous la Vᵉ République, André Malraux, nommé en 1959 ministre chargé des Affaires culturelles par le général de Gaulle, déclare à la tribune de l'Assemblée nationale qu'il s'agit de faire, pour la démocratisation de la culture, ce que la IIIᵉ République avait réalisé, dans sa volonté républicaine, pour l'enseignement.

À la veille du XXIᵉ siècle, cette triple dimension des politiques culturelles n'a rien perdu de son actualité. Bien au contraire, chacun de ces objectifs peut à présent s'appuyer sur des moyens accrus. Mais l'État n'agit plus seul dans ce domaine.

Les acteurs

L'État

Les sommes allouées au ministère de la Culture ont progressivement augmenté au cours des années, approchant en 1998 le seuil symbolique de 1 % du budget de l'État, soit 15,1 milliards de francs (2,5 milliards de dollars). Si l'on y ajoute les dépenses de nature culturelle effectuées par d'autres ministères (ministères de l'Éducation nationale, de la Jeunesse et des sports, par exemple) ou déléguées à des organismes tiers (CNRS, Centres d'action culturelle subventionnés pour un tiers par l'État), ainsi que les crédits qui passent par le canal de l'action sociale, de l'aménagement de la ville et des espaces ruraux et du développement touristique, on peut considérer que près de 40 milliards de francs par an sont consacrés par l'État au financement de la culture.

Parallèlement à cette augmentation des crédits, les services du ministère de la Culture ont été réorganisés. Ils emploient en 1998 près de 15 000 personnes et couvrent patrimoine et architecture, musées, archives, musique, danse, théâtre et spectacles, arts plastiques, livres et lecture. La formation des experts et des responsables de cette administration a également été l'objet d'efforts dont témoigne, par exemple, l'ouverture en 1993 de l'École nationale du patrimoine.

Les collectivités locales

Les compétences des collectivités locales en matière culturelle et leurs moyens d'intervention ont été élargis par les lois de décentralisation de 1982-1983. Les budgets culturels des départements et des régions ont été multipliés par cinq au cours des années quatre-vingt et ceux des communes par plus de deux. Globalement, la contribution des collectivités locales au financement de la culture dépasse aujourd'hui celle de l'État (50,3 % contre 49,7 %). La mise en commun de leurs moyens et de ceux de l'État exerce, incontestablement, un effet multiplicateur et la culture bénéficie ainsi d'environ 80 milliards de francs par an.

Les villes jouent un rôle primordial, assurant 40 % du financement public de la culture, avec une contribution annuelle de plus de 30 milliards de francs (5 milliards de dollars). À elle seule, la municipalité de Paris consacre un budget de 2 milliards de francs (0,3 milliard de dollars) à la culture, mais de nombreuses villes de province ont aussi consenti de gros efforts financiers tant pour sauvegarder le patrimoine que pour développer des animations spécifiques. Plusieurs villes abritent aussi des institutions culturelles de rang national, voire international : Musées d'art moderne à Lyon, Saint-Étienne et Grenoble, École nationale de la photographie à Arles, École nationale supérieure de danse à Marseille, Centre national de la bande dessinée à Angoulême, Archives du monde du travail à Roubaix, musée Matisse à Nice. L'épanouissement progressif de la culture sur tout le territoire national contraste ainsi avec une longue tradition d'hégémonie parisienne.

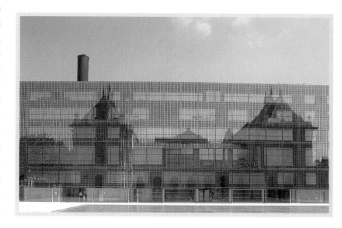

Le Musée des Beaux-Arts de Lille (Nord-Pas-de-Calais) conçu et restauré par les architectes Ibos et Vitart

Associations et entreprises

L'engagement des associations et des entreprises en faveur de la culture doit aussi être souligné. Les premières emploient près de 20 000 salariés et sont le plus souvent subventionnées par l'État et les collectivités locales. Elles contribuent à drainer le public vers les manifestations les plus diverses et aident à former des amateurs susceptibles de devenir de véritables professionnels. C'est à leur initiative, le plus souvent, que de nombreux festivals sont organisés un peu partout en France. Certaines associations sont spécifiques à un monument ou un musée et sont parties prenantes dans des opérations de restauration qui associent souvent des partenaires étrangers et des actions de mécénat, comme c'est le cas pour la longue et patiente restauration du château de Versailles.

La Fondation Cartier à Paris, mécène de jeunes créateurs

Le mécénat privé est un phénomène ancien en matière culturelle mais le développement du mécénat d'entreprise, à l'image de ce qui se passe depuis longtemps aux États-

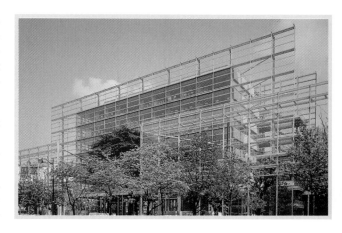

Unis, est plus récent. Par la loi du 23 juillet 1987, l'État a d'ailleurs institué un cadre légal pour ces opérations qui représentent une contribution annuelle globale de plus d'un milliard de francs au profit des arts. La création de fondations ou le financement d'opérations de prestige font aujourd'hui partie de la politique de communication de beaucoup de grands groupes. Les fondations Cartier pour les arts plastiques, Vuitton pour l'art lyrique, GAN pour le cinéma, ainsi que bien d'autres, jouent un rôle important dans l'organisation de manifestations et l'aide aux jeunes créateurs. De même, de coûteuses opérations de sauvegarde du patrimoine sont prises en charge ou cofinancées par des entreprises : EDF a ainsi participé à la restauration du dôme des Invalides, Kodak à la reproduction de la grotte de Lascaux et, en 1998, la NTV japonaise s'est engagée dans un programme de rénovation de la salle de la Joconde au musée du Louvre.

La culture, un secteur d'activité à part entière

Chaque année, les Français dépensent près de 150 milliards de francs (25 milliards de dollars) dans l'acquisition de matériel et de supports audiovisuels, ainsi que dans l'achat de livres, de journaux, de revues et de places de spectacles. À cette consommation culturelle des ménages, il faut ajouter celle des entreprises, de l'État et des collectivités territoriales, ce qui représente au total un marché proche de 200 milliards de francs (33 milliards de dollars). Les industries et les services qui satisfont à cette demande sont donc devenus un secteur à part entière de l'économie, qui emploie plus de 300 000 personnes et connaît, de plus, une croissance soutenue.

Au nombre des activités économiques touchant à la culture et aux arts, on trouve en tête la presse, l'édition et les industries graphiques (avec un chiffre d'affaires de plus de 100 milliards de francs – 16,6 milliards de dollars), suivies par les activités audiovisuelles : télévision, industries du disque, cinéma (chiffre d'affaires annuel de l'ordre de 70 milliards de francs – 11,6 milliards de dollars). Le marché de l'art représente, lui aussi, un enjeu économique non négligeable : le chiffre d'affaires des ventes aux enchères, porté par l'augmentation des ventes d'œuvres contemporaines, est de l'ordre de 5 milliards de francs par an (0,8 milliard de dollars). Le nombre des galeries d'art a doublé en province au cours des années quatre-vingt, tandis qu'apparaissaient à Paris, aux côtés des secteurs traditionnels du faubourg Saint-Honoré et de Saint-Germain-des-Prés, deux nouveaux quartiers pour le commerce de l'art : celui de Beaubourg et, plus récemment, celui de la Bastille.

Mémoire et patrimoine

La notion de patrimoine s'est progressivement élargie pour recouvrir désormais de nombreux témoignages du passé jusqu'ici négligés mais comporte aussi une dimension esthétique, qui touche en particulier aux paysages. Les missions traditionnelles de conservation du patrimoine concernant les monuments publics, les édifices religieux et les sites archéologiques restent cependant centrales et s'appuient sur des moyens accrus et la mise en œuvre de techniques de plus en plus sophistiquées.

Conservation, restauration, archéologie

D'importants programmes thématiques, engagés notamment en faveur des cathédrales et des parcs et jardins, montrent que le patrimoine classique n'est pas négligé. Globalement le nombre d'inscriptions à l'Inventaire des monuments historiques s'est accru au rythme de plusieurs centaines par an depuis 1980 et on compte actuellement près de 40 000 bâtiments classés ou inscrits.

La restauration est au cœur de l'activité de la Direction du patrimoine du ministère de la Culture, qui s'appuie sur les techniques élaborées par des laboratoires français et étrangers. Tous les supports traditionnellement fragiles ou menacés par les outrages du temps – pierres, vitraux, parois ou murs peints, tissus..., bénéficient de l'attention des chercheurs. Quelques réalisations exemplaires montrent les progrès réalisés dans ce domaine : le nettoyage au laser de la cathédrale d'Amiens, la restauration des vitraux de Chartres ou de Troyes, la remise en état des orgues de Notre-Dame ou de l'église Saint-Eustache à Paris. Recours à la technique, également, pour l'étude des

Au service de restauration des musées nationaux, inspection au microscope de «La résurrection de Lazare», œuvre de Gérard Saint-Jean (fin XVIᵉ siècle)

diverses pollutions subies, avant leur réfection, par les soixante-neuf statues de la cour Napoléon du Louvre ou pour la restauration du dôme des Invalides, selon un procédé de dorure à la feuille destiné à résister aux intempéries.

Dans le domaine de l'archéologie, plus de 200 000 sites sont actuellement répertoriés sur l'ensemble du territoire ; leur exploitation permet d'explorer jusqu'aux origines du patrimoine national. Des découvertes importantes ont permis de renouveler notre connaissance de la période néolithique et de l'âge du fer : sur les rives de la Seine, en amont de Paris, trois pirogues miraculeusement conservées ont été mises au jour ; sur le chantier du lac de Chalain, dans le Jura, ont pu être reconstituées les maisons sur pilotis caractéristiques de cette période ; à la Combe d'Arc (Ardèche) enfin, un somptueux bestiaire mis au jour fin 1994 égale celui de Lascaux. L'archéologie médiévale a profité des travaux d'urbanisme réalisés dans plusieurs villes : à Paris, les travaux d'aménagement du Grand Louvre ont donné lieu à des fouilles sans précédent et ont permis de trouver d'importants vestiges de cette époque, notamment ceux du donjon érigé par Philippe Auguste à la fin du XIIᵉ siècle.

Nouveaux objets

Insensiblement, la notion même de patrimoine s'est élargie au cours des dernières décennies, pour englober tout un ensemble de repères autrefois négligés : les arts et traditions populaires, l'architecture urbaine de la fin du XIXᵉ et du XXᵉ siècle, l'architecture industrielle et finalement tous les lieux de l'activité humaine qu'il convient d'arracher à l'oubli, y compris actuellement les paysages ruraux emblématiques de certaines provinces. L'impulsion est d'abord venue des ethnologues, soucieux de préserver le témoignage des modes de vie des sociétés rurales. C'est à l'un d'entre eux, Georges-Henri Rivière, aidé par Claude Lévi-Strauss, que l'on doit la création, sur le site du Jardin d'acclimatation à Paris, du musée des Arts et Traditions populaires. Cet exemple a été suivi partout en France afin de conserver la mémoire des pratiques régionales et locales : c'est l'objet du Musée camarguais, entre Provence et Languedoc, du Musée dauphinois dans les Alpes, ou encore des nombreux écomusées qui se sont ouverts récemment dans la plupart des régions. La mission du Patrimoine ethnologique veille à préserver la mémoire de ces traditions séculaires.

Le Palais du Luxembourg ouvre ses portes au public lors des Journées du Patrimoine qui connaissent chaque année un succès grandissant, 20 septembre 1998

Les centres-villes font l'objet de protections spécifiques depuis la loi Malraux de 1962, qui instaure les procédures de réhabilitation dans les programmes d'aménagement du tissu urbain. Mais l'ancienneté ou la présence de monuments ne sont plus les seuls critères de préservation et les paysages industriels et urbains, caractéristiques des deux derniers siècles, sont aujourd'hui sauvegardés. Dans les bassins houillers de l'Est et du Nord, l'État et les collectivités locales se sont efforcés de préserver les lieux symbolisant l'histoire de la mine et des luttes sociales qui lui sont attachées : le carreau Simon à Forbach (Moselle), ou celui de Denain qui inspira à Zola l'atmosphère de son roman *Germinal*. Enfin, de nombreux

bâtiments ou sites urbains présentant un intérêt architectural ou historique sont à leur tour entrés dans le champ du patrimoine : gares, restaurants, salles de spectacles et même anciennes maisons closes peuvent être classés monuments historiques s'ils sont un témoignage caractéristique d'une époque et d'une société.

Nouveaux supports

La France, patrie de Niepce, de Daguerre, de Nadar, de Doisneau et de Cartier-Bresson, ne peut négliger l'art de la photographie dont elle demeure une terre d'élection. Au fort de Saint-Cyr, près de Versailles, sont stockés depuis 1981 plus de cinq millions de négatifs, œuvres des plus grands photographes.

L'une des tâches de la mission du Patrimoine photographique est d'acquérir ou de gérer des fonds qui ont marqué l'histoire de la photographie, comme la collection de missions photographiques conduites partout dans le monde au début de ce siècle à l'initiative d'Albert Kahn ou comme la collection Harcourt. Elle a également bénéficié de la générosité de photographes illustres, celle de Jacques-Henri Lartigue laissant plus de quatre-vingts années de clichés allant de la République d'Émile Loubet (1899-1906) à celle de François Mitterrand ; celle d'Amélie Galup, qui fixa sur quelque 2 800 plaques de verre une société rurale au travail ou en fête entre 1895 et 1920 ; ou encore celle de Willy Ronis, témoin des quartiers populaires de Paris dans les années cinquante. Par ailleurs, afin d'assurer son rôle de témoin, le Centre Georges Pompidou pratique une politique d'achat systématique de photographies contemporaines.

Le cinéma a, lui aussi, un patrimoine à défendre. Henri Langlois, fondateur de la cinémathèque française, fut l'un des précurseurs de la mémoire du cinéma. Les copies de films sont systématiquement confiées au Centre national de la cinématographie (CNC), mais leur support photochimique soulève de délicats problèmes de conservation et, le cas échéant, de restauration. Lancé en 1990, un plan d'urgence sur quinze ans a été établi afin d'arracher à la corrosion les pellicules de 250 000 films tournés avant 1954. Parmi les œuvres qui ont pu ainsi échapper à la destruction et ont été restaurées figurent des chefs-d'œuvre du cinéma comme le *Napoléon* d'Abel Gance ou *L'Atalante* de Jean Vigo.

La France bénéficie d'une longue tradition de conservation systématique des archives et des documents imprimés, qui a été étendue au XXᵉ siècle à la photographie et au cinéma : c'est ce que l'on appelle le dépôt légal (dépôt d'un exemplaire de chaque document à la Bibliothèque nationale). Ce système, réorganisé par la loi de 1992, paraît une fois encore symptomatique de l'extension de la notion de patrimoine : le dépôt légal s'étend désormais aux documents audiovisuels, diffusés par les principales chaînes de radio et de télévision, ainsi qu'aux logiciels informatiques. Le besoin de conserver une mémoire photographique pour les générations futures n'est pas oublié et, depuis sa création en 1992, l'Observatoire photographique du territoire répertorie les modifications de l'environnement de sites caractéristiques de la géographie nationale.

Le goût de l'histoire

Peut-être cet intense effort de conservation du patrimoine doit-il être rapproché de l'engouement aujourd'hui manifesté en France pour l'Histoire, qu'elle soit nationale, régionale ou même familiale avec le développement des recherches généalogiques. Ces dernières années ont été ponctuées par de nombreuses manifestations commémorant de grands événements nationaux : millénaire capétien (1987), bicentenaire de la Révolution française (1989), centenaire de la naissance du général de Gaulle (1990), cinquantième anniversaire des débarquements de Normandie et de la Libération de la France (1994-1995). Ces célébrations ont eu un large succès public, attesté par la multiplication des initiatives locales : plus de mille manifestations décentralisées – expositions, colloques, concerts, fêtes et reconstitutions – ont été recensées entre 1986 et 1992. On a pu parler d'« ère de la commémoration » et même de « ruée vers le passé » pour décrire ce nouvel attachement des Français à leur mémoire collective.

La création contemporaine

Ce souci de protéger le patrimoine ne signifie pas cependant que la culture française soit aujourd'hui enfermée dans l'exaltation de ses œuvres passées. Les dernières décennies du XXe siècle sont marquées par le dynamisme renouvelé de la création.

La place des Terreaux à Lyon (Rhône) aménagée par les artistes Buren et Drevet

Arts plastiques et architecture

Depuis la fin du XIXe siècle, les créateurs français ont joué un rôle décisif dans l'éclosion de la peinture moderne : ainsi les œuvres des Impressionnistes, de Cézanne et des Fauves ont inspiré le mouvement cubiste. En témoigne aujourd'hui l'afflux des amateurs se rendant par millions chaque année visiter le Louvre, le Musée d'Orsay, le Musée national d'art moderne du Centre Georges Pompidou ou le Musée Picasso. L'évocation de ce dernier montre assez l'exceptionnel pouvoir d'attraction que Paris a longtemps exercé sur les artistes comme Van Gogh, Miro, Van Dongen, Modigliani, Soutine, Chagall, Brancusi, Giacometti et bien d'autres, venus du monde entier poursuivre leurs travaux dans les ateliers de Montparnasse ou de Montmartre.

Au lendemain des années cinquante, à la faveur du bouillonnement des tendances et des écoles picturales qui, de l'abstraction géométrique au pop'art, révolutionne une nouvelle fois l'art moderne, Paris a sans doute cédé la place à New York comme foyer des avant-gardes plastiques. Mais la création française n'en est pas moins active ; les œuvres de Daniel Buren, Pierre Soulages, César ou Ipoustéguy ont acquis une reconnaissance internationale. La jeune génération continue d'apporter sa contribution aux grandes tendances de l'art contemporain.

L'encouragement qu'apportent les pouvoirs publics à cette activité créatrice s'exprime d'abord à travers l'enseignement artistique et les facilités accordées aux jeunes artistes : allocations d'études et bourses de prestige, comme celle qui ouvre l'accès à l'Académie de France à Rome, établie à la Villa Médicis ; il se manifeste aussi par différentes aides à l'édition ou à la première exposition gérées par le Fonds d'incitation à la création (FIACRE) du ministère de la Culture. Enfin, au cours des dernières années, le soutien de l'État-mécène s'est traduit par la relance d'une pratique tombée en désuétude, la commande publique, et par une politique de grands travaux.

Le Conservatoire de musique de La Villette (Paris) conçu par l'architecte C. de Portzamparc

Certaines des commandes publiques passées aux artistes contemporains ont connu un retentissement spectaculaire : les colonnes de Daniel Buren au Palais-Royal ont été, des mois durant, l'objet de polémiques vivifiantes, rappelant l'émoi qu'avait suscité, un siècle plus tôt, l'érection de la statue de Balzac par Rodin. Pour s'en tenir à Paris, on peut également mentionner les accumulations d'Arman sur le parvis de la gare Saint-Lazare (1985), l'hommage à Picasso par César (1985), la Tour aux figures de Jean Dubuffet dans l'île Saint-Germain (1988) ou le rideau de scène du théâtre de l'Athénée peint par Jean-Pierre Chambas (1989).

Enfin les grands travaux, entrepris depuis le début des années quatre-vingt, répondent à la volonté de stimuler l'imagination d'architectes venus du monde entier : le Centre national d'art et de culture Georges Pompidou avait été construit, dans les années soixante-dix, par le Britannique Richard Rogers et l'Italien Renzo Piano. L'ancienne gare d'Orsay, symbole de l'architecture ferroviaire de la fin du siècle dernier, a été transformée pour accueillir les collections du XIXe siècle au Musée d'Orsay, œuvre de trois architectes français et d'une architecte italienne. À son tour, le plus célèbre des musées parisiens a fait peau neuve à l'occasion de son bicentenaire : le Grand Louvre a été entièrement réaménagé par l'architecte américain Pei. Symbolisé par sa pyramide de verre, cet ouvrage forme l'axe de la somptueuse perspective qui traverse les jardins des Tuileries et les Champs-Élysées et débouche sur la Grande Arche de La Défense conçue par l'architecte danois Von Spreckelsen. Au nord de la ville, le parc de La Villette, imaginé par Bernard Tschumi, se présente comme une ville-jardin intégrant toute une série d'édifices : du Zénith qui accueille les grands spectacles de variétés, à l'étonnante Géode (salle de « cinéma total ») d'Adrien Fainsilber et à la Cité de la Musique, architecture pour le son selon la formule de son auteur, Christian de Portzamparc. Enfin les rives de la Seine, en amont de Notre-Dame, retiennent elles aussi l'attention, désormais bordées par l'Institut du monde arabe de Jean Nouvel et par le nouveau siège du ministère des Finances de Paul Chemetov à Bercy. En retrait se dressent l'Opéra-Bastille, construit par l'architecte Carlos Ott, et les quatre tours de la Bibliothèque nationale de France, conçue par Dominique Perrault, qui a ouvert ses portes au public en 1996.

La musique

L'engouement collectif pour la musique recouvre les préférences les plus diverses. Toutes les formes musicales, des plus classiques aux plus populaires, comme le rock, la variété, le raï ou le rap, sont encouragées par les pouvoirs publics. L'État soutient aussi bien le Centre de musique baroque de Versailles que le Centre national du patrimoine de la chanson et des variétés, l'Orchestre national de jazz ou le Centre d'information du rock.

Dans le domaine de la musique savante, la création contemporaine a gagné de nouveaux publics à travers les œuvres d'Olivier Messiaen, de Pierre Boulez, Yannis Xenakis ou Henri Dutilleux. Cette activité créatrice se poursuit au sein de l'IRCAM (Institut de recherche et de coordination acoustique/musique). L'Ensemble intercontemporain permet la promotion de ce répertoire du XXᵉ siècle grâce à ses tournées en France et à l'étranger.

Le compositeur et chef d'orchestre Pierre Boulez dirige l'Ensemble Court-circuit, juin 1998, à Aix-en-Provence

L'art lyrique a également bénéficié de la sollicitude publique ces dernières années. L'Opéra-Bastille, ouvert en 1988, dispose des équipements techniques les plus modernes et peut accueillir dans sa grande salle 2 700 auditeurs. L'Opéra-Comique se consacre au répertoire français et le Châtelet, ancien temple de l'opérette, alterne récitals, concerts et opéras tandis que le Palais-Garnier est voué davantage à l'art chorégraphique. En province, signalons l'activité du Théâtre français de la musique à Compiègne, qui s'affirme comme un lieu d'importance pour le patrimoine lyrique français. Les Opéras de Lyon, Toulouse, Rouen, Nantes, etc., continuent d'offrir des productions de haute qualité.

La danse

À l'instar de la musique, la danse échappe de plus en plus aux classifications rigides entre classique et moderne. Le Ballet de l'Opéra de Paris a conservé sa longue tradition d'excellence et son école de danse est devenue, sous l'impulsion de Claude Bessy, l'une des premières au monde. Grâce à de nombreuses compagnies, créées depuis vingt ans, la chorégraphie a été renouvelée en profondeur. Maurice Béjart a réinventé à sa manière l'univers de la danse. D'autres, à sa suite, ont marqué cet art de leur empreinte, de Régine Chopinot à Jean-Claude Gallota, de Dominique Bagouet à Angelin Preljocaj. La danse en France s'est enrichie également des expériences menées à l'étranger par William Forsythe, Merce Cunningham ou Pina Bausch, régulièrement accueillis et fêtés sur les scènes de Paris et de province.

« Shazam », un spectacle du chorégraphe Philippe Decouflé et de la compagnie DCA

Le cinéma

Juliette Binoche, lauréate de l'Oscar de la meilleure actrice 1997 pour son rôle dans le film « Le patient anglais »

En 1995, le cinéma a fêté ses 100 ans : c'est en effet le 28 décembre 1895 qu'eut lieu sur les grands boulevards de Paris, au « Grand Café », la première projection payante organisée par les frères Lumière, qui avaient enregistré sur pellicule les premières images animées de la « Sortie des usines Lumière ». Cette date étant considérée comme celle de la naissance du spectacle cinématographique, l'année a vu se succéder des manifestations organisées sur l'ensemble du territoire français. Berceau du Septième Art, la France demeure une de ses terres d'élection et lui a donné quelques-unes de ses figures légendaires : de Méliès, génial précurseur, à la génération du réalisme poétique des années trente (Renoir, Carné, Prévert), puis à la nouvelle vague des années soixante (Truffaut, Godard, Chabrol, Malle, Rohmer). Cette tradition française du cinéma d'auteur s'est également enrichie de brillantes réussites industrielles (Pathé, Gaumont) et de stars revêtues

d'une aura internationale : Brigitte Bardot, Yves Montand ou Alain Delon hier, Gérard Depardieu, Isabelle Adjani ou Juliette Binoche aujourd'hui.

En 1997, le cinéma a enregistré 148 millions d'entrées sur le territoire national et réalisé 5,14 milliards de francs (0,85 milliard de dollars) de recettes en salle ; 57 % des Français sont allés au cinéma au moins une fois dans l'année et 39 % au moins une fois par mois. La fréquentation connaît ainsi une embellie et retrouve le niveau qu'elle atteignait dans les années 80 mais, sur la longue durée, elle connaît un recul tendanciel du fait de la concurrence de la télévision et de la vidéo.

Le cinéma français continue ainsi à jouer un rôle international reconnu. Il a bénéficié d'un système très complet de soutien à la création, à la production et à la distribution, organisé sous l'égide du Centre national de la cinématographie (CNC). Celui-ci redistribue les ressources tirées d'une taxe sur les recettes en salles, sur les ventes de cassettes-vidéo et sur la diffusion des films par la télévision. La procédure d'avance sur recettes, symbole de ce dispositif de soutien, permet aussi d'encourager les nouveaux talents et de compléter, pour des projets ambitieux, les financements classiques du circuit normal de la production. Cette politique se traduit en termes quantitatifs. Équipée de 4 400 salles de cinéma, la France a le second parc européen après la Russie. De nombreux établissements ont pu engager des travaux de modernisation. La baisse des recettes liée à une moindre fréquentation, inquiétante jusqu'à la fin des années soixante-dix,

L'équipe du film « La vie rêvée des anges », du réalisateur Erick Zonca, présenté au Festival de Cannes, 17 mai 1998, pour lequel E. Bouchez et N. Régnier ont reçu le Prix d'interprétation féminine

a pu être enrayée avec succès au cours de la décennie suivante. Le nombre des longs métrages produits chaque année se situe aux alentours de 100, dont à peu près un tiers de premiers films. Ainsi la France arrive au troisième rang mondial après l'Inde et les États-Unis pour la production de films. Enfin, situation unique en Europe, les films français représentaient en 1997 près de 35 % des entrées en salles, ce qui traduit une bonne résistance de la production française face aux films américains, qui ont une situation quasi monopolistique sur de nombreux marchés étrangers.

La vitalité de la création cinématographique française est symbolisée par quelques réalisateurs dont l'œuvre est très personnelle, qu'il s'agisse de Bertrand Tavernier (*Que la fête commence, Un dimanche à la campagne, Coup de torchon, L 627, La vie et rien d'autre, Capitaine Conan*), de Maurice Pialat (*À nos amours, Loulou, Sous le soleil de Satan, Van Gogh*), de Bertrand

Blier (*Buffet froid, Tenue de soirée, 1, 2, 3, Soleil, Mon homme*), d'André Téchiné (*Rendez-vous, Ma saison préférée, Les roseaux sauvages*), ou de Jean-Jacques Beineix (*Diva, 37°2 le matin, IP 5*). Le cinéma populaire de qualité a aussi ses talents avec Jean-Paul Rappeneau (*Cyrano de Bergerac, Le Hussard sur le toit*) et Claude Berri (*Jean de Florette, Manon des sources, Germinal*), dont les films ont reçu du public un accueil enthousiaste. Réussite aussi, pour les films comiques dans lesquels se sont illustrés des comédiens comme Josiane Balasko, Michel Blanc, Christian Clavier, Gérard Jugnot, Thierry Lhermitte, le genre ayant renoué en 1993, avec *Les Visiteurs*, avec un succès qu'il n'avait pas connu depuis les années soixante. Par ailleurs, quelques réalisateurs se sont forgés une réputation internationale tels Jean-Jacques Annaud (*L'Ours, Le Nom de la rose, L'Amant, Sept ans au Tibet*) et Luc Besson (*Le Grand Bleu, Nikita, Léon, Le cinquième élément*). Enfin, une nouvelle génération s'affirme avec Olivier Assayas, Léos Carax, Cédric Klapisch, Manuel Poirier, Éric Rochant, Christian Vincent, etc., tandis que la relève se prépare au sein de la FEMIS, Fondation européenne des métiers de l'image et du son, école installée au Palais de Tokyo à Paris.

Le théâtre

Selon une tradition qui remonte au Théâtre libre d'Antoine et qui s'est poursuivie avec l'œuvre du Cartel (Gémier, Copeau, Baty, Jouvet) dans l'entre-deux-guerres, puis avec le Théâtre national populaire (TNP) de Jean Vilar après la Libération, le dynamisme de l'art dramatique français doit beaucoup aux grands metteurs en scène qui inspirent ses orientations. Antoine Vitez, prématurément disparu en 1990, a formé des générations d'acteurs et renouvelé l'approche du répertoire, de Molière à Hugo, d'Aragon à Claudel. D'autres personnalités ont également enrichi la scène française de leurs expériences : Roger Planchon à Lyon, Marcel Maréchal à Marseille,

Une représentation
de « Phèdre »
de Jean Racine, au
théâtre de l'Odéon à
Paris, septembre 1998,
mise en scène par
L. Bondy, avec ici
N. Dréville et D. Sandre

Ariane Mnouchkine à la Cartoucherie de Vincennes, Peter Brook aux Bouffes du Nord (Paris), Jean-Pierre Vincent au Théâtre des Amandiers de Nanterre, Jorge Lavelli au Théâtre de la Colline à Paris, Georges Lavaudant à Villeurbanne, Jacques Nichet à Montpellier, Jérôme Savary au Théâtre de Chaillot, Bernard Sobel à Gennevilliers. Comme Daniel Mesguich, Patrice Chéreau, Gildas Bourdet ou Jacques Lassalle, tous continuent d'animer avec passion les scènes françaises.

Cette énumération ne donne qu'une faible idée du nombre et de la diversité des spectacles présentés chaque année. Il existe en effet 42 centres dramatiques nationaux, 170 compagnies conventionnées, 398 compagnies subventionnées. Globalement, le nombre des compagnies indépendantes a triplé au cours des années quatre-vingt et dépasse largement le millier. Enfin, de nombreuses salles ont été ouvertes, modernisées ou restaurées ces dernières années, que ce soit à Paris (Théâtre national de la Colline) ou en province (Théâtre du Port de la Lune à Bordeaux, Théâtre de la Salamandre à Lille, Nouveau Théâtre de Nice, etc).

Autre spectacle vivant, le cirque s'est renouvelé. Des compagnies comme le cirque Plume, Archaos et le Cabaret équestre Zingaro ont bouleversé ce genre. Plusieurs écoles ont fleuri et le cirque Gruss, soucieux de la tradition des chapiteaux, a su reprendre le flambeau.

Les lettres françaises : tradition et modernité

Les écrivains d'aujourd'hui doivent assurer la relève d'une brillante génération de classiques contemporains : Gide, Sartre, Camus, Céline, Malraux, Mauriac, Anouilh, Beckett, Genet ou Montherlant. La tâche est d'autant plus ardue que l'époque n'est pas marquée, comme au temps du surréalisme, par l'existence de courants clairement identifiés, moins encore d'écoles. Certes la tribu des « hussards », orpheline de Roger Nimier, d'Antoine Blondin et de Jacques Laurent, compte encore sur Michel Déon pour prolonger la tradition anti-conformiste forgée dans l'immédiat après-guerre. De leur côté, les écrivains du nouveau roman des années cinquante tels Michel Butor, Alain Robbe-Grillet et Nathalie Sarraute ont poursuivi leurs expériences littéraires, tandis que l'œuvre de Claude Simon trouvait une ultime consécration avec l'attribution du prix Nobel de littérature en 1985.

L'impression dominante est aujourd'hui celle d'un champ d'expériences singulières, chacun traçant d'œuvre en œuvre un sillon personnel. Julien Gracq qui poursuit, depuis la publication du *Château d'Argol*, un dialogue solitaire avec la grande tradition classique, est de ce point de vue exemplaire. Mentionnons également Marguerite Yourcenar, première femme élue à l'Académie française, décédée en 1987 en laissant une œuvre profondément enracinée dans l'histoire (*Mémoires d'Hadrien*, *L'Œuvre au noir*), Marguerite Duras, décédée en 1996, qui rencontra finalement le grand public avec la publication de *L'Amant*, Michel Tournier aussi, avec *Vendredi ou les limbes du Pacifique* et *Le Roi des aulnes*. Au sein de la génération suivante, Philippe Sollers, Jean-Marie Le Clézio, Patrick Modiano, Patrick Grainville,

Le Salon du Livre, qui se tient chaque année à Paris, est l'occasion d'une rencontre entre lecteurs et auteurs : le philosophe Michel Serres dédicaçant un de ses ouvrages, 22 mars 1998

Pascal Quignard, figurent parmi les valeurs les plus reconnues mais depuis les années quatre-vingt se sont révélés des auteurs talentueux comme Erik Orsenna, Jean Rouault, Patrick Chamoiseau, Didier Van Cauwelaert, Andrei Makine, Patrick Rambaud...

Le roman reste le genre le plus apprécié du public, mais la France n'oublie pas la poésie : Aragon, Saint-John Perse, René Char, Jacques Prévert et Francis Ponge ne sont pas les derniers poètes français. Jean Tardieu, décédé en 1995, mais aussi Jacques Roubaud, Michel Deguy, Yves Bonnefoy, Jacques Reda, transforment cet immense héritage et résistent avec bonheur à un climat malheureusement peu propice à ce genre littéraire.

Publics et pratiques

Au renouvellement de la création s'ajoute l'élargissement des publics. D'une part, la consommation de biens culturels continue à être inégalement répartie selon l'âge, le niveau d'études, l'appartenance sociale ou l'origine géographique ; d'autre part, l'essor de la demande culturelle au sein de toutes les catégories sociales se traduit aussi bien par un équipement croissant des ménages en matériel audiovisuel que par l'augmentation de la fréquentation des musées et des salles de spectacles.

L'accès à la culture

Les pouvoirs publics mènent une politique active de diffusion culturelle qui passe d'abord par un effort d'éducation et de formation auprès des plus jeunes. La place réservée aux apprentissages artistiques – musique et arts plastiques principalement –, autrefois modeste, s'est fortement étendue au cours des années quatre-vingt. Un réseau très dense de conservatoires régionaux et municipaux permet, moyennant un faible coût, de pratiquer la musique, le théâtre et la danse. Enfin, plusieurs établissements d'excellence se consacrent à la formation des futurs professionnels : les deux Conservatoires nationaux supérieurs de musique, l'École nationale des beaux-arts, le Conservatoire national supérieur d'art dramatique, l'École nationale de la photographie et la Fondation européenne des métiers de l'image et du son (FEMIS).

Les chaînes de télévision publiques ont depuis longtemps réservé une partie – même minime – de leurs programmes à la culture : l'émission littéraire Apostrophes, animée chaque ven-

Le « Mur des mots » de l'École des Beaux-Arts de Blois (Loir-et-Cher) imaginé par l'artiste Ben

dredi pendant dix ans par Bernard Pivot, a été reprise sous le nom de Bouillon de culture en élargissant le champ des événements culturels qui y sont présentés. Depuis 1992, le public bénéficie d'une chaîne spécifiquement consacrée à la culture, Arte, qui constitue la première expérience européenne de cette nature menée conjointement par la France et l'Allemagne, avec des programmes bilingues. Par ailleurs, Arte n'émettant qu'en soirée, une chaîne à vocation éducative, La Cinquième, occupe désormais ce canal tout au long de la journée.

Les lieux de la culture

Pour attirer un public plus large de citadins, André Malraux avait conçu dès le début des années soixante les Maisons des jeunes et de la culture. Trente ans plus tard, les espaces à vocation culturelle se sont multipliés. Dans le domaine du théâtre, des efforts ont été consentis avec succès afin de monter ou de restaurer partout en France des lieux de création. Pour leur part, les salles de concert de rock et de music-hall accueillent en moyenne chaque année quinze millions de spectateurs. Le Parc omnisports de Paris-Bercy a une capacité d'accueil de 15 000 personnes, mais des concerts géants peuvent aussi être organisés dans des stades, comme celui des Rolling Stones au Grand Stade de France en 1998. Les salles de type Zénith à Paris, Montpellier et Toulon connaissent un grand succès et se multiplient en France (Lyon, Marseille, Nancy, Caen, Tours...).

Les musées jouent eux aussi un rôle déterminant : une discipline nouvelle, la muséologie, s'est constituée afin de faire de ces temples du beau, voués à la conservation, des lieux de circulation et de promotion, largement ouverts au public. L'ouverture du Centre Georges Pompidou, pour l'art contemporain, puis celles du Musée d'Orsay, consacré à la seconde moitié du XIXe siècle, du musée Picasso à l'hôtel Salé, de la Cité des sciences et de l'industrie, ont stimulé l'ensemble des musées français. En vingt-cinq ans, près de quatre-vingts musées ont été créés ou rénovés, à Paris et en province. On peut ainsi citer le musée des Beaux-Arts de Lyon, qui occupe l'intégralité du Palais Saint-Pierre, ancienne abbaye du XVIIe siècle rénovée par les architectes Philippe Dubois et Jean-Michel Wilmotte. Inauguré en avril 1998 après 9 ans de travaux pour un coût de 400 millions de francs (66,6 millions de dollars), ce musée est désormais le plus important et le plus riche de France, après le Louvre, et expose 6 300 œuvres sur 15 000 m^2, avec en particulier le legs de peintures impressionnistes de Jacqueline Delubac. La réalisation de certains musées de province a été confiée à des architectes importants, par exemple le musée d'Art contemporain de Lyon, installé

Les bibliothèques restent l'un des lieux de culture les plus fréquentés en France

depuis 1995 dans un édifice conçu par Renzo Piano, ou le Carré d'art à Nîmes, confié à Norman Foster.

L'œuvre majeure reste cependant le Grand Louvre. L'aile Richelieu dont le volume est comparable, à lui seul, à celui de tout le Musée d'Orsay, a été ouverte en 1993. Depuis l'automne 1994, l'aile Denon réaménagée est accessible au public et présente les collections de sculptures italiennes, espagnoles et d'Europe du Nord, dont les deux célèbres *Esclaves* de Michel Ange. L'ensemble a été achevé en 1997, avec l'ouverture de trente-cinq nouvelles salles consacrées à la peinture française du XVIIe au XIXe siècle et le réaménagement des salles des Antiquités. Au total, il existe 34 musées nationaux, dont 19 hors de Paris, et près de 900 musées contrôlés, qui appartiennent le plus souvent aux collectivités locales. Leur succès est à la hauteur de l'attente : plus de 70 millions de visiteurs par an. Ceux-ci se pressent pour admirer des chefs-d'œuvre qui font partie du patrimoine mondial de l'humanité mais aussi de grandes expositions temporaires dont les plus récentes furent consacrées à Matisse, Poussin, Cézanne, de La Tour, etc.

Les bibliothèques restent l'un des lieux de culture les plus fréquentés en France. Outre les bibliothèques scolaires et universitaires, il existe environ 3 000 bibliothèques municipales. Chaque département gère aussi une bibliothèque de prêt, l'ensemble des bibliothèques départementales disposant de près de 21 000 points de desserte dont 17 000 fixes et 4 000 itinérants, du type « bibliobus ». Paris dispose de bibliothèques prestigieuses comme celles du Centre Georges Pompidou, de l'Arsenal, les bibliothèques Sainte-Geneviève et Mazarine. La capitale s'est dotée de la Bibliothèque nationale de France, ouverte en 1996, d'une capacité de 30 millions d'ouvrages et qui accueille les fonds des départements livres, imprimés, des périodiques et de la phonothèque de l'ancienne Bibliothèque nationale Richelieu.

Les fêtes de la culture

La culture a aussi ses moments privilégiés. La Fête de la musique, lancée en 1982, symbolise un peu une nouvelle approche tendant à dépasser les habituels clivages entre le spectacle officiel organisé et la pratique populaire spontanée. Tous les 21 juin, elle rassemble des dizaines de milliers de musiciens professionnels ou amateurs, partout à travers les villes. Aujourd'hui, près de 80 pays ont repris

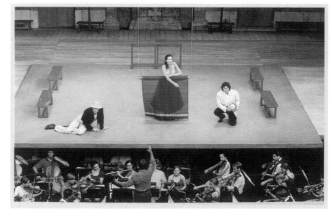

Lors du festival lyrique d'Aix-en-Provence (Bouches-du-Rhône), en juillet 1998, répétition du « Don Giovanni » de Mozart, mis en scène par P. Brook et dirigé par Cl. Abbado

cette initiative. Elle ne doit pas faire oublier les grands festivals d'été consacrés à l'opéra (Aix-en-Provence), au chant choral (Vaison-la-Romaine), au théâtre (Avignon) et à la musique contemporaine (Strasbourg). Les variétés et le rock ont également leurs grand-messes : le Printemps de Bourges est devenu une tradition et les Trans-Musicales de Rennes ont révélé Étienne Daho, Niagara ou Stéphan Eicher.

La Fête du cinéma, elle, a été créée en 1985. Manifestation de promotion exceptionnelle longue d'une semaine environ, elle permet, pour le prix d'une entrée, d'assister à une journée complète de projections. Elle tente de s'exporter à l'étranger, par le canal des ambassades et des Alliances françaises. Également importants, les festivals internationaux, et d'abord le Festival de Cannes, dont la Palme d'Or constitue sans doute la plus prestigieuse des consécrations. Les manifestations cinématographiques se sont multipliées ces dernières années : festival d'Avoriaz du film fantastique et de science-fiction, festival de Deauville consacré au cinéma américain et qui a pour pendant, aux États-Unis, le festival du film français à Sarasota, festival du film policier de Cognac ou encore festival du court-métrage de Biarritz. Ces festivals constituent aussi de puissants leviers pour le développement du tourisme régional.

La littérature est également fêtée : Lire en fête, qui succède au Temps des livres en 1998, développe chaque année au mois d'octobre une série d'initiatives destinées à faire partager au plus grand nombre la passion de l'écrit. L'organisation du Salon du livre est par ailleurs l'occasion de présenter au public, chaque année depuis 1981, la plus grande librairie de France : 1 200 éditeurs présentent sur 450 stands toute la gamme de leurs produits éditoriaux, de la littérature aux encyclopédies, du livre d'art aux collections pour la jeunesse. Stimulés par cette réussite, une dizaine d'autres salons se sont implantés en province, à Brive, Bordeaux, Nantes, Le Mans, Saint-Etienne, Saint-Malo, Lyon ou Strasbourg... Il faut aussi noter, dans un domaine proche, le festival de la bande dessinée d'Angoulême.

Le patrimoine, enfin, a une occasion privilégiée de dévoiler ses trésors au public. Une fois par an, les monuments ouvrent leurs portes aux visiteurs qui déambulent gratuitement dans les salons de l'Élysée ou de l'Institut de France, de l'Hôtel Matignon ou du Palais-Bourbon, de la Bibliothèque nationale ou de l'Opéra-Bastille. Deux millions de personnes profitent de l'occasion pour pénétrer dans quelque 8 300 édifices nationaux. C'est le même principe qui inspire la campagne « Visitez un jardin en France », destinée chaque printemps à faire connaître cet aspect trop peu connu du patrimoine français.

L'ouverture sur le monde

La Joconde est le plus célèbre des tableaux exposés au Louvre : le chef-d'œuvre de Léonard de Vinci symbolise ainsi ce que la culture française doit, depuis toujours, aux créateurs des autres pays et aux influences étrangères. À l'orée du troisième millénaire, cette tradition d'ouverture réciproque ne se dément pas.

Accéder à toutes les cultures

Le public manifeste avec régularité son goût pour les œuvres venues du monde entier : près de la moitié des ventes de disques et cassettes en France concerne les variétés internationales, tandis que les deux-tiers des recettes des salles de cinéma proviennent de films étrangers. Ceux-ci sont le plus souvent américains, mais Paris est sans doute la seule ville du monde où le cinéphile peut, selon ses goûts et sa curiosité, visionner les œuvres, classiques ou récentes, venues d'Inde, d'Afrique, de Chine ou d'Amérique latine, ainsi que de tous les pays européens.

Cet éclectisme se confirme dans de nombreux autres domaines. En témoigne l'accueil enthousiaste que trouvent en France les chorégraphes d'origine étrangère, suisse comme Gallotta, américains comme Merce Cunningham, William Forsythe ou Carolyn Carlson qui a dirigé le groupe de recherches de l'Opéra de Paris. La même remarque vaut pour le théâtre : Peter Brook, Lucian Pintillé, Jorge Lavelli, animent plusieurs scènes françaises d'importance. L'ancien théâtre de l'Odéon, rebaptisé Théâtre de l'Europe et placé sous la direction du Catalan Luis Pasqual, est destiné à accueillir en priorité les spectacles représentant les grandes traditions scéniques étrangères. La même volonté d'ouverture prévaut dans le domaine des arts plastiques, comme le montre le succès rencontré par les expositions d'écoles ou d'artistes étrangers régulièrement organisées dans le cadre des musées nationaux. Le Centre Georges Pompidou s'est fait, depuis sa création, une spécialité des grandes rétrospectives consacrées à l'influence réciproque des cultures : de Paris-New York et Paris-Moscou voici quinze ans, jusqu'aux hommages plus récemment rendus aux figures cosmopolites de Borgès, d'Amado ou de Brancusi.

La chanteuse Patricia Kaas au Parc des Princes (Paris), lors d'un concert célébrant la Fête de la musique, 21 juin 1997

Les pouvoirs publics encouragent à leur tour ce goût des œuvres étrangères et s'efforcent de les faire mieux connaître du public français. Dans le domaine de la littérature, des efforts sont faits pour permettre aux éditeurs de s'affranchir des surcoûts résultant de la traduction : un Collège international des traducteurs a été créé à Arles en 1989 et a aidé à la publication de centaines de titres en langues étrangères. Par ailleurs, les opérations « Belles étrangères » permettent, deux à trois fois par an, de présenter aux lecteurs français telle ou telle littérature étrangère en invitant ses représentants les plus réputés : les écrivains des Pays-Bas, d'Israël, d'Égypte, de Suède et de Corée ont ainsi été fêtés, 1998 étant l'année de la littérature brésilienne.

Des affinités électives

Aucune culture, aucun continent n'est donc négligé. Il n'en existe pas moins certaines affinités électives qui expriment, aujourd'hui encore, la vitalité d'anciennes traditions d'échanges et de solidarités. Dans cette perspective, une place particulière doit être faite

à la francophonie. Depuis que les ministres de la Culture de tous les pays francophones se sont réunis pour la première fois, en 1981 à Cotonou, se multiplient les initiatives destinées à renforcer les liens entre les créateurs et les publics de l'espace francophone. Le Festival international des francophonies de Limoges est ainsi devenu le rendez-vous annuel des théâtres francophones du monde entier, tandis que les Francofolies de La Rochelle

Une représentation
chorégraphique devant le
Palais des Papes
en Avignon (Vaucluse)

accueillent toutes les tendances de la chanson d'expression française. La littérature de langue française n'est pas en reste, tant est importante la contribution que lui ont apportée les écrivains du monde entier. Sur les cinq continents, elle affirme une vitalité retrouvée : une dimension épique dans les récits des Antilles et de l'océan Indien, une gravité nouvelle chez les prosateurs du Maghreb et du Levant, un sens renouvelé du mystère chez les poètes africains. Il n'est qu'à évoquer pour s'en convaincre les œuvres de Léopold Sedar Senghor, Aimé Césaire, Tahar Ben Jelloun ou Ampathé Bâ.

Qu'ils aient ou non la langue française en partage, de nombreux pays du Sud entretiennent avec la France des relations culturelles privilégiées. Quelques lieux, quelques événements voués à la promotion de ces échanges méritent d'être évoqués : ainsi l'Institut du monde arabe ou la Maison de l'Amérique latine, à Paris, rappellent tout ce qui rapproche la culture française de la Méditerranée et de la latinité. Le festival Musiques métisses d'Angoulême a également permis au public français de découvrir des groupes africains comme Touré Kounda ou Mory Kante, qui ont depuis acquis une véritable notoriété internationale. Le festival des Trois Continents à Nantes, chaque automne, présente une sélection de films d'Afrique, d'Asie et d'Amérique du Sud. Enfin, la Maison des cultures du monde, créée en 1982, adresse ses invitations aux musiciens, artistes, danseurs et peintres du monde entier afin de leur permettre de se produire en France.

Au moment où les peuples d'Europe nouent des liens politiques et économiques toujours plus étroits, la France fait en sorte que la dimension culturelle ne soit pas négligée : dans ce but, elle soutient quelques grandes initiatives institutionnelles comme le rendez-vous annuel des capitales européennes de la culture, la création du prix littéraire européen ou la mise en place du programme de soutien au cinéma et à l'audiovisuel. Mais l'Europe de la culture, c'est également le foisonnement spontané des initiatives, des complicités et des rencontres : la multiplication des traductions, les coproductions cinématographiques en nombre croissant, la formation commune des jeunes créateurs... Ou encore, pour ne retenir que quelques exemples symboliques, l'accueil régulier du Piccolo teatro de Milan sur les scènes françaises, l'organisation d'une Semaine de la musique suédoise à Paris, la reconstitution des chemins de Saint-Jacques de Compostelle, la présentation des chefs-d'œuvre de la peinture anglaise au sein des collections françaises, etc.

Exception culturelle

La France, agissant de concert avec ses partenaires de l'Union européenne et de la communauté francophone, a insisté, lors de la phase finale des négociations du GATT, pour qu'un traitement particulier soit réservé aux biens et services culturels.

On comprendra, à la lumière de ce qui précède, que cette attitude de principe ne pouvait être dictée par la volonté de limiter si peu que ce fût les échanges culturels. Bien au contraire, en affirmant que la culture ne pouvait être considérée comme une banale marchandise, en réclamant pour chaque État le droit d'encourager ses créateurs, la France entendait aider au maintien des diverses traditions qui constituent le patri-

moine culturel de l'humanité. C'est la même ambition qui inspire son action au sein des enceintes internationales vouées à la promotion de la culture, comme le Conseil de l'Europe et l'UNESCO : favoriser la libre circulation des œuvres de l'esprit, tout en veillant à ce que chaque culture, bénéficiant d'une égale dignité, puisse assurer les conditions de sa survie et de son constant renouvellement.

Le château de Chambord (1519-1537), bâti pour François Ier, chef-d'œuvre de la Renaissance

Pour en savoir plus :

Ministère de la Culture et de la Communication, *Chiffres clés 1997 - Statistiques de la culture* (sous la dir. de J. Cardona et C. Lacroix), La Documentation française, 1998.

O. Donnat, *Les Français face à la culture. De l'exclusion à l'éclectisme*, La Découverte, 1994.

P. Goetschel, E. Loyer, *Histoire culturelle et intellectuelle de la France au XXe siècle*, Armand Colin, 1994.

P. Urfalino, *L'invention de la politique culturelle*, Ministère de la Culture, La Documentation française, 1996.

Institutions et vie culturelles, La Documentation française - CNFPT, collection Les Notices, 1996.

« Culture et société », in *Cahiers français*, La Documentation française, 1993.

O. Donnat, *Les pratiques culturelles des Français. 1997*, Ministère de la Culture et de la Communication, La Documentation française, 1998.

Ministère de la Culture, Direction des Archives de France, *Célébrations nationales*, 1996.

Ministère de la Culture, Département des études et de la prospective, *Les jeunes et les sorties culturelles*, 1995.

P. Fouché, *L'édition française depuis 1945*, Édition du Cercle de la Librairie, 1998.

Les 300 mannequins du défilé Yves Saint-Laurent présentant une rétrospective des 40 ans de création du couturier avant le coup d'envoi de la finale France-Brésil au Stade de France (Seine-Saint-Denis), 12 juillet 1998

19

Les médias

En France, la liberté d'expression est un droit. L'article 11 de la Déclaration des Droits de l'homme et du citoyen dispose que tout citoyen peut parler, écrire, imprimer librement, sauf à répondre de l'abus de cette liberté dans les cas déterminés par la loi. Sans liberté de la presse, il ne peut y avoir de démocratie. Pourtant la conquête de cette liberté ne s'est pas faite sans heurts. Après 1789 alternent périodes libérales et périodes autoritaires, et il faut attendre la loi du 22 juillet 1881 pour consacrer définitivement le principe d'une presse libre. La loi supprime toutes sortes d'entraves (autorisation, caution, timbre...) et limite la portée des délits de presse. On assiste alors à une multiplication des titres.

Pendant l'Occupation, une partie de la presse soutient la politique de collaboration avec l'Allemagne nazie. Elle fait l'objet d'une épuration rigoureuse à la Libération. Le Gouvernement provisoire de la République édicte, entre juin et août 1944, trois ordonnances afin de protéger la presse des interventions du pouvoir politique, mais aussi des pressions financières et des servitudes commerciales.

La logique du marché n'étant pas toujours favorable au pluralisme, les lois du 23 octobre 1984, puis des 1er août et 27 novembre 1986 ont pour objectifs de garantir la pluralité de la presse, essentielle au débat démocratique, et d'empêcher la concentration d'un trop grand nombre de titres au sein d'un même groupe. Le seuil maximum de diffusion des quotidiens contrôlés – par fusion ou acquisition – par un seul groupe de presse est depuis limité à 30 %.

Un des nombreux kiosques à journaux parisiens

Parallèlement, au fil des décennies, le législateur a mis au point un dispositif susceptible de protéger les personnes, de garantir la paix publique et d'assurer l'indépendance et le statut des journalistes. C'est dans ce cadre juridique qu'évolue aujourd'hui la presse française.

Il y avait en France, fin 1997, quelque 30 000 journalistes titulaires de

la carte de presse, dont 37,5 % de femmes. Plus de la moitié d'entre eux avait moins de quarante ans.

La presse écrite : un tableau contrasté

Avec 3 100 titres environ et un tirage annuel de 8 milliards d'exemplaires, la presse écrite connaît des difficultés. Le tableau est cependant très contrasté : les quotidiens nationaux se battent avec acharnement et les plus importants d'entre eux, *Le Monde*, *Libération*, *Le Parisien-Aujourd'hui*, se sont remis en question depuis 1994 et ont tenté de mieux répondre aux nouvelles attentes du public. Avec succès semble-t-il puisque, depuis lors, leurs ventes connaissent une embellie.

La presse régionale, quant à elle, a su s'adapter plus tôt aux nouvelles demandes et reste le premier média français, devant la télévision. La presse spécialisée, enfin, est en plein essor.

La presse quotidienne nationale et régionale, non compris les quotidiens spécialisés, représente une petite centaine de titres et un tirage de l'ordre de 12 millions d'exemplaires.

La presse quotidienne nationale

La plupart des journaux sortent le matin ; seuls *Le Monde* et *La Croix* paraissent l'après-midi. Ils ont, dans l'ensemble, renoncé à afficher une couleur politique tranchée. Le ton général est devenu plus neutre, à l'exception de l'éditorial et des pages d'opinions.

La presse quotidienne d'opinion, si puissante avant-guerre, a quasiment disparu : demeurent *La Lettre de la Nation*, organe du Rassemblement pour la République (RPR), *L'Humanité*, fondée par Jean Jaurès en 1904, organe du Parti communiste français, *Présent*, tribune de l'extrême droite. *La Croix*, quotidien catholique, appartient au premier groupe français de presse religieuse, Bayard Presse, mais il est plus un quotidien d'informations générales qu'un quotidien d'opinion à proprement parler.

Au journal *Le Monde*, le directeur, Jean-Marie Colombani, assiste à la mise en place de la nouvelle maquette du quotidien, décembre 1994

Les titres phares de la presse quotidienne d'information dite de qualité sont *Le Monde*, *Le Figaro* et *Libération*. Leur influence est importante non seulement sur l'opinion mais aussi sur les autres médias. Leur diffusion globale (nombre d'exemplaires vendus), proche d'un million d'exemplaires pour près de cinq millions de lecteurs en 1997, est pourtant inférieure à celle des autres grands journaux européens. Le fleuron de la presse populaire est *Le Parisien-Aujourd'hui*. Conservateur à l'origine, il a pris des mesures radicales pour se redresser et renouveler son lectorat. Il s'est politiquement recentré, ouvrant ses colonnes à des éditorialistes de centre-gauche, et a développé une stratégie de presse régionale ; il propose aussi une édition nationale baptisée *Aujourd'hui*. Ces efforts ont été couronnés de succès puisque *Le Parisien-Aujourd'hui*, avec une diffusion de l'ordre de 500 000 exemplaires et deux millions de lecteurs, est devenu le numéro deux de la presse quotidienne nationale.

À l'inverse, le quotidien d'information populaire *France Soir* n'a pu redresser la barre et est passé de 1,5 million d'exemplaires en 1955 à 400 000 en 1985 et 173 000 en 1997. Avec le format tabloïd adopté en 1998, *France Soir* se donne une nouvelle chance pour retrouver un lectorat plus fidèle.

Les quotidiens thématiques connaissent plus de succès. C'est notamment le cas de la presse quotidienne d'informations économiques et financières, *Les Échos* (129 000 exemplaires diffusés en 1997), *La Tribune* (90 000 exemplaires), et de la presse quotidienne sportive avec *L'Équipe*, premier quotidien français, et ses deux millions de lecteurs (381 000 exemplaires en moyenne, près de 500 000 le lundi).

Apparue en 1993, la « presse de rue » annonçait alors un tirage situé entre 45 000 et 50 000 exemplaires. Vendue entre 10 et 15 francs le numéro dans les lieux publics (métro, gare...) par des chômeurs et des sans-logis qui conservent une part du produit de la vente et obtiennent ainsi une couverture sociale, elle traverse aujourd'hui des difficultés financières et une baisse de ses ventes. Parmi les titres phares de ces mensuels ou hebdomadaires, *Macadam-Journal*, *La Rue*, *Sans-Abri* et *L'Itinérant* continuent de paraître au prix d'une baisse de leur tirage et de leurs ventes.

La presse quotidienne régionale

Cette presse a mieux résisté à la crise que la presse nationale, avec 409 titres et une diffusion annuelle de 2,2 milliards d'exemplaires. Elle bénéficie souvent d'une situation d'exclusivité territoriale et donc d'un marché publicitaire protégé ; ses informations de proximité et de services, ses pages locales la protègent de la concurrence de la radio et de la télévision.

La presse régionale a commencé à se moderniser au début des années soixante-dix avec l'offset, la télématique et le fac-similé, ce qui a exigé des moyens financiers considérables qui n'ont pu être réunis que par le regroupement des titres et la concentration. Quelques grands groupes dominent aujourd'hui : le groupe Hersant contrôle ainsi environ 30 % du marché (*Le Dauphiné Libéré*, *Paris-Nor-*

mandie, *Le Progrès de Lyon*, *Les Dernières Nouvelles d'Alsace*, *Nord-Matin*, *Nord-Éclair*, *Le Havre-Libre*, *Midi-Libre*, etc.). Hachette-Filipacchi Presse est également très présent (*Le Provençal*, *Le Méridional*, *La République*) aux côtés de groupes plus modestes constitués autour d'un titre phare (*Ouest-France*, *Sud-Ouest*, *La Dépêche du Midi*, *La Voix du Nord*). *Ouest-France*, le premier des quotidiens français (17 éditions, soit plus de 800 000 exemplaires), est diffusé dans douze départements en Bretagne, en Normandie et dans les Pays de la Loire. Avec environ 7 millions d'exemplaires vendus quotidiennement, soit plus de 20 millions de lecteurs, la presse quotidienne régionale dispute à la télévision le titre de premier média national.

Une étude menée par Ipsos Médias montre que 45,4 % des Français âgés de plus de 15 ans lisent régulièrement un quotidien régional et que 43,8 % d'entre eux sont des lecteurs fidèles. Les lecteurs âgés de 35 à 59 ans, pour la plupart des actifs, se partagent équitablement entre hommes et femmes. Enfin, tandis que le taux de pénétration de la presse quotidienne régionale atteint seulement les 17 % en région parisienne, il dépasse généralement les 50 % dans l'ensemble des autres régions de France.

L'économie de la presse

La presse écrite française occupe la vingt-deuxième place dans le monde et la septième en Europe, avec 157 exemplaires pour 1 000 habitants. 49 % des Français lisent un quotidien tous les jours, contre 55 % il y a vingt ans. En 1998, le budget « presse » moyen d'un ménage français est de l'ordre de 793 francs (132 dollars).

À la crise économique et à la concurrence de la télévision, qui ont eu pour conséquence la désaffection des annonceurs publicitaires, s'est ajoutée l'interdiction ou la stricte limitation de la publicité sur les tabacs et alcools. En 1980, la presse écrite recevait encore 60 % des recettes publicitaires, 20 % revenant à la télévision. En 1996, la part de la presse est tombée à 47,3 % (petites annonces comprises) contre 33,5 % pour la télévision.

Par ailleurs, la presse française souffre d'un cruel manque de fonds propres et, partant, supporte des frais financiers élevés. Or, elle a dû, et doit encore, investir massivement pour se moderniser et survivre. L'augmentation du prix du papier et le coût de la diffusion (qui absorbe les deux tiers des recettes de vente) pèsent sur le prix de revient d'un produit qu'il faut vendre deux fois, aux lecteurs et aux annonceurs. Comparé à ceux pratiqués en Grande-Bretagne et en Allemagne, le prix de vente des quotidiens français est sensiblement plus élevé, malgré les aides de l'État : 7,50 francs (1,25 dollar) pour *Le Monde* contre 1,70 franc (0,30 dollar) pour son homologue britannique *The Times*. Jadis aligné sur le prix du timbre-poste, le prix de vente des journaux a été multiplié par huit entre 1970 et 1980 alors que le coût de la vie n'était multiplié que par quatre.

Le poids économique de la presse en France (60 milliards de francs de chiffre d'affaires en 1997, soit 10 milliards de dollars) est inférieur à celui de la presse britannique et allemande qui ont subi et affronté la crise plus tôt. En 1996, environ 2 000 titres de la presse française ont été exportés vers 107 pays pour un chiffre d'affaires de 2,74 milliards de francs (45 millions de dollars).

La presse hebdomadaire

La presse magazine, pour sa part, est très dynamique. Avec 1 354 exemplaires vendus pour 1 000 habitants, les Français sont les premiers lecteurs de magazines dans le monde. 95,5 % des Français sont, en 1998, lecteurs, réguliers ou non, de ce type de presse.

Les hebdomadaires d'information

La France ne compte pas moins de sept grands hebdomadaires d'information générale et ces publications, *Le Nouvel Observateur*, *L'Express*, *Le Point*, *L'Événement du Jeudi*, *Paris-Match*, *VSD* et, le dernier né, *Marianne*, créé en 1997, sont globalement en bonne santé. Grâce à des restructurations économiques et des changements de formule bien menés, mais aussi grâce à leur appartenance à de grands groupes, elles sont diffusées à près de 2 320 000 exemplaires, dont 828 600 pour le seul *Paris-Match*. Ce magazine, né en 1949, mêle actualité, culture et rubriques sur les grands de ce monde (artistes, hommes politiques, familles royales) ; il accorde une grande place au reportage photographique. *Courrier International* a célébré son huitième anniversaire en 1998. Cet hebdomadaire traduit et publie en français des articles d'actualité de la presse internationale. Il est diffusé à 100 000 exemplaires. Les prix de ces magazines s'échelonnent de 12 à 30 francs (2 à 5 dollars).

Aux côtés de ces titres, une place existe aussi pour une presse hebdomadaire d'information et d'opinion plus originale. *Le Canard Enchaîné* en est sans doute l'exemple le plus vivace ; cet hebdomadaire satirique, indépendant puisqu'il n'accepte aucune publicité, est, à lui seul, un baromètre de la liberté de la presse en France. Né en 1916, vendu 8 francs (1,3 dollar), il incarne l'irrévérence et la liberté d'informer, quel que soit le pouvoir en place. Il critique les abus de pouvoir et dénonce, avec force caricatures et jeux de mots mais dans un grand respect de la langue française, les scandales, malversations ou anomalies en tout genre

Quelques-uns des titres de la presse française

grâce à un redoutable réseau d'informateurs et d'enquêteurs. Ses lecteurs sont nombreux (plus de 2,5 millions, 550 000 exemplaires vendus chaque semaine). *Charlie Hebdo* est lui aussi un hebdomadaire satirique dont le lectorat atteint les 200 000 personnes.

▮ Les magazines thématiques

Une extraordinaire floraison de magazines thématiques a vu le jour en France ces dernières années, plusieurs dizaines de titres nouveaux apparaissant chaque année. La presse enfantine et la presse de loisirs sont particulièrement dynamiques.

La presse économique est passée, entre 1979 et 1991, de sept à dix-huit titres, très florissants pour la plupart. La crise économique, la bonne santé de la Bourse, l'intérêt accordé à l'épargne et aux placements et celui, plus récent, porté à la vie des entreprises, ont stimulé ce secteur. *Capital*, qui appartient au groupe allemand Prisma et attire chaque mois 440 000 acheteurs, est le plus important succès de ces dernières années ; il répond aux préoccupations des cadres par des articles courts et pratiques. *Challenges* (212 000 exemplaires diffusés), *Enjeux-les Échos* (130 000), *Le Revenu français* (170 000), *Mieux vivre votre argent* (230 000), *Investir Magazine* (115 000), *L'Expansion* (145 000), *Valeurs actuelles* (85 000) témoignent, parmi d'autres, de ce dynamisme de la presse économique et financière.

La presse scientifique connaît un succès croissant avec des titres solidement implantés comme *Science et Vie* (320 000 exemplaires), *Ça m'intéresse*, *Science et Avenir* et des publications de haut niveau atteignant de bons tirages, comme *La Recherche* et *Pour la science*.

Les hebdomadaires de radio-télévision figurent parmi les plus forts tirages de la presse française. En 1997, ils représentaient une diffusion de 20 millions d'exemplaires chaque semaine. En tête, *TV Magazine* attirait 13,5 millions de lecteurs, *Télé 7 Jours*, 11,4 millions et *Télé Star*, *Télé Z* et *Télé Loisirs*, près de 7 millions de lecteurs chacun.

Individualistes, les Français ont une presse qui leur ressemble : pas une mode, un courant, un sport, une culture, un art, un mode de vie qui n'ait sa publication. Ainsi, plus d'une quinzaine de magazines sont consacrés à la voiture, six à la moto, neuf à la photographie ou au cinéma, vingt à la gastronomie, au tourisme et aux voyages, sept aux sciences, six à la musique, une vingtaine à l'informatique, près de quarante aux sports les plus divers, onze à la littérature, à l'histoire et aux beaux-arts, vingt-trois à la maison et au jardin, onze à la chasse et à la pêche, etc. La presse destinée à la jeunesse, du tout-petit à l'étudiant, est elle aussi en plein essor avec près de 80 titres en 1997. De la naissance d'un enfant (*Famille magazine*, *Parents*, *Enfants magazine*...) à la retraite (*Notre Temps*, 1 054 000 exemplaires), chaque âge a son magazine.

La presse féminine, héritière d'une tradition très ancienne, est florissante et a souvent essaimé à l'étranger où elle contribue à propager l'image traditionnelle de la France (la mode, la beauté, l'art de vivre). Très ciblée, elle a su fidéliser lecteurs et annonceurs. Ces dernières années, elle s'est recentrée. Renonçant au « parisianisme », elle a su toucher un public plus large et plus familial. Les magazines tels que *Femme actuelle* (1 735 000 exemplaires), *Prima* (1 110 000), *Modes et Travaux* (800 000), *Madame Figaro* (545 000), *Marie-Claire* (540 000) figurent parmi les vingt-huit titres français dépassant les 500 000 exemplaires. La plus prestigieuse et la plus influente de ces publications est sans doute *Elle*. Créé en 1945, ce magazine a su suivre l'évolution de la vie, les luttes des femmes, tant en France qu'à l'étranger, tout en magnifiant la mode et le style. Vendu 13 francs (2 dollars) à 345 000 exemplaires, *Elle* existe en 29 éditions étrangères : américaine, canadienne, anglaise, allemande, italienne, espagnole, mexicaine, brésilienne, argentine, chilienne, grecque, néerlandaise, portugaise, suédoise, tchèque, norvégienne, polonaise, roumaine, taïwanaise, coréenne, singapourienne, thaïlandaise, vietnamienne, indienne, australienne, sud-africaine, hongkongaise, japonaise et russe.

Les agences de presse

Journaux, télévisions et radios ne pourraient fonctionner sans les agences de presse. Celles-ci sont les grossistes de l'information : elles fournissent aux organes de presse et aux institutions des informations de toutes natures – textes, photos, graphiques – moyennant un abonnement dont le coût varie en fonction du tirage ou de l'audience. Dans certains journaux, plus de 80 % des informations publiées proviennent d'une ou de plusieurs agences de presse. Les agences ne rapportent que des faits, d'une manière rigoureusement neutre, afin que leurs informations puissent être reprises par des abonnés de tendances politiques et de nationalités diverses.

Salle de rédaction de l'Agence France-Presse, à Paris

L'Agence France-Presse (AFP) est l'une des trois grandes agences mondiales (avec les agences américaine *Associated Press* et britannique *Reuter*). Avec 150 bureaux dans le monde, elle est la seule agence mondiale francophone. Elle emploie 1 200 journalistes titulaires dont 200 photographes et plus de 2 000 pigistes dans 165 pays. Elle diffuse deux millions de mots par jour en six langues et 70 000 photos par an. Elle compte parmi ses clients 650 journaux, 400 radios et télévisions, 1 500 administrations et entreprises, 100 agences de presse nationales. Elle touche ainsi, directement ou indirectement, trois milliards de personnes et informe 10 000 médias. Elle propose également des chroniques et reportages radio, des infographies et des prestations multimédias sur Internet et Intranet.

Il existe également des agences de presse photographiques : les trois premières du monde, Sygma, Gamma et Sipa, sont françaises.

L'explosion de l'audiovisuel

La presse écrite a reculé devant la montée de l'audiovisuel et, dans une moindre mesure, devant le livre qui s'est emparé de l'histoire immédiate, traditionnelle chasse gardée de la presse. En 1997, les Français passaient en moyenne 3 h 20 par jour devant la télévision, alors qu'ils ne consacraient que 30 minutes à la lecture de la presse.

La radio et la télévision ont été, jusqu'en 1982, soumises à un monopole d'État. Cette année-là, dix-huit radios privées obtiennent l'autorisation d'émettre. Puis, afin d'assurer l'indépendance des moyens de communication, en particulier à l'égard du pouvoir politique, la loi du 29 juillet 1982 place l'ensemble des réseaux télévisuels et radiophoniques français, à l'exception de la chaîne franco-allemande Arte, sous l'autorité d'un organisme administratif indépendant, comme il en existe aux États-Unis ou au Canada. Celui-ci prend le nom de Conseil supérieur de l'audiovisuel (CSA) en 1989.

Le Conseil supérieur de l'audiovisuel

L'une des missions du Conseil supérieur de l'audiovisuel est le contrôle du temps de parole de chaque candidat ou de chaque parti, lors des campagnes électorales

Le Conseil supérieur de l'audiovisuel est chargé de contrôler le respect par les entreprises de radio et de télévision de leurs obligations légales. Il lui revient également d'attribuer les fréquences, de nommer les présidents des chaînes publiques, de donner un avis

lorsque le gouvernement ou le Parlement le lui demande. Il doit assurer le respect du pluralisme politique, favoriser la libre concurrence, veiller à la protection de l'enfance et défendre la langue française. Il est doté par la loi d'un pouvoir de sanction (amendes, suspension de diffusion, etc).

Les neuf membres du CSA sont nommés par tiers par les trois plus hautes autorités de la République : le président de la République, le président du Sénat et le président de l'Assemblée nationale. Le président du CSA est nommé par le chef de l'État. Les conseillers sont désignés pour six ans et renouvelés par tiers tous les deux ans. Pour mieux préserver leur indépendance, ils ne sont pas révocables et ne peuvent être reconduits dans leurs fonctions.

La multiplication des chaînes de télévision

Depuis 1982, l'audiovisuel est entré dans l'ère de la concurrence avec la création et la multiplication de chaînes de télévision privées. En dix ans, l'offre française est passée de trois à plus de trente chaînes (câble compris).

Toutes chaînes confondues, les téléspectateurs français aiment avant tout les films, la fiction télévisuelle, les émissions de divertissement et d'information (journaux, magazines, documentaires). Les journaux de 20 heures de TF1 et de France 2, notamment, sont de grands rendez-vous nationaux. Cependant, comme ce fut le cas pour la presse écrite, on voit fleurir, à côté d'un nombre limité de chaînes généralistes, des chaînes de plus en plus spécialisées et payantes visant un public intéressé, qu'il s'agisse de sport, de musique et de concerts, de films, etc.

Il existe actuellement, outre une vingtaine de chaînes de télévision par câble, sept chaînes de télévision diffusées par voie hertzienne : quatre appartiennent au secteur public et sont financées par la redevance (d'un montant de 735 francs en 1998, 122 dollars), par des subventions de l'État et par la publicité. Ce sont France 2, France 3, la chaîne franco-allemande Arte et La Cinquième. Trois relèvent du secteur privé : TF1 et M6, financées par des actionnaires privés et qui ne vivent que de la publicité, et Canal Plus, chaîne cryptée payante, qui perçoit aussi des recettes publicitaires.

Le nouveau siège de France Télévision à Paris

Depuis 1989, France 2 et France 3 sont regroupées au sein de France Télévision ; elles dépendent d'une présidence unique afin d'assurer une plus grande cohérence et de favoriser leur complémentarité. France 2 est une chaîne généraliste nationale dont la mission est d'informer, de distraire et d'éduquer. Elle détient environ 25 % de part de marché. Elle accorde une grande place, en première partie de soirée, à la fiction française et européenne.

France 3 est une chaîne à vocation nationale et régionale puisqu'elle diffuse, à certaines heures de la journée, des informations et des émissions régionales et locales. Grâce au renforcement de son identité nationale et à la qualité de sa programmation, France 3 progresse régulièrement et s'approche de 20 % de part de marché. Le 19-20, son journal d'information, est en tête de l'audience de début de soirée, grâce notamment aux « décrochages » régionaux.

Arte, qui occupe le cinquième canal de 19 heures à 3 heures du matin, est une chaîne culturelle haut de gamme, diffusée également en Allemagne par le câble, qui propose notamment des soirées complètes, films, débats, reportages, autour d'un thème unique. Issue du Traité franco-allemand du 2 octobre 1990, Arte a une vocation européenne : la Radio-télévision belge l'a d'ores et déjà rejointe ; d'autres pourraient suivre prochainement. Son audience est encore modeste mais progresse régulièrement : 19 millions de téléspectateurs réguliers en France en 1997, 5,6 millions en Allemagne et 27 millions en Europe.

Le 14 décembre 1994, la première chaîne éducative française consacrée au « savoir, à la formation et à l'emploi », La Cinquième, a vu le jour. Elle diffuse aux heures laissées libres par Arte, de 6 heures à 19 heures, et propose des programmes éducatifs et de nombreux documentaires accessibles au plus grand nombre, et en particulier au milieu scolaire.

Deux chaînes généralistes appartiennent au secteur privé, TF1 et M6. TF1, privatisée en 1987, est la première chaîne française avec une audience moyenne de 35 %. Elle a bénéficié de l'ancienneté, de la réputation et du savoir-faire de ce qui fut la première et pendant longtemps la seule chaîne publique de télévision existant en France. C'est une chaîne populaire généraliste qui met l'accent sur les jeux, le sport, les variétés et les films grand public. Elle draine 55 % des recettes publicitaires de la télévision et est contrôlée par le groupe de BTP Bouygues associé à Bolloré.

M6, dont les actionnaires principaux sont la Compagnie luxembourgeoise de télédiffusion (CLT) et la Lyonnaise des Eaux-Dumez, fait la part belle aux fictions en première partie de soirée et à la musique. Elle diffuse des journaux spécifiques à destination de douze grandes villes françaises. La moitié de son public a moins de trente-cinq ans.

Née en 1984, Canal Plus est la plus ancienne des chaînes privées. Elle est payante et cryptée (il est nécessaire de louer un décodeur pour regarder ses émissions, sauf lorsque celles-ci sont diffusées en clair). Créée dans le scepticisme général, Canal Plus est un succès : avec près de 5 millions d'abonnés et un chiffre d'affaires de 13,5 milliards de francs en 1997 (2,25 milliards de dollars), elle est la plus belle réussite de l'audiovisuel français et a exporté son succès vers certains pays européens comme l'Espagne, la Belgique et la Pologne. Ses points forts sont le cinéma et le sport. Elle diffuse également une des plus célèbres émissions télévisées du pays, Les guignols de l'info, dont les marionnettes en latex parodient avec la plus grande irrévérence les personnalités du monde politique, artistique et sportif. Canal Plus est passée sous le contrôle de la Générale des Eaux, qui organise son « pôle communication » autour de la chaîne pour les activités audiovisuelles, de Havas pour les activités d'édition, de multimédias et de publicité et de Cégétel pour les industries de télécommunications.

Outre ces sept chaînes hertziennes, quelque 250 chaînes françaises et étrangères sont accessibles par câble et par satellite. Concrètement, toutefois, la plupart des foyers ne reçoivent pour le moment que les ensembles de programmes thématiques émanant d'un seul satellite. Plus de 3 millions de foyers sont équipés d'antennes paraboliques ou sont câblés et la moitié environ d'entre eux sont abonnés au service de base, qui permet d'accéder à une quinzaine de chaînes : les télévisions hertziennes, les chaînes thématiques françaises et des chaînes étrangères (BBC, MTV, CNN, TVE, RAI, ZDF, etc.), sans oublier la chaîne européenne d'information Euronews.

Les principales chaînes thématiques françaises sont aujourd'hui Canal J (programmes destinés à la jeunesse) qui émet tous les jours de 7 à 20 heures avant de passer le relais à Canal Jimmy et à ses émissions principalement destinées aux nostalgiques des années soixante et soixante-dix, Planète (documentaires et reportages d'actualité), Eurosport, MCM (musique) et LCI (La Chaîne Info), première chaîne d'information continue française, née en juin 1994. Cette dernière, filiale de TF1, diffuse un journal complet toutes les demi-heures ainsi que des journaux en continu lorsque l'actualité l'exige. Elle propose aussi des débats et

des interviews. Par ailleurs deux chaînes de cinéma, Ciné-Cinéma et Ciné-Cinéfil, sont accessibles sur le réseau câblé moyennant un abonnement supplémentaire.

Le plateau de LCI (La Chaîne Info), filiale de TF1 et première chaîne française d'information continue, née en juin 1994

La télévision numérique a démarré en force en France en 1996 et le million d'abonnés a été dépassé en moins de deux ans. Il est essentiel pour la France de développer la diffusion par satellites de bouquets de programmes afin, d'une part, de conserver sa place, son rang et son influence dans le monde de demain - avec les enjeux culturels et économiques inhérents -, de contrer la concurrence de chaînes étrangères et, d'autre part, d'aller au-delà de l'offre des chaînes hertziennes actuelles dans un souci de diversification. C'est ce que fait déjà Canal Satellite, bouquet géré par Canal Plus, qui propose à 750 000 abonnés (en 1998) un ensemble de neuf chaînes thématiques.

Sur ces traces, TPS (filiale de TF1, de France Télévision, de M6 et de la Compagnie luxembourgeoise de télécommunications) a proposé à son tour un bouquet de chaînes auquel 200 000 foyers se sont abonnés. Parmi les nouveaux venus, on trouve aussi AB Sat, qui compte déjà 50 000 abonnés. Tous ces opérateurs se livrent une guerre commerciale sans merci sur un marché en plein développement : le chiffre d'affaires de la télévision par satellite est de l'ordre de 5 milliards de francs en 1998 et a dépassé celui du câble (4 milliards de francs). La compression numérique va également faciliter le développement de la télévision payante à la carte, grâce à laquelle le téléspectateur pourra visionner le programme désiré à l'heure où il le souhaite, service que proposent déjà Multivision 1, reliée à plus de vingt-cinq réseaux câblés, et Multivision 2, qui a vu le jour en janvier 1995.

Enfin, les chaînes de télévision française soutiennent activement le cinéma grâce à une politique dynamique de pré-achat et de coproduction. En 1996, Canal Plus a ainsi pré-acheté plus d'une centaine de films long métrage pour un montant total de 605 millions de francs (100,8 millions de dollars) et participé à la coproduction de 22 films. TF1 a pour sa part coproduit 17 films (221,2 millions de francs d'investissement, soit 36,8 millions de dollars), France 2 a co-financé 23 films (120,9 millions de francs, soit 20,1 millions de dollars), France 3 15 films (99 millions de francs, soit 16,5 millions de dollars), La Sept 11 films et M6 15.

Tournage sur les berges de la Dordogne, dans le Lot, du téléfilm « La rivière Espérance » qui a connu un grand succès sur France 2

L'Institut national de l'audiovisuel : la mémoire audiovisuelle

Depuis plus de vingt ans, l'Institut national de l'audiovisuel (INA), établissement public, est chargé de gérer les archives télévisées de la France. Architecte de « la mémoire du futur », l'INA entend bien poursuivre et renforcer cette mission patrimoniale de conservation et d'exploitation, en s'appuyant sur de nouveaux outils informatiques, notamment sur les réseaux à haut débit numérique et sur l'Inathèque de France qui a débuté ses activités le 1ᵉʳ janvier 1995. Cette nouvelle entité a pour mission de conserver et d'ouvrir à la consultation, à des fins de recherche, les documents télévisuels et radiophoniques français, à partir desquels les chercheurs, les universitaires et les étudiants en doctorat peuvent travailler, grâce à des outils informatiques et multimédias comme le système « Vidéoscribe ». Ce dernier permet en effet d'analyser, image par image, des documents télévisés avec des variations de lumière, de plan et de son. Par ailleurs, la publication des travaux et des études des universitaires qui accèdent à l'Inathèque de France rend possible l'élaboration d'une réflexion critique sur les médias audiovisuels dont la présence et le rôle vont croissant.

L'engouement pour la radio

Le succès de la télévision n'a pas entraîné de repli de la radio, bien au contraire. La multiplication des radios, rendue possible par la loi de 1982, et leur diversité croissante, ont redonné un nouvel élan à ce support de communication qui constitue encore le média préféré des Français, sauf en soirée où la télévision arrive en tête. En revanche, le succès de la radio et de la télévision s'est fait au détriment de la presse écrite. En moyenne, tous âges confondus, les Français écoutent la radio plus de 2 heures par jour, les repas, les tâches ménagères et les déplacements étant les moments de plus forte écoute.

Le journal de 13 heures
sur Europe 1

Le secteur radiophonique public est regroupé au sein de la société nationale de radiodiffusion Radio France, qui conçoit et programme des émissions diffusées sur un réseau de cinquante-trois radios : cinq radios nationales, trente-neuf radios locales et une dizaine de radios dites « d'accompagnement », créées à partir de 1971 (FIP) et qui diffusent 24 heures sur 24 des informations, des messages de service (météo, spectacles, circulation routière, offres d'emploi, programmes de télévision et de radio) sur un fond musical ininterrompu. Radio France emploie plus de 3 000 personnes dont près de 450 journalistes et dispose de 124 studios, dont plus de la moitié situés en province. Elle s'appuie aussi sur deux orchestres, l'Orchestre national de France et l'Orchestre philarmonique, ainsi que sur le Chœur et la Maîtrise de Radio France. Au total, Radio France assure un volume d'émissions de près de 500 000 heures par an. Les radios du service public sont financées par la redevance audiovisuelle, éventuellement par l'État, et la publicité y est strictement limitée.

Parmi les cinq radios nationales figure France Inter, créée en 1947. Deuxième radio de France derrière RTL, elle émet 24 heures sur 24. France Culture présente des programmes très variés associant des émissions musicales, des entretiens, des grands reportages et des débats. France Musique diffuse plus de mille concerts par an, notamment ceux produits par Radio France. Radio Bleue privilégie les auditeurs de plus de cinquante ans, à qui elle propose des chansons françaises. Quant à France Info, créée en 1987, elle constitue la première radio française et européenne d'information continue et elle a connu un succès rapide. Elle émet 24 heures sur 24, proposant un rappel fréquent des grands titres de l'actualité et un journal complet toutes les demi-heures.

Radio France Internationale (RFI) est diffusée en France et sur les cinq continents. Elle est l'une des pièces-maîtresses de l'action audiovisuelle extérieure du pays. RFO, Société nationale de Radio et de Télévision d'Outre-mer, programme, produit et diffuse des émissions de télévision et de radio dans les départements et les territoires d'outre-mer.

Le secteur privé est constitué de trois stations nationales généralistes : RTL, Europe 1 et Radio Monte-Carlo. Il existe aussi des radios nationales à dominante musicale en modulation de fréquence (FM), NRJ, Radio-Nostalgie, Fun radio, Skyrock, etc., une trentaine de radios régionales privées, telles Sud-Radio, Radio-Service, Radio-1, etc., et plus de 350 radios associatives, soit 450 programmes sur environ 2 650 fréquences. À la fin des années quatre-vingt, les radios généralistes privées ont constaté une baisse importante de leur audience. Pour faire face à ce défi, RTL, Europe 1 et RMC ont tissé des liens plus étroits et plus personnalisés avec leurs auditeurs, en jouant sur la proximité et l'interactivité. C'est ainsi que les auditeurs sont invités à s'exprimer en direct, lors de certaines émissions. Elles ont, par ailleurs, racheté des réseaux FM (Radio-Montmartre et Nostalgie pour RMC, Fun Radio pour la CLT, RFM pour Europe 1) ou créé leur propre radio FM (Europe 2 pour Europe 1, RTL 2 pour RTL).

Pour protéger la culture française, la loi du 1er février 1994 impose aux programmes de musique de variétés de comporter au moins 40 % de chansons en langue française, dont la moitié émanant de «nouveaux talents ou de nouvelles productions». Par ailleurs, cette même loi prévoit qu'une personne physique ou morale ne peut disposer de plusieurs réseaux que dans la mesure où la somme des populations desservies n'excède pas 150 millions d'habitants.

Le domaine de compétence du Conseil supérieur de l'audiovisuel (CSA, voir plus haut) s'étend également aux radios.

L'action audiovisuelle extérieure de la France

La France a été l'un des premiers pays à exercer une véritable diplomatie culturelle par le biais des écoles, des centres culturels, des Alliances françaises, de la coopération scientifique et technique. Aujourd'hui, elle passe également par l'action audiovisuelle extérieure pour laquelle le gouvernement a choisi de nouvelles orientations ; celles-ci doivent permettre le développement des grands canaux de communication mondiaux que sont TV5, Canal France International (CFI), Radio France Internationale (RFI) et les filiales radiophoniques de la SOFIRAD, qui regroupe les participations de l'État dans les entreprises audiovisuelles publiques ou mixtes. Ces orientations s'articulent autour de trois axes : faire de TV5 la vitrine de l'action télévisuelle extérieure de la France, soutenir à l'exportation les programmes audio-visuels français et renforcer l'aide financière des chaînes par satellites.

À cette fin, le financement public de l'action audiovisuelle extérieure française est passé de 900 millions de francs (150 millions de dollars) à 1,4 milliard de francs en 1998. TV5, qui portera désormais l'essentiel des efforts de diffusion des programmes français vers l'étranger, est une chaîne de télévision francophone multilatérale diffusée par satellite et sur des réseaux câblés. Née en 1984, elle associe le secteur audiovisuel public français (France 2, France 3, la Sofirad, l'Institut national de l'audiovisuel) aux télévisions publiques suisse romande, belge, canadienne et québécoise, d'où son nom de TV5. En 1998, TV5, dotée d'un budget de 350 millions de francs (58 millions de dollars), est reçue dans plus de 80 millions de foyers dans une centaine de pays d'Europe, d'Amérique, d'Afrique et d'Asie, grâce à une vingtaine de satellites. Elle diffuse, 24 heures sur 24, des programmes haut de gamme, à 75 % français : des journaux spécifiques produits par la chaîne, les journaux des télévisions publiques françaises, suisse, belge, québécoise et canadienne, des magazines, des fictions, des films, des variétés, des jeux, etc.

Canal France International (CFI) est depuis sa création, en 1989, une banque d'images des chaînes françaises diffusée par satellite et destinée essentiellement aux chaînes nationales africaines. Elle a diffusé, en 1997, 27 500 heures de programmes dans plus de 80 pays via plus de 100 télévisions partenaires. Grâce à six canaux satellitaires couvrant les cinq continents, elle dispose d'une audience potentielle de 354 millions de téléspectateurs. Dotée d'un budget de 180 millions de francs en 1998 (30 millions de dollars), CFI diffuse onze journaux d'information quotidiens, dont deux en anglais, ainsi que de nombreux événements sportifs en direct (tournoi de tennis de Roland-Garros, Coupe du monde de football, Tour de France cycliste, etc.). CFI propose également plus de 150 films longs métrages par an ainsi que des documentaires, des fictions, des magazines d'actualité, des variétés et des programmes pour la jeunesse. Dans le nouveau dispositif de l'audiovisuel extérieur, CFI recentre son action sur ses missions de banque de programmes et d'instrument de coopération technique et son rôle de diffuseur vers l'Afrique est maintenu.

Enfin, pour favoriser la synergie entre les deux pôles de l'action télévisuelle française à l'étranger, CFI et TV5 sont placées sous une présidence commune.

RFI, la radio mondiale

Autre pilier de l'action audiovisuelle extérieure, Radio France Internationale (RFI) présente aux auditeurs du monde entier l'actualité française et internationale, du point de vue de la France et de l'Europe. RFI se fait entendre depuis 1931. Elle est aujourd'hui une radio aux programmes multiples, qui utilise tous les moyens de diffusion et dont les journalistes ont su faire la preuve de leur professionnalisme. Elle a 45 millions d'auditeurs réguliers, en français et en 18 langues étrangères.

Depuis l'automne 1996, RFI a lancé un programme d'information en continu 24 heures sur 24 en français, avec des bulletins d'information de 10 minutes toutes les demi-heures et des programmes qui présentent tous les aspects de la vie culturelle, économique et sociale française. La construction européenne, les questions africaines, les relations économiques internationales occupent également une place importante. Ces programmes existent également, sur des durées plus courtes, en 18 langues étrangères.

RFI diffuse aussi un programme spécifique dédié à la chanson francophone et dispose de deux sites Internet, l'un consacré à l'actualité et l'autre à la chanson. Son budget est de l'ordre de 775 millions de francs (129 millions de dollars).

S'appuyant sur une couverture satellitaire de qualité numérique, RFI a constitué un réseau de relais fonctionnant 24 heures sur 24, et de reprises partielles en FM, en ondes moyennes ou sur le câble dans plus de 140 villes du monde. Parmi elles figure la quasi-

Le réseau mondial de diffusion de Radio France Internationale

Source : RFI

Zone balayée par les émetteurs ondes courtes   ● Relais RFI 24h/24   Zone desservie par chacun des onze satellites

totalité des capitales de l'Afrique francophone et de l'Europe centrale et orientale. Elle est aussi présente, par exemple, à New York, à Amman ou à Phnom Penh.

Depuis 1991, RFI a repris RMC Moyen-Orient, radio qui émet 16 heures 30 par jour en langue arabe et 1 heure 30 en français et dont les émissions sont reçues par 13 millions d'auditeurs sur ondes moyennes au Proche et Moyen-Orient et, en FM, dans un nombre croissant de capitales arabes.

Il faut ajouter à ce dispositif Medi 1 qui émet 19 heures de programmes par jour en arabe et en français en direction de 11 millions d'auditeurs dans les pays du Maghreb.

La France à l'heure d'Internet

Les Français sont entrés dans l'ère du multimédia avec un temps de retard sur les Américains et sur leurs voisins européens en raison, notamment, des performances du Minitel. Avec plus de deux milliards d'appels par an et 115 millions d'heures de connexion, la France est le premier consommateur mondial de services en ligne (annuaire électronique, services professionnels, services de vie pratique, cotations boursières, messageries, loisirs et jeux).

À la mi-1996, 21 % des foyers étaient équipés d'un ordinateur, dont 17 % d'un ordinateur multimédia, et cette proportion devrait s'accroître fortement d'ici l'an 2000, grâce notamment à la baisse du prix des équipements, à une politique volontariste des différents gouvernements en faveur de l'informatique à l'école et à la baisse des prix des communications, due à l'ouverture à la concurrence du marché du téléphone en 1998.

À la mi-1997, la France comptait 1,12 million d'utilisateurs d'Internet, soit 2,4 % des Français de plus de 15 ans. Le taux de croissance devait être, selon les prévisions, de 90 % au cours des 12 mois suivants et l'Hexagone comptait, à la mi-1998, 2,1 millions d'internautes, soit 5 % de la population âgée de plus de 15 ans, et plus de 25 000 sites. Les sites français représentaient, en juin 1997, la moitié des temps de connexion, contre un tiers en 1996. La quasi-totalité des quotidiens et des hebdomadaires nationaux sont aujourd'hui présents sur Internet. Le site du quotidien économique *Les Échos* est le plus visité avec 350 000 visiteurs par mois, suivi par celui du quotidien d'information générale *Libération*.

Pour en savoir plus :

Les réseaux de la société d'information, rapport du Commissariat général du Plan sous la direction de T. Miléo, Éditions Aspe, 1997.

D'Internet aux autoroutes de l'information, in *Regards sur l'actualité*, n° 217, La Documentation française, 1996.

L'Internet, un vrai défi pour la France, La Documentation française, collection des Rapports officiels, 1997.

Programme d'action gouvernemental, *Préparer l'entrée de la France dans la société de l'information*, Premier Ministre, Service d'information du gouvernement, La Documentation française, 1998.

L'abrégé du droit de la presse, Éditions du Centre de formation et de perfectionnement des journalistes (CFPJ), 1994 (abondante bibliographie).

Indicateurs statistiques de la radio, SJTI, CSA, La Documentation française, 1997.

Indicateurs statistiques de l'audiovisuel. Cinéma, télévision, vidéo. Données 1995, SJTI, La Documentation française, 1997.

Chiffres clés de la télévision et du cinéma. France 1995, INA, CNC, CSA, La Documentation française, 1996.

Daniel Junqua, *La presse écrite et audiovisuelle*, Éditions du CFPJ, collection Connaissance des médias, 1997.

Pierre Albert, *La presse française*, La Documentation française, collection Les Études, 1998.

H. Pigeat, *Les agences de presse. Institutions du passé ou médias d'avenir ?* La Documentation française, collection Les Études, 1996.

Internet et les réseaux numériques, La Documentation française, collection des Rapports du Conseil d'État, 1998.

Les sites Internet de La Documentation française :
http://www.ladocfrancaise.gouv.fr
http://www.admifrance.gouv.fr

ANNEXES

Index

Index des noms propres

Crédits photographiques

Les numéros renvoient aux pages ;
h = haut, m = milieu, b = bas.

7 D. Repérant / Rapho

8h La Documentation française / ph. D. Taulin-Hommell ; **8m** T. Perrin / Hoa-qui ;

8b La Documentation française / Interphotothèque ph. Sodel-M. Brigaud

9 G. Sioen / Rapho

10 D. Repérant / Rapho

11 La Documentation française / ph. D. Taulin-Hommell

12 Office national des forêts / J.-P. Chasseau

13 F. de la Mure / Ministère des Affaires étrangères. Diffuseur La Documentation française

19h F. de la Mure / Ministère des Affaires étrangères ;

19b La Documentation française / ph. F. Saur-Visum

20 La Photothèque EDF

21 La Documentation française / ph. D. Taulin-Hommell

25 F. de la Mure / Ministère des Affaires étrangères. Diffuseur La Documentation française

31h Yan / Rapho ; **31m** D. Repérant / Rapho ;

31b La Documentation française / ph. J.-F. Marin-Editing

32 La Documentation française / ph. J.-F. Marin-Editing

34 E. Valentin / Hoa-qui

36 Debaisieux / Rapho

37 X. Richer / Hoa-qui

41 Photo Josse

43 Photo Josse

45h Fournier / Rapho ; **45b** CNDP-collection historique

46 Photo Willy Ronis / Rapho

47 Archives La Documentation française

49 Ministère des Affaires étrangères

51 Photo A.F.P.

53 Photo A.F.P.

54 Photo A.F.P.

56 Premier Ministre / Service photographique

58 L.-N. Bonaparte : La Documentation française, d'après nature/Lafosse ; **A. Thiers** : La Documentation française ; **Mac-Mahon** : La Documentation française ; **J. Grévy** : Bibliothèque nationale de France, diffuseur La Documentation française ; **S. Carnot** : Présidence de la République, diffuseur La Documentation française ; **J. Casimir-Périer** : Présidence de la République, diffuseur La Documentation française ; **F. Faure** : Présidence de la République, diffuseur La Documentation française ; **E. Loubet** : Présidence de la République, diffuseur La Documentation française ; **A. Fallières** : Présidence de la République, diffuseur La Documentation française ; **R. Poincaré** : Présidence de la République, diffuseur La Documentation française ; **P. Deschanel** : Bibliothèque nationale de France, diffuseur La Documentation française ; **A. Millerand** : Bibliothèque nationale de France, diffuseur La Documentation française ; **G. Doumergue** : Bibliothèque nationale de France, diffuseur La Documentation française ; **P. Doumer** : Bibliothèque nationale de France, diffuseur La Documentation française ; **A. Lebrun** : Présidence de la République, diffuseur La Documentation française ; **V. Auriol** : photo Harcourt, diffuseur La Documentation française ; **R. Coty** : Présidence de la République, diffuseur La Documentation française ; **C. de Gaulle** : La Documentation française, photo J.-M. Marcel ; **G. Pompidou** : La Documentation française, photo F. Pagès / Paris Match : **V. Giscard d'Estaing** : La Documentation française, photo J.-H. Lartigue ; **F. Mitterrand** : La Documentation française, photo G. Freund ; **J. Chirac** : La Documentation française, photo B. Rheims.

61 Présidence de la République

63 Premier Ministre / Service photographique

65 Premier Ministre / Service photographique

66 La Documentation française / ph. F. Le Diascorn

67 D. Repérant / Rapho

68 La Documentation française / ph. R. Allard-Vu

72h Epamarne / Ph. Morency. Diffuseur La Documentation française ; **72b** SAN de Sénart / J. Dupeyrat. Diffuseur La Documentation française

73 La Documentation française / ph. S. Challon

75 A. Le Bot / DIAF

78 Photo Branger / Viollet

79 Photo A.F.P.

80 Moschetti / Réa

84 B. Bisson / Sygma

85 J.-B. Vernier / Sygma

94 F. De la Mure / Ministère des Affaires étrangères

97 F. De la Mure / Ministère des Affaires étrangères

98h F. De la Mure / Ministère des Affaires étrangères ; **98b** Commission européenne

99 F. De la Mure / Ministère des Affaires étrangères

100 V. Maaski

102 Premier Ministre / Service photographique

103 Trois Têtes. A l'Amitié. Henri Matisse 1951-52. Héritiers Matisse 1998

107 Droits réservés

109 Ministère des Affaires étrangères / DGRCST

112 Ministère des Affaires étrangères

113 J. Marces / SIRPA / ECPA

115 F. De la Mure / Ministère des Affaires étrangères

116 ECPA

117 ECPA

118 ECPA

119 ECPA

124 S. Cuisset / Réa

125 D. Faget / A.F.P.

129 Th. Rousseau / Sygma

131 J.-P. Amet / Sygma

133 P. Wang / Hoa-qui

134 D. Maillac / Réa

135 La Documentation française / ph. J.-F. Marin-Editing

136 Ministère de l'Emploi et de la Solidarité

138 J.E. Pasquier / Rapho

140 Sygma / Tempsport / T. Orban

141 J. Van Hasselt / Sygma

144 J.-P. Amet / Sygma

145 J.-P. Amet / Sygma

146 La Documentation française / ph. P. Dewarez

147 La Documentation française / ph. J.-P. Bajard-Editing

149 D. Giry / Sygma

154 La Documentation française / ph. F. Ivaldi-Viva

155 La Documentation française / ph. J. Guillaume-Editing

156 La Documentation française / ph. F. Boucher

157 Epamarne / Ph. Morency. Diffuseur La Documentation française

158 Epamarne / Ph. Morency. Diffuseur La Documentation française

159 La Documentation française / ph. F. Boucher

160 M. Denance / Archipress

171 Bartoli / Réa

178 Conseil régional du Centre / B. Voisin. Diffuseur La Documentation française

180 La Documentation française / J.-F. Marin-Editing

183 La Documentation française / Interphotothèque ph. Sodel-M. Brigaud

185 B. Decoux / Réa

CRÉDITS
PHOTOGRAPHIQUES

187h Peterson / Saba / Réa ; **187b** La Documentation française / ph. Ph. Guignard

188 D. Maillac / Réa

189 S. Cuisset / Réa

190 M. Fourmy / Réa

192 A. Devouard / Réa

194 P. Sittler / Réa

196 C. Ena / Réa

197 A. Wolf / Hoa-qui

200 M. Fourmy / Réa

203 J.-M. Charles / Sygma

209 D. Repérant / Rapho

210 M. Denance / Archipress

214 P. Sittler / Réa

215 A. Devouard / Réa

216 Allard / Réa

218h Ministère des Affaires étrangères ; **218b** V. Macon / Réa

220 B. Marguerite / RATP-Audiovisuel

221 A. Devouard / Réa

223 La Documentation française / ph. P. Dewarez

225h F. Eustache / Archipress ; **225b** Archipress

227 Delluc / Réa

228 B. Annebicque / Sygma

230 Archipress

231 La Documentation française / ph. T. Carre

232 C. Masson / Enguérand

233h Q. Bertoux / Enguérand ; **233b** A.F.P. / ph. T.A. Clary

234 S. Cardinale / Sygma

235 F. Fogel / Sygma

236 D. Sauveur / Sygma

237 F. Eustache / Archipress

238 C. Stephan / Ministère des Affaires étrangères

239 F. Fogel / Sygma

241 M. Attar / Sygma

242 Photo M. Enguérand

243 D. Thierry / Maison de la France

244 Sygma / Tempsport / S. Compoint

245 Ministère des Affaires étrangères

246 G. Leimdorfer / Réa

249 Ministère des Affaires étrangères

251 G. Leimdorfer / Réa

252 G. Leimdorfer / Réa

253 Photo France 2 / G. Schrempp

255 G. Leimdorfer / Réa

256 D. Repérant / Hoa-qui

257 G. Leimdorfer / Réa

Infographie : Graffito, Paris

Compogravure - Impression : S.N. imb IMPRIMEUR - 70000 Vesoul - Dépôt légal n° 4483 - Décembre 1998 - Imprimé en France